A·N·N·U·A·L E·D·I·T·I·O·N·S

Urban Society
Twelfth Edition

EDITORS

Fred Siegel
The Cooper Union for Science and Art, New York

Fred Siegel, a professor of history at The Cooper Union for Science and Art in New York is also a senior fellow at the Progressive Policy Institute in Washington. The author *The Future One Happened Here*: New York, D.C., L.A. and, he is currently writing a book about Rudy Giuliani and New York.

Harry Siegel
Editor of New Partisan.com

Harry Siegel, editor of New Partisan.com, has written extensively on cities for publications including the *New York Sun,* where he was the chief urban affairs editorial writer, *Commentary*, the *Public Interest*, and the *New York Post*. He is writing a book on gentrification in New York for Ivan R. Dee, publisher.

McGraw-Hill/Dushkin
2460 Kerper Blvd., Dubuque, IA 52001

Visit us on the Internet
http://www.dushkin.com

Credits

1. **The Urban Frame**
   Unit photo—© Getty Images/Daisuke Morita (BU005572)
2. **Sprawl: Challenges to the Metropolitan Landscape**
   Unit photo—© Getty Images/Hisham F. Ibrahim (TR007278)
3. **Urban Economies**
   Unit photo—© CORBIS/Royalty-Free (BPE025)
4. **Urban Revival**
   Unit photo—© Getty Images/PhotoLink/Scenics of America (TR001954)
5. **Urban Politics and Policies**
   Unit photo—© Getty Images/PhotoLink (SO001055)
6. **Urban Neighborhoods**
   Unit photo—© Getty Images/Ryan McVay (AA0338414)
7. **Urban Problems: Crime, Education, and Poverty**
   Unit photo—© Getty Images/PhotoLink/S. Meltzer (SO000273)
8. **Urban Futures: Cities After September 11, 2001**
   Unit photo—© 2003 by PhotoDisc, Inc.

Copyright

Cataloging in Publication Data
Main entry under title: Annual Editions: Urban Society 12/E.
1. Urban Society—Periodicals. I. Siegel, Fred, *comp*. II. Title: Rosenberg, Jan, *comp*. III. Title: Urban Society.
ISBN 0–07–3012610   658'.05   ISSN 0735–2425

Twelfth Edition

Cover image © John A Rizzo and PhotoLink/Getty Images.
Printed in the United States of America   1234567890QPDQPD987654   Printed on Recycled Paper

Editors/Advisory Board

Members of the Advisory Board are instrumental in the final selection of articles for each edition of ANNUAL EDITIONS. Their review of articles for content, level, currentness, and appropriateness provides critical direction to the editor and staff. We think that you will find their careful consideration well reflected in this volume.

To the Reader

In publishing ANNUAL EDITIONS we recognize the enormous role played by the magazines, newspapers, and journals of the public press in providing current, first-rate educational information in a broad spectrum of interest areas. Many of these articles are appropriate for students, researchers, and professionals seeking accurate, current material to help bridge the gap between principles and theories and the real world. These articles, however, become more useful for study when those of lasting value are carefully collected, organized, indexed, and reproduced in a low-cost format, which provides easy and permanent access when the material is needed. That is the role played by ANNUAL EDITIONS.

To properly address urban issues, from crime and poverty to gentrification and urban revival, this twelfth edition of Annual Editions: Urban Society has had to reach past the boundaries of the city and consider the rapid growth of exurbia and the broader state of the "knowledge economy" to examine the impact of these trends on America's cities. We've also had to consider the impact of the terror attacks of September 11, 2001, on America's cities. That is addressed in the final unit.

As of early 2004, it remains unclear whether America's cities will hold on to their hard-earned gains of the 1990s, or fall back into what had seemed the intractable decline of the previous 30 years. It is still too early to discern the full long-term economic and demographic fallout of the terror attacks, let alone what the effect of additional attacks might bring.

Still, the problems cities face are far different than they were just a decade ago. Sprawl and gentrification have replaced crime and chaos as the urban "plagues" of the day. Such problems, it has been remarked, are serious, but they beat the alternatives of depopulation and poverty. Both are the inevitable result of economic prosperity. Sprawl draws life from the city. Gentrification revives neighborhoods but at the price of generating social resentments. Neither is likely to slow down. In both cases urbanites move into areas where they can purchase more space for less money as surely as water flows downhill.

City governments, on the other hand, are once again faced with tough choices. The long recessions set off by the tech bust and exacerbated by 9/11, have exhausted the record surpluses most cities built up in the 1990s. But fiscal problems not withstanding, the renewed desire for densely trafficked public spaces—parks, commercial and residential centers, and downtowns—in cities as diverse as Newark and Cincinnati, Kansas City and Denver heralds a new national affection for urban life.

The continued decline of manufacturing and industrial jobs has reduced the urban dependence on highly cyclical industries in favor of more stable service sector work. But the loss of such jobs has left the cities with a social structure resembling an hourglass. Cities are attracting young single professionals and immigrants. But the still unresolved problems of failing schools continue to push middle class families with young children to suburbia.

Population decentralization, an inevitable and continued result of first the electric grid and the automobile, and later the internet, has contributed to the urban sprawl that eats up farmland and creates competing corridors of power and influence that threaten both the central cities and those smaller cities that fail to retain and attract a middle-class population. A number of articles deal with alternatives to decentralization; they elaborate the core ideas of the "new urbanism," such as the virtues of density and the elements of urban design that encourage civic life.

Without immigrants continuing to flood into cities—especially New York, Los Angeles, Miami and Chicago—over the past two decades, filling jobs and neighborhoods that many others had fled, the urban revival of the 1990s would have been far more limited. They have rebuilt down-and-out city neighborhoods building by building, and reshaped and revived local economies. Without the demographic renewal these immigrants provided, entire urban neighborhoods would now be largely depopulated. But immigrants bring to our cities and our country problems as well as benefits. Post-9/11 security issues, notably INS screening and the tension between police and communities of illegal immigrants, remain unresolved.

Urban America, then, is at a crucial junction. Having made major gains in the war on crime, the cities are in many ways on the front lines of the war on terror. The funding for first responders in case of a terror attack, however, is deeply skewed by the demography of the Senate. This means that the cities most at risk like New York and Los Angeles are receiving a fraction of what unlikely targets like Wyoming are receiving on a per capita basis.

With school reform progressing but slowly and terror suggesting the dangers of density, it is unclear whether or not the gains of the 1990s can be sustained. Hopefully, the 1990s will be remembered more as a turning point than passing phase in the longer trend of urban decline.

Fred Siegel

Fred Siegel
Editor

Harry Siegel

Harry Siegel
Editor

Contents

UNIT 1
The Urban Frame

Three articles review some of the dynamics of urban living that need to be stressed if cities are to regain their appeal.

UNIT 2
Sprawl: Challenges to the Metropolitan Landscape

Five selections explore some of the factors that define the urban scene.

The concepts in bold italics are developed in the article. For further expansion, please refer to the Topic Guide and the Index.

UNIT 3
Urban Economies

Five selections discuss some of the forces that drive the economies of urban centers.

The concepts in bold italics are developed in the article. For further expansion, please refer to the Topic Guide and the Index.

UNIT 4
Urban Revival

Nine articles look at how cities are being resurrected and rejuvenated.

The concepts in bold italics are developed in the article. For further expansion, please refer to the Topic Guide and the Index.

UNIT 5
Urban Politics and Policies

UNIT 6
Regentrification and Urban Neighborhoods

The concepts in bold italics are developed in the article. For further expansion, please refer to the Topic Guide and the Index.

UNIT 7
Urban Problems: Crime, Education, and Poverty

Ten articles examine the inherent problems of urban growth.

The concepts in bold italics are developed in the article. For further expansion, please refer to the Topic Guide and the Index.

The concepts in bold italics are developed in the article. For further expansion, please refer to the Topic Guide and the Index.

UNIT 8
Urban Futures: Cities After September 11, 2001

Three articles examine the meaning of memorials, views of New York after the terrorist attack; and the implications of a rapidly rising urban population.

The concepts in bold italics are developed in the article. For further expansion, please refer to the Topic Guide and the Index.

Topic Guide

This topic guide suggests how the selections in this book relate to the subjects covered in your course. You may want to use the topics listed on these pages to search the Web more easily.

On the following pages a number of Web sites have been gathered specifically for this book. They are arranged to reflect the units of this *Annual Edition*. You can link to these sites by going to the DUSHKIN ONLINE support site at *http://www.dushkin.com/online/*.

ALL THE ARTICLES THAT RELATE TO EACH TOPIC ARE LISTED BELOW THE BOLD-FACED TERM.

City history
1. Fear of the City, 1783 to 1983
2. The Man Who Loved Cities
3. The Death and Life of America's Cities
15. Ground Zero in Urban Decline
18. The Fall and Rise of Bryant Park
21. Saving Buffalo From Extinction
23. Mayors and Morality: Daley and Lindsay Then and Now
31. Rocking-Chair Revival
40. Chief Bratton Takes on L.A.
43. The Rise, Fall, and Rise Again of Public Housing
44. Time to Think Small?

Crime
1. Fear of the City, 1783 to 1983
18. The Fall and Rise of Bryant Park
21. Saving Buffalo From Extinction
29. Windows Not Broken
34. Broken Windows
35. How an Idea Drew People Back to Urban Life
36. Murder Mystery
37. Crossing the Line
40. Chief Bratton Takes on L.A.
41. Police Line—Do Cross
43. The Rise, Fall, and Rise Again of Public Housing

Culture
4. Patio Man and the Sprawl People
9. The Rise of the Creative Class
10. Too Much Froth
12. Packaging Cities
14. Financing Urban Revitalization
16. Return to Center
17. New Village on Campus
19. Culture Club
20. Midwestern Momentum
22. Movers & Shakers
24. Beyond Safe and Clean
26. Brain-Gain Cities Attract Educated Young
29. Windows Not Broken
37. Crossing the Line

Disorder
1. Fear of the City, 1783 to 1983
18. The Fall and Rise of Bryant Park
21. Saving Buffalo From Extinction
29. Windows Not Broken
34. Broken Windows
35. How an Idea Drew People Back to Urban Life
36. Murder Mystery
37. Crossing the Line
40. Chief Bratton Takes on L.A.
41. Police Line—Do Cross
43. The Rise, Fall, and Rise Again of Public Housing

Downtown
6. Downtown Struggles While Neighbor Thrives
17. New Village on Campus
19. Culture Club
24. Beyond Safe and Clean

26. Brain-Gain Cities Attract Educated Young

Economic development
9. The Rise of the Creative Class
16. Return to Center
24. Beyond Safe and Clean
44. Time to Think Small?
46. Model Cities; What New York Can Learn from the Economic Recoveries in Houston and L.A.

Future
1. Fear of the City, 1783 to 1983
15. Ground Zero in Urban Decline
21. Saving Buffalo From Extinction
26. Brain-Gain Cities Attract Educated Young
31. Rocking-Chair Revival
40. Chief Bratton Takes on L.A.
42. An Inner-City Renaissance
43. The Rise, Fall, and Rise Again of Public Housing
44. Time to Think Small?
46. Model Cities; What New York Can Learn from the Economic Recoveries in Houston and L.A.

Gentrification
18. The Fall and Rise of Bryant Park
27. The Gentry, Misjudged as Neighbors
28. The Essence of Uptown
29. Windows Not Broken
30. Amid Office Shuffle in San Francisco, Bohemian Rhapsody
33. The Best of Mates
37. Crossing the Line
42. An Inner-City Renaissance

Government
5. Is Regional Government the Answer?
11. As Cities Move to Privatize Water, Atlanta Steps Back
15. Ground Zero in Urban Decline
16. Return to Center

Housing
16. Return to Center
17. New Village on Campus
24. Beyond Safe and Clean
30. Amid Office Shuffle in San Francisco, Bohemian Rhapsody
42. An Inner-City Renaissance
43. The Rise, Fall, and Rise Again of Public Housing

Immigration
2. The Man Who Loved Cities
21. Saving Buffalo From Extinction
22. Movers & Shakers
38. Segregation in New York Under a Different Name

Neighborhoods
16. Return to Center
17. New Village on Campus
20. Midwestern Momentum
21. Saving Buffalo From Extinction
27. The Gentry, Misjudged as Neighbors

World Wide Web Sites

The following World Wide Web sites have been carefully researched and selected to support the articles found in this reader. The easiest way to access these selected sites is to go to our DUSHKIN ONLINE support site at *http://www.dushkin.com/online/*.

AE: Urban Society 05/06

The following sites were available at the time of publication. Visit our Web site—we update DUSHKIN ONLINE regularly to reflect any changes.

General Sources

Library of Congress

http://www.loc.gov

Examine this extensive Web site to learn about the wonderful resource tools, library services/resources, exhibitions, and databases in many different subfields of urban studies.

National Geographic Society

http://www.nationalgeographic.com

This site provides links to National Geographic's huge archive of maps, articles, and other documents. There is a great deal of material of interest to students of urban society.

UNIT 1: The Urban Frame

Manchester, N.H., Open Urban Space Website

http://www.mv.com/ipusers/env/

At this site, read about the "urban open space philosophy" and explore specific initiatives in various communities.

WNET/Tenement Museum

http://www.wnet.org/archive/tenement/eagle.html

The Tenement Museum in New York City's Lower East Side is a unique place. Visit this Public Broadcasting Service site to learn the history of a tenement building as housing during subsequent waves of immigration.

UNIT 2: Sprawl: Challenges to the Metropolitan Landscape

American Studies Web

http://www.georgetown.edu/crossroads/asw/

This eclectic site provides links to a wealth of Internet resources for research in American studies, from rural and urban development, to federalism, to race and ethnic relations.

Sprawl Guide

http://www.plannersweb.com/sprawl/home.html

The online Sprawl Guide is designed to explain the key issues associated with sprawl: housing density, urban sprawl, and growth management. See the Sprawl Resource Guide to link to the wealth of information that is available on the Web.

Yahoo/Social Science/Urban Studies

http://www.yahoo.com/Social_Science/Urban_Studies/

Yahoo's page provides many valuable links to resources on various topics in urban studies and development, such as urban planning and urban sprawl.

UNIT 3: Urban Economies

IISDnet

http://iisd1.iisd.ca

This site of the International Institute for Sustainable Development, a Canadian organization, presents links on business and sustainable development, developing ideas, and Hot Topics. Linkages is its multimedia resource for environment and development policymakers.

The International Center for Migration, Ethnicity, and Citizenship

http://www.newschool.edu/icmec/

The Center is engaged in scholarly research and public policy analysis bearing on international migration, refugees, and the incorporation of newcomers in host countries. Explore this site for current news and to learn of resources for research.

National Immigration Forum

http://www.immigrationforum.org/index.htm

This pro-immigrant organization examines the effects of immigration on the U.S. economy and society. Examine the links for discussion of underground economies, immigrant economies, and other topics.

School of Labor and Industrial Relations

http://www.lir.msu.edu

This MSU/SLIR Hot Links page takes you to sites regarding industrial relations throughout the world. It has links from U.S. government and statistics, to newspapers and libraries, to international intergovernmental organizations.

U.S. Equal Employment Opportunity Commission

http://www.eeoc.gov

The EEOC's mission "is to ensure equality of opportunity by vigorously enforcing federal legislation prohibiting discrimination in employment." Consult this site for small business information, facts about employment discrimination, and enforcement and litigation.

UNIT 4: Urban Revival

Connect for Kids/Workplace

http://www.connectforkids.org/info-url1564/info-url_list.htm?section=Workplace

Browse here to learn about how employees, employees' families, society in general, and management can help a company and a community become more family-friendly. It provides useful hints and guidelines.

WWW Virtual Library: Demography & Population Studies

http://demography.anu.edu.au/VirtualLibrary/

This is a definitive guide to demography and population studies with important links to information about the urban environment and the quality of life worldwide.

www.dushkin.com/online/

UNIT 5: Urban Politics and Policies

Munisource.org
http://www.munisource.org

Hundreds of links to government bodies and agencies at all levels and from countries all over the world may be accessed here.

U.S. Department of Housing and Urban Development
http://www.hud.gov

Explore this government site for information on public housing, community development, and other topics. Click on Communities for links to state and local government sites.

Virtual Seminar in Global Political Economy/Global Cities & Social Movements
http://csf.colorado.edu/gpe/gpe95b/resources.html

This site of Internet resources is rich in links to subjects of interest in urban studies, covering topics such as sustainable cities, megacities, and urban planning. Links to many international nongovernmental organizations are included.

UNIT 6: Regentrification and Urban Neighborhoods

Center for Democracy and Citizenship
http://www.publicwork.org

This site from the Center for Democracy and Citizenship, associated with the Hubert H. Humphrey Institute of Public Affairs, provides information on current projects and research aimed at strengthening citizenship and civic education. Click on the links to stories describing various such endeavors.

Civnet/CIVITAS
http://www.civnet.org/index.htm

CIVITAS is an international, nongovernmental organization dedicated to promoting civic education and civil society. Find news from around the world related to civic education and civil society, a journal, and Web links here. Resources include a number of great historical documents.

The Gallup Organization
http://www.gallup.com

Open this Gallup Organization home page for links to an extensive archive of public opinion poll results and reports on a variety of topics related to urban life.

UNIT 7: Urban Problems: Crime, Education, and Poverty

The Center for Innovation in Education, Inc.
http://www.center.edu

This is the home page of the Center for Innovation in Education, self-described as a "not-for-profit, non-partisan research organization" focusing on K–12 education reform strategies. Click on its links for information about and varying perspectives on various reform initiatives such as the voucher system.

Justice Information Center
http://www.ncjrs.org

Provided by the National Criminal Justice Reference Service, this JIC site connects to information about corrections, courts, crime prevention, criminal justice, statistics, drugs and crime, law enforcement, and victims—among other topics—and presents news and current highlights.

National Institute on the Education of At-Risk Students
http://www.ed.gov/offices/OERI/At-Risk/

The At-Risk Institute supports a range of research and development activities designed to improve the education of students at risk of educational failure due to limited English proficiency, race, geographic location, or economic disadvantage. Access its work and links at this site.

The Urban Institute
http://www.urban.org

Visit this home page of the Urban Institute, an organization that investigates social and economic problems and analyzes efforts to solve these problems. Click on the links provided to access information on such topics as welfare reform and health care financing.

UNIT 8: Urban Futures: Cities After September 11, 2001

Department of State International Information Programs
http://usinfo.state.gov

A wide-ranging page, which is prepared by the Department of State, this site leads to discussions of topics of global concern such as urbanization. The site addresses today's Hot Topics as well as ongoing issues that form the foundation of the field. Many Web links are provided.

Metropolis Archives: Sustainability
http://www.metropolismag.com/html/content_1001/sup/index_b.html

At this site find many articles from the *Metropolis* journal's archives, which discuss issues of sustainability worldwide.

SocioSite: University of Amsterdam
http://www.pscw.uva.nl/sociosite/TOPICS/

This huge sociological site provides access to many discussions and references of interest to students of urban studies, such as links to information on inner cities and the effects of rapid urbanization.

United Nations
http://www.unsystem.org

Visit this Official Web Site Locator for the UN to learn about programs and plans related to urban development and urbanization around the world.

Urban Education Web
http://iume.tc.columbia.edu

Dedicated to urban students, their families, and the educators who serve them, this site is a clearing house on urban education.

We highly recommend that you review our Web site for expanded information and our other product lines. We are continually updating and adding links to our Web site in order to offer you the most usable and useful information that will support and expand the value of your Annual Editions. You can reach us at: *http://www.dushkin.com/annualeditions/*.

UNIT 1
The Urban Frame

Unit Selections

1. **Fear of the City, 1783 to 1983**, Alfred Kazin
2. **The Man Who Loved Cities**, Nathan Glazer
3. **The Death and Life of America's Cities**, Fred Siegel

Key Points to Consider

- Why have Americans traditionally feared big cities? Are these fears well founded?

- What are the different ways to define a city? To define urban life?

- What are the best-designed public spaces in your city or town? What makes a well-designed public space?

- Could merging these cities with their suburbs solve the social problems centered in America's big cities?

- How are Americans re-sorting themselves geographically? What effect will these population shifts have on social tensions?

 **Links: www.dushkin.com/online/**
These sites are annotated in the World Wide Web pages.

Manchester, N.H., Open Urban Space Website
http://www.mv.com/ipusers/env/
WNET/Tenement Museum
http://www.wnet.org/archive/tenement/eagle.html

Historically, the rapid growth of cities was largely a consequence of the developments of agricultural surpluses and factory systems. When farms produced surpluses, they needed a center for exchange. When factories were developed, the need for a concentrated labor supply and services was apparent. Thus, the city came into existence and became the center of both economic and cultural activity. While scholars agree that cities have existed for many centuries and in most parts of the world, only about 3 percent of the world's population lived in towns of more than 5,000 inhabitants before 1800. Even today, less than 30 percent of the world's population live in cities larger than 20,000 people. Nevertheless, urbanization has profoundly influenced the course of global development.

Urbanization is a complex and continuous process. It involves the movement of people from rural to urban areas, the creation of new patterns of living, and the communication of these new patterns to both urban and rural populations. In the Western world, the emergence of cities as a dominant force in the lives of people has been so rapid that it has been characterized as an explosion.

Social scientists have been fascinated with the process of urbanization. For the historian, the dynamics of urban growth illustrated the ways in which entire cultures and nations change over time. For the sociologist, the nature of urbanization became a way of explaining social arrangements and transforming social structures. The psychologist saw urbanization as a force in the ways that individuals learned to cope with new threats to survival. Through the process of urbanization, the economist came to recognize cities, and more recently suburbs, as important units for generating wealth and for allocating resources. The political scientists, too, studied urbanization in order to gain a better understanding of the ways in which order and change were maintained in these dynamic units. The change was more gradual for the anthropologist, but, nevertheless, urbanization proved to be a rich resource for observing and understanding the nature and importance of subcultural groups within the larger urban culture.

Opening a new chapter in American urban history, the relative decline of big cities has dominated American political and economic life since the 1960s. Alfred Kazin examines the anti-urban threads that weave through American culture and literature; Nathan Glazer pays tribute to William H. Whyte, one of America's most original and insightful urban analysts, singling out his prescient appreciation of density and public space in city life at a time when these qualities were widely viewed as social problems. Fred Siegel's "The Death and Life of America's Cities" reviews the misguided perspectives and policy choices that drove cities down, and the new generation of reformist mayors in the 1990s who debunked the conventional wisdom and seized

control of local taxes, quality of life issues, police strategies, and even improved local public schools in some instances. Now that these reformist mayors have left office, it remains to be seen whether cities can consolidate these gains, or if the 1990s will prove a fleeting recovery in the midst of a longer decline.

FEAR of the CITY
1783 to 1983

The city has been a lure for millions, but most of the great American minds have been appalled by its excesses. Here an eminent observer, who knows firsthand the city's threat, surveys the subject.

Alfred Kazin

EVERY THURSDAY, when I leave my apartment in a vast housing complex on Columbus Avenue to conduct a university seminar on the American city, I reflect on a double life—mine. Most of the people I pass on my way to the subway look as imprisoned by the city as my parents and relatives used to look in the Brooklyn ghetto where I spent my first twenty years. Yet no matter where else I have traveled and taught, I always seem to return to streets and scenes like those on New York's Upper West Side.

Two blocks away on Broadway there is daily carnage. Drunks outside the single-room-occupancy hotel dazedly eye me, a professor laden with books and notes trudging past mounds of broken glass, hills of garbage. Even at eight in the morning a craps game is going on in front of the hydrant that now gives off only a trickle. It has been left open for so many weeks that even the cover has vanished. On the benches lining that poor polluted sliver of green that runs down the center of Broadway, each drunk has his and her bottle in the regulation brown paper bag. A woman on crutches, so battered looking that I can't understand how she stands up, is whooping it up—totally ignored by the cars, trucks, and bicycles impatiently waiting at the red light. None of the proper people absorbed in their schedules has time to give the vagrants more than a glance. Anyway, it's too dangerous. No eye contact is the current rule of the game.

I left all this many times, but the city has never left me. At many universities abroad—there was even one improbable afternoon lecturing in Moscow—I have found myself explaining the American city, tracing its history, reviewing its literature—and with a heavy heart, more and more having to defend it. The American city has a bad reputation now, though there was a time, as the violinist Yehudi Menuhin said during World War II, when one of the great war aims was to get to New York.

There is no general fear of the city. While sharing it, I resent it, for I have never ceased feeling myself to be one of the city's

people, even as I have labored in libraries to seize the full background to my life in the city. But when in American history has there not been fear of the city—and especially on the part of those who did not have to live in it?

BEFORE THERE WERE American cities of any significance, the best American minds were either uninterested in cities or were suspicious of them. The Puritans thought of Boston as another Jerusalem, "a city upon a hill," but even their first and deepest impression was of the forest around it. This sense of unlimited space was bewitching until the end of the nineteenth century. In his first inaugural address in 1801, Thomas Jefferson pronounced, as if in a dream, that Americans possessed "a chosen country, with room enough for our descendants to the hundredth and thousandth generation." What was "chosen" was not just an endless frontier but the right people to go with it. This, as a matter of course to a great country squire like Jefferson, surveying the future from his mountaintop at Monticello, meant excluding the mobs he associated with European cities. Jefferson's attitude may have been influenced by the European Philosophes whom Louis XVI blamed for the French Revolution. Jefferson was a Philosophe himself; he would have agreed with a leader of the revolution, Saint-Just, that oppressed people "are a power on the earth." But he did not want to see any oppressed people here at all—they usually lived to become the kind of mob he detested and feared. "The mobs of great cities," he wrote in *Notes on Virginia*, "add just so much to the support of pure government, as sores do to the strength of the human body."

Jefferson knew what the city mob had done to break down ancient Rome as well as feudal France. America was a fresh start, "the world's best hope," and must therefore start without great cities. As a universal savant of sorts, as well as a classicist and scientist, Jefferson knew that Athens and Rome, Florence and Venice, Paris and London, had created the culture that was his proudest possession. And since he was an eighteenth-century skeptic, this cosmopolitan world culture was his religion. But anticipating the damage that "manufactures" could inflict on the individual, he insisted that on an unsettled continent only the proudly self-sustaining American "cultivator" could retain his dignity in the face of the Industrial Revolution.

It is not easy now to appreciate all Jefferson's claims for the rural life, and his ideas were not altogether popular with other great landowners and certainly not with such promoters of industry as Hamilton. Jefferson was a great traveler and world statesman who hardly limited himself to his country estate. Monticello, with its magnificent architecture, its great library, its array of inventions and musical and scientific instruments, more resembled a modern think tank (but imagine one this beautiful!) than the simple American farm he praised as a bastion of virtue.

But "virtue" was just what Jefferson sought for America. Whatever else they did, cities corrupted. The special virtue of rural folk rested on self-reliance, a quality unobtainable in "manufactures and handicraft arts" because these depended "on casualties and caprice of customers. Dependence begets subservience and venality, suffocates the germ of virtue, and prepares fit tools for the designs of ambition."

A few years later Emerson had a more complicated view of his society. The Sage of Concord was no farmer (Thoreau was his handyman) and did not particularly think the farmers in his neighborhood were the seat of all virtue. They were just of the earth, earthy. But believing in nothing so much as solitude, *his* right to solitude, his freedom only when alone to commune with Nature and his own soul ("Alone is wisdom. Alone is happiness."), Emerson found the slightest group to be an obstruction to the perfect life.

There is an unintentionally funny account in Emerson's journal for 1840 of just how irritating he found his fellow idealists. There was a gathering in some hotel—presumably in Boston, but one Emerson likened to New York's Astor House— to discuss the "new Social Plans" for the Brook Farm commune: "And not once could I be inflamed, but sat aloof and thoughtless; my voice faltered and fell. It was not the cave of persecution which is the palace of spiritual power, but only a room in the Astor House hired for the Transcendentalists.... To join this body would be to traverse all my long trumpeted theory, and the instinct which spoke from it, that one man is a counterpoise to a city—that a man is stronger than a city, that his solitude is more prevalent and beneficent than the concert of crowds."

Emerson finally agreed to help found Brook Farm but he could not have lived there. Hawthorne tried it for a while and turned his experiences into the wry novel *The Blithedale Romance.* Hawthorne was another Yankee grumpily insisting on his right to be alone but he did not take himself so seriously; he was a novelist and fascinated by the human comedy. A twentieth-century admirer of Emerson, John Jay Chapman, admitted that you can learn more from an Italian opera than from all the works of Emerson; in Italian opera there are always two sexes.

But Emerson is certainly impressive, bringing us back to the now forgotten meaning of "self-reliance" when he trumpets that "one man is a counterpoise to a city—that a man is stronger than

a city...." This was primary to many Americans in the nineteenth century and helped produce those great testaments to the individual spirit still found on the walls of American schoolrooms and libraries. Power is in the individual, not in numbers; in "soul," not in matter or material conglomeration. And "soul" is found not in organized religion, which is an obedience to the past, but in the self-sufficient individual whose "reliance" is on his inborn connection, through Nature, with any God it pleases him to find in himself.

CERTAINLY IT WAS EASIER then to avoid the "crowd." Thoreau, who went back many an evening to his family's boardinghouse for meals when he was at Walden Pond writing a book, said that the road back to Concord was so empty he could see a chicken crossing it half a mile off. Like Thoreau's superiority to sex and—most of the time—to politics, there is something truly awesome in the assurance with which he derogates such social facts as the city of New York: "I don't like the city better, the more I see it, but worse. I am ashamed of my eyes that behold it. It is a thousand times meaner than I could have imagined.... The pigs in the street are the most respectable part of the population. When will the world learn that a million men are of no importance compared with *one* man?"

To which Edgar Allan Poe, born in Boston and fated to die in Baltimore, could have replied that Thoreau had nothing to look at but his reflection in Walden Pond. Poe would have agreed with his European disciple Baudelaire on the cultural sacredness of great cities. He would have enjoyed Karl Marx's contempt for "rural idiocy." Poe was a great imagination and our greatest critic; as an inventor of the detective story and a storyteller, he was as dependent on the violence and scandal of New York in the 1840s as a police reporter. "The Mystery of Marie Roget," based on the actual murder of a New York shop assistant named Mary Rogers who was found dead in the Hudson after what is now believed to have been a botched abortion, was the first detective story in which an attempt was made to solve a real crime. Even the more than usual drunkeness that led to his death in Baltimore on Election Day of 1849 was typical of his connection with "low" urban life. He was found in a delirious condition near a saloon that had been used for a voting place. He seems to have been captured by a political gang that voted him around the town, after which he collapsed and died.

Yet just as Abraham Lincoln was proud of having a slow, careful countryman's mind, so Poe would have denied that *his* extraordinary mind owed anything to the cities in which he found his material. In the same spirit, John Adams from once rural Quincy, his gifted son John Quincy, and his even more gifted great-grandson Henry, all hated Boston and thought of the financial district on State Street as their antithesis. Herman Melville, born in New York, and forced to spend the last twenty-five years of his life as a customs inspector on the docks, hated New York as a symbol of his merchant father's bankruptcy and of his own worldly failure as an author. In a poem about the Civil War, when the worst insurrection in American history broke out in New York as a protest against the Draft Act, Melville imagined himself standing on the rooftop of his house

(From "Americans shall rule America," c. 1856–1860) Maryland Historical Society, Baltimore, MD

To prevent immigrants from voting, squads of Know-Nothing party members rampaged through Baltimore on Election Day in 1856. The city had a nationwide reputation for political violence.

on East Twenty-sixth Street listening to the roar of the mob and despising it:

> *... Balefully glares red Arson—there—and there.*
> *The Town is taken by its rats—ship-rats*
> *And rats of the wharves. All civil charms*
> *And priestly spells which late held hearts in awe—*
> *Fear-bound, subjected to a better sway*
> *Than sway of self; these like a dream dissolve,*
> *And man rebounds whole aeons back in nature.*

BEFORE THE Civil War there was just one exception among the great American writers to the general fear and resentment of the city. Whitman was to be prophetic of the importance of New York as a capital of many races and peoples and of the city as a prime subject in modern American writing. Whitman found himself as man and poet by identifying with New York. None of the gifted writers born and bred in New York—not Melville or Henry James or Edith Wharton—was to make of the city such an expression of personal liberation, such a glowing and extended fable of the possibilities released by democracy. "Old New York," as Edith Wharton called it (a patriciate that Melville could have belonged to among the Rhinelanders and Schuylers if his father had not failed in business), still speaks in Melville's rage against the largely Irish mob burning and looting in 1863. But Whitman, his exact contemporary, did not despair of the city's often lawless democracy when he helped put the first edition of *Leaves of Grass* into type in a shop off Brooklyn's Fulton Street.

Whitman found himself by finding the city to be the great human stage. Unlike earlier and later antagonists of the city, who feared the masses, Whitman saw them as a boundless human fellowship, a wonderful spectacle, *the* great school of ambition. The masses, already visible in New York's population of over a million, were the prime evidence Whitman needed to ground his gospel of American democracy as "comradeship." Formerly a schoolteacher, printer, carpenter, a failure at many occupations who was born into a family of failures and psychic cripples, Whitman felt that the big anonymous city crowd had made it possible for *him* to rise out of it.

One's self I sing, a simple separate person,
Yet utter the word Democratic, the word En-Masse.

Whitman found the model and form of *Leaves of Grass*, the one book he wrote all his life, in the flux and mass of the city—he even compared his book *to* a city. He never reached his countrymen during his lifetime, and the Gilded Age took the foam off his enthusiasm for democracy, but in decline he could still write, "I can hardly tell why, but feel very positively that if anything can justify my revolutionary attempts & utterances, it is such *ensemble*—like a great city to modern civilization & a whole combined clustering paradoxical unity, a man, a woman."

Whitman was that "paradoxical unity, a man, a woman." His powerful and many-sided sexuality gave him friends that only a great city can provide; his constant expectation of love from some stranger in the street, on the ferryboat, even his future reader—"I stop somewhere waiting for you"—made stray intimacies in the city as sweet to him as they were repellent to most Americans.

The trouble with the city, said Henry James, Henry Adams, and Edith Wharton, *is* democracy, the influx of ignorant masses, their lack of manners, their lack of standards. The trouble with the city, said the angry Populist farmers and their free-silver standard-bearer Bryan in 1896, is Wall Street, the "moneyed East," the concentration of capital, the banking system that keeps honest, simple farmers in debt. Before modern Los Angeles, before Dallas, Phoenix, and Houston, it was understood that "the terrible town," as Henry James called New York, could exist only in the crowded East. The West, "wild" or not, was land of heart's ease, nature itself. The East was the marketplace that corrupted Westerners who came East. There was corruption at the ballet box, behind the bank counter, in the "purlieus of vice." The city was ugly by definition because it lacked the elemental harmony of nature. It lacked stability and relentlessly wrecked every monument of the past. It was dirt, slums, gangsters, violence.

Above all it was "dark." The reporter and pioneer photographer Jacob Riis invaded the East Side for his book *How the Other Half Lives* (1890) because he was "bent on letting in the light where it was much needed."

Look at Riis's photograph "Bandit's Roost," 59 Mulberry Street, taken February 12, 1888. "Bandit's Roost" did not get its name for nothing, and you can still feel threatened as your eye travels down the narrow alley paved with grimy, irregularly paved stone blocks that glisten with wet and dirt. Tough-looking characters in derbies and slouch hats are lining both sides of the alley, staring straight at you; one of them presses a stick at the ground, and his left knee is bent as if he were ready, with that stick, to go into action at a moment's notice. The women at the open windows are staring just as unhelpfully as the derbied young fellow in the right foreground, whose chin looks as aggressive as the long, stiff lines of his derby.

CONSIDER NEW YORK just a century ago: the rooftops above the business district downtown are thick with a confusion of the first telephone lines crossing the existing telegraph wires. The immigrant John Augustus Roebling has built a suspension bridge of unprecedented length over the East River, thanks to the wire rope he has invented. This wire makes for a rooted strength and airy elegance as Roebling ties his ropes across one another in great squares. Brooklyn Bridge will be considered stronger as well as infinitely more beautiful than the other bridges to be built across the East River. But a week after opening day in 1883, the crowd panics as vast numbers cross the bridge, crushing several people to death—and exposing a fear of numbers, of great bridges, of the city itself, that even city dwellers still feel. What they thought of New York in the prairie West and the cotton South may easily be imagined.

But here is Central Park, the first great public park in the New World, finally completed after decades of struggle to reclaim a horrid waste. Unlike the European parks that were once feudal estates, Central Park has been carved, landscaped, gardened, built, and ornamented from scratch and specifically for the people. And this by a Connecticut Yankee, Frederick Law Olmsted, the most far-seeing of democratic visionaries, who saw in the 1850s that New York would soon run out of places in which city dwellers could escape the city. Though he will never cease complaining that the width of his park is confined to the narrow space between Fifth Avenue and what is now Central Park West, he will create a wonderland of walks, "rambles," lakes, gardens, meadows. All this is designed not for sport, political demonstrations, concerts, the imperial Metropolitan Museum, but for the contemplative walker. As early as 1858, before he was chosen superintendent but after having submitted the winning design, "Greensward," in a competition, Olmsted wrote of his park: "The main object and justification is simply to produce a certain influence in the minds of the people and through this to make life in the city healthier and happier. The character of this influence is a poetic one, and it is to be produced by means of scenes, through observation of which the mind may be more or less lifted out of moods and habits in which it is, under the ordinary conditions of life in the city, likely to fall…."

Alas, Central Park is not enough to lift some of us out of the "moods and habits" into which we are likely to fall. Even Walt Whitman, who truly loved New York, acidly let it drop in *Democratic Vistas* (1871) that "the United States are destined either to surmount the gorgeous history of feudalism, or else prove the most tremendous failure of time." The "great experiment," as some English sardonically call the democratic Republic, may very well depend on the city into which nearly a million immigrants a year were to pour at the beginning of the next century. Whitman was not prepared to estimate the effect on America of the greatest volunteer migration recorded in history. It was the eclipse of virtue that surprised him at the end of the century. As if he were Jefferson, he wrote: "The great cities reek with respectable as much as nonrespectable robbery and scoundrelism. In fashionable life, flippancy, tepid amours, weak infidelism, small aims, or no aims at all, only to kill time. In business (this all-devouring modern word business), the one sole object is, by any means, pecuniary gain. The magician's serpent in the fable ate up all the other serpents; and money-making is our magician's serpent, remaining today sole master of the field."

"Bandit's Roost, 39 1/2 Mulberry St.," by Jacob Riis (c.1888). Riis later found that five of nine children who lived in one of these houses were dead by the end of the year.

ARE CITIES all that important as an index of American health and hope? The French sociologist Raymond Aron thinks that American intellectuals are too much preoccupied with cities. He neglects to say that most Americans now have no other life but the life in those cities. Paris has been the absolute center of France—intellectually, administratively, educationally—for many centuries. America has no center that so fuses government and intellect. Although Americans are more than ever an urban people, many Americans still think of the city as something it is necessary to escape from.

In the nineteenth century slums were the savage places Jacob Riis documented in his photographs, but on the whole the savagery was confined to the slums. The political scientist Andrew Hacker has shown that "there was actually little crime of the kind we know today and in hardly any cases were its victims middle class. The groups that had been violent—most notably the Irish—had by 1900 turned respectable. The next wave of immigrants, largely from Eastern Europe and southern Italy, were more passive to begin with and accepted the conditions they found on their arrival… they did not inflict their resentments on the rest of society…."

What has finally happened is that fear of the city on the part of those who live in it has caught up with the fear on the part of those who did not have to live in it.

American fear of the city may seem ungrateful, since so much of our social intelligence depends on it. But the tradition of fear persists, and added to it nowadays—since all concern with the city is concern with class—has been fear of the "underclass," of blacks, of the youth gangs that first emerged in the mid-fifties. Vast housing projects have become worse than the slums they replaced and regularly produce situations of extreme peril for the inhabitants themselves. To the hosts of the uprooted and disordered in the city, hypnotized by the images of violence increasingly favored by the media, the city is nothing but a state of war. There is mounting vandalism, blood lust, and indiscriminate aggressiveness.

The mind reels, is soon exhausted, and turns indifferent to the hourly report of still another killing. In Brooklyn's 77th precinct a minister is arrested for keeping a sawed-off shotgun under his pulpit. On Easter Sunday uniformed police officers are assigned to protect churchgoers from muggers and purse snatchers. In parts of Crown Heights and Bedford-Stuyvesant, the *Times* reports that "there, among the boarded-up tenements, the gaudy little stores and the residential neighborhoods of old brownstones and small row houses, 88 people were killed in one year—16 in one three-block area." A hundred thousand people live and work in this precinct, but a local minister intones that "Life has become a mean and frightening struggle." Gunshots are heard all the time.

I was born and brought up alongside that neighborhood; the tenement in which my parents lived for half a century does not exist and nothing has replaced it. The whole block is a mass of rubble; the neighborhood has seen so much arson that the tops of the remaining structures are streaked with black. Alongside them whole buildings are boarded up but have been broken into; they look worse than London did after the blitz.

Democracy has been wonderful to me and for me, and in the teeth of the police state creeping up elsewhere in the world, I welcome every kind of freedom that leaves others free in the city. The endless conflict of races, classes, sexes, is raucous but educational. No other society on earth tolerates so many interest groups, all on the stage at once and all clamoring for attention.

Still, the subway car I take every day to the city university definitely contains a threat. Is it the young black outstretched across the aisle? The misplaced hilarity proceeding from the drinking group beating time to the ya-ya-ya that thumps out of their ghetto blaster? The sweetish marijuana fumes when the train halts too long in this inky tunnel and that make me laugh when I think that once there was no more absolute commandment in the subway than NO SMOKING?

Definitely, there is a threat. Does it proceed from the unhelpful, unsmiling, unseeing strangers around me? The graffiti and aggressive smears of paint on which I have to sit, and which so thickly cover every partition, wall, and window that I cannot make out the stations? Can it be the New York *Post*—"Post-Mortem" as a friend calls it—every edition of which carries the news MOM KILLS SELF AND FIVE KIDS? The battle police of the transit force rushing through one car after another as the motorman in his booth sounds the wailing alarm that signifies trouble?

What a way to live! It is apartness that rules us here, and the apartness makes the threat. Still, there is no other place for me to work and live. Because sitting in the subway, holding the book on which I have to conduct a university seminar this afternoon, I have to laugh again. It is *Uncle Tom's Cabin, or Life Among the Lowly.*

Alfred Kazin was Distinguished Professor of English at the City University of New York Graduate Center. He was the author of several books, including An American Procession, *a book about American writers from Emerson to T. S. Eliot.*

From *American Heritage*, February/March 1983, pp. 14–23. Reprinted by permission of *American Heritage* magazine, a division of Forbes, Inc.
© 1983 by Forbes, Inc.

The Man Who Loved Cities

by Nathan Glazer

William H. Whyte seems fated to be known as *The Organization Man* man. His death, on January 12, 1999, inspired numerous reflections on his sociological bestseller of 1956. Recognized as a benchmark in its own time, *The Organization Man* gave new meaning to a watchword of the decade, "conformity": Whyte's book put a carefully tailored suit of clothes on a vaguely defined but worrisome phenomenon of midcentury America. He identified what he saw as a "major shift in American ideology" away from an individualist Protestant Ethic. But his book was not a nostalgic lament. Rather, Whyte's mission was to reveal the dilemmas at the heart of a new group ethos—which he called the Social Ethic—that he saw emerging in the corporate and social world of the postwar era. The organization man was expected to be loyal to his organization, and the organization to be loyal to him. This was hardly a recipe for stability, however. He was required to pull up roots at a moment's notice and relocate himself and his family wherever the corporation thought it needed him. For these "transients," a new ideology of adaptive harmony beckoned.

The "tremendous premium on 'adjustment,'" on the "co-operative," on the "social," promised to make life and work proceed smoothly in "an age of organization"—and, Whyte observed, often did indeed help to do so. Yet he believed that the new group imperative, enshrined in social science and pop psychology and management theory, had also become "an ethic that offers a spurious peace of mind" and that should be resisted. And could be resisted: Whyte was convinced that "we are not hapless beings caught in the grip of forces we can do little about." The burden of his book was that "the fault is not in organization... it is in our worship of it. It is in our vain quest for a utopian equilibrium, which would be horrible if it ever did come to pass; it is in the soft-minded denial that there is a conflict between the individual and society. There must always be, and it is the price of being an individual that he must face these conflicts."

Four decades later, amid alarms about "downsizing," remembering Whyte has meant revisiting the well-known classic of his career: what changes have occurred in the relationship between corporations and those who serve them since Whyte first described the rather uninspiring bond? A great deal, was the not very surprising consensus. On the *New York Times* op-ed page, Virginia Postrel, the editor of the libertarian magazine *Reason*, and the sociologist Arlie Hochschild rendered opposing verdicts on the transformations that have left us with a world in which neither newly lean corporations nor those who serve them feel very deep loyalties.

We can conceive of the change as opening new vistas of freedom, as Virginia Postrel did. (Consider the entrepreneurs of Silicon Valley, no organization men they.) Or one can still find Whyte's portrait of the unanchored organization man affecting and relevant, as Hochschild did. And one can argue, as the sociologist and social critic Richard Sennett does in his new book *The Death of Character*, that the decay of the old ties uniting corporations and employees has introduced new strains into the life of the uncertain organization man and woman. This late-century anxiety is different from the old conformist strictures, which could so easily crimp creativity and autonomy, but it is no less damaging.

There is no question that Whyte's book had an enormous impact when it appeared. When the paperback came out, I was an editor at the then-young Anchor Books—which had also published the other great sociological bestseller of the 1950s, David Riesman's *Lonely Crowd* (of which I was a junior author). Sales of *The Organization Man* were explosive. It was remarkable in the exhaustiveness of its research. Who else would have read "every single one of the social notes" that appeared in a suburban newspaper over three-and-a-half years ("believe me," Whyte wrote, "that's a lot of social notes"), in order to find out whether meaningful patterns emerged from the parties and other gatherings that took place? Whyte did, and made a significant discovery: that physical layout-arrangements of cul de sacs, courtyards, driveways—dictated "a set of relationships... that were as important in governing behavior as the desires of the individuals in them." *The Organization Man* wove such data into an ambitious and very readable analysis that shed light on the erosion of the entrepreneurial ethos so central to American identity. It was misleading, Whyte emphasized, to see the problem as a new demand for conformity. The real danger was an alluring, and unrealistic, promise of group harmony, which all too easily tempted corporate Americans to surrender their independence.

Whyte's book identified tensions between the demands of organizational loyalty—which meant an often dizzying degree of mobility—and the desire for stability that certainly have not disappeared from corporate life in America. Yet events have moved beyond the book, as Whyte himself moved beyond it. The truth is that *The Organization Man* was more a prelude than the pinnacle of his career. Whyte deserves to be remembered, I believe, more for a second endeavor that was in many ways less sweeping than his signature book—a project that quite literally kept him much closer to the ground.

In the 1960s and 1970s, after leaving *Fortune*, where he'd been assistant managing editor, Whyte emerged as one of America's most influential observers of the city and the space around it, an observer whose distinctive contribution to our understanding of the American metropolis lay in his avoidance of anything so grandiose as a vision. Whyte, who became a distinguished professor at Hunter College of the City University of New York, advised Laurance S. Rockefeller on environmental issues and served as a planning consultant for various cities. What he set out to do was to become the best kind of expert, concerned with improving the way we live by paying close attention to the details: how we build our suburbs, how we choose sites for our houses, how we arrange our streets and plazas. This was a man who couldn't wait, on his many visits to many cities, to rush to a downtown street corner at midday and count the passersby! It was his way of taking a city's pulse.

Whyte began his career as an analyst, and became an activist. He turned his attention to the fate of cities and their surrounding countryside in the late 1950s, when the suburban boom was well under way, and when the errors of planners and developers were beginning to become evident to sharp observers. In his writing on the city, Whyte ranks with Jane Jacobs, though her efforts to show the way cities work when they work well are better known. Indeed, they both began writing on the city in the same volume, *The Exploding Metropolis*, a joint work by the editors of *Fortune* (where Whyte and Jacobs were working at the time) published in 1958. Whyte edited the book, and also contributed an introduction and two chapters, "Are Cities Un-American?" and "Urban Sprawl?" Jacobs wrote a chapter titled "Downtown Is for People," which set forth the main lines of her criticism of postwar city rebuilding, which she went on to develop in her classic 1961 book, *The Death and Life of Great American Cities*.

Whyte's second career grew naturally out of the blockbuster that launched him. Part of *The Organization Man* is devoted to examining one of the large planned developments sprouting up on the suburban fringes in the 1950s. These new bedroom communities were "the packaged villages that have become the dor-

mitory of the new generation of organization men." Whyte viewed them, and so (he found) did their self-conscious inhabitants, as "social laboratories" where "we can see in bolder relief than elsewhere the kind of world the organization man wants and may in time bring about." What most interested him was the way the transient inhabitants went about creating, "through a sort of national, floating co-operative,… a *new* kind of roots"—a kind of tie that gave them security and at the same time encroached on their autonomy.

Social connections in these classless communities, Whyte showed, were all-pervasive yet shallow, linking wives and children into a conveniently encompassing support system that demanded and rewarded constant group participation, from coffee klatches to school boards. "Suburbia is the ultimate expression of the interchangeability so sought by the organization," Whyte wrote, and of the social adaptability required to thrive within it. When the time came to move, families could be sure they would be spared a jolt in settling into another, not very different habitat. The suburban development in question was Park Forest, near Chicago, which plays an important role in the history of American sociology. (Herbert Gans was also studying it for his master's thesis at the University of Chicago, and he went on to write a classic work on the new planned suburb, *The Levittowners*.) Whyte moved on from Park Forest to ask the key question: Was this the best way for our cities to expand? He asked it in a pragmatic spirit, rather than in a despairing one.

It was easy enough to denounce the suburbs, the eating up of fields and farmland for individual plots to serve single-family houses, the homogeneity of the new communities, the absence of many urban amenities and of urban diversity. Such attacks were all too common, as were the parallel denunciations of the crowded city, with its noise, dirt, packed subways, and helter-skelter mix of housing. Whyte could appreciate both critiques. But he was skeptical of the received answers of the time, whether they issued from another major city and landscape observer, Lewis Mumford, or emerged in the work of the era's great visionary architect, Le Corbusier.

To Mumford, who was an admirer of the compact feudal city and a leader of the "garden city" movement, and to other critics, what was happening to the city and countryside was simply capitalism run wild, development without the restraint that sound community living required. Whyte was no enemy of capitalism and the free market. In studying what had gone wrong, he was as critical of the planners and the "new town" vogue, which Mumford believed could save us, as he was of shortsighted developers. Together, he believed, they made a terrible team. In *The Last Landscape* (1968), the book Whyte published the year before he began helping the New York City Planning Commission draft a comprehensive plan for the city, he criticized the diagnoses and the utopian desires that he felt were leading America astray:

> New town proposals are generally prefaced with a sweeping indictment of the city as pretty much of a lost cause. We tried, the charge goes, but the city is a hopeless tangle. Medical analogies abound. The city is dis-

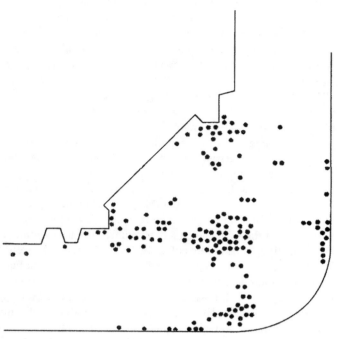

A White's-eye view of the world: a 1988 study showed where New Yorkers paused in front of Alexander's Department Store.

eased, cancerous, and beyond palliatives. The future is not to be sought in it, but out beyond, where we can start afresh.

The possibility of working with a clean slate is what most excites planners and architects about new towns. Freed from the constraints of previous plans and buildings and people, the planners and architects can apply the whole range of new tools. With systems analysis, electronic data processing, game theory, and the like, it is hoped, a science of environmental design will be evolved and this will produce a far better kind of community than ever was possible before....

To offer all this, a new town would really have to be a city.... But these are not to be like cities as we have known them. There is not to be any dirty work in them. There are not to be any slums. There are not to be any ethnic concentrations.... Housing densities will be quite low. There will be no crowded streets.... It will have everything the city has, in short, except its faults.

[But] you cannot isolate the successful elements of the city and package them in tidy communities somewhere else.... The goal is so silly it seems profound.

But denunciation was not Whyte's style. Rather, the question was what could be done, and he believed that much could. His 1964 book *Cluster Development* was a handbook on how developers could plot their new suburban tracts to save land, reduce the need for expensive roads, bring houses somewhat closer together, with no loss to what new suburb dwellers were looking for. His most substantial work, *The Last Landscape*, lays out in detail the many mechanisms, public and semipublic and private,

by which urban sprawl could be contained and the pleasures of the countryside saved.

As that book showed, Whyte's specialty was realism, not utopianism or alarmism. He did not simply wring his hands in despair or cry in outrage, though there was much to be outraged by. Instead, he aimed at what was practically possible, and he showed that a great deal was. For example, he observed that the trouble wasn't so much that America lacked countryside as that it was "becoming a hidden countryside." And unsightly billboards did not deserve all the blame. Greenery itself, as cleared land became second-growth forest, sealed off open vistas from the eye. "Landscape is not beautiful if you do not see it" was Whyte's point. He was just as practical about open spaces in the city. They were not the salvation so many planners believed, but they were well worth salvaging—and patchwork reclaiming was what it would take, Whyte insisted. "The most pressing need now," he wrote, "is to weave together a host of seemingly disparate elements—an experimental farm, a private golf course, a local park, the spaces of a cluster subdivision, the edge of a new freeway right-of-way." *The Last Landscape* remains a remarkably useful book.

Whyte's forte in his study of the city was close observation, indeed very close observation. He used time-lapse photography to capture the daily reality of urban places—parks, storefronts, sidewalks. He minutely analyzed what drew people, what repelled them, and how they were affected by small changes in the urban environment. It was the "eye-level view, the way people see it," not the bird's-eye view favored by grand planners, that interested Whyte. Thanks to him, we now understand that people are not repelled by crowding—up to a point—but excited by it, eager and able to adapt to it. Much of his work was pure scientific ethnography, but much of it gave hints and guidance on how we should build and rebuild in cities.

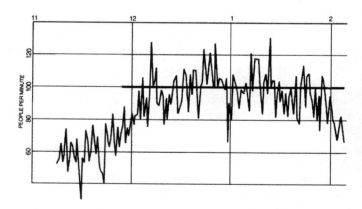

A connoisseur of sidewalks, Whyte bolstered his case for wider ones with his graph of heavy pedestrian traffic on Lexington Avenue near Grand Central Station.

Possibly Whyte's greatest achievement was to revise our thinking about urban density. He took issue with the prevailing wisdom: planners and critics, he felt, had gone too far in attacking urban crowding and disorder. According to the reigning view, the key to improved planning was to thin out the city and insist on more open space. But Whyte argued that density worked—it made the city attractive. His midday pedestrian counts downtown were his gauge of a city's prospects: if fewer than 1,000 people passed in an hour, "the city could pave the streets with gold for all the difference it would make. The city is one that is losing its center or has already done so."

In the 1930s, Mumford had written that New York was saved by the Depression, because the city would have ground to a halt had it continued to build skyscrapers and increase the number of jobs downtown. Nonsense, said Whyte. See how energetically people behave in crowds. They manage and, more than that, they love the easy access to so many facilities and specialized providers that their numbers make possible. Indeed New York later added tens of millions of square feet of office space, with almost no increase in public transit facilities, in a succession of postwar building booms. Far from grinding to a halt, as Mumford expected, the city thrived. It became clear that the planning theorists had missed some important things. In his *Social Life of Small Urban Spaces* (1980), and in many lectures and consultations with city officials, developers, and planners in which he tried to put his insights to good use, Whyte pointed out how much had been overlooked.

It was Whyte who helped to identify and remedy a fundamental misunderstanding of the life of city and streets that planners of the 1960s embedded in the zoning codes of New York and other cities. The codes rewarded office tower developers who pulled their buildings back from the street, creating spaces rather grandiloquently called plazas. The idea was to open up crowded city streets, admitting light and air. But the new plazas often became little more than dead zones between streets and building lobbies, spaces that derelicts and other undesirable people were only too happy to occupy. Other plazas became all but inaccessible, to protect them from just such users. Whyte pointed out that the plazas broke up the continuous street front that is an identifying characteristic of the good city, providing entertainment and a sense of security for the strolling pedestrian.

The key to reclaiming these plazas, Whyte explained, was to attract more people to them. Then the derelicts and unappealing users would be crowded out or stay away. His research uncovered small but key details that draw people: movable seats are important, for example, and the availability of food and drink, even from a pushcart, is helpful. Any fixed seating—a designer's or architect's arrangement of space, whatever it was and whatever its formal virtues—imposed itself on those who tried to use the space. People wanted to feel in control, and one way they could feel in control was to be able move their chairs, whether to get closer to someone to whom they were talking, or further away from someone to whom they didn't want to talk,

or to catch a ray of sun, or simply to shift around for no reason at all. And so the lightweight, unattached chair became a fixture in the New York City plazas and similar city spaces elsewhere.

For an example of Whyte's ideas at work, it is hard to do better than New York City's Bryant Park, recently restored after years of neglect. Lying along 42nd Street and behind the city's grand public library, the park was originally cut off from the street, physically and visually isolated from passing pedestrians and motorists by shrubs. The design worked in New York's earlier, more placid days, creating a sense of shelter and privacy for harried New Yorkers. But in a high-crime city it was a disaster, providing a well-concealed haven for miscreants. Now the park has been opened up and transformed into one of the best-used open spaces in New York City. If you can find an empty chair, you can move it wherever you want, and there are almost as many food vendors as pigeons.

T*he Exploding Metropolis* was recently reprinted—40 years after its original appearance!—by the University of California Press. Whyte is restored to the title page as editor (the original volume was "by the editors of *Fortune*"). It says something about Whyte's enduring contribution that in 1999 *The Organization Man* is out of print, but his books on the city and on open spaces are still available. In his last book, *City: Rediscovering the Center* (1988), Whyte wrote with typical realism that "I am eschewing prophecy in this book. It is hard enough to figure out what is happening now, let alone what might or might not 20 years hence." But he was optimistic that "the center is going to hold."

Indeed, the signs since then are that, thanks not least to advice he had offered 20 years before in *The Last Landscape*, downtown revitalization is alive and well—and often it is much the sort of motley enterprise he favored. As Whyte urged then, invoking San Francisco's waterfront as a model, even touristy rehabilitation can work. "Almost every city with a waterfront has a pier or shoreside structure that could be refashioned for restaurants and shops," he pragmatically observed. "They are slightly fraudulent—the seafood is apt to be flown in from somewhere else and not very well prepared—but the view is good, and people do love the honky tonk." *The Exploding Metropolis* and the works that followed are urban history, but they are more than that. Whyte's work remains a living and usable handbook for improving our cities, our countryside, and our lives.

NATHAN GLAZER *is professor of education emeritus at Harvard University and the author of many books, including* Ethnic Dilemmas *(1983),* The Limits of Social Policy *(1988), and most recently,* We Are All Multiculturalists Now *(1998). He co-edited* The Public Face of Architecture *with Mark Lilla (1987). Copyright © 1999 by Nathan Glazer.*

From *The Wilson Quarterly*, Spring 1999, pp. 27-33. © 1999 by Nathan Glazer. Reprinted by permission.

The death and life of America's cities

FRED SIEGEL

IN the wake of the events of September 11, American cities are basking in the reflected glory of New York and its courageous mayor, Rudolph Giuliani. Giuliani's ascent to the status of a national hero, "America's mayor," has eclipsed not only his own accomplishments but the mixed if hopeful condition of big-city America.

America's larger cities are on the upswing after a wave of reformist mayors in the 1990s. Even before the economic boom of that decade took hold, Cleveland's mayor Mike White, Chicago's Richard Daley, Milwaukee's John Norquist, Indianapolis's Steven Goldsmith, Denver's Wellington Webb, and Philadelphia's Ed Rendell had begun to turn their cities around. While the federal government was locked in a decade of trench warfare, reform currents flowed through city halls. Innovations in school, welfare, and crime policy all had a local address. When George Bush described himself as a "compassionate conservative" during the 2000 presidential campaign, he was following in the path of Los Angeles's highly effective Republican mayor, Richard Riordan, who called himself "a bleeding heart conservative." Bush's rival, Al Gore, wrapped himself in the success of Democratic mayors such as Daley, Webb, and Detroit's Dennis Archer.

But for all the accomplishments associated with these men, most cities will need several more successful administrations to repair the damage done over the past 40 years. For the revival to be sustained, it must transform the big cities' dysfunctional political culture. The danger, in the words of a world-weary veteran of Philadelphia politics, is that "Rendell improved things here just enough to make it safe to go back to the policies that produced the problems in the first place."

Unlike the crusading mayors of the Progressive era, none of these recent reformers were part of a broad social movement to institutionalize reform. Thus few of the reformers groomed successors. The new-wave chief executives who left office in Philadelphia, Los Angeles, Jersey City, and Cleveland have been replaced by back-to-business-as usual mayors, though in the first two cities reform currents haven't been entirely stilled. Reform continues in Indianapolis and to a lesser extent in New York while the situation in Detroit is ambiguous.

Big-city revival

Before we consider the problem of sustaining the urban revival, let's consider the nature of the revival itself. The prosperity of the 1990s was different from earlier expansions. The 1960s boom had been accompanied by riots, rapidly rising crime rates, and social breakdown. In the 1980s, many major cities, including Detroit and Baltimore, never caught the economic wave, while those that did still suffered from increasing crime and welfare dependency. In the 1990s, by contrast, urban home ownership achieved historic highs, and poverty dropped sharply to its lowest rate since 1979. This trend was particularly pronounced in New York, where the greatest gains occurred in poor outer-borough neighborhoods.

New Orleans mayor Marc Morial captured the spirit of the urban renewal when he announced last year that the city was reviving the streetcar route along the Desire corridor. "People," he exulted, will once again "be able to ride a streetcar named Desire." "We're returning to the future." The 2000 Census suggests that cities all across America have been "returning to the future" as incubators of new businesses and catalysts of upward mobility for immigrants. Fueled by immigration, New York, Los Angeles, and Miami reached record population levels. Prosperity hit not only these and other fast-growing cities like Denver, Charlotte, and Columbus, but also so-called "dinosaurs" like Chicago, Boston, and Kansas City, all once given up for dead. Eight of the ten largest cities posted growth, and even those that continued to shrink, including Detroit, Philadelphia, and Cleveland, did so at much slower rates or in some cases nearly held even.

It would be a mistake to assume that the big cities can ever again achieve the dominant position they once held. America continues to become more suburban, as city populations continue to decline relative to their surrounding areas. For every three households that "returned" to the city, notes demographer Bill Frey, five households departed for the suburbs. Growth was fastest in overwhelmingly white exurbia, but minorities joined the move out of the cities as well. Still, as recently as the early 1990s, rising crime, welfare, and unemployment rates as well as riots in Los Angeles and New York led many to assume that central cities were dying if not already dead. What happened to turn things around? Some of the credit goes to the surging economy, some to immigration. But both of those elements were present in the 1980s and failed to spur an urban revival at that time.

Three broad social changes made an enormous difference. First, the storm created by the rise of black political power in the 1960s has largely passed. Day-to-day racial tensions have eased, and African-American leaders have been incorporated into the political classes of all the major cities. Race remains a major factor in local politics, but after three decades of black mayors, whites are far less fearful of blacks in power, and blacks have, for the most part, come to recognize that black mayors are fully capable of failing their own core constituency.

Secondly, the decline of manufacturing finally began to pay off in many cities. The reduction of manufacturing production in the past half-century occurred almost entirely within city boundaries, as nonurban manufacturing has held steady. Deindustrialization, a disaster for some cities, has been an opportunity for others to upgrade their quality of life by turning manufacturing lofts into living spaces and once-polluted waterways into recreation areas. Old manufacturing districts, like Soho in New York and Lodo in Denver, are now hip places to live. College graduates have flocked back to the center cities, which have become the place to meet other young, single twenty-somethings. Refurbished lofts and a newly developed nightlife like that of Baltimore's intriguing harbor neighborhood, Fell's Point, attract young professionals, while empty-nesters are drawn to the city's museums, restaurants, and theaters.

Many of those who work in Fell's Point are part of the software and graphics industry. The first phase of the high-tech revolution occurred largely in exurbia, but the second phase, involving designing software content, has found a natural home in the creative quarters of our older cities. Even famously conservative Cincinnati, a city torn apart by recent riots, is home to a thriving software sector.

Thirdly, retailers have discovered the untapped buying power of the underserved inner-city market. Cities have benefited from the saturation of suburban markets. One developer explained that he was looking at Brooklyn locations because "if we put up one more shopping center on the [New Jersey] Route 1 corridor, the whole place is going to sink into the ground, if it isn't killed off by traffic congestion first." Insurance companies have similarly awakened to the potential of what the *Wall Street Journal* has called "the last untapped insurance market in the U.S."

Policies that made a difference

But these structural changes would not have brought about the resurgence of the big city in the 1990s without a concurrent reconceptualization of urban issues. Washington, D.C., mayor Marion Barry captured the essence of many 1980s mayoralties when he insisted that he should not be held accountable for the mayhem in his city. He blamed the federal government for not giving the District enough money and exclaimed, "I'm not going to let murder be the gauge, since we're not responsible for murders, we can't stop the murders." Barry's portrait of a victim mayor presiding over a victimized population was challenged in the Reagan years, but to little effect. In the summer of 1982, the Reagan administration created a firestorm with a report written by Housing and Urban Development staffer Steven Savas. Savas, a veteran of the disastrous mayoral administration of John Lindsay, used his New York experience to challenge every major assumption of 1960s urban liberalism. Guarantees of federal support, Savas wrote, have created "crippling dependency rather than initiative and independence." Federal programs, he argued, have transformed local officials "from leaders of self-reliant cities to wily stalkers of federal funds." But Savas insisted that "cities can learn to become masters of their own destinies—regardless of the level of federal support."

The Savas argument was received with hostility, but it slowly gained currency. By the early 1990s, a group dubbed "the new mayors" had embraced his approach to city governance. Over the course of the 1990s, the federal government's involvement in cities declined while the cities, newly skeptical of Washington, have revived. If Barry depicted himself as a cork on the ocean, the reform mayors of the 1990s, beginning with Milwaukee's John Norquist, assumed responsibility for the condition of their cities. Denver mayor Wellington Webb encapsulated their approach when he described mayors as "CEOs," fully accountable for the performance of city government. He argued that mayors "need to bury forever the old image of mayors with a tin cup and an extended palm asking for handouts to sustain and expand cumbersome bureaucracies." Providence's roguish but enormously effective mayor Buddy Cianci summed up the change in attitude: "I've been a mayor in the 70s, 80s, and 90s, and it used to be that being a big city mayor meant being a social worker.... Now mayors are entrepreneurs."

All the new mayors recognized that the central cities would continue to lose population and jobs to their suburbs unless steps were taken to bring taxes under control and improve the quality of life. This conclusion has led to a new concern with the details of daily existence. Daley planted trees throughout the city, even on the roof of City Hall, and Cleveland's mayor Mike White attacked graffiti and potholes. John Norquist has encouraged excellence in the architectural design for new projects in Milwaukee, arguing that cities' strong suit is their public spaces. Cities offer pleasures of public life unavailable in suburbs, he notes, where "life is filtered through a two screen experience—the TV and the windshield."

Less dramatic, but almost as significant, has been the new attention paid to neighborhood vitality by mayors like Thomas Menino of Boston, Norquist, Daley, and Webb. Menino recognizes that retail is crucial to a neighborhood's revival. "You can't just do housing," he argues. "Commerce isn't the last step in a community's comeback; more often, it has to be the first." Many mayors speak of new convention centers or stadiums, but Menino endorses a different strategy. He proudly told *Governing Magazine* that "in the eight years I've been in office, Boston has built 12 new supermarkets." He explained that "a supermarket is the focal point of a community; you need it to get the foot traffic."

But the greatest achievement of the last decade was bringing crime under control. New York led the way through a combination of the "broken windows" policing strategy and the Comstat crime-mapping program. Broken-windows policing takes seriously small crimes, such as public drinking and urination, that can make a neighborhood seem threatening to residents and inviting to would-be felons. In the most famous example of the broken-windows approach, the New York City Transit Police began arresting turnstile jumpers in the early 1990s and found that one in seven was wanted on outstanding felony warrants. Before Comstat, a method of charting crime trends, the information that police used was sometimes weeks or even months old. Now crime patterns are tracked daily so that problems can be quickly addressed and precinct commanders held responsible for the crime rates in their districts.

Baltimore's innovative mayor Martin O'Malley has taken the Comstat principles and applied them to a range of services. In the case of sanitation, he has used the Comstat mapping principles to target emerging problems and hold district managers accountable. O'Malley's innovations have introduced an unaccustomed transparency to government agencies, whose operations were once understood only by a few insiders. Baltimore's success has led mayors and other officials from more than one hundred cities to visit and learn how it was done.

How much of the legacy of the new mayors will endure? How much of their success has been institutionalized? After a decade of strong, successful mayors, cities such as Los Angeles, Oakland, Spokane, and Cincinnati have enhanced the power of the executive office relative to city councils and school boards. The experience of recent years suggests that mayors need the authority to override the parochial interests that dominate city councils and boards of education. In Chicago, Detroit, and Philadelphia, mayors now have more power over the educational system, and New York is also likely to move in that direction. But a strong mayor doesn't guarantee a strong city: Detroit's Coleman Young ruled virtually without opposition but sent his city deeper and deeper into failure.

George Musgrove, Oakland's deputy city manager, not too long ago took an optimistic view of the future, claiming that "a movement of good government for cities has swept the country, and all good mayors—African-American, white, Latino—are governing that way." New Orleans mayor Marc Morial sounded a more cautious note: "The last few years have been tremendous for most of the mayors." But looking at the mayoral campaigns then underway in Atlanta, Cincinnati, Cleveland, Detroit, Hartford, Houston, New York, and Seattle, Morial mused that there was no guarantee that the sort of people and policies that had made for the 1990s revival would continue to hold sway. Morial was right to worry. The recent rounds of elections suggest, at best, a range of possibilities for continued urban revitalization.

The good and the bad

Indianapolis and Philadelphia represent the best- and worst-case scenarios, respectively. With a string of four consecutive effective mayors, Indianapolis is the envy not only of misbegotten neighbor Cincinnati but of much of the country. In the 1990s, Steve Goldsmith transformed Indianapolis government by opening up city services to competition with private-sector vendors. The result has been a more efficient government, as union workers now have the opportunity to compete to perform city services. But despite his successes on services ranging from bus routes to waste-water management to the upkeep of the parks, Goldsmith had scant luck in reforming the hidebound police department and the schools, which are under an independent board of education. Democrat Bart Peterson, picking up where Goldsmith left off, is trying to circumvent the board of education by supporting charter schools. He is the first mayor in the country to be given state authorization to approve charter schools on his own.

Following the record levels of homicide of the Goldsmith era, Peterson has also promised to hire 200 more police officers over four years. But his reform efforts are likely to be hampered by a system that allows a new administration to appoint only the chief and deputy chief of police, while everyone else in the department, officers and patrolmen alike, belong to the same strong union.

In Philadelphia, by contrast, the reform impetus of the 1990s, already fading during the second term of Mayor Ed Rendell, has been replaced by a return to patronage and process-driven politics. Rendell saved Philadelphia from collapse, but whether he permanently altered the city's self-defeating political culture is not yet clear.

In the early 1990s, Mayor Rendell made a reputation for himself as an urban reformer by rescuing Philadelphia—which was losing jobs and population—from near bankruptcy. This was a city that had raised taxes 19 times in 11 years, and in which municipal workers could take off one workday in five. Rendell knew that Philadelphia's traditional patronage politics had come to a dead end. He faced down the city's powerful unions, which he said hadn't "had a bad day in 30 years," by trimming paid holidays and eliminating work rules that required, for example, three workers to change a light bulb at the city-owned airport.

But successor John Street, who was elected in 1999 with the support of those same unions and interest groups, has shown little inclination to buck the city's permanent political class. Street, the city's second African-American mayor, was elected by the same racially mixed public-sector coalition that former tough-guy mayor Frank Rizzo tried to put together just before his death in 1991. Mayor Street is a brilliant tactician and negotiator. But while his allies and donors are doing well, Philadelphia as a whole has very little to show for the first two years of his administration.

Philadelphia lost 68,000 people—4 percent of its population—in the 1990s. Ten percent of the city's land is unoccupied, and about 14,000 abandoned buildings blight the landscape. The obstacles to redeveloping abandoned land for new uses are numerous. Before confronting the city's rococo zoning rules and permit processes, a prospective builder must get legal possession of the abandoned lots. According to the *Philadelphia Daily News*, "Anyone wanting to take over a tax-delinquent vacant lot in Philadelphia must go through 54 steps at 12 agencies, a process that takes at least two years and often many more. The job is only slightly easier if the city already owns the lot: 30 steps at nine agencies." If persistent enough to acquire the land, builders will then face labor costs that make construction 60 to 80 percent more expensive than in the suburbs. And after overcoming all those hurdles, they will find that the building-trades member of the zoning board—an ally of Mayor Street and a representative of the sheet-metal workers—requires that all new homes, no matter how modest in price, have central air-conditioning.

But instead of acknowledging the obvious fact that the city's permit and zoning system is designed to produce public-sector jobs rather than new construction, Street and the city council got bogged down in a lengthy fight over control of the money set aside for cleaning abandoned lots and buildings. Street wanted council permission to float $250 million worth of bonds before receiving public or city-council sanction. But the council, well aware of Street's history on this matter, balked. As Rendell's council president, Street had controlled Philadelphia's empowerment-zone monies. He produced consulting contracts and several large holes in the ground, but virtually no new development. In fact, the population inside Philadelphia's empowerment zone dropped 17 percent in the 1990s, or four times the city's overall rate of decline, despite an infusion of $79 million in federal funds. Suspicions were therefore aroused that

the blight money was intended largely for Street's friends and donors. The mayor himself, never bashful on this point, has explained that "the people who support me in the general election have a greater chance of getting business from my administration."

Mayor Street appears to view all policy choices through a special-interest lens. This year the state threatened a takeover of the city's violence-ridden, financially bankrupt school system, in which fewer than half of the students graduate and the teachers' workday is among the shortest in the country. Street initially welcomed the takeover as a chance for reform. But when the NAACP, the strike-prone teachers, and the contractors and suppliers objected, Street changed his tune. His staff and allies devised a secret plan to subvert reform. The 67-page plan explained how Street could undermine the state by shifting key educators to the city payroll to "cripple" school operations. But the report warned that the city must "avoid the public perception that the mayor does not care about improving education and is using the city's schoolchildren as pawns in a political power struggle."

Street largely succeeded in derailing major school reform. The new school commission run by the city and the state quickly moved to divide the spoils by awarding $675,000 worth of consulting and legal contracts to Pennsylvania Republicans and Street's Democratic backers. But Street's "victory" so aroused the ire of the state legislature that limited change in the form of several new charter schools will now go ahead. In the words of one Philadelphia insider, "School reform has gone from promising to fraudulent to weak."

After Street's early manipulation of school-reform politics, a local political insider claimed that "John Street has just removed the last obstacle to his reelection in two years." But in March, 2002 the overconfident mayor provoked an unexpected civic storm by announcing that he was suspending the small scheduled reductions in the city's onerous wage tax. This levy gives Philadelphia the highest family-tax burden in the country. Economists at the Federal Reserve estimate that Philadelphia has lost more than 200,000 jobs to the wage tax since 1970. During the 1990s, when other cities were enjoying an employment boom, Philadelphia lost 33,662 private-sector jobs.

With his announcement, Street ignited a very public fight with the usually moribund business leadership. Philadelphia politics is defined by an exquisite cynicism: Columnists brag that the city is a model of democracy because everyone can afford the $10 bribes necessary to buy off city plumbing inspectors. But when the mayor insisted that even a small tax cut would lead to library and recreation-center closings and possibly even a shortage of police bullets, he tapped an unexpected wellspring of anger in a city where the population has shrunk even as the city workforce continues to grow. The city chamber of commerce, its members shod in wing-tipped loafers, led a march on city hall that was joined by Teamsters and a bevy of black ministers. Loudspeakers blared the Beatles'

"Taxman" and "Revolution" and, of course, the theme from *Rocky*. Conceding that the wage tax "has become symbolic of something that is fundamentally wrong with our city and its tax structure," Street backed off and allowed the tax cut to go through.

To Street's surprise, it wasn't possible to go all the way back to business as usual. The rising expectations produced by the Rendell years had become a factor to be reckoned with. But even with the tiny cuts in the wage tax restored, Philadelphia is still uncompetitive. And it remains uncertain whether this will be the end of tax relief or the beginning of a more promising future.

Los Angeles

Richard Riordan, who became mayor of Los Angeles in 1992, restored the confidence of his riot-torn city. In the early 1990s, Los Angeles was struck by a series of blows. The city was particularly hard hit by the 1991 recession, which coincided with the end of the Cold War and a sharp decline in the area's defense employment. The administration of Tom Bradley, mayor since 1973, was shaken by scandals. Additionally, in a city where the two-party system usually refers to the mayor's party and the police chief's party, Bradley and his police chief—the imperious Daryl Gates—were not on good terms. They hadn't spoken for a year when the 1992 Los Angeles riots broke out, and their freud left the city government paralyzed.

Riordan, a businessman with a long history of civil involvement, inherited a dispirited city and an office with sharply limited powers. Los Angeles had a uniquely organized city government—a strong council, a commission system that ran the port and the water and power systems, and a police chief who was virtually independent. But Riordan used his limited powers to calm and reassure the city. He recognized that the loss of military contractors, as well as other major corporations, meant the city was going to have to pay a great deal more attention to small and medium-sized businesses. He was particularly effective at restoring business confidence by reducing the red tape that had built up during Bradley's long reign.

Despite his campaign promises, Riordan was never able to bring the LAPD up to full strength. Demoralized by the 1992 Rodney King riots, rogue cops, threats of a federal consent decree, and intense hostility between the chief and the police union, the force was perennially short-staffed. Los Angeles has roughly 40 percent of New York's population, but only about 21 percent of the Big Apple's police officers. Riordan spoke with admiration of New York's broken-windows and Comstat policing but was never able to push through similar reforms in Los Angeles. Riordan was successful, however, in using his own considerable fortune to win public approval of a new charter that expanded the powers of the mayoralty. The

1999 city charter limited the executive power of the city council and gave the mayor the ability to replace department heads, subject to a council veto. It represented, asserted the *Los Angeles Times*, "the most profound change in the structure of government since the 1920s." Furthermore, the office of the police chief was stripped of its right to tenure and was made subject to oversight by a police commission, which now can terminate the chief's contract after a five-year term.

By restructuring the institutions of city government, the new charter held out the promise of continued reform. But Riordan's chosen heir, Republican businessman Steve Soboroff, was eliminated in the first round of the 2001 nonpartisan primary. Neither of two leading candidates, Democrat James Hahn, a cautious career politician whose father had been a great favorite of African-American voters, nor the charismatic Antonio Villaraigosa, a former state assembly speaker bidding to be the city's first Latino mayor, campaigned on the continuation of Riordan's policies. Instead, both invoked the memory of the late Tom Bradley.

The year 2001 was an important one for Los Angeles. The city was to elect a new mayor, a new controller, and new city attorney, and, due to term limits, six of eleven council members. Furthermore, the city had gone through an unprecedented demographic change. Over the course of 40 years, Los Angeles had been transformed from the whitest major city in the United States to a city with a Latino majority.

After the first round of voting, it appeared that Villaraigosa would be the victor. Backed by a labor-Latino alliance, the candidate spoke of using the mayor's enhanced powers to remake the city. "Villaraigosa," explained influential journalist Harold Meyerson, promised to turn "Los Angeles into the next great proving ground for American progressivism, the place where the great wave of new immigrants stakes its claim on the nation's conscience, bounty and future." But it was a false denouement. Villaraigosa was defeated in the run-off by Hahn, who assembled a *mesalliance* of black voters from South Los Angeles and white moderates from the San Fernando Valley.

Hahn, who grew up as a part of the political class of this apolitical city, has continued and even enhanced policies designed by Riordan that aimed at supporting small businesses. But Hahn's tenuous electoral coalition has fractured. The perennial contest for control over the police department has roiled his relationship with blacks, even as a strong secession movement suggests that much of the city assumes that Los Angeles is unreformable.

Los Angeles, with its 466 square miles, is *de facto* a regional city. The downtown area, where city government is located, is only one of a half-dozen business centers and is remote from the lives of most people. Like Riordan, Hahn was elected with the support of the San Fernando Valley, which is separated from the rest of the city by a low-lying mountain chain. The Valley sees itself as forever shortchanged when it comes to city services, comparing unfavorably the services it receives with those in the nearby small cities of Burbank, Glendale, and Pasadena, where city government is accessible and responsive. Like Riordan, Hahn has paid lip service to Valley concerns, and in the campaign, he implied that he would stay neutral in the secession fight. But as mayor, Hahn has aligned himself with the city's public-sector unions, which bitterly oppose a divorce, eliciting cries of betrayal. As of mid-March of this year, polls show that support for secession has grown by 10 percent and now leads 55 to 36 percent in the Valley and 46 to 38 percent in the city as a whole. There is even a growing secession movement in Hahn's home territory, the port neighborhood of San Pedro.

Secessionists are not the only ones crying foul. The crime rate, driven by a revival of gang activity, is rising rapidly. But this has been overshadowed by the hostilities between two of Hahn's core constituencies, African Americans and the Police Protective League (PPL). Hahn, who seems unaware of, and uninterested in, the methods that have made other cities more successful in reducing crime, promised both to retain African-American Bernard Parks as police chief and to grant the PPL a three-day work week. But the PPL has been at war with Parks, who has cited 6,000 of the 9,000 officers for one infraction or another. Hahn has had personal difficulties with Parks, who often overshadows him, and ultimately sided with the PPL, agreeing not to reappoint Parks. His once-loyal black supporters were angered, seeing his decision as a dangerous erosion of their political power.

In other cities these two developments might produce enormous turmoil. Hahn supporters fear that an alliance between anti-Hahn secessionists and blacks angry over Parks's dismissal might allow the secessionists to break away. But government tends to be at best a secondary matter in this sunshine city where politics is derided as a profession for people without the good looks to make it in the movies. Hahn, who to date has made but limited use of his enhanced powers, seems to have little in the way of an agenda other than hanging on. If he falters, he may be replaced in the next election by the new city attorney Rocky Delgadillo, a Latino centrist. Delgadillo, who appeals to African Americans, has a strong probusiness agenda and has promoted New York-style police practices.

Detroit

In Detroit, the successor administration has been slow to reveal its character. It remains to be seen whether the reforms of former mayor Dennis Archer will be sustained, let alone advanced. Detroit's population had declined from 2 million in 1950 to a little under 1 million in 2000, but like Philadelphia, the city caught a bit of the 1990s rising tide. The city Archer inherited from five-term mayor Coleman Young in 1993 was near collapse. The government barely functioned: "When I walked into the city hall," Archer has commented, "I didn't even have a computer. We still had rotary dial phones in some departments." But that was hardly the worst of it. Coleman Young, who liked to think of himself as a "badass," had taken pleasure in cursing at the suburbanites beyond Eight Mile road, whom he accused of "pillaging the city." They returned the sentiment in kind, leaving Detroit economically isolated. Young was similarly hostile to the police, arguing that "crime is a problem but not the problem. The police are the major threat… to the minority community." Murder and arson soared. As one observer put it, "It is as if the [1967] riot never ended, but goes on in slow motion."

Young created a cult of personality, but he was never able to deliver basic services—the city didn't even plow residential streets after snowstorms. The subject of numerous federal investigations, Young was never found guilty of anything, though his former police chief, the chief's top deputy, and a Young business partner were convicted of embezzling about $2.5 million each from a Detroit Police Department fund. Detroit's downtown was so vacant that it was proposed that the empty skyscapers be turned into a necropolis, a monument to urban failure. When the city cut back on power for lighting to save money, people joked that the "last one to leave should turn off the lights."

Unlike Young, Archer consistently maintained a high standard of conduct and kept his administration largely free of scandals. He reduced Detroit's growth-stunting business and income taxes and balanced its budgets. He put the city's fiscal house in order, rescuing it from near junk-bond status. Archer's most important accomplishment was to reconnect Detroit to the surrounding region. He enticed General Motors and the Compuware Corporation to move their headquarters into downtown Detroit, bringing back more than 10,000 jobs. The city's baseball team, the Tigers, has returned to the downtown, and its football team, the Lions, is soon to follow. Archer also repaired relations with both the state government, which responded with "brownfields" legislation, making it easier to clean up polluted industrial sites, and with the local county governments, which pitched in to help Detroit when it was unable to cope with a major snowstorm.

But for all this progress, Detroit still can't plow its streets. Having foresworn competitive bidding to appease the city's powerful unions, Archer struggled to improve city services. He pushed through a $10 million modernization of the streetlight system, boosting the number of working lights from 60 percent to 95 percent. But when he left office, more than a third of the city's traffic signals were still out of commission. Archer was also unable to reform a police department that leads the country in fatal shootings, in a city that is near the top in homicides. Detroit's crime statistics are so unreliable that the FBI has refused to include them in its uniform crime surveys. And in June of 2000, Detroit suffered a two-day blackout when the city-owned power system failed.

Like Philadelphia, Detroit has a massive government of 44 departments, built up when the city's population was far larger. Archer has made some progress in straightening out the land titles for the city's 44,000 abandoned lots. But as in Philadelphia, getting a title is only the start of a builder's problems, as some 350 different permits, issued by 11 different city agencies, are required. In addition, 5 separate agencies issue 83 different licenses, and responsibility for environmental inspections is split among 13 operations across 6 departments. In short, as Archer's successor Kwame Kilpatrick enters office, Detroit still hasn't decided whether city government exists to provide jobs for organized interests or services to citizens.

Kilpatrick won the mayoralty this past November in an election dominated not by Archer's incremental achievements but by the long shadow of Coleman Young. Archer, a Catholic in a city of Baptists, was dogged by charges that he "wasn't black enough," and was always more popular in the suburbs than at home. He was even subject to a failed recall effort in 1999. Neither Kilpatrick nor his rival, former police officer Gil Hill, talked about building on what he had achieved. The public, explained Bill Johnson of the *Detroit News*, "still buys Coleman Young's argument that the psychic benefits of a black autonomy outweigh the material gains of rejoining the region." To underscore that point in the midst of the mayoral election, the city council unanimously voted to create a holiday honoring Coleman Young.

The 31-year-old Kilpatrick, the country's youngest big-city mayor, is a former star football player who comes from the city's leading political family. His mother is a congresswoman, his father a key advisor to the Wayne County executive. He worked well with Republicans when he was House minority leader in Lansing, earning a reputation as a moderate. But running for mayor in Detroit, Kilpatrick found it necessary to establish his Coleman Young credentials by blasting his home state as "the Mississippi of the north."

Kilpatrick enjoys the backing of the business community, but with the auto economy slumping and Ford laying off workers, he has a formidable task ahead. He enters office with a growing budget deficit and a host of union contracts up for renewal. In his inaugural address, the crowd responded with enthusiasm when Kilpatrick promised to root out city workers with a "quit-and-stay mentality"—those who, as he put it, "quit a long time ago, but they come to work every single day." But it's not clear how he can accomplish this, having won office with the backing of public-sector unions and having all but promised never to submit city services to managed competition.

If the new mayor sticks to his campaign platform, it is likely that Detroit will revert once again to being Coleman Young's city. But there are some indications that Kilpatrick, a man with higher ambitions, might surprise. Jerry Oliver, his choice to head the dysfunctional police force, told the press that public-sector "unions are about maintaining the status quo and mediocrity." Kilpatrick himself has made a point of firing very publicly city workers caught on camera goofing off on the job. To date, notes George Canto of the *Detroit News*, Kilpatrick "has been successful at symbolism," but the city is "waiting to see what the substance of the administration will be like."

New York

The mayor who most inspired these others was New York's Rudy Giuliani. Giuliani exerted an enormous influence on American cities through New York's broken-windows policing and its Comstat computer-tracking model, which has been adapted by other cities for a wide range of services. But these successes were only the precondition for his greatest achievement, the restoration of upward mobility as the social norm in New York. Before Giuliani, New York politics was mostly about striking caring poses. Giuliani's predecessors, from John Lindsay to David Dinkins, spoke endlessly of what the city owed the poor but delivered instead rising rates of crime and welfare.

Dinkins' New York was organized around the unspoken assumption that poverty was a permanent condition, and that the best that could be done was to make it bearable. In Giuliani's words, "We blocked the genius of America for the poorest people in New York." Under Giuliani, the city restored the ideal of upward mobility. Giuliani spoke not only of the rights of the poor but also of their obligations to society. As mayor, he delivered greater safety and a rising standard of living in the city's most blighted areas, from Mott Haven in the South Bronx to Brooklyn's East New York. New York's poorest neighborhoods experienced the sharpest drop in crime and the biggest rises in income and property values. None of this was predestined. No other city has made comparable gains, let alone sustained them. New York's crime rates continue to decline even as they have been rising in other big cities. Turning the tables on those who would substitute intentions for outcomes, writer James Traub has asked of Giuliani's critics, "Isn't preserving people's lives, well-being, and property the most compassionate policy of all?"

But Giuliani cultivated no heir. Near the end of a mayoral campaign overshadowed by the terrorist attacks and the war in Afghanistan, he endorsed the eventual victor, billionaire Michael Bloomberg. A lifelong Democrat and a self-proclaimed liberal, Bloomberg spent his way to the Republican nomination and went on to burn through a record-shattering $75 million (plus untold dollars in the form of charitable donations) in the course of defeating the favorite, Democrat Mark Green. Insulated from criticism and scrutiny by a wall of money and advisors,

Bloomberg put together a *mesalliance* easily as strange as that which elected Hahn in Los Angeles. He won the votes both of Giuliani's most fervent admirers and his angriest detractors. One of these partners is likely to be disappointed.

The new mayor, who has brought a gentler style to City Hall, has made a point of stressing cooperation and partnership whenever he speaks. To date, this emphasis on teamwork seems to be paying off. His efforts to cut the $4.8 billion budget deficit produced by the stock-market slowdown, the destruction of the World Trade Center, and the cost of new hires brought on in Giuliani's second term, have brought what for New York is a relatively minor reaction. Bloomberg's pledge to impose no new broad-based taxes has drawn uncharacteristically mild criticism from the city council, which is dominated by representatives of public-sector unions and social-service agencies funded by the city.

Bloomberg has reached out to interests shut out of City Hall during the Giuliani years, and he has, for the most part, continued Giuliani's policing practices. The mayor will no doubt use his personal fortune, estimated at $4 billion, to keep many of the city's often ferocious interest groups in his corner, through ongoing "charitable" donations. Like Nelson Rockefeller, he has his own system of rewards and punishment independent of the public treasury.

The new mayor's first big policy initiative and the first major test of his consensual style has been his continuation of Giuliani's fight to abolish the dysfunctional board of education. The board, which has seen its funding rise from $8 to $12 billion annually over the past four years to little educational effect, has been described by Bloomberg as a "rinky-dink operation." But in order to assume mayoral control, Bloomberg needs the cooperation of the state legislature, traditionally a handmaiden to the city's powerful teachers' union. His effort is also complicated by the fact that the teachers' contract is up for renegotiation. Bloomberg declares that his administration should be judged in large measure by its educational achievements. It's a fair measure, and his commitment partially undercuts those critics who worry that by softening the hard edges of "Rudyism," Bloomberg may revert to treating the poor with the paternalism and condescension associated with Nelson Rockefeller and John Lindsay in the 1960s. But if Bloomberg's cooperative approach fails, he may have little choice but to return to a Rudy-style politics.

No turning back?

The reform mayors of the 1990s made a sharp break with the past. Once-standard arguments that poverty was the root cause of urban problems, and that therefore crime could not be reduced until poverty was eliminated, largely fell by the wayside. With the declining crime rates and the broad national prosperity of the 1990s, poverty became less a proof of oppression than evidence of failed social and economic policies.

While reform currents have been slowed in some cities, they are unlikely to be entirely displaced. The new urban reformism has no ideological competition. Some of the policy successes of the 1990s in the areas of taxes, policing, and welfare reform have come under attack, but the critics have offered little in the way of alternatives. Furthermore, as in Philadelphia, the 1990s awakening created a change in expectations, an updraft, that makes citizens less likely to accept ongoing failure. Cincinnati, for instance, looks with envy at the success of nearby Indianapolis, while Detroiters talk about how it's done in Cleveland.

Still, some mayors and cities will continue to fail. It is hard to be optimistic about the future of Philadelphia and Detroit, where the gravitational pull of a patronage-driven parochialism—more intent on preserving old jobs than creating new ones—may be too strong for mayors to escape from its orbit. It may be that the reforms of the 1990s will turn out to be merely an Indian summer in those cities where failed political cultures undermine the self-correcting mechanisms of democracy. But failure now exacts a political price. In both Philadelphia and Detroit, state governments have shown an increasing willingness to take over city institutions such as schools, parking authorities, and the courts.

For nearly 70 years—from roughly 1920 to 1990—the broad trends of American life ran against the country's big cities. Federal efforts to bolster urban areas in the 1960s tended to make matters worse, as cities waited passively for the federal government to rescue them. In the 1990s, the tides shifted and urban America, once stranded, rejoined the rest of the country. A new generation of mayors stopped relying on Washington and broke out of old orthodoxies. In those cities that remain on the path of self-reliance and economic growth, progress will continue.

From *The Public Interest*, Summer 2002, No. 148, pp. 3-22. © 2002 by National Affairs, Inc.

UNIT 2

Sprawl: Challenges to the Metropolitan Landscape

Unit Selections

4. **Patio Man and the Sprawl People**, David Brooks
5. **Is Regional Government the Answer?**, Fred Siegel
6. **Downtown Struggles While Neighbor Thrives**, Michael Brick
7. **Unscrambling the City**, Christopher Swope
8. **Are Europe's Cities Better?**, Pietro S. Nivola

Key Points to Consider

- Should the country build more highways to encourage growth beyond cities?

- Sould cities and regional planning bodies develop extensive public transportation systems to ease the burden that uncontrolled sprawl has on the highway system? If this were to happen, how could it best be implemented?

- Why do city dwellers choose to move to suburbs and exurbs? Why do people move into cities from less dense areas?

- What effect does planning have on city life? Can cities cooperate with the regions they are part of, or must they compete with their suburbs for people and money?

 **Links: www.dushkin.com/online/**
These sites are annotated in the World Wide Web pages.

American Studies Web
http://www.georgetown.edu/crossroads/asw/
Sprawl Guide
http://www.plannersweb.com/sprawl/home.html
Yahoo/Social Science/Urban Studies
http://www.yahoo.com/Social_Science/Urban_Studies/

Problems come in cycles. In the early 1990s when the country, in general, and the cities, in particular, were mired in high unemployment and slow growth, all attention turned to restarting the economic engine. The country is now in its tenth year of economic growth and growth itself has at times become the problem. Decentralizing cities have spread into the countryside, replacing millions of acres of farmland and open space with new development.

What to do about sprawl? What about the social, political, and economic implications? Is it possible to control the impact that sprawl has on highway systems? How can rampant development be slowed? Are there effective ways to balance development without upsetting the environment? None of these questions have easy or universal answers. Only a few places in the country have had the political will to control sprawl; in many communities zoning boards have been slow to react to the flood of extensive development. The economic enticement of new taxes that are generated by the large corporations that move into small suburban towns close to urban centers overcomes any resistance. With it, however, comes an exponential increase in population and services that quickly outstrips the community's capacity to effectively handle the new requirements.

"Patio Man and the Sprawl People" and "Downtown Struggles While Neighbor Thrives" examine the centrifugal social and economic forces that are drawing people and businesses from cities into exurbs and suburbs. Two other articles in this section look at how cities and regions are planned, and the effect of these plans on the competition between city and suburb.

Patio Man and the Sprawl People

America's newest suburbs

BY DAVID BROOKS

I don't know if you've ever noticed the expression of a man who is about to buy a first-class barbecue grill. He walks into a Home Depot or Lowe's or one of the other mega hardware complexes and his eyes are glistening with a faraway visionary zeal, like one of those old prophets gazing into the promised land. His lips are parted and twitching slightly. Inside the megastore, the grills are just past the racks of affordable- house plan books, in the yard-machinery section. They are arrayed magnificently next to the vehicles that used to be known as rider mowers but are now known as lawn tractors, because to call them rider mowers doesn't really convey the steroid-enhanced M-1 tank power of the things.

The man approaches the barbecue grills and his face bears a trance-like expression, suggesting that he has cast aside all the pains and imperfections of this world and is approaching the gateway to a higher dimension. In front of him are a number of massive steel-coated reactors with names like Broilmaster P3, The Thermidor, and the Weber Genesis, because in America it seems perfectly normal to name a backyard barbecue grill after a book of the Bible.

The items in this cooking arsenal flaunt enough metal to suggest they have been hardened to survive a direct nuclear assault, and Patio Man goes from machine to machine comparing their features—the cast iron/porcelain coated cooking surfaces, the 328,000-Btu heat-generating capacities, the 1,600-degree-tolerance linings, the multiple warming racks, the lava rock containment dishes, the built-in electrical meat thermometers, and so on. Certain profound questions flow through his mind. Is a 542-square-inch grilling surface really enough, considering that he might someday get the urge to roast an uncut buffalo steak? Though the matte steel overcoat resists scratching, doesn't he want a polished steel surface on his grill so he can glance down and admire his reflection as he is performing the suburban manliness rituals, such as brushing tangy sauce on meat slabs with his right hand while clutching a beer can in an NFL foam insulator ring in his left?

Pretty soon a large salesman in an orange vest who looks like a human SUV comes up to him and says, "How-yadoin'," which is, "May I help you?" in Home Depot talk.

Patio Man, who has so much lust in his heart it is all he can do to keep from climbing up on one of these machines and whooping rodeo-style with joy, manages to respond appropriately. He grunts inarticulately and nods toward the machines. Careful not to make eye contact at any point, the two manly suburban men have a brief exchange of pseudo-scientific grill argot that neither of them understands, and pretty soon Patio Man has come to the reasoned conclusion that it really does make sense to pay a little extra for a grill with V-shaped metal baffles, ceramic rods, and a side-mounted smoker box. Plus the grill he selects has four insulated drink holders. All major choices of consumer durables these days ultimately come down to which model has the most impressive cup holders.

Patio Man pays for the grill with his credit card, and is told that some minion will forklift his machine over to the loading dock around back. It is yet another triumph in a lifetime of conquest shopping, and as Patio Man heads toward the parking lot he is glad once again that he's driving that Yukon XL so that he can approach the loading dock guys as a co-equal in the manly fraternity of Those Who Haul Things.

He steps out into the parking lot and is momentarily blinded by sun bouncing off the hardtop. The parking lot is so massive that he can barely see the Wal-Mart, the Bed Bath & Beyond, or the area-code-sized Old Navy glistening through the heat there on the other side. This mall is in fact big enough to qualify for membership in the United Nations, and is so vast that shoppers have to drive from store to store, cutting diagonally through the infinity of empty parking spaces in between.

As Patio Man walks past the empty handicapped and expectant-mother parking spots toward his own vehicle, wonderful grill fantasies dance in his imagination: There he is atop the uppermost tier of his multi-level backyard patio/outdoor recreation area posed like an admiral on the deck of his destroyer. In his mind's eye he can see himself coolly flipping the garlic and pepper T-bones on the front acreage of his new grill while carefully testing the citrus-tarragon trout filets that sizzle fragrantly in the rear. On the lawn below he can see his kids, Haley and

Cody, frolicking on the weedless community lawn that is mowed twice weekly by the people who run Monument Crowne Preserve, his townhome community.

Haley, 12, is a Travel Team Girl, who spends her weekends playing midfield against similarly pony-tailed, strongly calved soccer marvels. Cody, 10, is a Buzz Cut Boy, whose naturally blond hair has been cut to a lawn-like stubble and dyed an almost phosphorescent white. Cody's wardrobe is entirely derivative of fashions he has seen watching the X-Games.

In his vision, Patio Man can see the kids enjoying their child-safe lawn darts with a gaggle of their cul de sac friends, a happy gathering of Haleys and Codys and Corys and Britneys. It's a brightly colored scene: Abercrombie & Fitch pink spaghetti-strap tops on the girls and ankle length canvas shorts and laceless Nikes on the boys. Patio Man notes somewhat uncomfortably that in America today the average square yardage of boys' fashion grows and grows while the square inches in the girls' outfits shrink and shrink, so that while the boys look like tent-wearing skateboarders, the girls look like preppy prostitutes.

Nonetheless, Patio Man envisions his own adult softball team buddies lounging on his immaculate deck furniture watching him with a certain moist envy in their eyes as he mans the grill. They are fit, sockless men in dock siders, chinos, and Tommy Bahama muted Hawaiian shirts. Their wives, trim Jennifer Aniston women, wear capris and sleeveless tops that look great owing to their many hours of sweat and exercise at Spa Lady. These men and women may not be Greatest Generation heroes, or earthshaking inventors like Thomas Edison, but if Thomas Edison had had a Human Resources Department, and that Human Resources Department had organized annual enrichment and motivational conferences for mid-level management, then these people would have been the marketing executives for the back office outsourcing companies to the meeting-planning firms that hooked up the HR executives with the conference facilities.

They are wonderful people. And Patio Man can envision his own wife, Cindy, a Realtor Mom, circulating amongst them serving drinks, telling parent-teacher conference stories and generally spreading conviviality while he, Patio Man, masterfully runs the grill—again, to the silent admiration of all. The sun is shining. The people are friendly. The men are no more than 25 pounds overweight, which is the socially acceptable male paunch level in upwardly mobile America, and the children are well adjusted. It is a vision of the sort of domestic bliss that Patio Man has been shooting for all his life.

And it's plausible now because two years ago Patio Man made the big move. He pulled up stakes and he moved his family to a Sprinkler City.

Sprinkler Cities are the fast-growing suburbs mostly in the South and West that are the homes of the new style American Dream, the epicenters of Patio Man fantasies. Douglas County, Colorado, which is the fastest-growing county in America and is located between Denver and Colorado Springs, is a Sprinkler City. So is Henderson,

Nevada, just outside of Las Vegas. So is Loudoun County, Virginia, near Dulles Airport. So are Scottsdale and Gilbert, Arizona, and Union County, North Carolina.

The growth in these places is astronomical, as Patio Men and their families—and Patio retirees, yuppie geezers who still like to grill, swim, and water ski—flock to them from all over. Douglas County grew 13.6 percent from April 2000 to July 2001, while Loudoun County grew 12.6 percent in that 16-month period. Henderson, Nevada, has tripled in size over the past 10 years and now has over 175,000 people. Over the past 50 years, Irving, Texas, grew by 7,211 percent, from about 2,600 people to 200,000 people.

The biggest of these boom suburbs are huge. With almost 400,000 people, Mesa, Arizona, has a larger population than Minneapolis, Cincinnati, or St. Louis. And this sort of growth is expected to continue. Goodyear, Arizona, on the western edge of the Phoenix area, now has about 20,000 people, but is projected to have 320,000 in 50 years' time. By then, Greater Phoenix could have a population of over 6 million and cover over 10,000 square miles.

Sprinkler Cities are also generally the most Republican areas of the country. In some of the Sprinkler City congressional districts, Republicans have a 2 or 3 or 4 to 1 registration advantage over Democrats. As cultural centers, they represent the beau ideal of Republican selfhood, and are becoming the new base—the brains, heart, guts, and soul of the emerging Republican party. Their values are not the same as those found in either old-line suburbs like Greenwich, Connecticut, where a certain sort of Republican used to dominate, or traditional conservative bastions, such as the old South. This isn't even the more modest conservatism found in the midwestern farm belt. In fact, the rising prominence of these places heralds a new style of suburb vs. suburb politics, with the explosively growing Republican outer suburbs vying with the slower-growing and increasingly Democratic inner suburbs for control of the center of American political gravity.

If you stand on a hilltop overlooking a Sprinkler City, you see, stretched across the landscape, little brown puffs here and there where bulldozers are kicking up dirt while building new townhomes, office parks, shopping malls, AmeriSuites guest hotels, and golf courses. Everything in a Sprinkler City is new. The highways are so clean and freshly paved you can eat off them. The elementary schools have spic and span playgrounds, unscuffed walls, and immaculate mini-observatories for just-forming science classes.

The lawns in these places are perfect. It doesn't matter how arid the local landscape used to be, the developers come in and lay miles of irrigation tubing, and the sprinklers pop up each evening, making life and civilization possible.

The roads are huge. The main ones, where the office parks are, have been given names like Innovation Boulevard and Entrepreneur Avenue, and they've been built for the population levels that will exist a decade from now, so that today you can cruise down these flawless six lane thoroughfares in traffic-less nirvana, and if you get a cell phone call you can just stop in the right lane and take the call because there's no one behind you. The smaller roads in the residential neighborhoods have pretentious names—in Loudoun County I drove down Trajan's Column Terrace—but they too are just as smooth and immaculate as a blacktop bowling alley. There's no use relying on a map to get around these places, because there's no way map publishers can keep up with the construction.

The town fathers try halfheartedly to control sprawl, and as you look over the landscape you can see the results of their ambivalent zoning regulations. The homes aren't spread out with quarter-acre yards, as in the older, close-in suburbs. Instead they are clustered into pseudo-urban pods. As you scan the horizon you'll see a densely packed pod of townhouses, then a stretch of a half mile of investor grass (fields that will someday contain 35,000-square-foot Fresh-Mex restaurants but for now are being kept fallow by investors until the prices rise), and then another pod of slightly more expensive detached homes just as densely packed.

The developments in the southeastern Sprinkler Cities tend to have Mini-McMansion Gable-gable houses. That is to say, these are 3,200-square-foot middle-class homes built to look like 7,000-square-foot starter palaces for the nouveau riche. And on the front at the top, each one has a big gable, and then right in front of it, for visual relief, a little gable jutting forward so that it looks like a baby gable leaning against a mommy gable.

These homes have all the same features as the authentic McMansions of the mid-'90s (as history flows on, McMansions come to seem authentic), but significantly smaller. There are the same vaulted atriums behind the front doors that never get used, and the same open kitchen/two-story great rooms with soaring palladian windows. But in the middle-class knockoffs, the rooms are so small, especially upstairs, that a bedroom or a master-bath suite would fit inside one of the walk-in closets of a real McMansion.

In the Southwest the homes tend to be tile and stucco jobs, with tiny mousepad lawns out front, blue backyard spas in the back, and so much white furniture inside that you have to wear sunglasses indoors. As you fly over the Sprinkler Cities you begin to see the rough pattern—a little pseudo-urbanist plop of development, a blank field, a plop, a field, a plop. You also notice that the developers build the roads and sewage lines first and then fill in the houses later, so from the sky you can see cul de sacs stretching off into the distance with no houses around them.

Then, cutting through the landscape are broad commercial thoroughfares with two-tier, big-box malls on either side. In the front tier is a line of highly themed chain restaurants that all fuse into the same Macaroni Grill Olive Outback Cantina Charlie Chiang's Dave & Buster's Cheesecake Factory mélange of peppy servers, superfluous ceiling fans, free bread with olive oil, and taco salad entrees. In the 21st-century migration of peoples, the food courts come first and the huddled masses follow.

Then in the back row are all the huge, exposed-air-duct architectural behemoths, which are the big-box stores.

Shopping experiences are now segregated by mood. If you are in the mood for some titillating browsing, you can head over to a Lifestyle Center, which is one of those instant urban streetscapes that developers put up in suburbia as entertainment/retail/community complexes, complete with pedestrian zones, outdoor cafés, roller rinks, multiplexes, and high-attitude retail concepts such as CP Shades, a chain store that masquerades as a locally owned boutique.

If you are buying necessities, really shopping, there are Power Malls. These are the big-box expanses with Wal-marts, K-Marts, Targets, price clubs, and all the various Depots (Home, Office, Furniture, etc.). In Sprinkler Cities there are archipelagoes of them—one massive parking lot after another surrounded by huge boxes that often have racing stripes around the middle to break the monotony of the windowless exterior walls.

If one superstore is in one mall, then its competitor is probably in the next one in the archipelago. There's a Petsmart just down from a Petco, a Borders nearby a Barnes & Noble, a Linens 'n' Things within sight of a Bed Bath & Beyond, a Best Buy cheek by jowl with a Circuit City. In Henderson, there's a Wal-Mart superstore that spreads over 220,000 square feet, with all those happy greeters in blue vests to make you feel small-town.

There are also smaller stores jammed in between the mega-outlets like little feeder fish swimming around the big boys. On one strip, there might be the ostentatiously unpretentious Total Wine & More, selling a galaxy of casual Merlots. Nearby there might be a Michaels discount women's clothing, a bobo bazaar such as World Market that sells raffia fiber from Madagascar, Rajasthani patchwork coverlets from India, and vermouth-flavored martini onions from Israel, and finally a string of storefront mortgage bankers and realtors serving all the new arrivals. In Sprinkler Cities, there are more realtors than people.

People move to Sprinkler Cities for the same reasons people came to America or headed out West. They want to leave behind the dirt and toxins of their former existence—the crowding and inconvenience, the precedents, and the oldness of what suddenly seems to them a settled and unpromising world. They want to move to some place that seems fresh and new and filled with possibility.

Sprinkler City immigrants are not leaving cities to head out to suburbia. They are leaving older suburbs—which have come to seem as crowded, expensive, and stratified as cities—and heading for newer suburbs, for the suburbia of suburbia.

One of the problems we have in thinking about the suburbs is that when it comes to suburbia the American imagination is motionless. Many people still have in their heads the stereotype of suburban life that the critics of suburbia established in the 1950s. They see suburbia as a sterile, dull, Ozzie and Harriet retreat from the creative dynamism of city life, and the people who live in the suburbs as either hopelessly shallow or quietly and neurotically desperate. (There is no group in America more conformist than the people who rail against suburbanites for being conformist—they always make the same critiques, decade after decade.)

The truth, of course, is that suburbia is not a retreat from gritty American life, it is American life. Already, suburbanites make up about half of the country's population (while city people make up 28 percent and rural folk make up the rest), and America gets more suburban every year.

According to the census data, the suburbs of America's 100 largest metro areas grew twice as fast as their central cities in the 1990s, and that was a decade in which many cities actually reversed their long population slides. Atlanta, for example, gained 23,000 people in the '90s, but its suburbs grew by 1.1 million people.

Moreover, newer suburbs no longer really feed off cities. In 1979, 74 percent of American office space was located in cities, according to the Brookings Institution's Robert Puentes. But now, after two decades in which the biggest job growth has been in suburban office parks, the suburbs' share of total office space has risen to 42 percent. In other words, we are fast approaching a time when the majority of all office space will be in the suburbs, and most Americans not only will not live in cities, they won't even commute to cities or have any regular contact with city life.

Encompassing such a broad swath of national existence, suburbs obviously cannot possibly be the white-bread places of myth and literature. In reality, as the most recent census shows, suburbs contain more non-family houses—young singles and elderly couples—than family households, married couples with children. Nor are they overwhelmingly white. The majority of Asian Americans, half of Hispanics, and 40 percent of American blacks live in suburbia.

And so now there are crucial fault lines not just between city and suburb but between one kind of suburb and another. Say you grew up in some southern California suburb in the 1970s. You graduated from the University of Oregon and now you are a systems analyst with a spouse and two young kids. You're making $65,000 a year, far more than you ever thought you would, but back in Orange County you find you can't afford to live anywhere near your Newport Beach company headquarters. So your commute is 55 minutes each way. Then there's your house itself. You paid $356,000 for a 1962 four-bedroom split level with a drab kitchen, low ceilings, and walls that are chipped and peeling. Your mortgage—that $1,800 a month—is like a tapeworm that devours the family budget.

And then you visit a Sprinkler City in Arizona or Nevada or Colorado—far from the coast and deep into exurbia—and what do you see? Bounteous roads! Free traffic lanes! If you lived here you'd be in commuter bliss—15 minutes from home on Trajan's Column Terrace to the office park on Innovation Boulevard! If you lived here you'd have an extra hour and a half each day for yourself.

And those real estate prices! In, say, Henderson, Nevada, you wouldn't have to spend over $400,000 for a home and carry that murderous mortgage. You could get a home that's brand new, twice the size of your old one, with an attached garage (no flimsy carport), and three times as beautiful for $299,000. The average price of a single-family home in Loudoun County, one of the pricier of the Sprinkler Cities, was $166,824 in 2001, which was an 11 percent increase over the year before. Imagine that! A mortgage under 200 grand! A great anvil would be lifted from your shoulders. More free money for you to spend on yourself. More free time to enjoy. More Freedom!

Plus, if you moved to a Sprinkler City there would be liberation of a subtler kind. The old suburbs have become socially urbanized. They've become stratified. Two sorts of people have begun to move in and ruin the middle-class equality of the development you grew up in: the rich and the poor.

There are, first, the poor immigrants, from Mexico, Vietnam, and the Philippines. They come in, a dozen to a house, and they introduce an element of unpredictability to what was a comforting milieu. They shout. They're less tidy. Their teenage boys seem to get involved with gangs and cars. Suddenly you feel you will lose control of your children. You begin to feel a new level of anxiety in the neighborhood. It is exactly the level of anxiety—sometimes intermingled with racism—your parents felt when they moved from their old neighborhood to the suburbs in the first place.

And then there are the rich. Suddenly many of the old ramblers are being knocked down by lawyers who proceed to erect 4,000-square-foot arts and crafts bungalows with two-car garages for their Volvos. Suddenly cars in the neighborhoods have window and bumper stickers that never used to be there in the past: "Yale," "The Friends School," "Million Mom March." The local stores are changing too. Gone are the hardware stores and barber shops. Now there are Afghan restaurants, Marin County bistros, and environmentally sensitive and extremely expensive bakeries.

And these new people, while successful and upstanding, are also… snobs. They're doctors and lawyers and journalists and media consultants. They went to fancy colleges and they consider themselves superior to you if you sell home-security systems or if you are a mechanical engineer, and in subtle yet patronizing ways they let you know it.

I recently interviewed a woman in Loudoun County who said she had grown up and lived most of her life in Bethesda, Maryland, which is an upscale suburb close to Washington. When I asked why she left Bethesda, she hissed "I hate it there now" with a fervor that took me by surprise. And as we spoke, it became clear that it was precisely the "improvements" she hated: the new movie theater that shows only foreign films, the explosion of French, Turkish, and new wave restaurants, the streets choked with German cars and Lexus SUVs, the doctors and lawyers and journalists with their educated-class one-upmanship.

These new people may live in the old suburbs but they hate suburbanites. They hate sprawl, big-box stores, automobile culture. The words they use about suburbanites are: synthetic, bland, sterile, self-absorbed, disengaged. They look down on people who like suburbs. They don't like their lawn statuary, their Hallmark greeting cards, their Ethan Allen furniture, their megachurches, the seasonal banners the old residents hang out in front of their houses, their untroubled attitude toward McDonald's and Dairy Queen, their Thomas Kinkade fantasy paintings. And all the original suburbanites who were peacefully enjoying their suburb until the anti-suburban suburbanites moved in notice the condescension, and they do what Americans have always done when faced with disapproval, anxiety, and potential conflict. They move away. The pincer movements get them: the rich and the poor, the commutes and the mortgages, the prices and the alienation. And pretty soon it's Henderson, Nevada, here we come.

George Santayana once observed that Americans don't solve problems, they just leave them behind. They take advantage of all that space and move. If there's an idea they don't like, they don't bother refuting it, they just go somewhere else, and if they can't go somewhere else, they just leave it in the past, where it dies from inattention.

And so Patio Man is not inclined to stay and defend himself against the condescending French-film goers and their Volvos. He's not going to mount a political campaign to fix the educational, economic, and social woes that beset him in his old neighborhood. He won't waste his time fighting a culture war. It's not worth the trouble. He just bolts. He heads for the exurbs and the desert. He goes to the new place where the future is still open and promising. He goes to fresh ground where his dreams might more plausibly come true.

The power of this urge to leave and create new places is really awesome to behold. Migration is not an easy thing, yet every year 43 million Americans get up and move. And it sets off a chain reaction. The migrants who move into one area push out another set of people, who then migrate to another and push out another set of people, and so on and so on in one vast cycle of creative destruction. Ten years ago these Sprinkler Cities didn't really exist. Fifteen years ago the institutions that dot them hadn't been invented. There weren't book superstores or sporting goods superstores or Petsmart or Petco, and Target was just something you shot arrows at. And yet suddenly metropolises with all these new stores and institutions have materialized out of emptiness. It's as if some Zeus-like figure had appeared out of the ether and slammed down a million-square-foot mall on the desert floor, then a second later he'd slammed down a 5,000-person townhome community, then a second later an ice rink and a rec center and soccer fields and schools and community colleges. How many times in human history have 200,000-person cities just materialized almost instantaneously out of nowhere?

The people who used to live in these empty places don't like it; they've had to move further out in search of valleys still pristine. But the sprawl people just love it. They talk to you like born-again evangelists, as if their life had undergone some magical transformation when they made the big move. They talk as if they'd thrown off some set of horrendous weights, banished some class of unpleasant experiences, and magically floated up into the realm of good climate, fine people, job opportunities, and transcendent convenience. In 2001, Loudoun County did a survey of its residents. Ninety-eight percent felt safe in their neighborhoods. Ninety-three percent rated their county's quality of life excellent or good. Only a third of the county's residents, by the way, have lived there for more than 10 years.

These people are so happy because they have achieved something that human beings are actually quite good at achieving. Through all the complex diversity of society, they have managed to find people who want pretty much the same things they want.

This is not to say they want white Ozzie and Harriet nirvana. The past 40 years happened. It never occurs to them to go back before rock, rap, women working, and massive immigration. They don't mind any of these things, so long as they complement the core Sprinkler City missions of orderly living, high achievement, and the bright seeking of a better future.

Recently three teams from the Seneca Ridge Middle School in Loudoun County competed in the National Social Studies Olympiad. The fifth grade team finished fifth out of 242 teams, while the eighth grade team finished twenty-third out of 210. Here are some of the names of the students competing for Loudoun: Amy Kuo, Arshad Ali, Samanth Chao, Katie Hempenius, Ronnel Espino, Obinna Onwuka, Earnst Ilang-Ilang, Ashley Shiraishi, and Alberto Pareja-Lecaros. At the local high school, 99 percent of seniors graduate and 87 percent go on to higher education.

When you get right down to it, Sprinkler Cities are united around five main goals:

★★ *The goal of the together life.* When you've got your life together, you have mastered the complexities of the modern world so thoroughly that you can glide through your days without unpleasant distractions or tawdry failures. Instead, your hours are filled with self-affirming reminders of the control you have achieved over the elements. Your lawn is immaculate. Your DVD library is organized, and so is your walk-in closet. Your car is clean and vacuumed, your frequently dialed numbers are programmed into your cell phone, your telephone plan is suited to your needs, and your various gizmos interface without conflict. Your wife is effortlessly slender, your kids are unnaturally bright, your job is rewarding, your promotions are inevitable, and you look great in casual slacks.

You can thus spend your days in perfect equanimity, the Sprinkler City ideal. You radiate confidence, like a professional golfer striding up the 18th fairway after a particularly masterful round. Compared with you, Dick Cheney looks like a disorganized hothead. George W. Bush looks like a self-lacerating neurotic. Professionally, socially, parentally, you have your life together. You may not be the most intellectual or philosophical person on the planet, but you are honest and straightforward. You may not be flamboyant, but you are friendly, good-hearted, and considerate. You have achieved the level of calm mastery of life that is the personality equivalent of the clean and fresh suburban landscape.

★★ *The goal of technological heroism.* They may not be stereotypical rebels, and nobody would call them avant-garde, but in one respect many Sprinkler City dwellers have the souls of revolutionaries. When Patio Man gets out of his Yukon, lowers his employee-badge necklace around his neck, and walks into his generic office building, he becomes a technological radical. He spends his long workdays striving to create some technological innovation, management solution, or organizing system breakthroughs that will alter the world. Maybe the company he works for has one of those indecipherable three-initial names, like DRG Technologies or SER Solutions, or maybe it's got one of those jammed together compound names that were all the rage in the 1990s until WorldCom and MicroStrategy went belly up.

Either way, Patio Man is working on, or longs to be working on, a project that is new and revolutionary. And all around him there are men and women who are actually achieving that goal, who are making that leap into the future. The biotech revolution is being conducted in bland suburban office parks by seemingly unremarkable polo-shirt-and-chino people at firms like Celera and Human Genome Sciences. Silicon Valley is just one long string of suburban office parks jutting out from San Jose. AOL is headquartered in Loudoun County. You walk down a path in a Sprinkler City corporate center and it leads you to a company frantically chasing some market-niche innovation in robotics, agricultural engineering, microtechnology, or hardware and software applications.

There are retail-concept revolutionaries, delivery-system radicals, market-research innovators, data-collection pioneers, computer-game Rembrandts, and weapons-systems analysts. They look like bland members of some interchangeable research team, but many of them are deeply engrossed in what they consider a visionary project, which if completed will help hurtle us all further into the Knowledge Revolution, the Information Millennium, the Age of MicroTechnology, the Biotech Century, or whatever transplendent future it is you want to imagine. They have broken the monopoly that cities used to have, and they have made themselves the new centers of creativity.

★★ *The goal of relaxed camaraderie.* The critics of suburbia believe that single-family homeowners with their trimmed yards and matching pansies are trying to keep up with the Joneses. But like most of what the critics assert, that's completely wrong. Sprinkler City people are competitive in the marketplace and on the sports field, but they detest social competition. That's part of why these people left inner-ring suburbs in the first place.

They are not emulating the rich; they are happy to blend in with each other. One of the comforts of these places is that almost nobody is far above you socially and almost nobody is far below. You're all just swimming in a pond of understated success.

So manners are almost aggressively relaxed. Everybody strives overtime to not put on airs or create friction. In style, demeanor, and mood, people reveal the language and values they have in common. They are good team members and demonstrate from the first meeting that they are team-able. You could go your entire life, from home to church to work to school, wearing nothing but Lands' End—comfortable, conservative, non-threatening activewear for people with a special fondness for navy blue. The dominant conversational tone is upbeat and friendly, like banter between Katie Couric and Matt Lauer on the "Today" show. The prevailing style of humor is ironic but not biting and owes a lot to ESPN's "SportsCenter."

★★ *The goal of the active-leisure lifestyle.* Your self-esteem is based on your success at work, but since half the time it's hard to explain to people what the hell it is you do, your public identity is defined by your leisure activities. You are the soccer family, engrossed by the politics and melodrama of your local league, or you are the T-ball coach and spend your barbecue conversations comparing notes on new $200 titanium bat designs (there's a new bat called The Power Elite—even C. Wright Mills has been domesticated for the Little League set). You are Scuba Woman and you converse about various cruises you have taken. You are Mountain Bike Man and you make vague references to your high altitude injuries and spills. Or you are a golfer, in which case nobody even thinks of engaging you in conversation on any topic other than golf.

Religion is too hot a subject and politics is irrelevant, so if you are not discussing transportation issues—how to get from here to there, whether the new highway exit is good or bad—you are probably talking about sports. You're talking about your kids' ice hockey leagues, NBA salary levels, or the competition in your over-70 softball league—the one in which everybody wears a knee brace and it takes about six minutes for a good hitter to beat out a double. Sports sets the emotional climate of your life. Sports provides the language of easy camaraderie, self-deprecating humor, and (mostly) controlled competition.

★★ *The goal of the traditional, but competitive, childhood.* Most everything in Sprinkler Cities is new, but much of the newness is in the service of tradition. The families that move here are trying to give their children as clean and upright and traditional a childhood as they can imagine. They're trying to move away from parents who smoke and slap their kids, away from families where people watch daytime TV shows about transvestite betrayals and "My Daughter is a Slut" confessions, away from broken homes and, most of all, away from the company of children who are not being raised to achieve and succeed.

They are trying to move instead to a realm of clean neighborhoods, safe streets, competitive cheerleading, spirit squads, soccer tots academies, accelerated-reader programs, and adult-chaperoned drug-free/alcohol-free graduation celebrations.

For the fifth consecutive year, the Henderson, Nevada, high school Marine Corps Junior ROTC squad has won the National Male Armed Drill Team championship. The Female Unarmed Drill Team has come in first six out of the past eight years. In Loudoun County the local newspaper runs notices for various travel team tryouts. In one recent edition, I counted 55 teams announcing their tryouts, with names like The Loudoun Cyclones, the Herndon Surge, the Loudoun Volcanoes. (It's not socially acceptable to name your team after a group of people anymore, so most of the teams have nature names.) As you drive around a Sprinkler City you see SUVs everywhere with cheers scrawled in washable marker on the back windows: "Go Heat!" "#24 Kelly Jones!" "Regional Champs!"

The kids spend their days being chaperoned from one adult-supervised activity to another, and from one achievement activity to the next. They are well tested, well trophied, and well appreciated. They are not only carefully reared and nurtured, they are launched into a life of high expectations and presumed accomplishment.

The dominant ideology of Sprinkler Cities is a sort of utopian conservatism. On the one hand, the people who live here have made a startling leap into the unknown. They have, in great numbers and with great speed, moved from their old homes in California, Florida, Illinois, and elsewhere, to these brand new places that didn't really exist 10 years ago. These places have no pasts, no precedents, no settled institutions, very few longstanding groups you can join and settle into.

Their inhabitants have moved to towns where they have no family connections, no ethnic enclaves, and no friends. They are using their imaginations to draw pictures for themselves of what their lives will be like. They are imagining their golf club buddies even though the course they are moving near is only just being carved out of the desert. They are imagining their successful children's graduation from high school, even though the ground around the new school building is still rutted with the tracks of construction equipment. They are imagining outings with friends at restaurants that are now only investor grass, waiting to be built.

And when they do join groups, often the groups turn out to be still in the process of building themselves. The migrants join congregations that meet in school basements while raising the money to construct churches. They go to office parks at biotech companies that are still waiting to put a product on the market. They may vote, or episodically pay attention to national politics, but they don't get drawn into strong local party organizations because the local organizations haven't been built.

But the odd thing is that all this imaginative daring, these leaps into the future, are all in the service of an extremely conservative ideal. You get the impression that these people have fled their crowded and stratified old suburbs because they really want to live in Mayberry. They have this image of what home should be, a historical myth or memory, and they are going to build it, even if it means constructing an old fashioned place out of modern materials.

It's going to be morally upstanding. It's going to be relaxed and neighborly. It's going to be neat and orderly. Sprinkler City people seem to have almost a moral revulsion at disorder or anything that threatens to bring chaos, including out-of-control immigration and terrorist attacks. They don't think about the war on terror much, let alone some alleged invasion of Iraq, but if it could be shown that Saddam Hussein presented a threat to the good order of the American homeland, then these people would support his ouster with a fervor that would take your breath away. "They have strong emotions when dealing with security," says Tom Tancredo, a congressman from suburban Denver. "Border security, the security of their families, the security of their neighborhoods."

Of course, from the moment they move in, they begin soiling their own nest. They move in order to get away from crowding, but as they and the tens of thousands like them move in, they bring crowding with them. They move to get away from stratification, snobbery, and inequality, but as the new towns grow they get more stratified. In Henderson, the $200,000 ranch homes are now being supplemented by gated $500,000-a-home golf communities. People move for stability and old fashioned values, but they are unwilling to accept limits to opportunity. They are achievement oriented. They are inherently dynamic.

For a time they do a dance about preserving the places they are changing by their presence. As soon as people move into a Sprinkler City, they start lobbying to control further growth. As Tancredo says, they have absolutely no shame about it. They want more roads built, but fewer houses. They want to freeze the peaceful hominess of the town that was growing when they moved there five minutes before.

But soon, one senses, they will get the urge to move again. The Hendersons and the Douglas Counties will be tomorrow what the Newport Beaches and the Los Altoses and the White Plainses are today, places where Patio Man no longer feels quite at home. And the suburban middle-class folks in these places will again strike out as the avant-garde toward new places, with new sorts of stores and a new vision of the innocent hometown.

So the dynamism and volatility will continue—always moving aggressively toward a daring future that looks like an imagined picture of the wholesome past, striving and charging toward that dream of the peaceful patio, the happy kids, the slender friends, and, towering over it all, the massive barbecue grill.

David Brooks is a senior editor at THE WEEKLY STANDARD.

Is regional government the answer?

FRED SIEGEL

SUBURBAN sprawl, the spread of low-density housing over an ever-expanding landscape, has attracted a growing list of enemies. Environmentalists have long decried the effects of sprawl on the ecosystem; aesthetes have long derided what they saw as "the ugliness and banality of suburbia"; and liberals have intermittently insisted that suburban prosperity has been purchased at the price of inner-city decline and poverty. But only recently has sprawl become the next great issue in American public life. That's because suburbanites themselves are now calling for limits to seemingly inexorable and frenetic development.

Slow-growth movements are a response to both the cyclical swings of the economy and the secular trend of dispersal. Each of the great postwar booms have, at their cyclical peak, produced calls for restraint. These sentiments have gained a wider hearing as each new upturn of the economy has produced an ever widening wave of exurban growth. A record 96 months of peacetime economic expansion has produced the strongest slow-growth movement to date. In 1998, antisprawl environmentalists and "not-in-my-backyard" slow-growth suburbanites joined forces across the nation to pass ballot measures restricting exurban growth.

Undoubtedly, the loss of land and the environmental degradation produced by sprawl are serious problems that demand public attention. But sprawl also brings enormous benefits as well as considerable costs. It is, in part, an expression of the new high-tech economy whose campus-like office parks on the periphery of urban areas have driven the economic boom of the 1990s. And it's sprawl that has sustained the record rise in home ownership. Sprawl is not some malignancy to be summarily excised but, rather, part and parcel of prosperity. Dealing with its ill effects requires both an understanding of the new landscape of the American economy and a willingness to make subtle trade-offs. We must learn to curb its worst effects without reducing the wealth and freedom that permit sprawl to develop.

Rising incomes and employment, combined with declining interest rates, have allowed a record number of people, including minority and immigrant families, to purchase homes for the first time. Home ownership among blacks, which is increasingly suburban, has risen at more than three times the white rate; a record 45 percent of African Americans owned their own homes in 1998. Nationally, an unprecedented 67 percent of Americans are homeowners.

Sprawl is part of the price we're paying for something novel in human history—the creation of a mass upper middle class. Net household worth has been increasing at the unparalleled annual rate of 10 percent since 1994, so that while in 1970, only 3.2 percent of households had an annual income of $100,000 (in today's dollars), by 1996, 8.2 percent of American households could boast a six-figure annual income. The new prosperity is reflected in the size of new homes, many of whose owners no doubt decry the arrival of still more "McMansions" and new residents, clogging the roads and schools of the latest subdivisions. In the midst of the 1980's boom, homebuilders didn't have a category for mass-produced houses of more than 3,000 square feet: By 1996, one out of every seven new homes built was larger than 3,000 square feet.

Today's tenement trail

Sprawl also reflects upward mobility for the aspiring lower-middle class. Nearly a half-century ago, Samuel Lubell dedicated *The Future of American Politics* to the memory of his mother, "who pioneered on the urban frontier." Lubell described a process parallel to the settling of the West, in which families on "the Old Tenement Trail" were continually on the move in search of a better life. In the cities, they abandoned crowded tenements on New York's Lower East Side for better housing in the South Bronx, and from there, went to the "West Bronx, crossing that Great Social Divide—the Grand Concourse—beyond which rolled true middle-class country where janitors were called superintendents."

Today's "tenement trail" takes aspiring working- and lower-middle class Americans to quite different areas. Kendall,

Florida, 20 miles southeast of Miami, is every environmentalist's nightmare image of sprawl, a giant grid carved out of the muck of swamp land that encroaches on the Everglades. Strip-malls and mega-stores abound for mile after mile, as do the area's signature giant auto lots. Yet Kendall also represents a late-twentieth-century version of the Old Tenement Trail. Kendall, notes the *New Republic*'s Charles Lane, is "the Queens of the late twentieth century," a place where immigrants are buying into America. Carved out of the palmetto wilderness, its population exploded from roughly 20,000 in 1970 to 300,000 today. Agricultural in the 1960s, and a hip place for young whites in the 1970s, Kendall grew increasingly Hispanic in the 1980s, as Cubans, Nicaraguans, and others who arrived with very little worked their way up. Today, it's half Hispanic and a remarkable example of integration. In most of Kendall, notes University of Miami geographer Peter Muller, "You can't point to a white or Latino block because the populations are so inter-mixed."

Virginia Postrel, the editor of *Reason*, argues that the slow-growth movement is animated by left-wing planners' hostility to suburbia. Others mock slow-growthers as elitists, as in the following quip:

> Q: What's the difference between an environmentalist and a developer?
> A: The environmentalist already has his house in the mountains.

But, in the 1990s, slow-growth sentiment has been taking hold in middle- and working-class suburbs like Kendall, as development turns into overdevelopment and traffic congestion becomes a daily problem.

Regional government

One oft-proposed answer to sprawl has been larger regional governments that will exercise a monopoly on land-use decisions. Underlying this solution is the theory—no doubt correct—that sprawl is produced when individuals and townships seek to maximize their own advantage without regard for the good of the whole community. Regionalism, however, is stronger in logic than in practice. For example, the people of Kendall, rather than embracing regionalism, are looking to slow down growth by *seceding* from their regional government. Upon examination, we begin to see some of the problems with regional government.

Kendall is part of Metro-Dade, the oldest major regional government, created in 1957. The largest of its 29 municipalities, Miami, the fourth poorest city in the United States, has 350,000 people; the total population of Metro-Dade is 2 million, 1.1 million of whom live in unincorporated areas. In Metro-Dade, antisprawl and antiregional government sentiments merge. Despite county-imposed growth boundaries, residents have complained bitterly of overdevelopment. The county commissioners—many of whom have been convicted of, or charged with, corruption—have been highly receptive to the developers

who are among their largest campaign contributors. As one south Florida resident said of the developers, "It's a lot cheaper to be able to buy just one government." The south Florida secessionists want to return zoning to local control where developers' clout is less likely to overwhelm neighborhood interests.

When Jane Jacobs wrote, in *The Death and Life of Great American Cities*, that "the voters sensibly decline to federate into a system where bigness means local helplessness, ruthless over-simplified planning and administrative chaos," she could have been writing about south Florida. What's striking about Metro-Dade is that it has delivered neither efficiency nor equity nor effective planning while squelching local self-determination.

The fight over Metro-Dade echoes the conflicts of an earlier era. Historically, the fight over regional versus local government was an important, if intermittent, issue for many cities from 1910 to 1970. From about 1850 to 1910, according to urban historian Jon Teaford, suburbanites were eager to be absorbed by cities whose wealth enabled them to build the water, sewage, and road systems they couldn't construct on their own. "The central city," he explains, "provided superior service at a lower cost." But, in the 1920s, well before race became a central issue, suburbanites, who had increasingly sorted themselves out by ethnicity and class, began to use special-service districts and innovative financial methods to provide their own infrastructure and turned away from unification. Suburbanites also denounced consolidation as an invitation to big-city, and often Catholic, "boss rule" and as a threat to "self-government."

In the 1960s, as black politicians began to win influence over big-city governments, they also joined the anticonsolidation chorus. At the same time, county government, once a sleepy extension of rural rule, was modernized, and county executives essentially became the mayors of full-service governments administering what were, in effect, dispersed cities. But they were mayors with a difference. Their constituents often wanted a balance between commercial development, which constrained the rise of taxes, and the suburban ideal of family-friendly semi-rural living. When development seemed too intrusive, suburban voters in the 1980s, and again in the 1990s, have pushed a slow-growth agenda.

The new regionalism

In the 1990s, regionalism has been revived as an effort to link the problem of sprawl with the problem of inner-city poverty. Assuming that "flight creates blight," regionalists propose to recapture the revenue of those who have fled the cities and force growth back into older areas by creating regional or metropolitan-area governments with control over land use and taxation.

The new regionalism owes a great deal to a group of circuit-riding reformers. Inspired by the arguments of scholars like Anthony Downs, one of the authors of the Kerner Commission report, and sociologist William Julius Wilson of Harvard, as well as the example of Portland, Oregon's metro-wide government, these itinerant preachers have traveled to hundreds of cities to spread the gospel of regional cooperation. The three most prominent new regionalists—columnist Neil Peirce, former

Albuquerque mayor David Rusk, and Minnesota state representative Myron Orfield—have developed a series of distinct, but overlapping, arguments for why cities can't help themselves, and why regional solutions are necessary.

Peirce, in his book *Citistates*, plausibly insists that regions are the real units of competition in the global economy, so that there is a metro-wide imperative to revive the central city, lest the entire area be undermined. Less plausibly, Orfield in *Metropolitics* argues that what he calls "the favored quarter" of fast-growing suburbs on the periphery of the metro area have prospered at the expense of both the central city and the inner-ring suburbs. In order [for] both to revive the central city and save the inner suburbs from decline, Orfield proposes that these two areas join forces, redistributing money from the "favored quarter" to the older areas. Rusk argues, in *Baltimore Unbound*, that older cities, unable to annex the fast growing suburbs, are doomed to further decline. He insists that only "flexible cities"—that is, cities capable of expanding geographically and capturing the wealth of the suburbs—can truly deal with inner-city black poverty. Regionalism, writes Rusk, is "the new civil rights movement."

There are differences among them. Orfield and, to a lesser degree, Rusk operate on a zero-sum model in which gain for the suburbs comes directly at the expense of the central city. Peirce is less radical, proposing regional cooperation as the means to a win-win situation for both city and the surrounding region. But they all share a desire to disperse poverty across the region and, more importantly, recentralize economic growth in the already built-up areas. The latter goal is consistent with both the environmental thrust of the antisprawl movement and the push for regional government. In a speech to a Kansas City civic organization, Rusk laid out the central assumption of the new regionalism. "The greater the fragmentation of governments," he asserted, "the greater the fragmentation of society by race and economic class." Fewer governments, argue the new regionalists, will yield a number of benefits, including better opportunities for regional cooperation, more money for cash-strapped central cities, less racial inequality, less sprawl, and greater economic growth. However, all of these propositions are questionable.

Better policies, not fewer governments

Consider Baltimore and Philadelphia, cities that the regionalists have studied thoroughly. According to the 1998 *Greater Baltimore State of the Region* report, Philadelphia has 877 units of local government (including school boards)—or 17.8 per 100,000 people. Baltimore has only six government units of any consequence in Baltimore City and the five surrounding counties—or 2.8 per 100,000 people. Greater Baltimore has fewer government units than any other major metro area in the United States. As a political analyst told me: "Get six people in a room, and you have the government of 2,200 square miles, because the county execs have very strong powers." We might expect considerable regional cooperation in Baltimore, but not in Philadelphia. Regionalism has made no headway in either city,

however. The failure has little to do with the number of governments and a great deal to do with failed policy choices in both cities.

Rusk does not mention the many failings of Baltimore's city government. He refers to the current mayor, Kurt Schmoke, just once and only to say that Baltimore has had "excellent political leadership." In Rusk's view, Baltimore is "programmed to fail" because of factors entirely beyond its control, namely, the inability to annex its successful suburbs. In the ahistorical world of the regionalist (and here, Peirce is a partial exception), people are always pulled from the city by structural forces but never pushed from the city by bad policies.

Baltimore is not as well financed as the District of Columbia, which ruined itself despite a surfeit of money. But Baltimore, a favorite political son of both Annapolis and Washington, has been blessed with abundant financial support. Over the past decade, Schmoke has increased spending on education and health by over a half-billion dollars. He has also added 200 police officers and spent $60 million more for police over the last four years. "His greatest skill," notes the *Baltimore Sun*, "has been his ability to attract more federal and state aid while subsidies diminished elsewhere." But, notwithstanding these expenditures, middle-class families continue to flee the city at the rate of 1,000 per month, helping to produce the sprawl environmentalists decry.

Little in Baltimore works well. The schools have been taken over by the state, while the Housing Authority is mired in perpetual scandal and corruption. Baltimore is one of the few cities where crime hasn't gone down. That's because Schmoke has insisted, contrary to the experiences of New York and other cities, that drug-related crime could not be reduced until drug use was controlled through treatment. The upshot is that New York, with eight times more people than Baltimore, has only twice as many murders. Baltimore also leads the country in sexually transmitted diseases. These diseases have flourished among the city's drug users partly owing to Schmoke's de facto decriminalization of drugs. According to the Centers for Disease Control and Prevention (CDC), Baltimore has a syphilis rate 18 times the national average, 3 or 4 times as high as areas where the STD epidemic is most concentrated.

Flexible cities

Rusk attributes extraordinary qualities to flexible cities. He says that they are able to both reduce inequality, curb sprawl, and maintain vital downtowns. Rusk was the mayor of Albuquerque, a flexible city that annexed a vast area, even as its downtown essentially died. The reduced inequality he speaks of is largely a statistical artifact. If New York were to annex Scarsdale, East New York's average income would rise without having any effect on the lives of the people who live there. As for sprawl, flexible cities like Phoenix and Houston are hardly models.

A recent article for *Urban Affairs Review*, by Subhrajit Guhathakurta and Michele Wichert, showed that within the elastic city of Phoenix, inner-city residents poorer than their outer-ring neighbors are subsidizing the building of new developments on the fringes of the metropolis. While sprawl is correlated with downtown decline in Albuquerque, in Phoenix it's connected with what *Fortune* described as "the remarkable rebound of downtown Phoenix, which has become a chic after-dark destination as well as a residential hot spot." There seems to be no automatic connection between regionalism and downtown revival.

Orfield's *Metropolitics* provides another version of an over-determined structuralist argument. According to him, the favored quarter is sucking the inner city dry, and, as a result, central-city blight will inevitably engulf the older first-ring suburbs as well. He is right to see strong pressures on the inner-ring suburbs, stemming from an aging housing stock and population as well as an influx of inner-city poor. But it is how the inner-ring suburbs respond to these pressures that will affect their fate.

When Coleman Young was mayor of Detroit, large sections of the city returned to prairie. But the inner-ring suburbs have done fairly well precisely by not imitating Detroit's practice of providing poor services at premium prices. "Much like the new edge suburbs," explains the *Detroit News*, "older suburbs that follow the proven formula of promoting good schools, public safety and well-kept housing attract new investment." Suburban Mayor Michael Guido sees his city's well developed infrastructure as an asset, which has already been bought and paid for. "Now," says Mayor Guido, "it's a matter of maintenance… and we offer a sense of history and a sense of community. That's really important to people, to have a sense of belonging to a whole community rather than a subdivision."

Suburb power

City-suburban relations are not fixed; they are various depending on the policies both follow. Some suburbs compete with the central city for business. In south Florida, Coral Gables more than holds its own with Miami as a site for business headquarters. Southfield, just outside Detroit, and Clayton, just outside St. Louis, blossomed in the wake of the 1960s' urban riots and now compete with their downtowns. Aurora, with a population of more than 160,000 and to the east of Denver, sees itself as a competitor, and it sees regional efforts at growth management as a means by which the downtown Denver elite can ward off competition.

Suburban growth can also help the central city. In the Philadelphia area, economic growth and new work come largely from the Route 202 high-tech corridor in Chester County, west of the city. While the city has lost 57,000 jobs, even in the midst of national economic prosperity, the fast growing Route 202 companies have been an important source of downtown legal and accounting jobs. At the same time, the suburbs are creating jobs for residents that the central city cannot produce, so that 20 percent of city residents commute to the suburbs while 15 percent of people who live in the suburbs commute to Philadelphia.

The "new regionalists" assume that the prosperity of the edge cities is a function of inner-city decline. But, in many cities, it is more nearly the case that suburban booms are part of

what's keeping the central-city economy alive. It is the edge cities that have taken up the time-honored urban task of creating new work.

According to *INC* magazine, the 500 fastest growing small companies are all located in suburbs and exurbs. This is because local governments there are very responsive to the needs of start-up companies. These high-tech hotbeds, dubbed "nerdistans" by Joel Kotkin, are composed of networks of companies that are sometimes partners, sometimes competitors. They provide a pool of seasoned talent for start-ups, where engineers and techies who prefer the orderly, outdoor life of suburbia to the crowds and disorder of the city can move from project to project. Henry Nicholas, CEO of Broadcom, a communications-chip and cable-modem maker, explained why he reluctantly moved to Irvine: "It's hard to relocate techies to LA. It's the congestion, the expensive housing—and there's a certain stigma to it."

Imagine what the United States would be like if the Bay Area had followed the New York model. In 1898, New York created the first regional government when it consolidated all the areas of the New York harbor—Manhattan, Brooklyn, Queens, the Bronx, and Staten Island—into the then-largest city in the world. The consolidation has worked splendidly for Manhattan, which thrives as a capital of high-end financial and legal services. But over time, the Manhattan-centric economy based on high taxes, heavy social spending, and extensive economic regulation destroyed Brooklyn's once vital shipping and manufacturing economy.

In 1912, San Francisco, the Manhattan of Northern California, proposed to create a unified regional government by incorporating Oakland in the East Bay and San Jose in the South. The plan for a Greater San Francisco was modeled on Greater New York and called for the creation of self-governing boroughs within an enlarged city and county of San Francisco. East Bay opposition defeated the San Francisco expansion in the legislature, and later attempts at consolidation in 1917, 1923, and 1928 also failed. But had San Francisco with its traditions of high taxation and heavy regulation succeeded, Silicon Valley might never have become one of the engines of the American economy. Similarly, it's no accident that the Massachusetts Route 128 high-tech corridor is located outside of the boundaries of Boston, even as it enriches the central city.

The Portland model

The complex and often ironic history of existing regional governments has been obscured by the bright light of hope emanating from Portland. It seems that in every generation one city is said to have perfected the magic elixir for revival. In the 1950s, it was Philadelphia; today, it's Portland. In recent years, hundreds of city officials have traveled to Portland to study its metropolitan government, comprehensive environmental planning, and the urban-growth boundary that has been credited with Portland's revival and success.

While there are important lessons to be learned from Portland, very little of its success to date can be directly attributed to the growth boundary, which was introduced too recently and with boundaries so capacious as not yet to have had much effect. Thirty-five percent of the land within the boundary was vacant when it was imposed in 1979. And, at the same time, fast growing Clark County, just north of Portland but not part of the urban-growth boundary, has provided an escape valve for potential housing pressures. The upshot, notes demographer Wendell Cox, is that even with the growth boundary, Portland still remains a relatively low-density area with fewer people per square mile than San Diego, San Jose, or Sacramento.

Portland has also been run with honesty and efficiency, unlike Metro-Dade. Blessed with great natural resources, Portland—sometimes dubbed "Silicon forest," because chipmakers are drawn to its vast quantities of cheap clean water—has conserved its man-made as well as natural resources. A city with more cast-iron buildings than any place outside of Manhattan, it has been a leader in historic preservation. Time and again, Portland's leadership has made the right choices. It was one of the first cities to reconnect its downtown with the riverfront. Portland never built a circumferential freeway. And, in the 1970s, under the leadership of mayor Neil Goldschmidt, the city vetoed a number of proposed highway projects that would have threatened the downtown.

In 1978, Portland voters, in conjunction with the state government, created the first directly elected metropolitan government with the power to manage growth over three counties. Portland metro government has banned big-box retailers, like Walmart and Price Club, on the grounds that they demand too much space and encourage too much driving. This is certainly an interesting experiment well worth watching, but should other cities emulate Portland's land-management model? It's too soon to say.

Good government is always important. But aside from that, it's hard to draw any general lessons from the Portland experience. The growth boundaries may or may not work, and there's certainly no reason to think that playing with political boundaries will bring good government to Baltimore.

Living with sprawl

What then is to be done? First, we can accept the consensus that has developed around preserving open space, despite some contradictory effects. The greenbelts around London, Portland, and Baltimore County pushed some development back toward the city and encouraged further sprawl as growth leapfrogged the open space. The push to preserve open space is only likely to grow stronger as continued growth generates both more congestion and more wealth, which can be used to buy up open land.

Secondly, we can create what Peter Salins, writing in *The Public Interest*,[1] described as a "level playing field" between the central cities and the suburbs. This can be done by ending exurban growth subsidies for both transportation as well as new

water and sewer lines. These measures might further encourage the revival of interest in old fashioned Main Street living, which is already attracting a new niche of home buyers. State and local governments can also repeal the land-use and zoning regulations that discourage mixed-use development of the sort that produces a clustering of housing around Main Street and unsubsidized low-cost housing in the apartments above the streets' shops.

Because of our strong traditions of local self-government, regionalism has been described as an unnatural act among consenting jurisdictions. But regional cooperation needn't mean the heavy hand of all-encompassing regional government. There are some modest, but promising, experiments already under way in regional revenue sharing whose effects should be carefully evaluated. Allegheny County, which includes Pittsburgh, has created a Regional Asset District that uses a 1 percent sales tax increase to support cultural institutions and reduce other taxes. The Twin Cities have put money derived from the increase in assessed value of commercial and industrial properties into a pot to aid fiscally weaker municipalities. Kansas and Missouri created a cultural district that levies a small increase in the sales tax across the region. The money is being used to rehabilitate the area's most treasured architectural landmark, Kansas City's Union Station.

Cities and suburbs do have some shared interests, as in the growing practice of reverse commuting which links inner-city residents looking to get off welfare with fast growing suburban areas hampered by a shortage of labor. Regionalism can curb sprawl and integrate and sustain central-city populations if it reforms the misguided policies and politics that have sent the black and white middle class streaming out of cities like Baltimore, Washington, and Philadelphia. Regional co-operation between the sprawling high-tech suburbs and the central cities could modernize cities that are in danger of being left further behind by the digital economy. In that vein, the District of Columbia's Mayor Anthony Williams has seized on the importance of connecting his welfare population with the fast growing areas of Fairfax County in Northern Virginia. The aim of focused regional policies, argues former HUD Undersecretary Marc Weiss, should be economic, not political, integration.

Sprawl isn't some malignancy that can be surgically removed. It's been part and parcel of healthy growth, and curbing it involves difficult tradeoffs best worked out locally. Sprawl and the movement against sprawl are now a permanent part of the landscape. The future is summed up in a quip attributed to former Oregon Governor Tom McCall, who was instrumental in creating Portland's growth boundary. "Oregonians," he said, "are against two things, sprawl and density."

Note

1. "Cities, Suburbs, and the Urban Crisis," *The Public Interest*, No. 113 (Fall 1993).

Downtown Struggles While Neighbor Thrives

By MICHAEL BRICK

HOUSTIN, MARCH 13—Gary Barnett does not trade natural gas and electricity futures for a living, and there is no indication that he plans to do so. This is something of a disappointment for many people in Houston. Should Mr. Barnett ever take a shine to the idea of trading energy futures, he is the new owner of an ideal place to start, a place that many people here had hoped would be used for that purpose.

He is president of the **Intell Management and Investment Company**, which bought the building formerly known as Enron Center South through a bankruptcy court auction for $102 million, about a third of its construction cost. The sale closed on Dec. 30, and Intell has renamed the building 1500 Louisiana, a name that makes its address redundant.

The only tenant, the power trading operation that UBS Warburg bought from Enron, plans to move in May.

Henry J. Terech, a senior vice president at Intell who manages the 40-story tower and who previously oversaw its development as an Enron employee, said he was marketing space to a range of potential tenants.

"The conventional wisdom was this place was going to sell to a Dynegy or a Duke," Mr. Terech said, naming companies that are, in fact, in the business of trading energy futures. "When the energy market melted down, that wasn't the case."

The problems of the power trading companies have steepened the downward slope of a boom-and-bust real estate cycle in the central business district, an echo of previous patterns driven by traditional energy companies. But Houston has diversified its economic base, developing a medical complex about four miles south of downtown. That part of town is thriving, but the traditional downtown remains hostage to boom or bust.

Vacancy rates for top-class office space downtown have risen to 13.75 percent at the end of 2002, not including sublease space, from 4.94 percent a year earlier, and asking rents have fallen to an average of $24.01 a square foot, from $27.35, the real estate services firm Insignia/ESG said.

"The hope is that there's some large energy companies that can take that space," said Jerald King, a director of Insignia, citing as an example Exxon Mobil, which has offices here in a building that is more than 40 years old.

"I don't know that any of them will," Mr. King said. "At least for the Enron building, there's still a stigma to it that people can't get over."

Mr. Terech, the manager of 1500 Louisiana, said he planned to market the space at rates comparable to other buildings downtown, emphasizing its modern amenities.

Inside, there are four trading floors, each with a 53,000-square-foot floorplate raised 18 inches to accommodate a maze of 1.3 million feet of data network cable. The cables connect with 475 trading positions, desktops with file cabinets, dwarfed beneath 55 plasma screens.

From just outside an office once intended for Jeffrey K. Skilling, who was once the chief executive of Enron, a luna pearl granite staircase leads down to one trading floor. The building's exterior wall is reinforced to withstand hurricane-force winds; backup generators sit atop the garage; and boardrooms are wired with microphones and videoconferencing equipment.

A few miles away, Houston's other downtown is booming.

The Texas Medical Center, with 22 million square feet of space, is a city within a city, not quite half the 47 million square feet of office space in the central business district.

The medical center has about 6,000 hospital beds and 60,000 workers. Another 11 million square feet is under construction at a cost of about $1.8 billion, according to the nonprofit group that manages the area.

The group, the Texas Medical Center Corporation, owns 250 undeveloped acres, and the complex is bordered by a bayou, a park and university land. Inside its zone, the corporation leases buildings to medical institutions for 198 years at a dollar a year, so commercial developers and brokers are effectively frozen out.

"We have driven up the price of land by our success," said Richard E. Wainerdi, chief executive of the corporation, noting that it spent $15.7 million in 2000 to buy 22 acres including a 600,000-square-foot building from Nabisco.

Much of this real estate is research space and hospital facilities, along with hotels and restaurants. But the center has 3.6 million square feet of office space, and its market is among the tightest in the country. Insignia places the vacancy rate at zero for top-class buildings, and 10.42 percent for buildings described as Class C, a designation typically applied to ̶l̶er buildings nearing economic ̶solescence.

"You've got fancy buildings down̶wn that can't get these kinds of ̶ntal rates," said Jeffrey P. Munger, a ̶nior director of Holliday Fenoglio ̶wler, a commercial mortgage bank̶g firm, standing outside Medical ̶wers, an 18-story building that ̶pened in 1954. Rental rates for older buildings in this part of the city range from $26 to $30 a square foot, Mr. Munger said.

Back downtown, brokers and building managers consistently cite its ever-increasing list of amenities as reason to think that tenants will return. A 7.5-mile, 16-station light rail system is being installed, and the city has promised that it will be complete, at least as far as the foot-

ball stadium, in time for the Super Bowl in January.

A $100 million convention center expansion is under way, and there is a new $85 million performing arts center.

In addition, a developer, Tilman J. Fertitta, has built what might be described as a permanent carnival, the Downtown Aquarium. His $38 million complex on the edge of the central business district has 500,000 gallons of water and 200 species of marine life, as well as seafood restaurants and games and rides not unlike a sanitized Coney Island. His aquarium complex is packed with visitors, mostly children, even on school days.

In Housten, vacancy rates rise downtown, but a nearby medical complex booms.

Downtown brokers and landlords do not expect the aquarium to lure office tenants, and neither does Mr. Fertitta, but they consistently say that another attraction cannot hurt.

"The problem is the oil," Mr. Fertitta said. "Maybe Houston still needs to be a little bit more diversified."

While energy still looms large, its dominance has been diminishing. More than 51 percent of economic activity drawing money into Houston these days comes from sources

other than energy, compared with 15.7 percent in 1981, according to the Institute for Regional Forecasting at the University of Houston.

Mr. Barnett, the owner of the former Enron Center South, is counting on that diversity. His building downtown is being marketed to companies in financial services, technology and traditional energy areas.

In addition to the former Enron building, Intell and its affiliates own or are developing 8 million square feet of commercial real estate around the country, including a 1.8-million-square-foot office building at 175 West Jackson Street in Chicago and the W Hotel in Times Square.

Mr. Barnett's hopes of developing an office tower near Times Square were frustrated last year when he and other property owners on the block lost a legal battle to prevent the state from condemning a site for a new headquarters for The New York Times Company.

Discussing his property in Houston, Mr. Barnett said, "We're seeing lots of interest in our building," adding that there are companies in the suburbs that want to move downtown and companies downtown that want to consolidate their space in more modern buildings.

"For years, there was no space in downtown Houston," he said. "You have the oil services business and the exploration and development, and those are doing really well now. The only ones that are hurting are the power traders."

Unscrambling the City

Archaic zoning laws lock cities into growth patterns that hardly anybody wants. Changing the rules can help set them free.

BY CHRISTOPHER SWOPE

Take a walk through Chicago's historic Lakeview neighborhood, and the new houses will jump right out at you. That's because they're jarringly incompatible with the old ones. On one quiet tree-lined street, you'll find a row of old two-story colonials with pitched roofs. Then you walk a little farther and it seems as though a giant rectangular box has fallen out of the sky. The new condominium building is twice as high as its older neighbors and literally casts shadows over their neat flower gardens and tiny front yards. Angry Lakeview residents have seen so many new buildings like this lately that they have come up with a sneering name for them. They call them "three-flats on steroids."

Listening to the complaints in Lakeview, you might wonder whether home builders are breaking the law and getting away with it, or at least bending the rules quite a bit. But that's not the case. If you take some time and study Chicago's zoning law, you'll find that these giant condos are technically by the book. It's not the new buildings that are the problem. The problem is Chicago's zoning ordinance. The code is nearly half a century old, and it is an outdated mishmash of vague and conflicting rules. Over the years, it has been amended repeatedly, to the point of nonsense. Above all, it's totally unpredictable. In Lakeview, zoning can yield anything from tasteful two-flats to garish McMansions, with no consideration at all for how they fit into the neighborhood.

Chicago's zoning problem lay dormant for decades while the city's economy sagged and population declined. Back in the 1970s and '80s, not much building was going on. But then the 1990s brought an economic boom and 112,000 new residents. While almost everyone is happy that the construction machine has been turned back on, so many Chicagoans are appalled by the way the new construction looks that Mayor Richard M. Daley decided it was time to rewrite the city's entire zoning code. Everything about Chicago land use is on the table: not just residential development but commercial and industrial as well. It is the largest overhaul of its kind in any U.S. city in 40 years.

But while few communities are going as far as Chicago, many are coming to a similar conclusion: The zoning laws on their books—most of them written in the 1950s and '60s—are all scrambled up. They are at once too vague and too complicated to produce the urban character most residents say they want.

The zoning problem afflicts both cities and suburbs and manifests itself in countless ways. It takes the form of oversized homes and farmland covered in cookie-cutter housing developments. It shows up as a sterile new strip mall opening up down the street from one that is dying. It becomes an obstacle when cities discover how hard it is to revive pedestrian life in their downtowns and neighborhood shopping districts. And it becomes a headache for city councils that spend half their time interpreting clumsy rules, issuing variances and haggling with developers.

What urban planners disagree about is whether the current system can be salvaged, or whether it should be scrapped altogether. Most cities are not ready to take the ultimate step. Chicago isn't going that far. Neither did Boston, Milwaukee, San Diego and San Jose. All of them retained the basic zoning conventions, even as they slogged through the process of streamlining the codes and rewriting them for the 21st century. According to researcher Stuart Meck, of the American Planning Association, there's a cyclical nature to all this. He points out that it's common for cities to update their laws after the sort of building boom many have enjoyed recently. "Cities are in growth mode again," Meck says, "but they're getting development based on standards that are 20, 30 or 40 years old."

MYRIAD CATEGORIES

For much of the past century, if you wanted to find out the latest thinking about zoning, Chicago was a good place to go. In 1923, it became one of the first cities, after New York, to adopt a zoning law. The motivation then was mostly health and safety. Smoke-spewing factories were encroaching on residential

PICTURE-BOOK ZONING

While Chicago and a few other large cities struggle to update old zoning laws for the new century, some places are going in a new direction. They are experimenting with zoning concepts percolating out of the New Urbanist movement, writing codes that bear a closer resemblance to picture books than to laws. Conventional zoning, they have decided, is based on an abstract language that leaves too much to chance. They would rather start with a question—what does the community want to look like—and then work back from there. "It's not enough to change the zoning," says New Urbanist author Peter Katz. "Cities have to move to a new system. They should look at the streets they like and the public spaces they like and then write the rules to get more of what they like and less of what they don't. Conventional zoning doesn't do that. It just gives a use and a density and then you hope for the best."

On jurisdiction currently buying in to this new idea is Arlington, Virginia, a suburb of 190,000 people just across the river from Washington D.C. A few months ago, Arlington's county board adopted a "form-based" zoning code for a 3.5-mile corridor known as Columbia Pike, making it one of the largest experiments yet with this new idea.

Columbia Pike is a typical traffic-choked suburban drag, lines mostly with strip malls, drive-throughs and apartment complexes ringed by parking lots. Developers have ignored the area for years. County planners want to convert it into a place that more closely resembles a classic American Main Street. They want a walk-able commercial thoroughfare, featuring ground-floor retail blended together with offices and apartments above. But the old zoning code made this nearly impossible.

Rather than starting with a clear vision of what Arlington wants Columbia Pike to look like, the old code starts with a letter and a number: "C-2." The "C" stands for commercial uses only, and the "2" means that development should be of a medium density. C-2 is so vague that it could yield any number of building types. But the code's ambiguities don't end there. Building size is regulated by "floor area ratio," a calculation that again says nothing about whether the building should be suitable for a Main Street or an interstate highway exit. Finally, the code doesn't say where on the lot the building should go—just that it shouldn't sit near the roadway. Mostly, developers have used this recipe to build strip malls. "The code is really absolute on things that don't matter to us at all," says Arlington board member Chris Zimmerman. "The tools are all wrong for the job we're trying to do."

The new code for Columbia Pike abandons these old tools. It begins with a picture: What does a Main Street look like? Rather than abstract language, the new code uses visuals to show the form that the buildings should take. Buildings are three to six stories tall. And they sit on the sidewalk, with ground-floor windows and front doors, not 50 feet back from the street.

Compared with traditional zoning, a form-based code doesn't focus on specific uses. It specifies physical patterns. Whether the buildings are occupied by coffee shops, law offices or upstairs renters makes little difference. "Traditionally," says Peter Katz, "zoning stipulates a density and a use and it's anyone's guess wheth-er you'll get what the planners' renderings look like. Form-based codes give a way to achieve what you see in the picture with precision."

One of the most prominent New Urbanists, Miami architect Andres Duany, advocates taking the form-based idea even further. In Duany's view, it's not only buildings along a road like Columbia Pike that should be coded according to physical form rather than use: entire metropolitan regions should be thought of this way. Duany is pushing an alternative he calls "Smart Code."

The Smart Code is based on the concept of the "transect." The idea is that there is a range of forms that the built environment can take. At one end is downtown, the urban core. At the other end is wilderness. In between are villages, suburbs and more dense urban neighborhoods. As Duany sees it, conventional zoning has failed to maintain the important distinctions between these types of places. Instead, it has made each of them resem-ble suburbia. When suburban building forms encroach on wilderness, the result is sprawl. When they encroach on urban areas, the result is lifeless downtowns.

Nashville-Davidson County, Tennessee, is one of the first places to begin incorporating these concepts into its planning process. The transect isn't a substitute for a zoning code, says planning director Rick Bernhardt. But it helps planners think about how one part of the city fits into the region, and how to zone accordingly. "It's really understanding what the purpose is of the part of the community you're designing," Bernhardt says, "and then making sure that the streetscape, the intensity and the mix of land use are all consistent with that."

—*C.S.*

neighborhoods, and the city's first ordinance sought to keep them out. By the 1950s, when more people drove cars, Chicago was a pioneer in rewriting the code to separate the places people live in from where they work and where they shop.

The 1957 zoning law was largely the creation of real estate developer Harry Chaddick, who proclaimed that the city was "being slowly strangled" by mixed uses of property. It classified every available parcel of land into myriad categories based on density. Residential neighborhoods, for example, were laid out in a range from "R1" (single family homes) to "R8" (high-rises). Land use rules were so strict as to dictate where ice cream shops, coin stores and haberdasheries could go. Chaddick's code was hailed in its time as a national model.

But over the years, one patch after another in the 1957 law made it almost impossible to use. Some parts contradicted other parts. Two attorneys could read it and come away with completely opposite views of what the code allowed. Finally, in 2000, the mayor tapped Ed Kus, a longtime city zoning attorney, to take charge of a full-scale rewrite. Kus thinks the law in the works will be equally as historic as Chaddick's—and more durable. "I hope the ordinance we come up with will be good for the next 50 years," Kus says.

Besides its rigidity, the old code has been plagued by false assumptions about population growth. Back in the 1950s, Chicago was a city of 3.6 million people, and planners expected it to reach a population of 5 million. Of course, it didn't work out that way. Like every other major city, Chicago lost a huge proportion of its residents to the suburbs. By 1990, it was down to fewer than 2.8 million residents. But it was still zoned to accommodate 5 million.

That's essentially how Lakeview got its three-flats on steroids. Had the city's population grown as the code anticipated, it would have needed a supply of large new residential buildings to replace its traditional two-flats and bungalows. The law made it possible to build these in lots of neighborhoods, regardless of the existing architecture or character.

For decades, this made relatively little difference, because the declining population limited demand for new housing in most of the city. Once the '90s boom hit, however, developers took advantage. They bought up old homes and tore them down, replacing them with massive condo projects. They built tall, and sometimes they built wide and deep, eating up front yards and side yards and often paving over the back for parking. "Developers are building to the max," Kus says. "We have all these new housing types and the zoning ordinance doesn't govern them very well."

There are other glaring problems. Although many people think of the 1950s as the decade when America went suburban, most retail business in Chicago was still conducted in storefronts along trolley lines, both in the city and the older close-in suburbs. The code reflects that mid-century reality. Some 700 miles of Chicago's arterial streets are zoned for commercial use, much more than the current local retail market can bear. Worse, the old code is full of anachronistic restrictions on what kinds of transactions can be conducted where. A store that sells computers needs a zoning variance to set up shop next door to one

that fixes them. "If you're in a 'B1' district"—a neighborhood business corridor—"you can hardly do any business," Kus says.

All of these archaic provisions are quietly being reconsidered and revised on the ninth floor of city hall, where Kus heads a small team that includes two planning department staffers and a consultant from the planning firm of Duncan Associates. Their work will go to the zoning reform commission, a panel whose 17 members were picked by the mayor to hold exhaustive public meetings and then vote on the plan. The commission includes aldermen, architects, planners, business representatives and a labor leader. Developers are conspicuously absent, which may come back to bite the whole project later. But for now, the rewrite is moving remarkably fast. The city council is expected to pass the new code this fall. That will set the stage for an even more difficult task: drawing new maps to fit the changed rules.

In the past, Chicago's zoning reforms sought nothing less than to transform the face of the city. This time, however, there is more of a conservationist bent. What the reformers are trying to do is to lock in the qualities Chicagoans like about their oldest, most traditional neighborhoods. That's not to say they want to freeze the city in place. The building boom is quite popular. But it's also widely accepted that the character of Chicago's neighborhoods is the reason why the city is hot again, and that zoning should require new buildings to fit in. "Cities that will succeed in the future are the ones that maintain a unique character of place," says Alicia Mazur Berg, Chicago's planning commissioner. "People choose to live in many of our neighborhoods because they're attractive, they have front yards and buildings of the same scale."

MADE FOR WALKING

The new rules being drafted for residential areas are a good example of this thinking. Height limits will prevent new houses from towering over old ones. Neighborhoods such as Lakeview will likely be "downzoned" for less density. New homes will be required to have a green back yard, not a paved one, and builders will not be allowed to substitute a new creation known as a "patio pit" for a front yard. Garages will be expected to face an alley—not the street—and blank walls along the streetscape will be prohibited.

In the same spirit, the creators of the new zoning code are also proposing a new category, the Pedestrian Street, or "P-street." This is meant for a neighborhood shopping street that has survived in spite of the automobile and still thrives with pedestrian life. The new code aims to keep things that way. Zoning for P-streets will specifically outlaw strip malls, gas stations and drive-throughs, or any large curb cut that could interrupt the flow of pedestrians. It also will require new buildings to sit right on the sidewalk and have front doors and windows so that people walking by can see inside.

There are dozens of other ideas. The new code aims to liven up once-vibrant but now-dying neighborhood commercial streets by letting developers build housing there. For the first time ever, downtown Chicago will be treated as a distinct place, with its own special set of zoning rules. The code will largely ignore meaningless distinctions between businesses, such as whether they sell umbrellas or hats.

The new code also will recognize that the nature of manufacturing has changed. Light manufacturing will be allowed to mix with offices or nightclubs. But heavy industry will get zones of its own, not so much for the health reasons that were important in 1923 and 1957, but because the big manufacturers want it that way and Chicago doesn't want to lose them.

For all the changes, Chicago is still keeping most of the basic zoning conventions in place. It is also keeping much of the peculiar language of zoning—the designations such as "R2" and "C3" that sound more like droids from Star Wars than descriptions of places where people live, work and shop.

On the other hand, the new code will be different from the old code in one immediately identifiable way: It will be understandable. Pages of text are being slimmed down into charts and graphics, making the law easier to use for people without degrees in law or planning. An interactive version will go up on the city's Web site. "Predictability is important," says Ed Kus. "The average person should be able to pick up the zoning code and understand what can and can't be built in his neighborhood."

From *Governing*, June 2003, pp. 30-33. © 2003 by Governing. Reprinted by permission.

Are Europe's cities better?

PIETRO S. NIVOLA

CITIES grow in three directions: *in* by crowding, *up* into multi-story buildings, or *out* toward the periphery. Although cities everywhere have developed in each of these ways at various times, nowhere in Europe do urban settlements sprawl as much as in the United States. Less than a quarter of the U.S. population lived in suburbia in 1950. Now well over half does. Why have most European cities remained compact compared to the hyperextended American metropolis?

At first glance, the answer seems elementary. The urban centers of Europe are older, and the populations of their countries did not increase as rapidly in the postwar period, In addition, stringent national land-use laws slowed exurban development, whereas the disjointed jurisdictions in U.S. metropolitan regions encouraged it.

But on closer inspection, this conventional wisdom does not suffice. It is true that the contours of most major urban areas in the United States were formed to a great extent by economic and demographic expansion after the Second World War. But the same was true in much of Europe, where entire cities were reduced to rubble by the war and had to be rebuilt from ground zero.

Consider Germany, whose cities were carpet bombed. Many German cities today are old in name only, and though the country's population as a whole grew less quickly than America's after 1950, West German cities experienced formidable economic growth and in-migrations. Yet the metropolitan population density of the United States is still about one-fourth that of Germany. New York, our densest city, has approximately one-third the number of inhabitants per square mile as Frankfurt.

Sprawl has continued apace even in places where the American population has grown little or not at all in recent decades. From 1970 to 1990, the Chicago area's population rose by only 4 percent, but the region's built-up land increased 46 percent.

Metropolitan Cleveland's population actually declined by 8 percent, yet 33 percent more of the area's territory was developed.

The fragmented jurisdictional structure in U.S. metropolitan areas, wherein every suburban town or county has control over the use of land, does not adequately explain sprawl either. Since 1950, about half of America's central cities at least doubled their territory by annexing new suburbs. Houston covered 160 square miles in 1950. By 1980, exercising broad powers to annex its environs, it incorporated 556 square miles. In the same 30-year period, Jacksonville went from being a town of 30 square miles to a regional government enveloping 841 square miles—two-thirds the size of Rhode Island. True, the tri-state region of New York contains some 780 separate localities, some with zoning ordinances that permit only low-density subdivisions. But the urban region of Paris—Ile de France— comprises 1,300 municipalities, all of which have considerable discretion in the consignment of land for development.

To be sure, European central governments presumably oversee these local decisions through nationwide land-use statutes. But is this a telling distinction? The relationship of U.S. state governments to their local communities is roughly analogous to that of Europe's unitary regimes to their respective local entities. Not only are the governments of some of our states behemoths (New York State's annual expenditures, for example, approximate Sweden's entire national budget) but a significant number have enacted territorial planning legislation reminiscent of European guidelines. Indeed, from a legal standpoint, local governments in this country are mere "creatures" of the states, which can direct, modify, or even abolish their localities at will. Many European municipalities, with their ancient independent charters, are less subordinated.

The enforcement of land-use plans varies considerably in Europe. In Germany, as in America, some *Länder* (or states) are more restrictive than others. The Scandinavians, Dutch, and British take planning more seriously than, say, the Italians. The ate Antonio Cederna, an astute journalist, wrote volumes about the egregious violations of building and development codes in and around Italy's historic centers. Critics who assume that land regulators in the United States are chronically permissive, whereas Europe's growth managers are always scrupulous and "smart," ought to contemplate, say, the unsightly new suburbs stretching across the northwestern plain of Florence toward Prato, and then visit Long Island's East End, where it is practically impossible to obtain a building permit along many miles of pristine coastline.

Big, fast, and violent

The more important contrasts in urban development between America and Europe lie elsewhere. With three and half million square miles of territory, the United States has had much more space over which to spread its settlements. And on this vast expanse, decentralizing technologies took root and spread decades earlier than in other industrial countries. In 1928, for example, 78 percent of all the motor vehicles in the world were located in the United States. With incomes rising rapidly, and the costs of producing vehicles declining, 56 percent of American families owned an automobile by that time. No European country reached a comparable level of automobile ownership until well after the Second World War. America's motorized multitudes were able to begin commuting between suburban residences and workplaces decades before such an arrangement was imaginable in any other advanced nation.

A more perverse but also distinctive cause of urban sprawl in the United States has been the country's comparatively high level of violent crime. Why a person is ten times more likely to be murdered in America than in Japan, seven times more likely to be raped than in France, or almost four times more likely to be robbed at gun point than in the United Kingdom, is a complex question. But three things are known.

First, although criminal violence has declined markedly here in the past few years, America's cities have remained dangerous by international standards. New York's murder rate dropped by two-thirds between 1991 and 1997, yet there were still 767 homicides committed that year. London, a mega-city of about the same size, had less than 130. Second, the rates of personal victimization, including murder, rape, assault, robbery, and personal theft, tend to be much higher within U.S. central cities than in their surroundings. In 1997, incidents of violent crime inside Washington, D.C., for instance, were six times more frequent than in the city's suburbs. Third, there is a strong correlation between city crime rates and the flight of households and businesses to safer jurisdictions. According to economists Julie Berry Cullen of the University of Michigan and Steven D. Levitt of the University of Chicago, between 1976 and 1993, a city typically lost one resident for every additional crime committed within it.

Opinion surveys regularly rank public safety as a leading consideration in the selection of residential locations. In 1992, when New Yorkers were asked to name "the most important reason" for moving out of town, the most common answer was "crime, lack of safety" (47.2 percent). All other reasons—including "high cost of living" (9.3 percent) and "not enough affordable housing" (5.3 percent)—lagged far behind. Two years ago, when the American Assembly weighed the main obstacles to business investments in the inner cities, it learned that businessmen identified lack of security as *the* principal impediment. In short, crime in America has further depopulated the cores of metropolitan areas, scattering their inhabitants and businesses.

The not-so-invisible hand

In addition to these fundamental differences, the public agendas here and in major European countries have been miles apart. The important distinctions, moreover, have less to do with differing "urban" programs than with other national policies, the consequences of which are less understood.

For example, lavish agricultural subsidies in Europe have kept more farmers in business and dissuaded them from selling their land to developers. Per hectare of farmland, agricultural subventions are 12 times more generous in France than in the United States, a divergence that surely helps explain why small farms still surround Paris but not New York City.

Thanks to scant taxation of gasoline, the price of automotive fuel in the United States is almost a quarter of what it is in Italy. Is it any surprise that Italians would live closer to their urban centers, where they can more easily walk to work or rely on public transportation? On a per capita basis, residents of Milan make an average of 350 trips a year on public transportation; people in San Diego make an average of 17.

Gasoline is not the only form of energy that is much cheaper in the United States than in Europe. Rates for electric power and furnace fuels are too. The expense of heating the equivalent of an average detached U.S. suburban home, and of operating the gigantic home appliances (such as refrigerators and freezers) that substitute for neighborhood stores in many American residential communities, would be daunting to most households in large parts of Europe.

Systems of taxation make a profound difference. European tax structures penalize consumption. Why don't most of the Dutch and Danes vacate their compact towns and cities where many commuters ride bicycles, rather than drive sport-utility vehicles, to work? The sales tax on a new, medium-sized car in the Netherlands is approximately nine times higher than in the United States; in Denmark, 37 times higher. The U.S. tax code favors spending over saving (the latter is effectively taxed twice) and provides inducements to purchase particular goods—most notably houses, since the mortgage interest is deductible. The effect of such provisions is to lead most American families into the suburbs, where spacious dwellings are available and absorb much of the nation's personal savings pool.

Tax policy is not the only factor promoting home ownership in the United States. Federal Housing Administration and Veterans Administration mortgage guarantees financed more than a quarter of the suburban single-family homes built in the immediate postwar period. In Europe, the housing stocks of many countries were decimated by the war. Governments responded to the emergency by erecting apartment buildings and extending rental subsidies to large segments of the population. America also built a good deal of publicly subsidized rental housing in the postwar years, but chiefly to accommodate the most impoverished city-dwellers. Unlike the mixed-income housing complexes scattered around London or Paris, U.S. public housing projects further concentrated the urban poor in the inner cities, turning the likes of Chicago's South Side into breeding grounds of social degradation and violence. Middle-class city-dwellers fled from these places to less perilous locations in the metropolitan fringe.

Few decisions are more consequential for the shape of cities than a society's investments in transportation infrastructure. Government at all levels in the United States has committed hundreds of billions to the construction and maintenance of highways, passenger railroads, and transit systems. What counts, however, is not just the magnitude of the commitment but the *distribution* of the public expenditures among modes of transportation. In the United States, where the share claimed by roads has dwarfed that of alternatives by about six to one, an unrelenting increase in automobile travel and a steady decline in transit usage—however heavily subsidized—was inevitable.

Dense cities dissipate without relatively intensive use of mass transit. In 1945, transit accounted for approximately 35 percent of urban passenger miles traveled in the United States. By 1994, the figure had dwindled to less than 3 percent—or roughly one-fifth the average in Western Europe. If early on, American transportation planners had followed the British or French budgetary practice of allocating between 40 and 60 percent of their transport outlays to passenger railroads and mass transit systems, instead of nearly 85 percent for highways, there is little question that many U.S. cities would be more compressed today.

Dense cities also require a vibrant economy of neighborhood shops and services. (Why live in town if performing life's simplest everyday functions, like picking up fresh groceries for supper, requires driving to distant vendors?) But local shopkeepers cannot compete with the regional megastores that are proliferating in America's metropolitan shopping centers and strip malls. Multiple restrictions on the penetration and predatory pricing practices of large retailers in various European countries protect small urban businesses. The costs to consumers are high, but the convenience and intimacy of London's "high streets" or of the corner markets in virtually every Parisian *arrondissement* are preserved.

"Shift and shaft" federalism

Europe's cities retain their merchants and inhabitants for yet another reason: European municipalities typically do not face the same fiscal liabilities as U.S. cities. Local governments in Germany derive less than one-third of their income from local revenues; higher levels of government transfer the rest. For a wide range of basic functions—including educational institutions, hospitals, prisons, courts, utilities, and so on—the national treasury funds as much as 80 percent of the expense

incurred by England's local councils. Localities in Italy and the Netherlands raise only about 10 percent of their budgets locally. In contrast, U.S. urban governments must largely support themselves: They collect two-thirds of their revenues from local sources.

In principle, self-sufficiency is a virtue; municipal taxpayers ought to pay directly for the essential services they use. But in practice, these taxpayers are also being asked to finance plenty of other costly projects, many of which are mandated, but underfunded, by the federal government. Affluent jurisdictions may be able to absorb this added burden, but communities strapped for revenues often cannot. To satisfy the federal government's paternalistic commands, many old cities have been forced to raise taxes and cut the services that local residents need or value most. In response, businesses and middle-class households flee to the suburbs.

America's public schools are perhaps the clearest example of a crucial local service that is tottering under the weight of unfunded federal directives. Few nations, if any, devote as large a share of their total public education expenditures to *non-teaching* personnel. There may be several excuses for this lopsided administrative overhead, but one explanation is almost certainly the growth of government regulation and the armies of academic administrators needed to handle the red tape.

Schools are required, among other things, to test drinking water, remove asbestos, perform recycling, insure "gender equity," and provide something called "special education." The latter program alone forces local authorities to set aside upwards of $30 billion a year to meet the needs of students with disabilities. Meanwhile, according to a 1996 report by the U.S. Advisory Commission on Intergovernmental Relations, the federal government reimburses a paltry 8 percent of the expense. Compliance costs for urban school districts, where the concentrations of learning-disabled pupils are high and the means to support them low, can be particularly onerous. Out of a total $850 million of local funds budgeted for 77,000 students in the District of Columbia, for instance, $170 million has been earmarked for approximately 8,000 students receiving "special education."

Wretched schools are among the reasons why most American families have fled the cities for greener pastures. It is hard enough for distressed school systems like the District's, which struggle to impart even rudimentary literacy, to compete with their wealthier suburban counterparts. The difficulty is compounded by federal laws that, without adequate recompense, divert scarce educational resources from serving the overwhelming majority of students.

Schools are but one of many municipal services straining to defray centrally dictated expenses. Consider the plight of urban mass transit in the United States. Its empty seats and colossal operating deficits are no secret. Less acknowledged are the significant financial obligations imposed by Section 504 of the Rehabilitation Act and subsequent legislation. To comply with the Department of Transportation's rules for retrofitting public buses and subways, New York City estimated in 1980 that it would need to spend more than $1 billion in capital improvements on top of $50 million in recurring annual operating costs.

As the city's mayor, Edward I. Koch, said at the time, "It would be cheaper for us to provide every severely disabled person with taxi service than make 255 of our subway stations accessible."

Although the Reagan administration later lowered these costs, passage of the Americans with Disabilities Act in 1990 led to a new round of pricey special accommodations in New York and other cities with established transit systems. Never mind that the Washington Metro is the nation's most modern and well-designed subway system. It has been ordered to tear up 45 stations and install bumpy tiles along platform edges to accommodate the sight impaired, a multi-million dollar effort. At issue here, as in the Individuals with Disabilities Education Act, is not whether provisions for the handicapped are desirable and just. Rather, the puzzle is how Congress can sincerely claim to champion these causes if it scarcely appropriates the money to advance them.

Nearly two decades ago, Mayor Koch detailed in *The Public Interest* what he called the "millstone" of some 47 unfunded mandates.[1] The tally of national statutes encumbering U.S. local governments since then has surpassed at least one hundred. And this does not count the hundreds of federal court orders and agency rulings that micromanage, and often drain, local resources. By 1994, Los Angeles estimated that federally mandated programs were costing the city approximately $840 million a year. Erasing that debit from the city's revenue requirements, either by meeting it with federal and state aid or by substantial recisions, would be tantamount to reducing city taxes as much as 20 percent. A windfall that large could do more to reclaim the city's slums, and halt the hollowing out of core communities, than would all of the region's planned "empowerment zones," "smart growth" initiatives, and "livability" bond issues.

Follow Europe?

To conclude that greater fiscal burden sharing and a wide range of other public policies help sustain Europe's concentrated cities is not to say, of course, that all those policies have enhanced the welfare of Europeans—and hence, that the United States ought to emulate them. The central governments of Western Europe may assume more financial responsibilities instead of bucking them down to the local level, but these top-heavy regimes also levy much higher taxes. Fully funding all of Washington's many social mandates with national tax dollars would mean, as in much of Europe, a more centralized and bloated welfare state.

Most households are not better off when farmers are heavily subsidized, or when anticompetitive practices protect microbusinesses at the expense of larger, more efficient firms. Nor would most consumers gain greater satisfaction from housing strategies that encourage renter occupancy but not homeownership, or from gas taxes and transportation policies that force people out of their cars and onto buses, trains, or bicycles.

In fact, these sorts of public biases have exacted an economic toll in various Western European countries, and certainly in Japan, while the United States has prospered in part because its economy is less regulated, and its metropolitan areas have been allowed to decompress. So suffocating is the extreme concentration of people and functions in the Tokyo area that government planners now view decentralization as a top economic priority. Parts of the British economy, too, seem squeezed by development controls. A recent report by McKinsey and Company attributes lagging productivity in key sectors to Britain's land-use restrictions that hinder entry and expansion of the most productive firms.

The densely settled cities of Europe teem with small shops. But the magnetic small-business presence reflects, at least in part, a heavily regulated labor market that stifles entrepreneurs who wish to expand and thus employ more workers. As the *Economist* noted in a review of the Italian economy, "Italy's plethora of small firms is as much an indictment of its economy as a triumph: many seem to lack either the will or the capital to keep growing." The lack of will is not surprising; moving from small to midsize or large means taking on employees who are nearly impossible to lay off when times turn bad, and it means saddling a company with costly mandated payroll benefits. Italy may have succeeded in conserving clusters of small businesses in its old cities and towns, but perhaps at the price of abetting double-digit unemployment in its economy as a whole.

Striking a balance

America's strewn-out cities are not without their own inefficiencies. The sprawling conurbations demand, for one thing, virtually complete reliance on automotive travel, thereby raising per capita consumption of motor fuel to four times the average of cities in Europe. That extraordinary level of fossil-fuel combustion complicates U.S. efforts to lower this country's considerable contribution to the buildup of greenhouse gases. Our seemingly unbounded suburbanization has also blighted central cities that possess irreplaceable architectural and historic assets. A form of metropolitan growth that displaces only bleak and obsolescent urban relics, increasingly discarded by almost everyone, may actually be welfare-enhancing. A growth process that also blights and abandons a nation's important civic and cultural centers, however, is rightfully grounds for concern.

Still, proposals to reconfigure urban development in the United States need to shed several misconceptions. As research by Helen Ladd of Duke University has shown, the costs of delivering services in high-density settlements frequently increase, not decrease. Traffic congestion at central nodes also tends to worsen with density, and more people may be exposed to hazardous levels of soot and smog. (The inhabitants of Manhattan drive fewer vehicle miles per capita than persons who inhabit New York's low-density suburbs. Nevertheless, Manhattan's air is often less healthy because the borough's traffic is unremittingly thick and seldom free-flowing, and more people live amid the fumes.) Growth boundaries, such as those circumscribing Portland, Oregon, raise real estate values, so housing inside the boundaries becomes less, not more, "affordable." Even the preservation of farmland, a high priority of managed growth plans, should be placed in proper perspective. The United States is the world's most productive agricultural producer, with ample capacity to spare. Propping up marginal farms in urbanizing areas may not put this acreage to uses most valued by society.

In sum, the diffuse pattern of urban growth in the United States is partly a consequence of particular geographic conditions, cultural characteristics, and raw market forces, but also an accidental outcome of certain government policies. Several of these formative influences differ fundamentally from those that have shaped European cities. Critics of the low-density American cityscape may admire the European model, but they would do well to recognize the full breadth of hard policy choices, and tough tradeoffs, that would have to be made before the constraints on sprawl in this country could even faintly begin to resemble Europe's.

Note

1. Edward I. Koch, "The Mandate Millstone," *The Public Interest*, Number 61, Fall 1980.

UNIT 3
Urban Economies

Unit Selections

Key Points to Consider

- Can cities prosper with manufacturing?

- Describe creative "knowledge workers." What draws this group to cities? What cities have suceeded in drawing this group, and what methods have they employed to attract them?

- Other than by attracting members of what Richard Florida calls the "creative class", what groups can cities attract or retain in order to prosper?

- What are the benefits and drawbacks of privatization for urban governments?

 **Links: www.dushkin.com/online/**
These sites are annotated in the World Wide Web pages.

IISDnet
http://iisd1.iisd.ca

The International Center for Migration, Ethnicity, and Citizenship
http://www.newschool.edu/icmec/

National Immigration Forum
http://www.immigrationforum.org/index.htm

School of Labor and Industrial Relations
http://www.lir.msu.edu

U.S. Equal Employment Opportunity Commission
http://www.eeoc.gov

America's cities have been in economic decline since the 1930s. The growth of new technologies such as the automobile and the telephone began to disperse the cities' functions over a wider and wider area. The changes were exacerbated by those that took off in the 1960s, particularly the painful dislocations brought by the shift from manufacturing to services and the accelerating loss of businesses as well as residents to the suburbs and smaller cities. These changes, in turn, created high rates of joblessness, particularly among black men in the inner city. Many analyses of and proposals for inner city economies focus on how to keep entry-level jobs in the city and attract entry-level workers to the jobs.

This section begins with a debate between Richard Florida on one side and Joel Kotkin and Fred Siegel on the other. In "The Rise of the Creative Class," Florida trumpets the tendency of highly-educated young "knowledge workers" to seek out cities like Boston and Seattle that offer the best lifestyle amenities. Attracting highly mobile members of this new creative class, he argues, is the key to building the post-industrial city. In "Too Much Froth," Kotkin and Siegel argue that Florida's proposals ignore the key qualities that make for a livable and prosperous city: lower taxes, intelligent zoning and quality schools. Both "Packaging Cities" and "Urban Warfare" report on the steps cities have taken to attract the creative class, and the effects of this competition on both its winners and its losers. In "As Cities Move to Privatize Water, Atlanta Steps Back," Douglas Jehl takes a different perspective on the urban economy, examining how cities have privatized basic services in order to save money and the consequences of such an approach in Atlanta.

The Rise of the Creative Class

*Why cities without gays and rock bands are losing
the economic development race.*

BY RICHARD FLORIDA

As I WALKED ACROSS THE CAMPUS OF PITTSBURGH'S CARnegie Mellon University one delightful spring day, I came upon a table filled with young people chatting and enjoying the spectacular weather. Several had identical blue T-shirts with "Trilogy@CMU" written across them—Trilogy being an Austin, Texas-based software company with a reputation for recruiting our top students. I walked over to the table. "Are you guys here to recruit?" I asked. "No, absolutely not," they replied adamantly. "We're not recruiters. We're just hangin' out, playing a little Frisbee with our friends." How interesting, I thought. They've come to campus on a workday, all the way from Austin, just to hang out with some new friends.

I noticed one member of the group sitting slouched over on the grass, dressed in a tank top. This young man had spiked multi-colored hair, full-body tattoos, and multiple piercings in his ears. An obvious slacker, I thought, probably in a band. "So what is your story?" I asked. "Hey man, I just signed on with these guys." In fact, as I would later learn, he was a gifted student who had inked the highest-paying deal of any graduating student in the history of his department, right at that table on the grass, with the recruiters who do not "recruit."

What a change from my own college days, just a little more than 20 years ago, when students would put on their dressiest clothes and carefully hide any counterculture tendencies to prove that they could fit in with the company. Today, apparently, it's the company trying to fit in with the students. In fact, Trilogy had wined and dined him over margarita parties in Pittsburgh and flown him to Austin for private parties in hip nightspots and aboard company boats. When I called the people who had recruited him to ask why, they answered, "That's easy. We wanted him because he's a rock star."

While I was interested in the change in corporate recruiting strategy, something even bigger struck me. Here was another example of a talented young person leaving Pittsburgh. Clearly, my adopted hometown has a huge number of assets. Carnegie Mellon is one of the world's leading centers for research in information technology. The University of Pittsburgh, right down the street from our campus, has a world-class medical center. Pittsburgh attracts hundreds of millions of dollars per year in university research funding and is the sixth-largest center for college and university students on a per capita basis in the country. Moreover, this is hardly a cultural backwater. The city is home to three major sports franchises, renowned museums and cultural venues, a spectacular network of urban parks, fantastic industrial-age architecture, and great urban neighborhoods with an abundance of charming yet affordable housing. It is a friendly city, defined by strong communities and a strong sense of pride. In the 1986 Rand McNally survey, Pittsburgh was ranked "America's Most Livable City," and has continued to score high on such lists ever since.

Yet Pittsburgh's economy continues to putter along in a middling flat-line pattern. Both the core city and the surrounding metropolitan area lost population in the 2000 census. And those bright young university people keep leaving. Most of Carnegie Mellon's prominent alumni of recent years—like Vinod Khosla, perhaps the best known of Silicon Valley's venture capitalists, and Rick Rashid, head of research and development at Microsoft—went elsewhere to make their marks. Pitt's vaunted medical center, where Jonas Salk created his polio vaccine and the world's premier organ-transplant program was started, has inspired only a handful of entrepreneurs to build biotech companies in Pittsburgh.

The Creativity Index

The key to economic growth lies not just in the ability to attract the creative class, but to translate that underlying advantage into creative economic outcomes in the form of new ideas, new high-tech businesses and regional growth. To better gauge these capabilities, I developed a new measure called the Creativity Index (column 1). The Creativity Index is a mix of four equally weighted factors: the creative class share of the workforce (column 2 shows the percentage; column 3 ranks cities accordingly); high-tech industry, using the Milken Institute's widely accepted Tech Pole Index, which I refer to as the High-Tech Index (column 4); innovation, measured as patents per capita (column 5); and diversity, measured by the Gay Index, a reasonable proxy for an area's openness to different kinds of people and ideas (column 6). This composite indicator is a better measure of a region's underlying creative capabilities than the simple measure of the creative class, because it reflects the joint effects of its concentration and of innovative economic outcomes. The Creativity Index is thus my baseline indicator of a region's overall standing in the creative economy and I offer it as a barometer of a region's longer run economic potential. The following tables present my creativity index ranking for the top 10 and bottom 10 metropolitan areas, grouped into three size categories (large, medium-sized and small cities/regions).

—Richard Florida

Over the years, I have seen the community try just about everything possible to remake itself so as to attract and retain talented young people, and I was personally involved in many of these efforts. Pittsburgh has launched a multitude of programs to diversify the region's economy away from heavy industry into high technology. It has rebuilt its downtown virtually from scratch, invested in a new airport, and developed a massive new sports complex for the Pirates and the Steelers. But nothing, it seemed, could stem the tide of people and new companies leaving the region.

I asked the young man with the spiked hair why he was going to a smaller city in the middle of Texas, a place with a small airport and no professional sports teams, without a major symphony, ballet, opera, or art museum comparable to Pittsburgh's. The company is excellent, he told me. There are also terrific people and the work is challenging. But the clincher, he said, is that, "It's in Austin!" There are lots of young people, he went on to explain, and a tremendous amount to do: a thriving music scene, ethnic and cultural diversity, fabulous outdoor recreation, and great nightlife. Though he had several good job offers from Pittsburgh high-tech firms and knew the city well, he said he felt the city lacked the lifestyle options, cultural diversity, and tolerant attitude that would make it attractive to him. As he summed it up: "How would I fit in here?"

This young man and his lifestyle proclivities represent a profound new force in the economy and life of America. He is a member of what I call the creative class: a fast-growing, highly educated, and well-paid segment of the workforce on whose efforts corporate profits and economic growth increasingly depend. Members of the creative class do a wide variety of work in a wide variety of industries—from technology to entertainment, journalism to finance, high-end manufacturing to the arts. They do not consciously think of themselves as a class. Yet they share a common ethos that values creativity, individuality, difference, and merit.

More and more businesses understand that ethos and are making the adaptations necessary to attract and retain creative class employees—everything from relaxed dress codes, flexible schedules, and new work rules in the office to hiring recruiters who throw Frisbees. Most civic leaders, however, have failed to understand that what is true for corporations is also true for cities and regions: Places that succeed in attracting and retaining creative class people prosper; those that fail don't.

Stuck in old paradigms of economic development, cities like Buffalo, New Orleans, and Louisville struggled in the 1980s and 1990s to become the next "Silicon Somewhere" by building generic high-tech office parks or subsidizing professional sports teams. Yet they lost members of the creative class, and their economic dynamism, to places like Austin, Boston, Washington, D.C. and Seattle—places more tolerant, diverse, and open to creativity. Because of this migration of the creative class, a new social and economic geography is emerging in America, one that does not correspond to old categories like East Coast versus West Coast or Sunbelt versus Frostbelt. Rather, it is more like the class divisions that have increasingly separated Americans by income and neighborhood, extended into the realm of city and region.

The Creative Secretary

The distinguishing characteristic of the creative class is that its members engage in work whose function is to "create meaningful new forms." The super-creative core of this new class includes scientists and engineers, university professors, poets and novelists, artists, entertainers, actors, designers, and architects, as well as the "thought leadership" of modern society: nonfiction writers, editors, cultural figures, think-tank researchers, analysts, and other opinion-makers. Members of this super-creative core produce new forms or designs that are readily transferable and broadly useful—such as designing a product that can be widely made, sold and used; coming up with a theorem or strategy that can be applied in many cases; or composing music that can be performed again and again.

Beyond this core group, the creative class also includes "creative professionals" who work in a wide range of knowledge-intensive industries such as high-tech sectors, financial

Large Cities Creativity Rankings

Rankings of 49 metro areas reporting populations over 1 million in the 2000 Census

The Top Ten Cities	Creativity Index	% Creative Workers	Creative Rank	High-Tech Rank	Innovation Rank	Diversity Rank
1. San Francisco	1057	34.8%	5	1	2	1
2. Austin	1028	36.4%	4	11	3	16
3. San Diego	1015	32.1%	15	12	7	3
3. Boston	1015	38.0%	3	2	6	22
5. Seattle	1008	32.7%	9	3	12	8
6. Raleigh–Durham–Chapel Hill	996	38.2%	2	14	4	28
7. Houston	980	32.5%	10	16	16	10
8. Washington–Baltimore	964	38.4%	1	5	30	12
9. New York	962	32.3%	12	13	24	14
10. Dallas	960	30.2%	23	6	17	9
10. Minneapolis	960	33.9%	7	21	5	29

The Bottom Ten Cities	Creativity Index	% Creative Workers	Creative Rank	High-Tech Rank	Innovation Rank	Diversity Rank
49. Memphis	530	24.8%	47	48	42	41
48. Norfolk–Virginia Beach, VA	555	28.4%	36	35	49	47
47. Las Vegas	561	18.5%	49	42	47	5
46. Buffalo	609	28.9%	33	40	27	49
45. Louisville	622	26.5%	46	46	39	36
44. Grand Rapids, MI	639	24.3%	48	43	23	38
43. Oklahoma City	668	29.4%	29	41	43	39
42. New Orleans	668	27.5%	42	45	48	13
41. Greensboro–Winston-Salem	697	27.3%	44	33	35	35
40. Providence, RI	698	27.6%	41	44	34	33

services, the legal and healthcare professions, and business management. These people engage in creative problem-solving, drawing on complex bodies of knowledge to solve specific problems. Doing so typically requires a high degree of formal education and thus a high level of human capital. People who do this kind of work may sometimes come up with methods or products that turn out to be widely useful, but it's not part of the basic job description. What they are required to do regularly is think on their own. They apply or combine standard approaches in unique ways to fit the situation, exercise a great deal of judgment, perhaps try something radically new from time to time.

Much the same is true of the growing number of technicians and others who apply complex bodies of knowledge to working with physical materials. In fields such as medicine and scientific research, technicians are taking on increased responsibility to interpret their work and make decisions, blurring the old distinction between white-collar work (done by decisionmakers) and blue-collar work (done by those who follow orders). They acquire their own arcane bodies of knowledge and develop their own unique ways of doing the job. Another example is the secretary in today's pared-down offices. In many cases this person not only takes on a host of tasks once performed by a large secretarial staff, but becomes a true office manager—channeling flows of information, devising and setting up new systems, often making key decisions on the fly. These people contribute more than intelligence or computer skills. They add creative value. Everywhere we look, creativity is increasingly valued. Firms and organizations value it for the results that it can produce and individuals value it as a route to self-expression and job satisfaction. Bottom line: As creativity becomes more valued, the creative class grows.

The creative class now includes some 38.3 million Americans, roughly 30 percent of the entire U.S. workforce—up from just 10 percent at the turn of the 20th century and less than 20 percent as recently as 1980. The creative class has considerable economic power. In 1999, the average salary for a member of the creative class was nearly $50,000 ($48,752), compared to roughly $28,000 for a working-class member and $22,000 for a service-class worker.

Not surprisingly, regions that have large numbers of creative class members are also some of the most affluent and growing.

The New Geography of Class

Different classes of people have long sorted themselves into neighborhoods within a city or region. But now we find a large-scale re-sorting of people among cities and regions nationwide, with some regions becoming centers of the creative class while others are composed of larger shares of working-class or service-class people. To some extent this has always been true. For instance, there have always been artistic and cultural communities like Greenwich Village, college towns like Madison and Boulder, and manufacturing centers like Pittsburgh and Detroit. The news is that such sorting is becoming even more widespread and pronounced.

In the leading centers of this new class geography, the creative class makes up more than 35 percent of the workforce. This is already the case in the greater Washington, D.C. region, the Raleigh-Durham area, Boston, and Austin—all areas undergoing tremendous economic growth. Despite their considerable advantages, large regions have not cornered the market as creative class locations. In fact, a number of smaller regions have some of the highest creative-class concentrations in the nation—notably college towns like East Lansing, Mich. and Madison, Wisc. (See chart, "Small-size Cities Creativity Rankings")

At the other end of the spectrum are regions that are being bypassed by the creative class. Among large regions, Las Vegas, Grand Rapids and Memphis harbor the smallest concentrations of the creative class. Members of this class have nearly abandoned a wide range of smaller regions in the outskirts of the South and Midwest. In small metropolitan areas like Victoria, Texas and Jackson, Tenn., the creative class comprises less than 15 percent of the workforce. The leading centers for the working class among large regions are Greensboro, N.C. and Memphis, Tenn., where the working class makes up more than 30 percent of the workforce. Several smaller regions in the South and Midwest are veritable working class enclaves with 40 to 50 percent or more of their workforce in the traditional industrial occupations.

These places have some of the most minuscule concentrations of the creative class in the nation. They are symptomatic of a general lack of overlap between the major creative-class centers and those of the working class. Of the 26 large cities where the working class comprises more than one-quarter of the population, only one, Houston, ranks among the top 10 destinations for the creative class.

Chicago, a bastion of working-class people that still ranks among the top 20 large creative centers, is interesting because it shows how the creative class and the traditional working class can coexist. But Chicago has an advantage in that it is a big city, with more than a million members of the creative class. The University of Chicago sociologist Terry Clark likes to say Chicago developed an innovative political and cultural solution to this issue. Under the second Mayor Daley, the city integrated the members of the creative class into the city's culture and politics by treating them essentially as just another "ethnic group" that needed sufficient space to express its identity.

The plug-and-play community is one that somebody can move into and put together a life—or at least a facsimile of a life—in a week.

Las Vegas has the highest concentration of the service class among large cities, 58 percent, while West Palm Beach, Orlando, and Miami also have around half. These regions rank near the bottom of the list for the creative class. The service class makes up more than half the workforce in nearly 50 small and medium-size regions across the country. Few of them boast any significant concentrations of the creative class, save vacationers, and offer little prospect for upward mobility. They include resort towns like Honolulu and Cape Cod. But they also include places like Shreveport, Lou. and Pittsfield, Mass. For these places that are not tourist destinations, the economic and social future is troubling to contemplate.

Plug-and-Play Communities

Why do some places become destinations for the creative while others don't? Economists speak of the importance of industries having "low entry barriers," so that new firms can easily enter and keep the industry vital. Similarly, I think it's important for a place to have low entry barriers for people—that is, to be a place where newcomers are accepted quickly into all sorts of social and economic arrangements. All else being equal, they are likely to attract greater numbers of talented and creative people—the sort of people who power innovation and growth. Places that thrive in today's world tend to be plug-and-play communities where anyone can fit in quickly. These are places where people can find opportunity, build support structures, be themselves, and not get stuck in any one identity. The plug-and-play community is one that somebody can move into and put together a life—or at least a facsimile of a life—in a week.

The list of the country's high-tech hot spots looks an awful lot like the list of the places with highest concentrations of gay people.

Creative centers also tend to be places with thick labor markets that can fulfill the employment needs of members of the creative class, who, by and large, are not looking just for "a job" but for places that offer many employment opportunities.

Cities and regions that attract lots of creative talent are also those with greater diversity and higher levels of quality of place. That's because location choices of the creative class are based

Medium-Size Cities Creativity Rankings

Rankings of 32 metro areas reporting populations 500,000 to 1 million in the 2000 Census

The Top Ten Cities	Creativity Index	% Creative Workers	Creative Rank	High-Tech Rank	Innovation Rank	Diversity Rank
1. Albuquerque, NM	965	32.2%	2	1	7	1
2. Albany, NY	932	33.7%	1	12	2	4
3. Tuscon, AZ	853	28.4%	17	2	6	5
4. Allentown–Bethlehem, PA	801	28.7%	16	13	3	14
5. Dayton, OH	766	30.1%	8	8	5	24
6. Colorado Springs, CO	756	29.9%	10	5	1	30
7. Harrisburg, PA	751	29.8%	11	6	13	20
8. Little Rock, AR	740	30.8%	4	10	21	11
9. Birmingham, AL	722	30.7%	6	7	26	10
10. Tulsa, OK	721	28.7%	15	9	15	18

The Bottom Ten Cities	Creativity Index	% Creative Workers	Creative Rank	High-Tech Rank	Innovation Rank	Diversity Rank
32. Youngstown, OH	253	23.8%	32	32	24	32
31. Scranton–Wilkes-Barre, PA	400	24.7%	28	23	23	31
30. McAllen, TX	451	27.8%	18	31	32	9
29. Stockton–Lodi, CA	459	24.1%	30	29	28	7
28. El Paso, TX	464	27.0%	23	27	31	17
27. Fresno, CA	516	25.1%	27	24	30	2
26. Bakersfield, CA	531	27.8%	18	22	27	19
25. Fort Wayne, IN	569	25.4%	26	17	8	26
24. Springfield, MA	577	29.7%	13	30	20	22
23. Honolulu, HI	580	27.2%	21	14	29	6

to a large degree on their lifestyle interests, and these go well beyond the standard "quality-of-life" amenities that most experts think are important.

For instance, in 1998, I met Gary Gates, then a doctoral student at Carnegie Mellon. While I had been studying the location choices of high-tech industries and talented people, Gates had been exploring the location patterns of gay people. My list of the country's high-tech hot spots looked an awful lot like his list of the places with highest concentrations of gay people. When we compared these two lists with more statistical rigor, his Gay Index turned out to correlate very strongly to my own measures of high-tech growth. Other measures I came up with, like the Bohemian Index—a measure of artists, writers, and performers—produced similar results.

Talented people seek an environment open to differences. Many highly creative people, regardless of ethnic background or sexual orientation, grew up feeling like outsiders, different in some way from most of their schoolmates. When they are sizing up a new company and community, acceptance of diversity and of gays in particular is a sign that reads "non-standard people welcome here."

The creative class people I study use the word "diversity" a lot, but not to press any political hot buttons. Diversity is simply something they value in all its manifestations. This is spoken of so often, and so matter-of-factly, that I take it to be a fundamental marker of creative class values. Creative-minded people enjoy a mix of influences. They want to hear different kinds of music and try different kinds of food. They want to meet and socialize with people unlike themselves, trade views and spar over issues.

As with employers, visible diversity serves as a signal that a community embraces the open meritocratic values of the creative age. The people I talked to also desired nightlife with a wide mix of options. The most highly valued options were experiential ones—interesting music venues, neighborhood art galleries, performance spaces, and theaters. A vibrant, varied nightlife was viewed by many as another signal that a city "gets it," even by those who infrequently partake in nightlife. More than anything, the creative class craves real experiences in the real world.

They favor active, participatory recreation over passive, institutionalized forms. They prefer indigenous street-level culture—a teeming blend of cafes, sidewalk musicians, and small galleries and bistros, where it is hard to draw the line between performers and spectators. They crave stimulation, not escape. They want to pack their time full of dense, high-quality, multi-

Small-Size Cities Creativity Rankings

Rankings of 63 metro areas reporting populations 250,000 to 500,000 in the 2000 Census

The Top Ten Cities	Creativity Index	% Creative Workers	Creative Rank	High-Tech Rank	Innovation Rank	Diversity Rank
1. Madison, WI	925	32.8%	6	16	4	9
2. Des Moines, IA	862	32.1%	8	2	16	20
3. Santa Barbara, CA	856	28.3%	19	8	8	7
4. Melbourne, FL	855	35.5%	1	6	9	32
5. Boise City, ID	854	35.2%	3	1	1	46
6. Huntsville, AL	799	35.3%	2	5	18	40
7. Lansing–East Lansing, MI	739	34.3%	4	27	29	18
8. Binghamton, NY	731	30.8%	12	7	3	60
9. Lexington, KY	717	27.0%	28	24	10	12
10. New London, CT–Norwich, RI	715	28.%1	23	11	13	33

The Bottom Ten Cities	Creativity Index	% Creative Workers	Creative Rank	High-Tech Rank	Innovation Rank	Diversity Rank
63. Shreveport, LA	233	22.1%	55	32	59	57
62. Ocala, FL	263	16.4%	63	61	52	24
61. Visalia, CA	289	22.9%	52	63	60	11
60. Killeen, TX	302	24.6%	47	47	51	53
59. Fayetteville, NC	309	29.0%	16	62	62	49
58. York, PA	360	22.3%	54	54	26	52
57. Fayetteville, AR	366	21.1%	57	57	42	17
56. Beaumont, TX	372	27.8%	25	37	56	55
55. Lakeland–Winter Haven, FL	385	20.9%	59	56	53	5
54. Hickory, NC	393	19.4%	61	48	32	30

dimensional experiences. Seldom has one of my subjects expressed a desire to get away from it all. They want to get into it all, and do it with eyes wide open.

Creative class people value active outdoor recreation very highly. They are drawn to places and communities where many outdoor activities are prevalent—both because they enjoy these activities and because their presence is seen as a signal that the place is amenable to the broader creative lifestyle. The creative-class people in my studies are into a variety of active sports, from traditional ones like bicycling, jogging, and kayaking to newer, more extreme ones, like trail running and snowboarding.

Places are also valued for authenticity and uniqueness. Authenticity comes from several aspects of a community—historic buildings, established neighborhoods, a unique music scene, or specific cultural attributes. It comes from the mix—from urban grit alongside renovated buildings, from the commingling of young and old, long-time neighborhood characters and yuppies, fashion models and "bag ladies." An authentic place also offers unique and original experiences. Thus a place full of chain stores, chain restaurants, and nightclubs is not authentic. You could have the same experience anywhere.

Today, it seems, leading creative centers provide a solid mix of high-tech industry, plentiful outdoor amenities, and an older urban center whose rebirth has been fueled in part by a combination of creativity and innovative technology, as well as lifestyle amenities. These include places like the greater Boston area, which has the Route 128 suburban complex, Harvard and MIT, and several charming inner-city Boston neighborhoods. Seattle has suburban Bellevue and Redmond (where Microsoft is located), beautiful mountains and country, and a series of revitalized urban neighborhoods. The San Francisco Bay area has everything from posh inner-city neighborhoods to ultra-hip districts like SoMa (South of Market) and lifestyle enclaves like Marin County as well as the Silicon Valley. Even Austin includes traditional high-tech developments to the north, lifestyle centers for cycling and outdoor activities, and a revitalizing university/ downtown community centered on vibrant Sixth Street, the warehouse district and the music scene—a critical element of a thriving creative center.

Institutional Sclerosis

Even as places like Austin and Seattle are thriving, much of the country is failing to adapt to the demands of the creative age. It is not that struggling cities like Pittsburgh do not want to grow or encourage high-tech industries. In most cases, their leaders are doing everything they think they can to spur innovation and high-tech growth. But most of the time, they are either unwilling or unable to do the things required to create an environment or habitat attractive to the creative class. They pay lip service to the need to "attract talent," but continue to pour resources into recruiting call centers, underwriting big-box retailers, subsidizing downtown malls, and squandering precious taxpayer dollars on extravagant stadium complexes. Or they try to create facsimiles of neighborhoods or retail districts, replacing the old and authentic with the new and generic—and in doing so drive the creative class away.

It is a telling commentary on our age that at a time when political will seems difficult to muster for virtually anything, city after city can generate the political capital to underwrite hundreds of millions of dollars of investments in professional sports stadiums. And you know what? They don't matter to the creative class. Not once during any of my focus groups and interviews did the members of the creative class mention professional sports as playing a role of any sort in their choice of where to live and work. What makes most cities unable to even imagine devoting those kinds of resources or political will to do the things that people say really matter to them?

The answer is simple. These cities are trapped by their past. Despite the lip service they might pay, they are unwilling or unable to do what it takes to attract the creative class. The late economist Mancur Olson long ago noted that the decline of nations and regions is a product of an organizational and cultural hardening of the arteries he called "institutional sclerosis." Places that grow up and prosper in one era, Olson argued, find it difficult and often times impossible to adopt new organizational and cultural patterns, regardless of how beneficial they might be. Consequently, innovation and growth shift to new places, which can adapt to and harness these shifts for their benefit. This phenomenon, he contends, is how England got trapped and how the U.S. became the world's great economic power. It also accounts for the shift in economic activity from the old industrial cities to newer cities in the South and West, according to Olson.

Olson's analysis presciently identifies why so many cities across the nation remain trapped in the culture and attitudes of the bygone organizational age, unable or unwilling to adapt to current trends. Cities like Detroit, Cleveland, and my current hometown of Pittsburgh were at the forefront of the organizational age. The cultural and attitudinal norms of that age became so powerfully ingrained in these places that they did not allow the new norms and attitudes associated with the creative age to grow up, diffuse and become generally accepted. This process, in turn, stamped out much of the creative impulse, causing talented and creative people to seek out new places where they could more readily plug in and make a go of it.

Most experts and scholars have not even begun to think in terms of a creative community. Instead, they tend to try to emulate the Silicon Valley model which author Joel Kotkin has dubbed the "nerdistan." But the nerdistan is a limited economic development model, which misunderstands the role played by creativity in generating innovation and economic growth. Nerdistans are bland, uninteresting places with acre upon acre of identical office complexes, row after row of asphalt parking lots, freeways clogged with cars, cookie-cutter housing developments, and strip-malls sprawling in every direction. Many of these places have fallen victim to the very kinds of problems they were supposed to avoid. The comfort and security of places like Silicon Valley have gradually given way to sprawl, pollution, and paralyzing traffic jams. As one technology executive told *The Wall Street Journal*, "I really didn't want to live in San Jose. Every time I went up there, the concrete jungle got me down." His company eventually settled on a more urban Southern California location in downtown Pasadena close to the CalTech campus.

Kotkin finds that the lack of lifestyle amenities is causing significant problems in attracting top creative people to places like the North Carolina Research Triangle. He quotes a major real estate developer as saying, "Ask anyone where downtown is and nobody can tell you. There's not much of a sense of place here.... The people I am selling space to are screaming about cultural issues." The Research Triangle lacks the hip urban lifestyle found in places like San Francisco, Seattle, New York, and Chicago, laments a University of North Carolina researcher: "In Raleigh-Durham, we can always visit the hog farms."

The Kids Are All Right

How do you build a truly creative community—one that can survive and prosper in this emerging age? The key can no longer be found in the usual strategies. Recruiting more companies won't do it; neither will trying to become the next Silicon Valley. While it certainly remains important to have a solid business climate, having an effective people climate is even more essential. By this I mean a general strategy aimed at attracting and retaining people—especially, but not limited to, creative people. This entails remaining open to diversity and actively working to cultivate it, and investing in the lifestyle amenities that people really want and use often, as opposed to using financial incentives to attract companies, build professional sports stadiums, or develop retail complexes.

The benefits of this kind of strategy are obvious. Whereas companies—or sports teams, for that matter—that get financial incentives can pull up and leave at virtually a moment's notice, investments in amenities like urban parks, for example, last for generations. Other amenities—like bike lanes or off-road trails for running, cycling, rollerblading, or just walking your dog—benefit a wide swath of the population.

There is no one-size-fits-all model for a successful people climate. The members of the creative class are diverse across the dimensions of age, ethnicity and race, marital status, and sexual preference. An effective people climate needs to emphasize openness and diversity, and to help reinforce low barriers to entry. Thus, it cannot be restrictive or monolithic.

Openness to immigration is particularly important for smaller cities and regions, while the ability to attract so-called bohemians is key for larger cities and regions. For cities and regions to attract these groups, they need to develop the kinds of people climates that appeal to them and meet their needs.

Yet if you ask most community leaders what kinds of people they'd most want to attract, they'd likely say successful married couples in their 30s and 40s—people with good middle-to-upper-income jobs and stable family lives. I certainly think it is important for cities and communities to be good for children and families. But less than a quarter of all American households consist of traditional nuclear families, and focusing solely on their needs has been a losing strategy, one that neglects a critical engine of economic growth: young people.

Young workers have typically been thought of as transients who contribute little to a city's bottom line. But in the creative age, they matter for two reasons. First, they are workhorses. They are able to work longer and harder, and are more prone to take risks, precisely because they are young and childless. In rapidly changing industries, it's often the most recent graduates who have the most up-to-date skills. Second, people are staying single longer. The average age of marriage for both men and women has risen some five years over the past generation. College-educated people postpone marriage longer than the national averages. Among this group, one of the fastest growing categories is the never-been-married. To prosper in the creative age, regions have to offer a people climate that satisfies this group's social interests and lifestyle needs, as well as address those of other groups.

Furthermore, a climate oriented to young people is also attractive to the creative class more broadly. Creative-class people do not lose their lifestyle preferences as they age. They don't stop bicycling or running, for instance, just because they have children. When they put their children in child seats or jogging strollers, amenities like traffic-free bike paths become more important than ever. They also continue to value diversity and tolerance. The middle-aged and older people I speak with may no longer hang around in nightspots until 4 a.m., but they enjoy stimulating, dynamic places with high levels of cultural interplay. And if they have children, that's the kind of environment in which they want them to grow up.

My adopted hometown of Pittsburgh has been slow to realize this. City leaders continue to promote Pittsburgh as a place that is good for families, seemingly unaware of the demographic changes that have made young people, singles, new immigrants, and gays critical to the emerging social fabric. People in focus groups I have conducted feel that Pittsburgh is not open to mi-

nority groups, new immigrants, or gays. Young women feel there are substantial barriers to their advancement. Talented members of racial and ethnic minorities, as well as professional women, express their desire to leave the city at a rate far greater than their white male counterparts. So do creative people from all walks of life.

Is there hope for Pittsburgh? Of course there is. First, although the region's economy is not dynamic, neither is it the basket case it could easily have become. Twenty years ago there were no significant venture capital firms in the area; now there are many, and thriving high-tech firms continue to form and make their mark. There are signs of life in the social and cultural milieu as well. The region's immigrant population has begun to tick upward, fed by students and professors at the universities and employees in the medical and technology sectors. Major suburbs to the east of the city now have Hindu temples and a growing Indian-American population. The area's gay community, while not large, has become more active and visible. Pittsburgh's increasing status in the gay world is reflected in the fact that it is the "location" for Showtime's "Queer as Folk" series.

Many of Pittsburgh's creative class have proven to be relentless cultural builders. The Andy Warhol Museum and the Mattress Factory, a museum/workspace devoted to large-scale installation art, have achieved worldwide recognition. Street-level culture has a growing foothold in Pittsburgh, too, as main street corridors in several older working-class districts have been transformed. Political leaders are in some cases open to new models of development. Pittsburgh mayor Tom Murphy has been an ardent promoter of biking and foot trails, among other things. The city's absolutely first-rate architecture and urban design community has become much more vocal about the need to preserve historic buildings, invest in neighborhoods, and institute tough design standards. It would be very hard today (dare I say nearly impossible) to knock down historic buildings and dismember vibrant urban neighborhoods as was done in the past. As these new groups and efforts reach critical mass, the norms and attitudes that have long prevailed in the city are being challenged.

For what it's worth, I'll put my money—and a lot of my effort—into Pittsburgh's making it. If Pittsburgh, with all of its assets and its emerging human creativity, somehow can't make it in the creative age, I fear the future does not bode well for other older industrial communities and established cities, and the lamentable new class segregation among cities will continue to worsen.

RICHARD FLORIDA *is a professor of regional economic development at Carnegie Mellon University and a columnist for* Information Week. *This article was adapted from his forthcoming book,* The Rise of the Creative Class: and How It's Transforming Work, Leisure, Community and Everyday Life *(Basic Books).*

First published in *The Washington Monthly*, May 2002, pp. 15-25, extracted from *The Rise of the Creative Class: and How It's Transforming Work, Leisure, Community and Everyday Life* by Richard Florida (2002, Basic Books/Perseus Books, L.L.C.). Copyright ©; 2002 by Richard Florida. Reprinted by permission of Perseus Books, L.L.C. and arrangement with Richard Florida and Susan Schulman, A Literary Agency, New York.

Too Much Froth

The latte quotient is a bad strategy for building middle-class cities.

by Joel Kotkin and Fred Siegel

Like smokers seeking a cure from their deadly habits, city politicians and economic development officials have a long history of grasping at fads to solve their persistent problems and rebuild middle class cities. In the 1960s and 1970s, the fad was for downtown malls. In the 1980s, it was convention centers and sports stadiums. But none of the fads came close to living up to their lofty billings.

Today, a new fad is bewitching urbanists and pols alike. Known as the "creativity craze," it promotes the notion that "young creatives" can drive an urban revival. It is a belated extension of the New Economy boom of the late 1990s. As with the idea of a New Economy, there is some merit to the focus on creativity. But as we learned from the dot-com bust that followed the boom, even the best ideas can be oversold.

Long before the current craze, Robert D. Atkinson of the Progressive Policy Institute wrote, "The ticket to faster and broader income growth is innovation." And one of the keys to innovation, he noted in describing his Metropolitan New Economy Indexes, is the ability to attract talented and innovative people. But he also emphasized the importance of school reform, infrastructure investments, work force development partnerships, public safety, and reinventing — and digitizing — city government. All these critical factors have been widely ignored by those who've discovered the magic bullet of "creative" urban development.

The new mantra advocates an urban strategy that focuses on being "hip" and "cool" rather than straightforward and practical. It is eagerly promoted by the Brookings Institution, by some urban development types, and by city pols from both parties in places like Cincinnati, Denver, Tampa, and San Diego. It seeks to displace the Progressive Policy Institute's New Economy Indexes with what might be called a "Latte Index" — the density of Starbucks — as a measure of urban success. Cities that will win the new competition, it's asserted, will be those that pour their resources into the arts and other cultural institutions that attract young, "with-it"

people who constitute, for them, the contemporary version of the anointed. Call them latte cities.

But, like all the old bromides that were supposed to save America's cities, this one is almost certain to disappoint. Based partly on the ideas in Carnegie Mellon professor Richard Florida's book, *Rise of the Creative Class*, the notion of hip *uber alles* reminds one of the confectionary world of earlier gurus such as Charles Reich, author of *The Greening of America*, and John Naisbitt, author of *Megatrends*. Both promised a largely painless path to a brave new world, but both now are largely forgotten.

It's not surprising that after 50 years of almost uninterrupted middle class and job flight to the suburbs — even with the partial urban revival of the 1990s — urban officials might be tempted to clutch at straws. The appeal of such fads is plain to see. They seem to offer a way around the intractable problems of schools that fail to improve, despite continuous infusions of money; contentious zoning and regulatory policies that drive out business; and politically hyperactive public-sector unions and hectoring interest groups that make investment in cities something most entrepreneurs studiously avoid.

The "creative solution" pointedly avoids such hurdles, suggesting that the key to urban resurgence lies in attracting the diverse, the tolerant, and the gay. Having such a population is well and good, but unlikely by itself to produce a revival, let alone a diversified economy. Those most outspoken about such a culture- and lifestyle-based urban revival have all the heady passion of a religious movement; indeed, they've organized themselves into something called the Creative Class. One hundred of them — they called themselves the "Creative 100" — met in Memphis last spring to lay out their principles in a document called the Memphis Manifesto. Their mission, it reads, is to "remove barriers to creativity, such as mediocrity, intolerance, disconnectedness, sprawl, poverty, bad schools, exclusivity, and social and environmental degradation." The 1934 Soviet constitution couldn't have said it better.

This is an urban strategy for a frictionless universe. There is no mention of government or politics or interest groups. There's no recognition of the problems produced by outmoded regulations, runaway public spending, or high taxes. Instead we get the following froth: "Cultivate and reward creativity. Everyone is part of the value chain of creativity. Creativity can happen at any time, anywhere, and it's happening in your community right now."

Why do supposedly serious people embrace such ideas? After decades of decline and often fruitless political combat, mayors, city councils, and urban development officials seem ready to embrace any notion that holds out hope without offending the entrenched constituencies that resist real reform.

"The economic development people will buy anything that makes it seem easy," suggests Leslie Parks, former chairwoman of the California Economic Development Corp. "They see a schtick that requires few hard choices, and they bought it."

Parks traces much of the current enthusiasm for the "creative" strategy to the late 1990s dot-com boom. In this period, there was a palpable economic surge in certain cities — San Francisco; Portland, Ore.; Seattle; Austin, Texas; New York — that also attracted bright, "creative" young people, and, incidentally, many gays. These are the cities that Florida and his acolytes have held up as models for other towns.

Yet virtually all these places have been hemorrhaging jobs and people since the boom busted. San Francisco, according to economist David Friedman, has actually lost employment at a rate comparable to that of the Great Depression. Roughly 4 percent of the population has simply left town, often to go to more affordable, if boring, places, such as Sacramento. San Francisco is increasingly a city without a real private-sector economy. It's home to those on the government or nonprofit payroll and the idle rich — "a cross between Carmel and Calcutta," in the painful phrase of California state librarian Kevin Starr, a San Francisco native.

As for the others, they are no bargain either. Seattle has also lost jobs at a far faster rate than the rest of the country and has its own litany of social problems, including a sizable homeless population; the loss of its signature corporation, Boeing; and growing racial tensions.

Although Portland is often hailed as a new urban paradise, it is in a region suffering very high unemployment. "They made a cool place, but the economy sucks," notes Parks, who conducted a major study for the Oregon city. "They forgot all the things that matter, like economic diversification and affordability."

New York City has also suffered heavy job losses. Gotham's population outflows, which slowed in the late 1990s, have accelerated, including in Manhattan, the city's cool core. In contrast, New York's relatively unhip suburbs, particularly those in New Jersey, quietly weathered the Bush recession in fairly fine fettle.

Today, economic growth is shifting to less fashionable but more livable locales such as San Bernardino and Riverside Counties, Calif.; Rockland County, N.Y.; Des Moines, Iowa; Bismarck, N.D.; and Sioux Falls, S.D.

In many cases, this shift also encompasses technology-oriented and professional service firms, whose ranks ostensibly dominate the so-called "creative class." This trend actually predates the 2000 crash, but it has since accelerated. Since the 1990s, the growth in financial and other business services has taken place not in New York, San Francisco, or Seattle, but in lower-cost places like Phoenix; Charlotte, N.C.; Minneapolis; and Des Moines.

Perhaps more important, the outflow from decidedly un-hip places like the Midwest has slowed, and even reversed. Employers report that workers are seeking more affordable housing, and, in many cases, less family-hostile environments.

To be sure, such cities are not without their share of Starbucks outlets, and they have put great stress on quality-of-life issues — like recreation and green space — that appeal to families and relocating firms. But the watchword is livability, not coolness. "It's gotten very easy to get workers to relocate here," notes Randy Schilling, founder and CEO of Quilogy, a St. Louis-area technology company. "You get a guy here from Chicago, New York, and San Francisco, and even if he gets a pay cut, he and his family lives better."

There is, fortunately, an alternative to a hollow urban politics that relies mainly on the hip and the cool. Such a politics lies not in trendy ideas that will be forgotten a decade from now, but in commonsense policies that stress basic services like police and firefighters, innovative public schools that are not beholden to teachers' unions, breaking down of barriers to new housing construction, and policies that lead local businesses to expand within the urban area. It's a politics that, to paraphrase the great urbanist Jane Jacobs, seeks not to "lure" a middle class with bars, bells, and whistles, but instead aims to create one at the grassroots level.

That's the kind of "creativity" that cities, and Democrats, really need to embrace.

Joel Kotkin is a senior fellow at the Davenport Institute for Public Policy at Pepperdine University. He is writing a history of cities for Modern Library. Fred Siegel is a professor at The Cooper Union and culture editor of BLUEPRINT.

As Cities Move to Privatize Water, Atlanta Steps Back

By Douglas Jehl

ATLANTA — Privatization has hit the water sector, which has remained mostly the bastion of public utilities. Over the last five years, hundreds of American communities, including Indianapolis, Milwaukee and Gary, Ind., have hired private companies to manage their waterworks, serving about one in 20 Americans.

The main reason is that the cities are facing enormous costs to repair aging sewer pipes, treatment plants and other water infrastructure. Federal officials say the total cost of repairs could outstrip current spending by more than $500 billion in the next 20 years. The utilities' hope has been that partnerships with private companies could generate savings and provide access to capital to help cover such staggering bills.

But a cautionary tale has emerged here in Atlanta, where the largest water privatization deal collapsed in January. Instead of public savings and private profit, a deal reached in 1999 between Atlanta and United Water resulted in bitter disappointments for all sides, not least of all consumers. Atlanta is now retaking control of a system that United Water was to have managed until 2019.

"This city had a motto for years, and it went something like 'Atlanta grows where water goes,'" said Jack Ravan, the city's commissioner of watershed management. "I think we've learned enough to know that we'd prefer to see the city in charge of that destiny."

The decision, in many ways, takes Atlanta back to square one. It will have a publicly controlled system that, on paper at least, will be more costly to ratepayers than the one it replaces. The arrangement offers no clear way to pay for extensive water-system repairs, estimated to cost $800 million over the next five years. (A separate bill to upgrade the city's sewers could exceed $3 billion.)

But Atlanta officials, along with customers like Gordon Certain, the head of a local neighborhood association, say almost any change seems preferable to existing service they call poor, unresponsive and fraught with breakdowns, including an epidemic of water-main breaks and occasional "boil only" alerts caused by brown water pouring from city taps.

"Is it possible to have private water work right?" Mr. Certain asked. "I'm sure it is. But if you have a political problem in your city, you can vote in a new administration. If you have a private company with a long-term contract, and they're the source of your problems, then it gets a lot more difficult."

The breakup comes as the question of privatized water is generating increased attention around the country, with advocacy groups like Public Citizen waging campaigns against the proposed deals. And while water privatization advocates describe the Atlanta failure as an aberration, all sides say that it is likely to weigh heavily in places like Stockton, Calif., which is considering whether to go down a similar path.

"This is a huge setback for privatization, and it's going to have to give both cities and companies pause," said Dr. Peter H. Gleick, president of the Pacific Institute, a nonpartisan environmental research organization in Oakland, Calif., that has written extensively about the risks and benefits of water privatization.

United Water, a subsidiary of the giant French company Suez, has acknowledged problems with its management of the Atlanta system. But it has also said it was stuck with trying to run a system in unexpected disrepair, while losing at least $10 million annually under a $22 million-a-year contract that the city refused to renegotiate.

"It was important to recognize reality in Atlanta," Michael Chesser, United Water's chairman and chief executive, said of his company's consenting to the breakup. Still, United Water, one of the country's two biggest private water companies, has contracts to operate more than 100 other municipal systems, and Mr. Chesser said he expected that number to grow. "This is a market with a huge potential," he said.

It was Atlanta's new mayor, Shirley Franklin, who forced an end to the partnership, demanding that United Water quit or be fired. But in announcing an end to the partnership in Atlanta on Jan. 24, Mr. Chesser and Ms. Franklin said each side had recognized that continuing the deal was in neither party's interest.

Across the country, 94 percent of water systems are publicly controlled, said William G. Reinhardt, editor of Public Works Financing, the leading trade journal covering the industry. Most are owned and operated by municipalities, in what remains the most fragmented of any American utility, divided into roughly 5,000 different pieces.

The number of publicly owned systems that, like Atlanta's, are operated under long-term contracts by private companies has increased to about 1,100, from about 400 in 1997.

"It all comes down to economics," said Debra Coy, a research analyst with Schwab Capital Markets. "In an environment where cities are paying much more attention to their problems with wastewater and water, you have an industry that's coming in and telling them, hey, we can help you do this."

A 1997 executive order helped to smooth the way for such public-private partnerships. But in cities already strapped for cash, the bigger factor has been the dark shadow cast by the need for new investment, to meet the needs of growing population or to keep aging systems in compliance with strict environmental laws.

Some federal estimates of the need for new spending for municipal water systems have reached as high as $1 trillion over the next 20 years. In Atlanta,

some water pipes date from the 19th century, and its water system has been in failing shape since the mid-1990's, when the federal government began to assess fines against the city for failing to meet water-safety standards. In striking the deal with United Water in 1999, city officials said they hoped to save as much as $20 million a year from the $42 million budgeted for the existing, bloated public utility, and to apply those savings to capital improvements.

But at most, Atlanta officials say, the city has managed to achieve only $10 million in annual savings, and only at what has been a significant political cost, with ratepayers blaming the city for United Water's shortcomings. At the same time, United Water said its expected profit had turned into heavy losses as operating costs soared. Atlanta's pipes, fire hydrants and water treatment plants turned out to be in much worse shape than the city had let on, the company said.

The return to public control that Atlanta has now embraced will send the city's water costs soaring back to about $40 million a year, compared with the

$22 million in direct costs it was paying United Water, Mr. Ravan said. But he said there would be other, less tangible savings. "What is the cost of a 'must boil' alert?" he asked.

But critics, including Hugh Jackson, a Nevada-based researcher with Public Citizen, are using the example of Atlanta to offer a broader indictment of a privatization process they regard as misguided from the start.

"Obviously, water is a basic necessity, to a degree that electricity isn't, when you get right down to it," Mr. Jackson said. "We do not feel that it should be managed for quarter-to-quarter returns for a corporation that is trying to satisfy a profit demand."

Some experts, including Adrian Moore, a privatization advocate who is a vice president at the Los Angeles-based Reason Foundation, say the main lesson of the Atlanta collapse is that cities and private companies needed to be realistic about what a partnership can achieve. "It's like a marriage," Mr. Moore said. "You've got to work to make it work."

Packaging Cities

How Lesser-Known Metro Areas Are Positioning
Themselves as the Next Hot Brands

By Rebecca Gardyn

Last year, Milwaukee's Chamber of Commerce, Visitors Bureau, Economic Development Office, and a variety of other local institutions pooled their resources to try to sell their city to the rest of the world in a cohesive way. Rather than continue individual marketing strategies with separate advertising themes, they hired Development Counsellors International (DCI), a Manhattan-based consulting firm specializing in regional marketing, to help them create the city's first integrated campaign. It is expected to be launched this May.

In the past, city tourism departments, economic development groups, and other government and civic organizations—each with different priorities and separate budgets—rarely combined their marketing efforts. Today, many municipal leaders, like those in Milwaukee, are sharing resources to come up with sharper, more professional strategies to sell their cities to diverse consumer audiences, among them business decision makers, conventioneers, and professionals. Whether making their market debuts, retooling their images, or repositioning themselves to reach new demographics, cities are beginning to regard themselves as the new brands, and everyone as their customer.

Choices of where to live, where to visit, and where to do business have expanded over the past decade, as advances in communications technology increasingly enable individuals and companies to operate efficiently pretty much anywhere, almost regardless of geography. Sensing the opportunity, some local leaders were beginning to take an integrated marketing approach even before September 11, promoting their communities as alternatives to big cities. But following the attacks, the apparent stability and quality of life offered by smaller and lesser-known cities well away from the national capitals of commerce and business have become even bigger selling points.

Mark Zandi, chief economist for Economy.com, an online provider of economic and financial research and analysis, says that now might be the perfect time for some oft-overlooked cities and regions to advertise. "Things that were weights on some economies two years ago are now assets, like the fact that

they are more removed from the hustle and bustle of urban areas," he says. "Now that big urban areas are having major problems financially, and people are more wary about being there in general, it's probably a good time for many of these places to be aggressive in marketing and positioning themselves as alternative places to visit, do business, and live."

That's because smaller and lesser-known cities are expected to be less affected economically by the tragedies than are the larger, flashier ones. For example, according to Economy.com's forecast of economic growth by metro area, prior to September 11, Milwaukee's annual gross domestic product (GDP) was expected to grow 2.29 percent through the second quarter of 2002. After the attacks, the company reduced the city's growth projections by 2.6 percentage points. Meanwhile, Chicago, Milwaukee's bigger and better-known competitor, was expected to grow 2.86 percent through he second quarter of 2002, and after the attacks, its projected GDP was lowered by 3.13 percentage points.

As *American Demographics* found in our December 2001 special report, Americans are undergoing a subtle reality shift in almost every fundamental aspect of their lives. As a result, quality of life attributes such as better commute times, access to public parks, and clean air may play bigger roles in where people choose to live, says Steve Higdon, president of Greater Louisville, Inc., an organization created to promote Louisville, Kentucky, and its surrounding regions. "What has happened to this country has really underscored the importance of Middle America," he says. "Of course, we will never take advantage of this tragedy in our marketing directly, but I do think our target audiences will look at our product different."

If it worked for Crest toothpaste, why not Milwaukee, Indianapolis, or Philadelphia? The concept of branding—the idea that one product is more valuable, has more "equity," than an alternative because it is attached to a recognizable name and promise of authenticity—began about 200 years ago, when Josiah Wedgwood realized that stamping his name on his pottery and naming his dinnerware after English nobility made it more desirable. Fast forward to the 1930s when Procter & Gamble's Neil McElroy, the company's promotion department manager, developed the "P&G brand management system," an organizational structure that assigned groups of people to handle specific marketing strategies for competing brands.

By the 1970s and '80s, "brand manager" was a coveted job title for the typical business school graduate, and by the mid-1990s, branding began to be applied not just to products but to the retailers that sell them, with names like Victoria's Secret and Bath & Body Works. "What has happened since the turn of the millennium is that everyone else is discovering branding," says Roger Blackwell, a marketing professor at the Fisher College of Business at Ohio State University. "It was inevitable that the people who market cities would turn to a concept that has been so productive and successful for others."

This push to integrate a city's disparate parts into one cohesive branding approach comes as competition among regions for tourists, conventioneers, and skilled workers has increased dramatically over the past 50 years. Alastair Morrison, director of the Purdue University Tourism and Hospitality Research Center, estimates that the number of city or regional visitors bureaus has grown from about 250 to 1,600 since 1950. Among economic development agencies, which specialize in industrial recruitment, the competition is even greater. According to the International Economic Development Council, for any given business relation or expansion, an estimated 15,000 cities, regions, or communities are in contention, and that's only in the U.S. Says Ted Levine, chairman of consulting firm DCI: "If you think about the fact that there are only about a half-dozen car manufacturers, it puts things into perspective. This is an extremely competitive field."

Cities and regions are also vying for permanent bodies, especially those with professional heads on their shoulders. With an estimated 80 percent of jobs and wealth created by privately owned companies or entrepreneurs, there's pressure on cities to keep and attract more educated workers and young entrepreneurs. While only 16 percent of the total U.S. population moved house in 1999, better-educated people are more likely to move longer distances, presumably for better-paying jobs, according to the Census Bureau's 2000 Current Population Survey. Forty-seven percent of movers with a college degree moved to a new county, either within the same state or in another state, compared with 34 percent of those with less than a high school education who did so. And the younger folks are the most mobile: 34 percent of 20- to 29-year-olds and 22 percent of 30- to 34-year-olds moved, making these demographics the primary target for many cities and regions.

For those doing the moving, whether they are employees looking for new digs or CEOs expanding or relocating their companies, image has become an important deal-breaker. According to Arthur Andersen's "Best Cities 2000" survey of 1,433 senior executives worldwide, conducted June through November 2000, a city's suitability for business is no longer just about geographic location, tax incentives, or cheap land. Instead, the top three factors mentioned are: "pro-business attitudes" (20 percent), "local availability of professionals" (12 percent), and "entrepreneurial activity" (10 percent).

"Thirty or 40 years ago, you just needed green grass by a railroad to set up shop," says Shari Barnett, senior manager of global location strategies at PricewaterhouseCoopers. Now there are so many variables, and there is never just one city that's right for a business or employee. Barnett says she is working with several companies that nixed her recommendation of a city she thought perfect because decision makers had an impression that its economy was failing or its quality of life was poor, even though the city was actually thriving. "Things like geography and tax incentives will get you on the short list, but at the end of the day, if the client doesn't perceive your city well, they'll move on."

Yet, lessons from the corporate boardroom extend only so far. Branding a city has its own set of challenges. The first is persuading city leaders, many of them with little or no marketing experience, that they need to do so. "You have to convince city councils that they need to spend money on something they know nothing about, and that's a tough sell," says Elizabeth Goodgold, CEO of The Nuancing® Group, a brand consultancy in San Diego.

Deborah Knudsen knows that dance. As president and CEO of the Traverse City, Michigan, Convention and Visitors Bureau, she spent 10 years trying to convince fellow civic leaders and small-business owners to participate in a branding effort before finally succeeding two years ago when she helped launch its brand— "A World Apart"—targeting affluent tourists. Raised in a family of restaurateurs, Knudsen grew up understanding the value of a brand maintaining consumer loyalty and ensuring repeat business. "I've followed what P&G and GM have been doing over the years and seen it work for them, so I knew we should be doing it too, at least at some level," she says. "But it's not easy when you're dealing with people from many different backgrounds."

Even when most leaders concur on the need for such activity, agreeing on strategy is another story. Unlike a corporation with one CEO calling the shots as to how to proceed, a city has multiple entities with very different, and often conflicting, priorities and target audiences. Indianapolis is struggling with this step in its current branding process, says Mike Lawson, president of the Indianapolis Regional Economic Development Partnership. In the past, the region was marketed as nine individual counties, with nine individual budgets. Now they've merged, but that has simply increased the number of cooks in the kitchen. What's more, there are a number of other private and nonprofit organizations in the area, all promoting the city differently to various consumers.

"The biggest challenge we face is coming to a consensus on an umbrella brand that will work for everyone's consumers," says Lawson. "It can be difficult to get people to see the big picture all the time, and there's a lot of 'protecting turf' going on." But they're working on it. Representatives of six entities, including Lawson's economic development group, the city's Arts Council, the Indiana Sports Corporation, and Indianapolis Downtown, Inc., met all through last summer, and have hired an independent facilitator, a marketing professor at Indiana University, to help.

Another obstacle to branding cities has to do with turnover in leadership, especially those in cities and counties with term limits for elected officials. "Often, you'll have political leaders who agree that someone should put the region on the map, but then say, 'It's not my job, I'm out of here in a few years,'" says Rod Underhill, chief executive of Spherical, Inc., the brand strategy consulting arm of The Richards Group, a Dallas-based advertising agency. That's why a good brand strategy has to be based and rigorously analyzed, he says. Otherwise, every mayoral election can bring a change in focus resulting in a stop-and-start marketing effort that is ineffective. "There has to be so much conviction among the other civic organizations and leaders that branding needs to get to withstand a turnover in leadership," he adds.

Underhill says that level of conviction exists in the Dallas-Fort Worth region—the Metroplex. The dual Chambers of Commerce hired Spherical to help brand the area. While details about their strategy are still under wraps, Underhill says that the biggest challenge has to do with reeling in and managing a brand that has been unmanaged for so long. "Most cities are a victim of their unmanaged reputations," he says. "In the absence of a brand strategy, Dallas-Fort Worth conjures images of J.R. Ewing and cheerleaders, but those cultural icons are not necessarily what the city would like to be known for."

And then there's the opposite problem. DCI's Levine estimates that 60 percent to 70 percent of all cities in the U.S. have no image at all in the public mind. Thus, finding a core distinguishable asset, or "unique selling proposition," as he terms it, becomes even more important. Nancy Koehn, marketing professor at Harvard and author of *Brand New: How Entrepreneurs Earned Consumers' Trust from Wedgwood to Dell* (Harvard Business School Press, 2001), recommends that decision makers turn to their city's unique histories. "Almost every city or region has some interesting piece of history that everyone can relate to," she says. "That can be your connection point with consumers. In any kind of branding, connecting on a personal level is always a very strong motivator."

But for some cities, history is double-edged. Leaders of nine public and private civic organizations in the Richmond, Virginia, region worked all through last summer, with Martin Branding Worldwide of "Virginia is for Lovers" fame, on an integrated branding effort. The region's rich ties to America's history were cited as a distinguishing asset in all its focus group sessions among all demographic groups, from tourists to business leaders to potential residents. Still, they debated as to whether or not that history was the best way to brand that area. Yes, the region is the birthplace of many U.S. presidents, but it was also once home to the country's largest slave port, notes Greg Wingfield, president of the Greater Richmond Partnership, the region's economic development organization. In the end, Richmond's leaders decided the positives about the area's five-century history outweighed any negatives, and in October 2001, its new brand was unveiled: "The Historic Richmond Region: Easy to Love."

Still, other cities continue to struggle with their identity crises. A nationwide study of 300 CEOs conducted by the Columbus, Ohio, Chamber of Commerce found that fewer than 10 percent of respondents knew anything about that city. And its municipal leaders are worried about the bigger picture. Columbus has consistently been a good place to live and work, with continuous growth, says Sally Jackson, president of the Greater Columbus Chamber of Commerce. But as business becomes more global and people become more mobile, that won't be enough if no one knows about it. "We need to get a lot better at projecting what we are all about," Jackson says. Because, for today's consumers, image is everything.

Urban Warfare

American cities compete for talent, and the winners take all

By Blaine Harden

In a Darwinian fight for survival, American cities are scheming to steal each other's young. They want ambitious young people with graduate degrees in such fields as genome science, bio-informatics and entrepreneurial management.

Sam Long was easy pickings. He was born, reared and very well educated in Cleveland. With a focus on early stage venture capital, he earned his MBA at Case Western Reserve University. Venture capital is in Long's blood. His great-great-grandfather invested in Standard Oil of Ohio, the company that John D. Rockefeller built in Cleveland in the late 19th century.

In the early 21st century, Cleveland desperately needs entrepreneurs, but it never had a shot at keeping Long. He wanted to sail in Puget Sound, ski in the Cascades and swim in Seattle's deep pool of money, ideas and risk-taking young investors.

He now runs a small venture capital company. It sniffs out software ideas, many of them incubated in the computer science department at the University of Washington. "Birds of a feather, you know," said Long, who arrived here in 1992, when he was 28. "There are more people like me in Seattle."

Long is part of an elite intercity migration that is rapidly remaking the way American cities rise and fall. In the 2000 Census, demographers found what they describe as a new, brain-driven, winner-take-all pattern in urban growth.

"A pack of cities is racing away from everybody else in terms of their ability to attract and retain an educated workforce," said Bruce Katz, director of the Center on Urban and Metropolitan Policy at the Brookings Institution. "It is a sobering trend for cities left behind."

The long economic downturn has stalled growth and increased unemployment in almost every U.S. city, and has brought a sense of near-desperation to the intercity fight for young talent. Mayors, business leaders and university presidents are scrambling to secure new technology companies and entice young people to live downtown.

"In our business, you have to cannibalize," said Ron Sims, the county executive of King County, which surrounds Seattle, and a Democratic candidate for governor of Washington state. "Many cities don't fight back very well."

In addition to Seattle, the largest brain-gain cities include Austin, Atlanta, Boston, Denver, Minneapolis, San Diego, San Francisco, Washington, and Raleigh and Durham, N.C.

The rising tide of well-schooled talent has created a self-reinforcing cycle. New-comers such as Sam Long have made a handful of cities richer, more densely populated and more capable of squeezing wealth out of the next big thing that a knowledge-based economy might serve up.

Some of these cities are blessed with relatively young, homegrown billionaires. They understand technology and are making huge bets to lure more talent. Seattle, with Microsoft Corp. co-founders Paul G. Allen and Bill Gates fronting much of the money, is probably making the most expensive such bet in the country—on bio-technology.

"If you have the resources," said Allen, the world's fourth-richest man ($20.1 billion), "you try to do positive things. You help keep momentum going."

Brain-gain cities are hardly immune to the economic cycle. In the tech-driven recession, Seattle, like San Francisco and Austin, endured wrenching levels of business failure and unemployment. The Seattle area lost more than 60,000 jobs in the past four years, as average wages declined and population growth stagnated. But this city and those like it remain national leaders in the availability of venture capital, and demographers say they appear to have kept most of their educated young people, who hang on even without good jobs.

THE WINNER-TAKE-ALL PATTERN of the past decade differs substantially from the Rust Belt decline and Sun Belt growth of the 1970s and '80s. Then, manufacturing companies moved south in search of a low-wage, nonunion workforce. Now, talented individuals are voting with their feet to live in cities where the work is smart, the culture is cool and the environment is clean.

Migrants on the move to winner-take-all-cities are most accurately identified by education and ambition, rather than by skin color or country of birth. They are part of a striving class of young Americans for whom race, ethnicity and geographic origin tend to be less meaningful than professional achievement, business connections and income.

The Sun Belt is no sure winner in this migration. Such cities as Miami and El Paso are struggling to keep college graduates, who are flocking to such foul-weather havens as Minneapolis, Seattle and Ann Arbor, Mich.

College Graduates

Among the 50 largest U.S. cities, Seattle ranks fifth in percentage of residents with college degrees. Cleveland ranks 49th.

Top 10

RANK/CITY	PERCENTAGE WITH COLLEGE DEGREE
1 Washington	81%
2 Atlanta	68
3 San Francisco	63
4 Oakland, Calif.	62
5 Seattle	**54**
6 Austin	52
7 Boston	49
8 Denver	48
9 New Orleans	48
10 Dallas	48

Bottom 10

RANK/CITY	PERCENTAGE WITH COLLEGE DEGREE
41 St. Louis	28%
42 Fresno, Calif.	28
43 Oklahoma City	28
44 Milwaukee	25
45 Philadelphia	24
46 Mesa, Ariz.	24
47 Jacksonville, Fla.	24
48 Las Vegas	22
49 Cleveland	**16**
50 Detroit	15

SOURCE: Brookings Institution Center on Urban and Metropolitan Policy

THE WASHINGTON POST

AMONG THE COUNTRY'S 100 LARGEST METRO areas, the 25 that entered the 1990s with the largest share of college graduates had, by the end of the decade, sponged up graduates at twice the rate of the other 75 cities, according to a Brookings analysis of the census.

Talent helps make these top-tier cities diverse, tolerant and rich with the cultural amenities that help them steal still more talent.

These cities tend to have a high percentage of residents who are artists, writers and musicians, as well as large and visible gay communities. They often have pedestrian neighborhoods, with good food, live music and theater. The percentage of foreign-born residents is also high in these cities, reflecting a significant population of college-educated imports.

"The great advantage of places like Seattle is that they have become the kind of place where young people want to freaking be," said Richard Florida, a professor of regional economic development at Carnegie Mellon University in Pittsburgh.

Florida is author of "The Rise of the Creative Class," an influential book among big-city politicians and urban planners. It tells them they can secure the future of their cities by tending to the care and feeding of smart young people.

Rapid population growth, by itself, does not guarantee that a city will experience a relative gain in college graduates. In most cases, extraordinary growth is a negative indicator.

With the exception of Austin, none of the 10 fastest-growing U.S. cities of the 1990s ranked among the top 25 cities for increases in the percentage of residents with college degrees. The fastest-growing city, Las Vegas, leads the nation in attracting more high school dropouts than college graduates.

"Really fast-growing places, like Las Vegas and Phoenix, have needs not associated with college education, like the construction industry and service workers for retirement communities," said William H. Frey, a demographer at the University of Michigan.

Another peculiarity of brain-gain cities is that they have a tendency to lose residents of lesser educational attainment, even as they vacuum up more college graduates.

In the second half of the 1990s, San Francisco experienced a 6.5 percent decline in residents who had only a high school degree, according to Frey's analysis of census data. At the same time, the number of college graduates rose by 2.8 per-

cent. Driven mostly by housing costs, a similar trend exists in Seattle and other brain-gain cities.

Frey said this demographic crosscurrent appears to have continued through the high-tech recession. It helps explain why—even as the college-educated young continue to cluster in a handful of cities—broader demographic trends show a substantial movement of people from large metropolitan centers to outer suburbs, small cities and rural areas.

"Clearly, as the economy got bad, lesser-educated folks had a harder time staying in San Francisco," Frey said. "My guess is that the higher-educated folks found a way to stay, or they circulated to one of the other idea-opolises, like Seattle."

New York, Chicago and Los Angeles are perennial magnets of high-end talent, but their size and the constant churning of their population make it difficult for demographers to discern the winner-take-all pattern identified in mid-size cities.

WHAT IS EASY—AND DEPRESSING— to see in brain-drain cities is the extraordinary cost of losing talent. The departure of people such as Sam Long from these cities has stalled growth, lowered per-capita income and prevented the formation of a critical mass of risk-takers who can create high-paying jobs.

Beside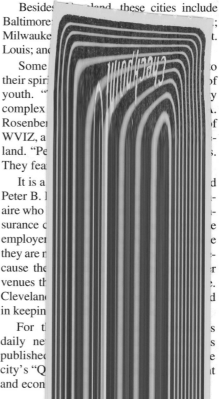 these cities include Baltimore Milwauke Louis; and

Some their spir youth. " complex Rosenber WVIZ, a land. "Pe They fea

It is a Peter B. aire who surance o employer they are r cause the venues th Clevelan in keepin

For t daily ne published city's "Q and econ

Cl
vat
fou
lik
ne
do
en
Ol

fo
the
co
co
on
po

pa
an
su

Cl
Gl
en
ha
Al

ur

in
w
to
lc
h
s
n
s

i

l

to leave the
d to inno-
Dealer
e more
ve. The
irds of
the sci-
out of

rt rein-
saying
single
of the
one of
metro-

become
losing,
rd cities

ival of
Manuel
ist and
that we
er yet?

ging—
ll city.
ful bio-
Genics,
down-
s in the
city's
wrote
anies to
s of re-

fast as
an com-
Glynias
arketing
od high-
year and
an Diego,
jobs left

tter places
t of way,"
n't find a
g my chil-
Diego or

O SET UP
Seattle, like
a has-been
comparison
ustin, Min-
poach tal-
n cities such
Hartford.

"It is a totally unfair fight, and it is the way the market works now," said Michael Fogarty, director of the School of Urban Studies at Portland State University and former professor of economics at Case Western.

Cleveland and Seattle are about the same size, with about a half-million residents inside the city limits and 2 million-plus in the metro region. Both cities have a history of big money. Each produced the richest men of its era (Rockefeller and Gates). In an explosion of capitalistic energy, they became world-famous centers for technical innovation, entrepreneurial creativity and a bullying business style that pushed—and sometimes broke—the limits of the law.

These bursts of prosperity, of course, were separated by nearly a century. Cleveland flowered in the second half of the 19th century and peaked by 1930, when productivity started to slide in steelmaking and metalworking.

As with many cities in the Rust Belt, the population began to decline in the 1960s. Racial segregation played a chronically corrosive role, as poverty rose, public schools nose-dived and whites fled to the suburbs.

Sprawl was encouraged and hugely subsidized by Ohio's tax policy. It sucked gas taxes out of Cleveland and other cities, and the state spent the money on roads in rural areas that often blossomed into affluent suburbs. At the same time, Cleveland failed to become a "gateway city" for new immigrants. Large waves of Asian or Latin American immigrants did not pour into the city or its close-in suburbs (as occurred in Seattle and Washington) to replace those who had been vacuumed out by subsidized sprawl.

Cleveland's population in 1950 was 914,808, but it lost 30 percent of its residents in the 1970s, 15 percent in the '80s and 5 percent in the '90s. Rockefeller left early, moving to New York before the turn of the century.

ALTHOUGH SEATTLE IS MIRED IN ITS worst recession in three decades and hobbled by the loss of about 17,000 jobs at Boeing Co., it is an altogether different story.

The city has succeeded in shifting its economic base over the years—from lumber and fishing to airplane manufacturing to high-tech enterprises and specialty retail. Its school system, although far from perfect, never collapsed. It does not have

intractable pockets of poverty. It does not have to clean up the festering environmental legacy of the industrial age. It is 70 percent white, 13 percent Asian, 5.4 percent black and 5 percent Hispanic. (Cleveland is 51 percent black, 41.5 percent white and 7.3 percent Hispanic.)

The success of U.S. cities, demographers agree, is not related to racial composition but rather to education levels. High levels of immigration by nonwhite college graduates in the 1990s to such cities as Seattle, Austin and San Francisco have been a major factor in their prosperity. At the same time, the relative dearth of college-educated immigrants of any race to cities such as Cleveland is viewed as a key reason for their decline.

Although Cleveland has sprawled without growth, Seattle has grown while winning a come-from-behind fight against sprawl. After losing population to the suburbs for 30 years, it turned a corner in the '90s, growing by 9 percent, with many newcomers moving to housing near the waterfront.

State law has forced more than 80 percent of new housing construction to occur inside designated urban zones in King County. Population growth continues in Seattle, although the recession slowed it to a crawl.

Thanks in large measure to the drawing power of such companies as Microsoft, Amazon.com Inc. and Starbucks Corp., Seattle ranks near the top on virtually every national index of knowledge-based urban muscle.

More than a half-million people moved to King County in the past two decades and about 10,000 millionaires were minted, mostly at Microsoft. Forty-seven percent of Seattleites have at least a bachelor's degree, about twice the national rate and four times higher than Cleveland's.

More households have access to the Internet (80.6 percent) than in any other U.S. city, and Seattle ranked second in the country (after Minneapolis) in a recent survey of literacy. The city also ranks among the top five high-tech cities in percentages of creative artists, foreign-born residents and gays.

THE EMERGENCE OF WINNER-TAKE-ALL CITIES is usually linked to the presence of a dominating research university. Seattle is no exception. The University of Washington, which is in the city, has doubled its research budget in the past decade and is the country's leading public university as measured by federal funding.

Among urban scholars, business leaders and big-city politicians, there is a chicken-and-egg debate over what exactly makes a high-tech city grow. Does technology come first and lure talent? Or does the mere presence of talent, through some creative alchemy, hatch technology that spawns high-paying jobs? A look at a recent software startup in Seattle suggests the answer is both.

The new company, called Performant Inc., emerged from an idea that Seattle investors quickly grasped and bathed in a nourishing pot of money. One of them was Sam Long, the venture capitalist who moved here from Cleveland. Three years ago, Long got a call from Ashutosh Tiwary, an Indian immigrant and doctoral student at the University of Washington's School of Computer Science and Engineering.

Tiwary had an idea that came to him while he was working part time at Boeing, where he was troubleshooting design software for new aircraft. He found a way to diagnose why computer systems at major companies often slow to a crawl. His software could speed them up.

He took the idea back to the university, where a professor and a senior software researcher from Microsoft (an adjunct professor) saw its potential. They helped him refine, patent and market a product. They also hooked him up with a venture capital company run by wealthy Microsoft retirees. That company, in turn, gave him Long's phone number.

Long quickly invested $750,000, part of the $10 million that Tiwary and his partners raised during the teeth of Seattle's recession. This spring, they sold the company, doubling their investors' money. Thirty jobs created by the company are staying in Seattle.

Tiwary said he never would have come up with the idea—or made money from it so quickly—had he not been in Seattle. He moved there in the late 1990s, by way of India, Texas and California.

"There is a business ecosystem here that is both creative and technical," said Tiwary, now a vice president at *Mercury Interactive Corp.*, the company that bought him out. "It starts with people who understand technology, have built successful things before and want to do it again. It is a little bit of an addiction."

AT THE VERY TOP OF THE ENTREPRENEURIAL food chain in Seattle, the addiction to risk-taking is being turned loose on biotech.

The city's two richest residents—with the backing of the University of Washington and enthusiastic help from the city and county governments—are bankrolling a bet that could supercharge the local economy for decades to come. Seattle is already a leader in biotech, but lags far behind Boston and San Francisco.

Paul Allen has spent $225 million of his own money to close the gap—fast. "You have to be ready to take advantage of the next big cycle," Allen said.

He said Seattle has strung together all the beads on that thread: a research university, a cooperative city government, lots of venture capital and "you have to be able to attract people.... That is just not a problem in Seattle."

In the past decade, Allen has bought 50 acres in downtown Seattle for a biotech research center. His company, Vulcan, is transforming a sterile stretch of parking lots, used-furniture stores and badly designed streets into what is expected to be the nation's largest urban life-science campus.

It will have the capacity to employ 20,000 scientists and technicians, according to Vulcan. If Allen's plan works, about 10,000 of them would live in a pedestrian neighborhood at the south end of the city's Lake Union, amid new restaurants, nightclubs and retail stores surmounted by apartments.

To help Seattle create a critical mass of biotech talent, Gates donated $70 million this spring to the University of Washington to build departments of genome science and bioengineering. For nearly a decade, Gates has used his money and his fame to recruit eminent biotech scientists from around the country.

"Gates and Allen are giving the city a real forward momentum," said Leroy Hood, whom Gates lured from the California Institute of Technology to start a biotechnology department at the University of Washington. "In 10 years, I think Boeing will be irrelevant to Seattle."

SCHOLARS WHO STUDY U.S. CITIES AGREE that Cleveland has probably tried harder—and achieved more—than any other major brain-drain city.

It has substantially rebuilt its downtown, winning national attention as a "comeback city" with the Rock and Roll Hall of Fame, as well as new complexes for professional baseball, basketball and football. The percentage of residents with high school degrees has increased and concentrated poverty has been reduced.

The fastest-growing neighborhood in Cleveland is the downtown core. There, city government has worked with developers to turn warehouses and abandoned department stores into apartments that appeal to young professionals. Cleveland's leading university, Case Western, is urging students and faculty to live in the city. It is spending hundreds of millions of dollars for new housing and for a retail neighborhood near the university. "You must position yourself as the place people want to move to, rather than from," said the school's new president, Edward M. Hundert.

He is demanding that the school's researchers work with, rather than compete against, other local research centers, such as the Cleveland Clinic and University Hospitals of Cleveland.

"This is a city that, against all odds, is getting its act together," said Katz, whose Urban Affairs Center at Brookings monitors most major U.S. cities. "I believe that if Cleveland had not tried so hard, it would look like St. Louis or Detroit."

And yet, in Cleveland—as in many other brain-drain cities that are trying to fight back—the loss of talent continues. Throughout the '90s, even as Cleveland made its highly publicized comeback, it continued to lose college graduates and income. It lost about $35 billion because it could not keep the people and maintain the per-capita income it had in 1990, according to an analysis in the Plain Dealer.

A critical mass of money, ideas and risk-taking has not coalesced in Cleveland, said David Morgenthaler, one of the country's most eminent venture capitalists. He manages $2 billion and lives in Cleveland. Morgenthaler said he would love to invest more money in his home town. But he does not do so because the city "does not breed enough good horses to bet on."

His judgment is echoed in Cleveland's dismal ranking among the 50 largest cities as measured by venture capital as a percentage of the metro economy. Cleveland ranks 42nd, while Seattle ranks second, behind San Francisco. "Cleveland lives off the past, and the executives from these old industries are still the community leaders," Morgenthaler said. "The city has made progress, but it is not close to where it has to be."

A   Cleveland for Seattle,   s his hometown well, but s   ot conceive of a reason he wou   here. He just built a four-bedroom he se near Lake Washington in one of Seattle's most expensive neighborhoods. At regular dinners with friends from the computer science department at the University of Washington, he schemes about turning ideas into money. "We talk of pie in the sky," he said.

In Seattle, unlike his home town and many other cities that keep losing young talent, pie in the sky has a way of turning into high-paying jobs and companies that own the future.

UNIT 4

Urban Revival

Unit Selections

Key Points to Consider

- Define urban revival.

- Describe the factors that have made it possible for many cities to think in terms of urban revival.

- Can urban revival be sustained? What do you see as the pitfalls to continuing progress?

- What are some possible ways to invigorate urban centers? Do you think these plans would work in any urban center in America? Why or why not?

- Pretend you have just been elected mayor of your city or the city nearest you. Articulate those issues that are most important to you, and then define how you intend to measure your success or failure in handling those issues.

 **Links: www.dushkin.com/online/**
These sites are annotated in the World Wide Web pages.

Connect for Kids/Workplace
http://www.connectforkids.org/info-url1564/info-url_list.htm?section=Workplace
WWW Virtual Library: Demography & Population Studies
http://demography.anu.edu.au/VirtualLibrary/

This section on Urban Revival is divided into three subsections: Financing and Costs, Downtown Renaissance: Culture, Tourism, and Education, and Immigration. Each aspect of the broader topic helps explain the large, complex processes of urban revival; while analytically distinct, these strands of the urban revival weave tightly together.

In "Ground Zero in Urban Decline," the author expresses serious skepticism about the long-term impact of publicly funded economic development schemes for revitalizing cities. Market forces can more successfully revitalize cities, he argues, if municipal governments can get out of their way by building and maintaining their infrastructures and ensuring the public safety. "Return to Center" shows how some states have deliberately moved their government offices back downtown from the suburbs in order to stimulate urban revitalization.

The subsection Downtown Renaissance: Culture, Tourism, and Education examines the expanded role of these institutions in twenty-first century cities. Numerous cities increasingly use cultural and educational institutions to attract the well-educated and well-heeled, and to market their lifestyle advantages. The implicit, unintended economic consequences of major cultural and educational institutions have been widely recognized and consciously used as levers of urban revitalization. Arts and educational institutions repeatedly calculate and publicize their economic benefits to their home cities. In New York, for instance, Julia Vitullo-Martin tells the remarkable story of how Bryant Park, once home to drug dealers and other criminals, became perhaps the most densely used park in America, and the symbolic and practical effects of this transformation for midtown Manhattan.

Lou Winick, an astute urban analyst, once said immigration is our most successful urban policy. This subsection of unit 4 acknowledges the positive consequences that immigrant residents and immigrant businesses have often had on American cities. It highlights major changes in Los Angeles, as well as smaller but significant developments in Buffalo.

FINANCING
Urban Revitalization

Beth Mattson-Teig

Urban revitalization projects often require a flowchart to track the many layers of financing. But neither the complexity of the transactions nor the sluggish economy appears to be deterring lenders. "Urban revitalization projects have always been tough deals to do because of higher costs of parcels, adaptive use, and multiple layers of debt and equity," says John Kastellic, a senior vice president and national manager for community development lending at Cleveland-based Key Community Development Corp.

Redevelopment is much more costly than building on open suburban acreage. Additional capital is required to assemble land, raze or renovate existing structures, and clean up any environmental contamination. As a result, revitalization projects typically involve multifaceted layering of bank and commercial mortgage financing, public grants or low interest loans, tax abatements, private equity, tax credits, and other forms of subordinated debt.

"There is no question that projects in an urban center take longer to put together," points out David St. Pierre, a senior vice president with Cleveland-based KeyBank and a district sales manager of Key Commercial Real Estate. Nevertheless, urban projects are in demand, he says, with some developers passing over suburban greenfields in pursuit of central business district projects in order to satisfy the demand for urban locales coming from both the residential and commercial sectors.

Retailers, in particular, are rediscovering urban markets due to the strong demographics and dense trade areas that they represent. "We used to have retailers expanding at breakneck speed," notes St. Pierre. "As retailers have started to struggle, they have taken a much more stringent approach to site selection." As a result, he says, retailers are targeting densely populated urban areas.

"We continue to see an increasing number of urban revitalization projects," comments Kastellic, who adds that those projects are not exclusive to major metropolitan areas. Revitalization projects are popping up in areas ranging from inner-city neighborhoods to mature suburban communities, he says, and municipalities play a key role in driving urban revitalization. Cities that are aggressive in courting developers with financial inducements are proving successful in attracting redevelopment, adds Kastellic.

Challenging urban deals require more patience and creativity to assemble financing.

"Unless you get assistance from the local municipality, these projects generally are not feasible," says Len Deering, a vice president in the Oakbrook, Illinois, office of ARCS Commercial Mortgage Co. "Because of their high costs, you need help to make them work."

Dayton, Ohio, is one city that has been proactive in its efforts to revitalize its downtown area, encouraging projects that include a minor league ballpark and an outdoor plaza. Another recent project involved the conversion of an old warehouse to condominiums. ARCS used the FannieMae Market Rate Forward Rate Lock Program to provide $7 million in permanent financing for the project. The St. Claire Lofts conversion project, which created 108 residential lofts and some commercial space on the first floor, also had a 12-year tax abatement from the local assessors, as well as historic tax credits. "All of that

helped to get equity that would not have been obtainabl otherwise," notes Deering.

Local lenders were reluctant to back the housing project, he says, because they did not think it would work. "They didn't think anyone would want to live downtown. But the success of similar conversions around the country shows that there is a definite niche for this type of housing," maintains Deering.

Loft conversions are favored because of their unique structure and urban setting. "The St. Claire Lofts have been leasing extremely well," Deering says. "There was a hidden demand for that type of product."

Los Angeles also is working to expand its financial resources to encourage revitalization. "We really need more sources here in L.A.," comments Eve Ryan, regional vice president and manager in the Community Lending Group at Wells Fargo Bank NA in Los Angeles. Los An-

geles has created a Downtown Rebound organization to initiate some studies and to obtain state grants for economic development. Ryan serves on one of the Downtown Rebound committees for housing that is working to identify ways to further encourage housing that will aid in downtown revitalization.

Bryson Apartments in Los Angeles succeeded in pooling public financing resources to renovate a 1920s hotel on Wilshire Boulevard into an 81-unit, family housing project. The housing development tapped several public financing sources, including $7.6 million in tax credits, $3.9 million in city money, and a $250,000 grant from the Federal Home Loan Bank. The project had a number of problems it had to deal with, such as lead paint and asbestos, before it was completed and opened in fall 2000.

Public and private entities are teaming up to provide the capital necessary to fund costly revitalization efforts. Some communities stand out as aggressive pursuers of economic development. "Those communities that are open and willing to think and to be creative are where you see these opportunities happen," Kastellic says.

One joint effort involves the 180,000-square-foot Lee-Harvard Shopping Center in Cleveland. Built in the 1950s, much of the space in the grocery-anchored neighborhood center had become outdated and run down. A neighborhood nonprofit group, New Village Corp., teamed up with Cleveland-based Forest City Enterprises Inc. to redevelop the center. About two-thirds of the center was razed and rebuilt.

KeyBank, acting as the agent bank, structured a $12.1 million facility using construction and mini-permanent loans from a three-bank consortium consisting of Key-Bank, National City Bank, and Bank One for the acquisition and renovation of the project. Other funding consisted of seven layers of subdebt totaling $4 million, tax increment financing (TIF) totaling $1 million, investor equity of $2.875 million, and owner equity of $4.5 million.

The goal was to rehabilitate the aging retail center, create additional office space for a neighborhood health clinic, and encourage continued investment and revitalization in the neighborhood. "The project was more of a response at the grass-roots level, but the city was eager to try to contribute whatever pieces of financing it could toward making this work," points out Kastellic.

Another Cleveland revitalization project involved the acquisition and rehabilitation of an old 1920s shopping center. The Shops at Shaker Square project, completed last summer, was a joint venture between Cleveland-based CenterPoint Properties and Miami-based Rosen Associates. "They have taken this remarkable real estate asset that most people in town avoided and created a vibrant, active retail center," says St. Pierre.

Key Commercial Real Estate provided a $14.3 million first mortgage for the $25.6 million project. Private equity totaled $3 million. The remaining $8.3 million comprised $3.9 million in TIF, a $1.3 million second mortgage from the city, a $1.3 million third mortgage from First Energy, a $1 million infrastructure grant, $700,000 in various Cleveland grants, and a $200,000 Ohio Development Grant. "Communities that want to see this type of development in their neighborhood are getting smarter, or at least becoming more open and encouraging developers to talk," notes St. Pierre.

Communities will have to work harder to keep economic development subsidies propped up in the slow economy. "Because cities rely on taxes for their funding, funding that is awarded really depends on the economy," says Ryan. The economic health of a city also affects bond ratings. Subsidies in cities such as Los Angeles that already are pretty small are likely to get smaller, she maintains. "There will have to be a reengineering of how things get done for affordable housing and urban revitalization as a whole," she adds.

Lining up public financing for urban projects could be more challenging—at least in the short term. "Everyone is having a problem keeping their tax base up," says Deering. However, many cities remain committed to revitalization efforts because redevelopment is essential to creating a vibrant downtown and expanding the business and residential base, he adds.

Although it might be more difficult to establish new TIF districts in the current economic climate, cities continue to make use of these tax-financing mechanisms. Dallas, Texas, for example, has not experienced a slowdown in redevelopment activity among the seven TIF districts it has established in and around downtown. The districts range in size from 65 to 400 acres. "The city of Dallas has experienced some belt tightening in recent years," notes Karl Stundins, area redevelopment manager for the city of Dallas. One way Dallas is alleviating the financial burden is by limiting terms on TIF districts. Some districts have 15- or 20-year limits, while other districts already have collected their allotted funds and will shut down, he notes.

Dallas also reduces the city's risk by requiring developers to put money upfront for infrastructure. Later, developers are reimbursed with a nominal interest rate through money raised in the TIF district. In addition, Dallas avoids bond sales to finance redevelopment. "If the level of development expected doesn't occur, or there is a real estate downturn, it can affect how bonds are repaid," says Stundins.

The recession has made it more difficult to assemble the various layers of financing that redevelopment projects demand. However, communities determined to move forward with urban revitalization efforts are tapping a variety of financial tools.

For example, Washington, D.C., currently has the authority to provide $330 million in tax increment financing, and it also is financing additional economic development through land sales. Government agencies are relocating, and the land is being sold to spark economic growth in what have become depressed areas, notes Gerry Widdicombe, development director for the Center City Part-

nership, a Washington, D.C.–based public/private partnership created to carry out the district's economic development agenda.

"We still have some big projects that seem to be on track," points out Widdicombe. One such project is the $225 million Gallery Place. Approximately $76 million in TIF is earmarked for the mixed-used redevelopment, which broke ground last July. The project is a key anchor to the revitalization occurring along the Seventh Street Corridor. Gallery Place spans 640,000 square feet, and will house a 14-screen, stadium-style theater; 200,000 square feet of retail space; 180,000 square feet of office space; 65,000 square feet of entertainment space; 193 apartments; and 650 new parking spaces. Washington, D.C.–based Western Development Corp. is developing Gallery Place in conjunction with the John Akridge Companies, also located in Washington, D.C.

Projects still on the drawing board may require more creative financing in the tougher economic climate. In Washington, a bill has been introduced to help the Shakespeare Theatre expand by providing tax abatement to a developer or owner who will house the theater in its building. Washington also continues to tap HOPE VI Program dollars. Public housing agencies with severely distressed housing are eligible to apply for the HOPE VI grants to revitalize their communities. "The district is availing itself of the tools it has to continue economic development throughout the city," says Widdicombe.

Public financing resources are being stretched amid a more conservative lending environment, meaning lenders are more cautious due to the slower economy. "We are being more careful on individual deals, and looking at each of the markets to see what is happening," says Jim Pape, a first vice president at LaSalle Bank N.A. in Chicago. In Chicago, for example, rising unemployment and increased homebuying have combined to push apartment vacancies higher. LaSalle is taking those higher vacancies into account when calculating deals, Pape notes. In some cases, the higher vacancies translate into requirements for additional equity to make a deal work, he adds.

Lenders such as ARCS are conducting more detailed analysis and research on projects. "Even a year ago, we would be thinking positive on everything, and today we are looking to make sure that we are not missing anything that could negatively affect the property," Deering says. Tenants are under more careful scrutiny regardless of whether a project is urban or suburban, or retail, industrial, or office, notes KeyBank's St. Pierre. For example, the Gap used to be the darling of a retail center. But nine consecutive quarters of declining earnings has shaken confidence even in this typically solid performer.

"We are being more cautious in our underwriting," agrees Ryan. Affordable housing projects in particular have the potential to be affected by deeply discounted apartment rents in some markets. "It is less of an issue here in Los Angeles, but when you get into other markets like Dallas or Austin, you may see rents dropping significantly in luxury units," she says. Market-rate properties could see rents drop to a point where the spread between market rate and affordable units is minimal. So properties are competing more avidly for renters. "We have always done a lot of due diligence, and now we are definitely looking deeply into what is happening in those local economies and those local markets," she explains.

"While lenders are looking for that credit quality to make sure they are in with the right deal, activity is still pretty robust," says Bob Imperato, a senior vice president at InterFirst, a subsidiary of ABN AMRO North American Mortgage in Waterbury, Connecticut. ABN AMRO Multifamily, a sister company, expects to produce $1.8 billion in multifamily transactions in 2001. That is a considerable amount considering the maximum loan size is $2 million, says Imperato.

Developers also are taking advantage of historically low interest rates to fix permanent rates at closing. "There has been a push by developers and syndicators not to hedge on what the interest is going to be two years out when they will be ready to convert to permanent fi-

nancing," observes Ryan. As a result, there has been more demand to get forward commitments on permanent financing. For example, a construction loan can close with a credit wrap provided by the construction financier. The forward funded product involves the permanent lender working closely with the construction lender to fund the permanent loan upfront at the closing of the construction loan, she notes.

Low interest rates will continue to drive urban revitalization projects well into the year. In addition, Fannie Mae, Freddie Mac, and the U.S. Department of Housing and Urban Development (HUD) all are very active in participating with municipalities and townships to create new housing opportunities. According to Imperato, "There is pent-up demand for revitalization opportunities in areas like Chicago, Minneapolis, Boston, and New York."

BETH MATTSON-TEIG is a freelance writer based in Minneapolis, Minnesota.

Ground Zero in Urban Decline

Cincinnati isn't just a town down on its luck. It's the future of the American city.

By Sam Staley

Welcome to ground zero in inner-city decline: the Over-the-Rhine district in Cincinnati, Ohio. This is the neighborhood, settled a couple hundred years ago and named for the predominantly German immigrants who once populated it, that was at the center of America's most recent spasm of social turmoil. In April, after police shot an unarmed black man, hundreds of Cincinnati residents took to the streets to protest entrenched racism and economic inequities. Cincinnati—once renowned as the Queen City of the Ohio River, once dubbed "Porkopolis" for its dominance in pig processing, once famous as the home of baseball's legendary Big Red Machine—is now known for civil disorder and a sagging population. The 2000 Census underscores that Cincinnati's glory days were somewhere in the past: During the 1990s, the city lost over 30,000 residents, or about 9 percent of its population.

Any prospects for revival in this Midwestern city were dealt a staggering setback by images of smoldering fires in the streets, angry men hurling bricks through storefront windows, and shop owners holding vigil over their property with shotguns. In less than a week, more than 600 people were arrested for disorderly conduct, vandalism, and assault. Urban decay—vacant buildings, declining population, few jobs—provided the tinderbox for the riots that thrust this famously staid city into the national headlines.

If the nation was shocked—this was a town known for its conservatism, restraint, and bedrock Midwestern val-

ues—so were Cincinnati's city leaders. Prior to the riots, the business community had been cultivating the city's reputation as a bastion of middle-class values and the German work ethic, regardless of the current residents' cultural heritages. The unrest provided a dramatic counterpoint to other recent development efforts. Earlier this year, in a bid to win the 2012 Summer Olympic Games, local activists and leaders put together an 800-page document touting Cincinnati's competitive advantages. In 1996, voters in Hamilton County, of which Cincinnati is a part, approved a sales tax increase to underwrite the construction of two new professional sports stadiums—a baseball-only stadium for the Reds (the nation's oldest professional baseball team) and a separate football facility for the Bengals. The city and county have also invested substantial public funds in redirecting Port Washington Way, a freeway providing easy access to downtown from the outer edge of the metropolitan area.

All told, those recent investments in downtown and riverfront improvements have cost Hamilton County residents close to $1 billion, and that's not counting the interest on bonds. The city lists 34 projects on its downtown development plan; if everything on that wish list gets built, the total price tag would be something like $4 billion. And yet Cincinnati has little to show for the effort, other than some white-elephant public works projects and the wreckage—physical and emotional—from this spring's riots. "The problems of the city," notes city councilman Phil Heimlich, "are not so much that white and black people don't get along; it's that white and black people don't stick around. I think the most important fact is that the city has lost almost 10 percent of its population over the last 10 years."

Cincinnati is a very specific place: Well-known for its steep hills and riverfront location, it has been built into its landscape in a singular and striking way (Winston Churchill once called it "America's most beautiful inland city"). Yet Cincinnati is also a very generic place in today's America. It's a city smack dab in the middle of a long, slow decline—not just in population but in prospects for the future. Its story—a sad one, though not without some measure of hope—is one that is being played out in urban centers throughout the country. The reasons for Cincinnati's decline and the misguided attempts to reverse it are all too representative of what's happening throughout the U.S. today. For good and ill, what's happening in Cincinnati may well be coming to a city near you. If, in fact, it's not already there.

In 2001, the Fannie Mae Foundation studied three dozen of the nation's largest cities and found that most have been losing population since the 1970s. While some cities gained population during the '90s—including such long-bleeding cosmopolises as New York and Chicago—more lost ground: Cincinnati, Cleveland, Milwaukee, Rochester, Syracuse, Toledo, Baltimore, Buffalo, Detroit, Philadelphia, St. Louis, and the District of Columbia, among others, continued long traditions of population decline.

A closer look inside Cincinnati's city limits reveals a more troubling trend: Only three of its 48 neighborhoods added people between 1990 and 2000. One of those neighborhoods—Queensgate—only grew because the city built a new jail. Twenty-six neighborhoods lost more than 10 percent of their population. The Over-the-Rhine area saw its population shrink from 9,572 people to 7,638.

A Long Line of Spenders

Cincinnati's recent orgy of high-profile, publicly funded projects is hardly its first. At the turn of the 19th century, public works projects served mainly to line the pockets of political boss George B. Cox's friends, earning Cincinnati the reputation of a corrupt frontier burg. The excesses of corrupt city bosses helped inspire a series of reform groups, including the Taxpayers' League, in 1880. By the early 20th century, the same sort of public works projects were carried out in the name of social welfare—whether the project in question entailed constructing a 15-mile commuter rail and subway system or taking over the local utilities. Despite its public profligacy, Cincinnati ranked among the nation's largest cities at the turn of the 19th century—a gateway to the West and a thriving commercial center sustained by the Ohio River and the Mi-

ami-Erie canal. The city quickly became a center for industry, hosting the nation's largest concentration of factories making soap, cleaners, shortening, candles, oils , and chemicals. The legacy is symbolically embodied in the twin towers of Procter & Gamble's world headquarters in the heart of the city's downtown. Pork processing and beer brewing rounded out the list of major industries.

The city's German history reaches back nearly two centuries. An ethnic German was elected its first mayor in 1802, and by the 1840s, the city was printing bilingual ordinances. By the mid-19th century, one-fifth of Cincinnati's population spoke German, and Germans are largely credited with the expansion of savings and loans, called "bauvereins," that created a foundation of homeownership among the middle and working classes. Even in the mid-20th century, high-rise apartment buildings were scarce, an architectural legacy that benefits even the poorest neighborhoods, including Over-the-Rhine.

In the wake of the riots, city leaders created a task force—Cincinnati Can—and charged it with developing recommendations to address the simmering problems of urban decline. The effort is strikingly similar to Rebuild LA, the largely ineffective effort to revitalize South Central Los Angeles after its riots in 1992. Whether Cincinnati Can actually does anything to revitalize the city, this much seems certain: It will provide cover for dozens of other projects that elected officials and prominent business leaders have trumpeted in recent years to stimulate the city. For instance, city leaders are pushing hard to expand the money-losing, municipally owned and operated Dr. Albert A. Sabin Convention Center. The proposal would double the size of the current convention center to more than 600,000 square feet.

Citizens for Civic Renewal, a nonprofit local urban reform organization, commissioned "regional government" guru Myron Orfield to do a study of the region. Orfield, an elected representative in the Minnesota state legislature, is best known for *Metropolitics*, an influential 1997 book published by the Brookings Institution that argued that declining inner suburbs were as much a victim of sprawl as central cities. Orfield's preliminary report, released earlier this year, highlighted growing inequalities among the city, its inner suburbs, and the growing outer suburbs, and called for regional planning to minimize them.

What seems to be missing in the mess of publicly financed projects is any rational—let alone balanced—debate on whether such endeavors have *any* positive effects, much less the pie-in-the-sky results proponents routinely claim.

If his past is any prologue, Orfield's final report, to be released later this year, will call for more regional government and revenue-sharing to redistribute income from relatively wealthy neighborhoods (and suburbs) to relatively poor inner-city neighborhoods (and suburbs). A multibillion-dollar light-rail project has also been proposed by the Ohio-Kentucky-Indiana council of governments (OKI), an organization that includes 105 representatives of government, business, social, and civic groups in an eight-county region. Proponents argue that the rail system will do just about everything—reduce regional congestion, promote economic development, revitalize inner-city neighborhoods, and constrain sprawl.

The Actual Effects

What seems to be missing in the mess of publicly financed projects is any rational—let alone balanced—debate on whether such endeavors have *any* positive effects, much less the pie-in-the-sky results proponents routinely claim. Sports stadiums have emerged as a classic case in point. "Adding professional sports teams and stadiums to a city's economy does not increase aggregate spending for the city," wrote Lake Forest College economist Robert Baade, a leading expert on the subject, in a 1996 study. In fact, according to Baade's research, adding teams "appears to realign leisure spending rather than adding to it and is, therefore, neutral with regard to job creation." Baade's conclusions are based on his analysis of economic growth in 48 cities between 1958 and 1987, some with and others without new professional sports stadiums. Other analysts go even further, arguing that public investment in a sports stadium might reduce economic growth by siphoning money away from other important projects, such as road improvements, or from lowering taxes.

Clemson political scientist David Swindell echoes Baade's concerns. Swindell has studied the general economic and neighborhood impacts of minor and major league professional sports stadiums in places as varied as Indianapolis; Fort Wayne, Indiana; Arlington, Texas; and Cincinnati. He stresses that stadiums and convention centers have a "marginal impact" and "might even be negative"; he has seen "no evidence to support subsidies for private companies" in this way.

"Part of the problem," says one frustrated elected official in Cincinnati who requested anonymity, is that "people in this city look around and ask what [nearby] Indianapolis has done and they want to do that better." There's no question that Indianapolis, just a couple of hours northwest of Cincinnati, has grown in a major way, adding more than 40,000 people to its population between 1990 and 2000. Although Indianapolis is more than four times larger than Cincinnati (362 square miles vs. 78 for Cincinnati), Cincinnatians still compare the cities since their respective metropolitan areas are about the same size: 1.5 million people. Between 1974 and 1992, the

period of the most intense investment in its downtown, Indianapolis funneled $2.76 billion into various development projects, most of which were centered on sports.

The civic leaders who cite these cases fail to check the peer-reviewed academic research that shows that Indianapolis' downtown development has largely failed. One of the most extensive studies of Indianapolis comes from Clemson's Swindell, Indiana University political scientists Michael Przybylski and Daniel Mullins, and Mark Rosentraub, author of *Major League Losers* and director of Indiana University's Center for Urban Policy and the Environment. Published in the *Journal of Urban Affairs* in 1994, the study found that such investments in Indianapolis increased sports-related employment by 60 percent. But since these jobs accounted for just 0.32 percent of all jobs in the Indianapolis economy, the overall effect on economic development was negligible.

"Indianapolis' focus on its downtown area and sports as a development strategy was associated with a general trend of increased employment and economic growth," conclude the authors. "However, Indianapolis' strategy did not result in more growth than was experienced by other Midwestern communities and did not lead to a concentration of higher paying jobs in the region." In short, Indianapolis' growth was the result of larger regional economic trends and the expansion of existing businesses, including a dramatic increase in Indiana University-Purdue University's employment base from 3,000 full-time faculty and staff to 8,200. Moreover, although the city's raw population grew from 1990 to 2000, its share of the region's population fell from 52.9 percent to 48.8 percent.

And even if public-sector investments did fuel job growth downtown, nearby neighborhoods would still be unlikely to see benefits. Consider Cleveland, the notorious Rust Belt city that pumped millions of public dollars into revitalizing its downtown during the 1980s. The value of commercial properties downtown doubled in value during that decade, but commercial property values outside the downtown fell by 4 percent overall.

Ironically, while local leaders look to other cities for new programs and projects, few look to those cities whose citizens have rejected such measures. Just two hours up I-71 from Cincinnati, voters in Columbus, Ohio, turned down a 1997 measure to publicly finance a new soccer stadium and a new hockey arena. Both facilities were eventually built anyway—with mostly private money—and both now house professional sports teams, despite predictions that public funding would be crucial to land the franchises.

Studies by the Pound

Cincinnati's emphasis on large, visible downtown development projects is in part a reflection of the "expert" advice proffered by consultants who have "studied" their "feasibility" and "economic benefits." In the case of the city's convention center, consultants concluded that Cincy needed a bigger (and more expensive) facility to compete with other cities. More recently, OKI released the results of its study from a national consulting firm "quantifying" the benefits of the first leg of the proposed multibillion dollar rail system, a light-rail trolley line extending from Northern Kentucky through the downtown of Cincinnati and up to its northern suburbs.

The studies seem endless at times, and the intent of most is transparent. One, written by Vanderbilt management professor Richard W. Oliver, purported to show the economic benefits of having the NHL Predators in Nashville. It was titled: *They Shoot! They Score! NHL Nashville Predators Score Winning Goal for Middle Tennessee!* Convention center expansions fit the same mold. "The rhetoric of convention center investment is drawn from 'feasibility studies' often developed by a national accounting or economic research firm," explains Heywood Sanders, a professor of political science at the University of Texas at San Antonio. Sanders has researched convention centers and their economic Impacts for almost two decades, reviewing dozens of feasibility studies and writing numerous professional articles and reports, including a highly regarded 1998 article in the policy journal *The Public Interest*. "These studies lay out an invariably positive market analysis, justifying more local convention space and lending visible, supposedly objective support to political pressures to spend more public money for convention centers."

The studies are little more than marketing tools for chambers of commerce pushing one project or another; despite popular local support, big and small cities across the nation are littered with failed economic development projects, almost all dramatically oversold by their proponents. What's too often missing is the bottom line.

In a study last year written for the Boston-based Pioneer Institute, a market-oriented think tank focusing on Massachusetts policy issues, Sanders documents the shrinking market for conventions, a harsh reality that is rarely acknowledged by gung-ho city big wigs and their consultants. Most forecasts during the 1990s for trade shows and conventions were "unreasonable and unreliable," Sanders writes. Total event counts declined from 1998 to 2001, and average tradeshow attendance dropped by more than 24 percent. Large, money-making conventions are gravitating toward a select few locations—Atlanta, Orlando, Las Vegas, Chicago, and New York. Other traditional destination spots, such as Boston, haven't fared well, with events there slipping from 71 in 1996 to just 63 in 2001. Even large, vibrant, expanding metropolitan areas such as Houston or Dallas don't have what it takes to be competitive in the current convention market.

Along with stadiums and convention centers, consultants tout light-rail transit projects with reports that project fantastic benefits. Untold in these "studies" is the fact that the benefits are the product of computer models

and have never been achieved in the real world. For example, in 1978, planners in Portland, Oregon, forecast that by 1990 the city's light-rail ridership would be 42,500. In reality, it was half that. In Sacramento, light-rail ridership was initially projected to be 50,000 on an average weekday. By 1998, average weekday boardings were 28,000 (slightly higher than a revised projection made once local officials had committed to the project). Studies typically highlight the congestion-relief benefits of rail transit, even as transportation planners refuse to argue that these benefits exist. Indeed, in his 1998 survey of rail transit investments built since 1980, Jonathan Richmond of Harvard's Taubman Center for Local Government concluded that none had appreciably reduced congestion in cities.

Nevertheless, OKI is pushing a 117-mile system of seven rail lines criss-crossing Cincinnati. The twin goals: to bring people back into the city and reduce road congestion. A 1998 estimate by OKI pegged the cost of the entire system at $1.8 billion. A single line running from Northern Kentucky through downtown Cincinnati to suburban Blue Ash might cost close to $900 million. And that's a conservative estimate: Large public investments are notorious for coming in over budget. A light-rail system being built in Jersey City, New Jersey, was supposed to cost $1 billion, but costs have exceeded the early estimates with just two-thirds of the track laid.

Real Development

This isn't the first time Cincinnati and Hamilton County have dabbled in rail—or been taken to the cleaners while doing so. In 1912, reformist mayor Henry Hunt proposed a 15-mile rapid rail transit system; ironically, he thought it would help relieve congestion in the inner city by letting people live farther apart from one another. By 1920, private contractors were digging tunnels in the drained Miami-Erie Canal bed. The project was abandoned in 1927, after the costs ramped up well beyond original estimates and the rampant corruption became public. The entrances to buried subway stations and rail lines are still visible for those who know where to look.

In the 1920s, when the reform-minded Charter Party was voted into office, Cincinnati became the first major city to adopt a comprehensive plan. "In this concept," notes Ohio State University professor Laurence Gerckens, one of the nation's leading authorities on the history of American planning, "legal control of community development is used as a tool for, and is subservient to, the realization of a set of long-range comprehensive community goals." Later, the city developed a freeway (the recently realigned Fort Washington Way) that was explicitly designed to bring people in from the edges of the city and dump them into the downtown.

Cincinnatians took this approach to heart. Throughout the 20th century, city leaders took on one scheme after another using public money. Urban renewal and federal dollars helped pave over and renovate the Union Terminal railroad station on the West Side of town in the 1970s. Cincinnati also poured millions into the perennially troubled convention center in the 1960s, giant Riverfront Stadium in the 1970s, and the Fountain Square and Fountain Square West developments in the 1980s. The '90s, of course, brought stadiums for the Reds and the Bengals.

It's tempting to blame such projects on the "edifice complex," well-known among elected officials who want to leave their mark on a landscape. But such projects aren't simply the brainchild of elected officials or faceless bureaucrats. The business community consistently provides very visible support. With corporate giants such as Procter & Gamble and Chiquita Banana headquartered downtown, the Cincinnati business community flexes its muscle for public largess, especially in the core city. "Cincinnati is one of the clearest cases of the 'Downtown will save us' approach," says one outside observer still advising local officials. "In any other context, the business community would be talking about the virtues of unfettered free markets. When it comes to protecting 'their' investments in the core city, they are unified in their belief the public sector should pay for it—anything goes."

There's always hope for down-on-their-heels urban areas. Even in Cincinnati, spontaneous economic development is happening right under the noses of local officials despite apparent "neglect" by the well-heeled big business sector.

Such efforts are not only ineffective and wasteful. They stand in stark contrast to the bottom-up economic development efforts that pop up in neighborhood after neighborhood, often right under the noses of local development officials. One of the most dramatic examples is "Toy Town" near downtown Los Angeles. As city leaders were throwing around millions of dollars in post-riot Los Angeles through the high-profile but ineffective Republic LA, Charlie Woo was taking advantage of a market opportunity. Mr. Woo, a Hong Kong-born former graduate student in physics at UCLA, realized the depressed downtown real-estate market allowed him buy or lease old warehouse space for $1 or $2 per square foot. He used those bargain-basement prices to get a foothold in the toy manufacturing and distribution industry. Over the ensuing decade, more and more toy distributors, manufacturers, and retailers took advantage of the accessible and affordable location, building the area into an economic juggernaut employing 5,000 people and generating half a billion dollars in sales annually. City officials were completely unaware of Toy Town until its presence was sim-

ply too large to ignore any longer (See "Movers & Shakers," December 2000.)

So there's always hope for down-on-their-heels urban areas. Indeed, even in Cincinnati, spontaneous economic development is happening right under the noses of local officials despite apparent "neglect" by the well-heeled big-business sector. About 80 technology-focused companies have located along a 10-block stretch of Main Street in Over-the-Rhine, making up what has become known as the "Digital Rhine" (digitalrhine.com). To some extent, the tech district is the product of Main Street Ventures, a private development company that owns five buildings and provides space to 13 businesses.

The Digital Rhine

Created in 1999, Main Street Ventures is a private effort to promote tech companies in the Digital Rhine. It is also a response to a market trend in Cincinnati. Tech businesses were sprouting up all across the region, but a few local leaders thought that concentrating the budding industry in one area would give it the synergies necessary to grow. By attracting similar businesses to the Digital Rhine, investors also felt they could get more attention from venture capitalists, banks, consultants, and technology providers. Main Street Ventures grabbed the attention of some tech-sector heavy hitters: Taft, Stettinius & Hollister, Procter & Gamble, Oracle, Whittman-Hart, Compaq, Microsoft, Broadwing, Lucent, Deloitte & Touche, Fifth Third Bank, and the Greater Cincinnati Chamber of Commerce all provided substantial resources that allowed it to expand its services.

Why is this happening in Over-the-Rhine, one of the poorest neighborhoods in the city? Access to technology is one factor. Cincinnati Bell, the local telephone utility, laid fiber optic cables here and, based on proximity, it was the easiest, least costly access point.

But location isn't the whole story. The district also has a key amenity in abundance: historic architecture, with many buildings dating to the 1840s and 1860s. As urban renewal was bulldozing other parts of the city, the Over-the-Rhine district maintained its architectural integrity. Rents were also affordable, typically half the going rate in other parts of the city, Artists, bars, and restaurants had pioneered a commercial foothold on the first floors of many buildings. Main Street Ventures leased a floor in a building and advertised for resident companies. In 1991, the first two—PlanetFeedback, an on-line consumer empowerment firm, and ConnectMail, an electronic video messaging company—moved in.

The spontaneous establishment of a commercial district in a hot new market, however, didn't prompt a flood of public money and support from city council. Which isn't to say that the city council completely neglected the fledgling commercial center. "The city has done a super job with infrastructure improvements," notes George

Molinsky, an attorney with Taft, Stettinius & Hollister who is widely credited with spearheading revitalization efforts in the district. The city has invested in new sidewalks, stepped up policing, buried wiring, provided decorative lighting, and created a façade program to spiff up several neglected buildings. "This helped create an environment conducive to additional investment by the private sector," notes Molinsky.

But in terms of public outlays, that's about it. While the Digital Rhine continues to get vocal and productive support from several city council members and local pols, the city has largely taken a hands-off approach, letting the private sector lead the way.

What of the riots? They were, after all, in Over-the-Rhine, though not in the high-tech end of the neighborhood. But Los Angeles has shown that riots do not have to be a death knell for neighborhoods. South Central's population climbed to almost 1 million in the 1990s. Almost 3,000 manufacturers are still located there, employing 80,000 people.

Similarly, the early signs after the Cincinnati riots are positive in the Digital Rhine. No companies left because of the unrest, and several have actually moved in. As long as the city provides the sort of minimal infrastructure it has in the past, there s no reason the Digital Rhine—and other entrepreneurial zones—can't flourish.

Yet cities such as Cincinnati make such development more difficult by continuing to focus on white elephants rather than the basic reforms that can help generate a broad economic base. Developers complain that many building inspectors are too narrowly focused on minimizing any risk when they should be letting the market innovate and diversify. Inspectors are focused on the narrowest interpretation of the law, and many rulings are arbitrary. Many developers in Cincinnati think of this as the cost of doing business, but it makes those areas less competitive than their suburban counterparts. Red tape shouldn't be considered simply another cost.

The city requires six complete documents to get a permit, and another week to process the permit once the documents are signed. On top of that, Hamilton County requires up to an additional two weeks. Obtaining a building permit takes only two days in nearby Clarmont County. Warren County, north of Cincinnati, requires one week. Developers expect four to six weeks in the city of Cincinnati. Builders also complain of not being able to find employees to start the permit application process in the city's Department of Public Works. Building standards sometimes double the costs of laying infrastructure on properties. "As a result," notes one large homebuilder, "we have made the decision to substantially limit our building in the city to projects that are financially feasible. Unfortunately, a project in the city rarely qualifies as being financially feasible. It simply isn't worth it for us."

Housing activists have also effectively created a moratorium on new construction in Over-the-Rhine. How? By passing ordinances that require developers to pony up the equivalent of $4 per square foot for low-income housing if they want to tear down an existing house. The unintended consequence is "demolition by neglect"—property owners let their properties deteriorate to the point where inspectors have to condemn the building, allowing them to circumvent the ordinance, tear down the building, and develop the property.

No Magic Bullets

Still, some key players are trying to improve the overall business climate and move away from the big-spending, big-ticket items that have historically plagued Cincinnati's development strategy. City Council member Pat DeWine pushed through legislation that eliminated entire classes of permits for minor repairs and renovations to homes. A bigger change, however, may come when the city reforms its 38-year-old zoning code. The city did little to overhaul the code before a comprehensive review process began in 2000. The goal, says Steven Kurtz, a planner in the city's land-use management division since 1991, is to create more certainty in the process by simplifying zoning and development review. Kurtz notes that the revised code should reduce the number of zoning districts, streamline the public hearing process, and allow more varied and mixed uses. Planners hope to send a draft ordinance to the planning commission by the end of the year. These are small steps, to be sure, but important ones.

The larger lesson for Cincinnati and other cities is to look beyond a single magic bullet—the one major project or set of projects that true believers think will pull a city into great times.

The larger lesson for Cincinnati and other cities is to look beyond a single magic bullet—the one major project or set of projects that true believers think will pull a city into great times. "I tell folks in Cincinnati the same thing I tell them in other medium-sized cities," says convention center expert Sanders. "You are pursuing a strategy that is essentially imitative; at the same time you're discussing expanding your convention center, so are all other cities."

David Swindell, the Clemson political scientist, reinforces the point. "Many politicians know full well that there are no magic bullets, but getting a new neighborhood grocery store is not front page news, and it takes a lot of work to create a climate so that one will locate in a given area." In the meantime, warns Swindell, politicians chase white elephants in their downtowns. The result is that a "lot of needs go unmet—streets are slow to be paved. More attention needs to be paid to the neighborhoods because they are important to providing a quality of life that can attract people to the inner city."

The best advice for urban renewal might come from the people actually investing in the Digital Rhine. "Do an exceptional job when it comes to the basic issues that cities are responsible for, such as infrastructure," says Molinsky. "Tax incentives are nice," he continues, but entrepreneurially minded people really want to live and work in neighborhoods that are "clean, safe, affordable, interesting, and eclectic, with valuable amenities."

Whether Cincinnati and other cities can learn this lesson is not clear. But their futures are riding on it.

Sam Staley (sams@rppi.org) is director of the Urban Futures Program at the Reason Public Policy institute and co-founder of the Buckeye Institute for Public Policy Solutions, a think tank based in Columbus, Ohio. Staley has written widely on planning and land use. He recently co-edited, with Randall G. Holcombe, Smarter Growth: Market-Based Strategies for Land Use Planning in the 21st Century *(Greenwood Press).*

RETURN TO CENTER

States that moved offices and jobs out to the suburbs are moving them back downtown.

BY CHRISTOPHER D. RINGWALD

Last spring, New York's Department of Environmental Conservation moved back where it started out: downtown Albany. After 30 years in a headquarters just off Interstate 87, in the suburb of Colonie, the agency and its 1,900 employees packed up and relocated to 625 Broadway, a few blocks from the state capitol.

Not every employee is happy—most had grown accustomed to off-ramp freeway access, massive parking lots and other accoutrements of a suburban location. On the other hand, there are compensations. "I like having sidewalks to walk on," says Franz Litz, a DEC attorney, standing outside his new 14-story office building after strolling back from lunch at a nearby restaurant. "I can walk to some meetings," says one of his colleagues. "Before, I used to have to drive to all of them."

Whether they approve of it or not, however, the return to downtown Albany is a change that thousands of New York State employees will need to get used to. The DEC is only one of the agencies involved. The state's Dormitory Authority, which finances and constructs major public facilities, has moved to a five-story glass-and-granite box at 515 Broadway, down the street from DEC. The state Comptroller's office is consolidat-

ing its workforce a few blocks away. In the past five years, more than 4,500 state employees have relocated into the city's center.

None of this is a coincidence. New York's General Services Commissioner, Kenneth Ringler, puts it succinctly. "The governor," he says, "has a downtown policy."

This is not the first time that major efforts have been launched to rescue downtown Albany. During the 1960s and 1970s, Governor Nelson Rockefeller—with the strong support of Democratic Mayor Erastus Corning II—cleared 80 acres in the center of the city and built the Empire State Plaza, nine giant buildings arrayed on a marble mall with vast reflecting pools. Grandiose, windswept and impersonal, the project has always generated more critics than admirers. Still, it did serve the purpose of concentrating thousands of state workers in the vicinity of the capitol.

But as the workforce ballooned in the 1980s, little effort was made to accommodate the new growth in the center of the city. Many agencies located in the suburbs. By the early 1990s, downtown Albany was again forlorn, Empire State Plaza notwithstanding. The new governor, George Pataki, decided it was time to try again.

That in itself might seem a little surprising. Pataki did not come into office with a reputation as a urbanist—all of his prior experience had been in Peekskill, a small village in northern Westchester County, where he was mayor and served as a state legislator. But Peekskill underwent its own miniature revival in the 1990s as artists from New York were enticed by cheap studio space and old houses.

This hometown experience had its effect on Pataki. In 1998, he proposed and the legislature approved a $240 million "Albany plan," built around returning the central city to its former role as the nerve center of state government. "By moving state facilities into downtown areas and neighborhoods," Pataki said, "we can revitalize the cities that are so important to the state, and particularly the city of Albany. We are committed to Albany being not just the capital, but being a revitalized capital."

The Pataki administration is trying not to repeat the mistakes of the previous era. "It is important how we locate in downtowns," Ringler says, "and not just that we do so." Instead of bulldozing vast sections of town to build a massive complex, the state has built at modest scale at various locations within the existing downtown grid. The buildings line up along the sidewalk; the new architecture blends reasonably well with historic appearances.

No state government is currently attempting anything as ambitious as New York's, but a surprising number of them have a similar idea. In New Jersey, where much of the state workforce moved to leased suburban space during the 1980s, the departments of Human Services and Education have both moved back to downtown Trenton. Former Governor Christine Todd Whitman halted construction of a Revenue Division building in suburban Hamilton Township "because it was going to move jobs out of the city," according to Robert Runciano, the state's former director of Property Management and Construction.

Two years ago, Kentucky was ready to build a new office for its Transportation Cabinet. Many state legislators favored moving it out of the capital area in central Frankfort. The business community wanted to keep it there. Business won. Construction started last month on the new Transportation center, a five-story, $113 million downtown building that will house several hundred workers. "The construction of it has spurred a lot of other developments, new water and sewer lines and also private development," says Don Speer, commissioner of the state Department of Administration. Meanwhile, a nearby public-private project, the Sullivan Square Office Building, has consolidated state workers from scattered spots and attracted a graphics firm with 50 employees.

Alabama's capital, Montgomery, lost so many state offices to the suburbs that, as one visitor put it, the city presented the image "of these gleaming alabaster government buildings up on a hill and down below it was a desperate scene" of urban decay. It was the state pension fund for civil servants and teachers that turned the tide by building six prime office buildings, one of them 26 stories, to lease to state agencies along Commerce Street, in the heart of downtown, and on Dexter Avenue, which leads up to the capitol. "It stabilized a deteriorating and dying central business district," says Tommy Tyson, the city's director of planning. The influx of money and workers has gener-

ated new restaurants and led to the opening of two hotels.

The phenomenon exists in even the smallest state capitals. In Montpelier, Vermont (population 8,000), rented state offices on the outskirts are being moved to retrofitted state-owned buildings downtown. And a $10 million state office project is on the drawing board. "The policy is to invest in downtowns whenever renovating or building state office space," says Thomas Torti, Vermont's Building and General Services commissioner. "If you're coming to see the tax people, drop something off at motor vehicles and then check on personnel, those are all near each other now." The new facilities in Montpelier aim to stimulate other development through multi-use buildings with room for retail and commerce. A new state parking complex is slated to include offices and housing.

In New York's case, the Albany plan is more complicated than just a one-way return to the city. It is actually a game of musical buildings. While some agencies head back downtown, others are being shuffled around to take advantage of the space being vacated. The Transportation Department will occupy the offices that the Department of Environmental Protection has given up. The Depression-era Alfred E. Smith building, an ornate downtown landmark badly in need of renovation, is being fixed up to house workers coming in from the 350-acre Harriman campus, built in the 1960s on the outskirts of the city. The state has yet to decide whether the 16 Harriman buildings will be sold to private developers. By preliminary estimates, the plan could save at least $86 million in renovation costs and recoup millions more from sales.

Albany is not the only city in the area benefiting from the urban commitment. Across the Hudson, in tiny, blue-collar Rensselaer, the state's Office of Children and Family Services consolidated its workers, previously spread across various sites, into a renovated felt factory. Ten miles upriver in Troy, the state restored two historic structures and a defunct mall and moved in more than 1,000 workers from the Health, Labor and Law

departments. About 20 miles west, Schenectady, already home to the headquarters of the state lottery, is gaining 450 Department of Transportation workers and a new office building. In distant Buffalo, an old windshield wiper factory was remodeled to create 60,000 square feet of space for the New York State Office of Temporary Disability Assistance and other tenants. "The local mayors are ecstatic," says Ringler, the General Services administrator.

Not everyone is on board. Critics trace the Troy moves to log-rolling, saying that these came at the behest of Joseph Bruno, the Senate majority leader who represents Troy. Others challenge the deal between Pataki and Jerry Jennings, the Democratic mayor of Albany, that led to the ongoing $11 million reconstruction of Pearl Street, the city's downtown backbone.

And there are those who complain that the Albany Plan relies too heavily on the buildings themselves, rather than on the less tangible investments needed for urban recovery. "State workers are downtown, and that's more people downtown," says Paul Bray, a local planning and environmental attorney and founder of a monthly civic forum, the Albany Roundtable. "But building a city is a much more nuanced, complex thing than moving offices."

Bray wants the state to provide incentives for its employees to live downtown, as well as work there, so that the city's core no longer will empty out after the work day. Critics also say the money spent on construction of bulky parking garages for each new building—a feature demanded by public employee unions—could have been used for improved bus lines or other alternatives to the automobile. "Cities make poor suburbs," Bray says. "You really need to concentrate on mass transit more than parking garages."

In truth, no one can guarantee that the return of state government to any downtown will generate a local economic revival. The sidewalks of downtown Troy, a treasure-trove of 19th-century buildings, are busier since the civil servants began arriving in 1995. But Mayor

Mark Pattison warns his counterparts in New York and elsewhere not to expect new government offices to work miracles. "They are not causing the economic boom that people thought they might," Pattison told a local newspaper reporter earlier this year. "The myth of the state worker is that they don't work hard. In fact, they have just a half-hour for lunch, and when they're done working, they go back home to the family and kids just like we all do. They bring a little bit of additional business but not quite the amount we expected."

Meanwhile, at the Stagecoach coffee and sandwich shop in downtown Albany, just across the park from the new Environmental Conservation building, a longtime employee concedes it is taking a while for the relocated workers to reorient themselves to city life. "It's been good for business, but not as great as we expected," she said last fall. "They complain because there's no mall to go to, they don't have enough shops to go to. A lot of them get an hour for lunch, and they don't know what to do with themselves."

But some of the restaurant's employees have been working longer hours since the Environmental Conservation building opened. And a couple of blocks away, the owners of Lodge's, a small department store dating back to the 1800s, are renovating four long-empty storefronts for interested retail and commercial tenants.

Whatever the economic impact turns out to be, long-suffering downtown Albany seems convinced that the plan will have been worth the effort, and the cost—if only for reasons of simple logic. "It's the capital," says Chungchin Chen, executive director of the Capital District Regional Planning Commission. "The agencies are supposed to be there— instead of dispersed in the suburbs."

New village on campus

A college town rises from the dust of Maxwell Street

Tribune photo by John Handley

A workman surveys the University Village construction site from the sixth floor of a loft building, one of the residential components of the 930-unit project.

By John Handley
Tribune staff reporter

The sizzle is gone.

Jim's hot dog stand at the corner of Halsted and Maxwell Streets is history.

Jim's place, founded in 1939, and most of the old buildings of Chicago's famous Maxwell Street market have been torn down to make way for a new "village." Rising from the dust and demolition is a new neighborhood just south of the University of Illinois at Chicago (UIC) on the Near West Side.

Now the sounds of construction resonate where old-time blues musicians—including the great Muddy Waters—used to play.

Preservationists fought to save the look of historic Maxwell Street, and they partly succeeded. The facades of 21 old buildings will be incorporated into the new development.

Even Jim's hot dog stand—now temporarily at Union and O'Brien Streets—will reappear near its original location.

The master plan for University Village calls for the 68-acre site to be developed with a mix of townhouses, midrise residences, dormitories, academic buildings, shops, restaurants, parking facilities and parks. Motorists driving the Dan Ryan Expressway have only to look west to view the construction. The property is along both sides of Halsted Street south of Roosevelt Road.

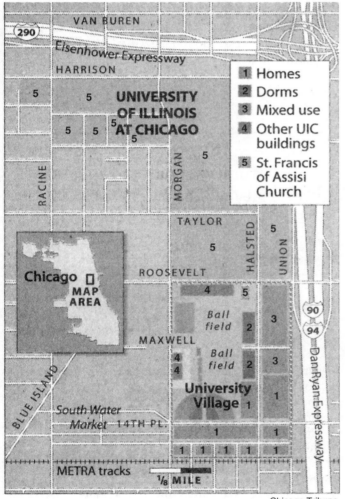

Chicago Tribune

Until building started, most of the land was vacant parking lots. The only people displaced were living in a battered school bus parked on Maxwell Street.

University Village is the name of the $700 million South Campus expansion at UIC, its largest construction project since the Circle Campus was built in 1965 and became UIC in 1982.

The university assembled the land just south of its 250-acre campus. Now the project is being built by the South Campus Development Team, a joint venture of Mesirow Stein Real Estate Inc., Harlem Irving Cos. and New Frontier Cos.

Residents of the new village will live in 930 units and two dorms for 755 students. Offering a college ambience, the for-sale residences are priced from $165,900 to $699,900. An agreement with the city calls for 21 percent of the units to be in the "affordable" range.

Projected for completion in 2005, University Village will have an estimated population of 2,000 at that time.

"The goal is to make this a 24-hour campus and enhance the social environment," said Mark Rosati, associate chancellor for public affairs at UIC.

Robinson Hall, the first new student dormitory in UIC's South Campus expansion, has a grassy interior courtyard. It opened last August with space for 340 students.

Known as a commuter college, UIC has just 11 percent of its 25,000 students living on campus. New dorms are projected to raise that to 25 percent by 2012, according to Rosati.

"There's a great demand for student housing. We have 800 on a waiting list," he said. The massive South Campus development also is intended to elevate the image of UIC. "This is a rising academic powerhouse," said Rosati.

"University Village is a new neighborhood, not a housing development," said Richard Stein, president of Mesirow Stein Real Estate. "It will tie together two existing neighborhoods—Pilsen to the south and Little Italy to the north."

A few residents already have moved into townhouses along 14th Place. The first new dorm opened last August.

Two buyers at University Village, Howard and Arden Powers, moved a month ago from Chinatown to a three-story, three-bedroom townhouse, which, they say, offers "incredible" views of the Loop's skyscraper skyline, a seven-minute drive away. Both are real estate attorneys working in the West Loop.

"We live in a construction zone, but you have to be flexible because buying early means we'll benefit from increased value later," said Arden. She added that property values near schools always maintain their value.

Green space at University Village covers more than 43 percent of the land, but the bulk of that is accounted for by university playing fields. Pocket parks will dot the new residential areas, and Gateway Park, with a water feature, will be built at Halsted and Roosevelt.

One of the last remaining buildings on Maxwell Street is slated for demolition, to make way for a parking garage and a streetscape that will resemble the look of the past.

Though University Village will be mostly new construction, reminders of the past will survive. Eight of the old storefronts along the east side of Halsted will be rehabbed and become a part of the 120,000 square feet of retail space in the new development.

Tribune file photo

Maxwell Street market as it appeared in March 1964. Facades of 21 buildings from the market will be saved and used in the development.

"Also, 13 facades of vintage buildings in the area that were deemed architecturally interesting were taken down and stored," said Larry Justice, project executive of the South Campus Development Team. "They will be attached to the front of the new parking facility to be built on both sides of Maxwell Street."

Adding to the flavor of this re-created streetscape will be first-floor shops and restaurants. Harkening back to yesteryear, live entertainment may return to the area.

"It will have a student character, with bookstores and coffee houses," Justice said.

A brick and limestone arch over Maxwell will be flanked by towers of the same material. A museum will commemorate the street's history.

The first stores are scheduled to open in May on the west side of Halsted.

The South Campus project is being financed in part by a tax increment financing (TIF) district approved by the Chicago City Council in 1999.

On the residential front, the new brick homes are certainly a cut above the modest frame houses that newly arrived immigrants lived in [in] this area around the turn of the 19th Century.

The architects of University Village—Roy Kruse, Papageorge & Haymes Ltd. and FitzGerald Associates—say they patterned the buildings after vintage Chicago styles.

The housing mix will include 186 lofts, 226 midrise condos in elevator buildings, 234 walkup condos and 284 townhouses.

New townhouses already are completed on 14th Place at University Village. The residential mix calls for the construction of 284 town-houses in the 930-unit development.

Condos will have one to three bedrooms with 796 to 1,866 square feet of living area with base prices from $165,900 to $513,900.

One- and two-bedroom lofts with 847 to 1,710 square feet are $182,900 to $461,900. Penthouses, some with three bedrooms, are $396,900 to $461,900.

The three-bedroom townhouses, with 2,154 to 3,000 square feet, range from $437,900 to $699,900.

Townhouses and condos are under construction, while two eight-story industrial loft buildings at the south end of the property are being converted to residences. Foundations have been laid for two additional eight-story buildings, which back up to the Metra tracks.

To date, more than 400 units have been sold, according to Terry Whitaker, a partner in New West Realty, the marketing agent for the homes.

A sales center is located at 1440 S. Halsted St.

Set aside in an "affordable" category (based on family income) are 21 percent of total units, or 196 homes. One- to three-bedroom "affordable" condos in the first phase were priced from $143,000 to $237,000, according to Whitaker.

While only 12 percent of buyers so far have been UIC faculty or staff, Rosati believes that number will rise to 15 to 20 percent.

Ken Brezinsky, professor of chemical engineering at UIC, has moved into a three-story townhouse with two bedrooms and a den.

"I wanted to be part of the new university development," he explained. "Now it's like living on the frontier, on the prairie, with civilization in the distance."

Brezinsky called the new development "exciting, better than I had envisioned."

Despite the proximity to the campus, he still drives to work. His commuting time is about the same as from his previous residence at Presidential Towers on West Madison Street.

UIC students moved into the first dorm, Robinson Hall, last summer. It houses 340 students.

Construction has begun on Beckham Hall, the second dorm. The $47.5 million structure is scheduled to open in June 2003. It will accommodate 415 students, who will pay $6,058 each to live there for an academic year.

Construction of two large academic buildings will start in 2004, according to Rosati.

The university has come a long way since its birth in 1946 as a two-year college at Navy Pier mainly catering to returning World War II veterans. But Navy Pier wasn't large enough, so the Circle Campus was built in 1965 on the Near West Side.

Now, as the South Campus development progresses, the question is whether there can be any future expansion for University Village.

One possible direction is toward the southwest, site of the 16-acre South Water Market. The wholesale produce market is relocating, and the site could become available.

"Over time, it is likely that the South Water Market will be developed for housing," Justice, the South Campus project executive, said. "But now we are staying focused on the mission of completing University Village."

From *Chicago Tribune,* April 28, 2002. © 2002 by the Chicago Tribune. Reprinted by permission.

The Fall and Rise of Bryant Park

By JULIA VITULLO-MARTIN

Shrewd developers often name their buildings for their neighborhood's most attractive asset. In this tradition, the Durst Organization recently announced that it was conferring the address of One Bryant Park on its flashy new Midtown tower, whose major tenant will be the Bank of America. On an average day in good weather, lovely, crime-free Bryant Park is wildly popular, drawing some 5,300 visitors at midday, or 900 people an acre. It is almost surely the most used urban open space in the world, exceeding even St. Mark's in Venice. The New York Times calls it "Manhattan's town square."

Yet associating any new building with Bryant Park would have been unthinkable just 20 years ago — akin to naming a building One Needle Park, which would pretty well summarize the drug den that was then Bryant Park. I remember this well because the Citizens Housing and Planning Council, my former employer, had offices on West 40th Street, Bryant Park's southern boundary. We had ringside seats for the sordid dealing and using that went on openly in the park, nestled behind the New York Public Library.

Entrepreneur Michael Fuchs, who was the first chairman of HBO, which was headquartered across the park on West 42nd Street, also remembers those days well. "It was the Wild West down there," he recalled recently. We had all come from uptown — Rockefeller Center, a good neighborhood. The Bryant Park area was so bad that people had no reason to go out. We developed a philosophy that we would make the HBO building self-sufficient, with a great cafeteria, gym, screenings, whatever people needed."

In retrospect, it may be hard to grasp that city government actually permitted the ongoing, daily degradation of such a magnificent asset. After all, the city-owned Bryant Park wasn't hidden in some obscure corner, far away from official eyes. It's been right there since the mid-19th century. It sits squarely in the middle of Midtown, surrounded by world-renowned landmarks. For example, the gorgeous Beaux-Arts New York Public Library, which opened in 1911 and uses two acres of Bryant Park, was designed by Carrère & Hastings. Raymond Hood's 1924 neo-Gothic American Radiator building, on West 40th Street, now the Bryant Park Hotel, is regarded by many architects as the finest building in New York.

The Beaux-Arts Bryant Park Studios Building, which opened in 1901, was built for a New York artist who had just returned from Paris, bringing with him the French emphasis on natural northern light. He commissioned lavish double-height workshop/residential studios with huge windows to capture the unobstructed light from Bryant Park. Yet in 1979, things were such a mess that the eminent urbanist, William Whyte, wrote about Bryant Park, "If you went out and hired the dope dealers, you couldn't get a more villainous crew to show the urgency of the situation."

Bryant Park had 150 reported robberies and 10 rapes annually, countless auto break-ins on the periphery, and a murder every other year. As a public park it was so mismanaged that it held down the property values of the surrounding neighborhood.

Today Bryant Park pumps up property values. Bank of America Senior Vice President John Saclarides says about the new tower, "Because of Bryant Park, we anticipate great employee happiness with our site. We think our employees will use the park for visitation, for reading, and for a remote office at lunch time." (The park now has free wireless fidelity Web access, known as "wi fi.") What happened?

In 1980 a group of civic-minded New Yorkers, property owners, and neighbors decided to rescue the park, and set up the Bryant Park Restoration Corporation. They spent seven years negotiating with the New York City Department of Parks and Recreation before they succeeded in getting a 15-year lease, which began in 1988. (The lease was subsequently renewed for another five years.) The BPRC immediately closed the park for five years of rebuilding.

The old design — a formal French garden — had dated from 1934, when Parks Commissioner Robert Moses, New York's master of public works, decided to elevate and isolate the park above the sidewalk. Instead of making

Bryant Park an elegant respite from the congestion of midtown as intended, the isolationist design deterred desirable users while attracting undesirable users.

The new BPRC design aimed to re-people the park while raising revenues to pay for the expensive planned maintenance of several million dollars annually — far more than the city spent. The designers cut new entrances, tore down the iron fencing, ripped out high hedges, restored the fixtures, and added neoclassical kiosks for concessions.

Fixed benches were replaced with some 3,200 movable, pretty French chairs and 500 tables, providing what Mr. Biederman calls "freemarket seating." The park's Upper Terrace, which had been its most active drug market, was leased to the trendy Bryant Park Grill, which became an instant hot spot.

High standards of behavior are enforced by the security officers, whom Mr. Biederman calls "friendly but firm." They deter "little pieces of disorder," as Mr. Biederman calls misdemeanors. The old laissez-faire attitude toward disruptive be-havior is gone. Neighboring business people and property owners are overjoyed.

The chairman of Mountain Development Corporation, which owns the now-landmarked Bryant Park Studios, Robert Lieb, recalled that crime was so bad in 1980 that his building could only be marketed by promising strong private security." The park should have been a positive for us, but the drug dealing and crime made it a negative," he said.

Today, he says, his company doesn't even have to work to rent space. "Our tenants, boutique designers, and manufacturers who specialize in sales to stores like Barney's and Nordstrom's, want to be on the park." Tenants include hip designers like Theory and Angel Zimick.

"Bryant Park proves that if you build something beautiful that people can enjoy," Mr. Lieb said. "They will pay a premium price to be there." And, indeed, rents soared to the mid-50s today from $14 a square foot in 1980.

Perhaps best of all, taxpayers aren't footing the bill for the park's $4 million annual budget, which is all privately raised. While $5 million of the $18 million spent on capital improvements came from public funds, no public money has been spent on the park since 1996. It may well be the only urban park in the world supported by neither government nor charitable funds.

"Because this park is integral to the functioning of Midtown, we ask commercial interests and users to pay for it," Mr. Biederman said.

Bryant Park's successful privatization is a tribute to a selfless innovation by the public sector — permitting the private sector to step in with resources and operational skills to restore and manage a splendid public space. Most public officials wouldn't have had the courage to let the private sector take over.

New York taxpayers owe heartfelt thanks to the four mayors, beginning with Edward Koch, and the four parks commissioners, finishing with Adrian Benepe, who made this happen.

Ms. Vitullo-Martin is a senior fellow at the Manhattan Institute .

CULTURE CLUB

Investments in Kansas City's arts and cultural community demonstrate confidence and commitment for the future.

MIKE SHERIDAN

On a vacant hillside south of Kansas City's convention center, work is beginning on one of the city's cultural crown jewels—the $300 million Metropolitan Kansas City Performing Arts Center (PAC). Designed by architect Moshe Safdie—who has helped transform urban areas internationally from Canada to Jerusalem to Wichita—the new facility is expected to turn the hilltop into a civic landmark when it opens in 2006. Kansas City Mayor Kay Barnes has called the center the anchor of SoLo, her $1.8 billion plan to revitalize the South Loop area of downtown. The center, located on 17.5 acres at Broadway and 16th Street, is expected to redefine Kansas City's cultural life for the 21st century and serve as a year-round educational complex, making the arts available to everyone. More important, the project is expected to stimulate further downtown development, providing an additional amenity to woo companies and their employees and conventions to the area.

Expansion of the Nelson-Atkins Museum of Art will make the facility one of Kansas City's foremost cultural attractions.

The Metropolitan Kansas City Performing Arts Center is the latest in an impressive series of arts and cultural projects undertaken in the region over the past several years. Nearly $1 billion in arts and cultural projects are either planned, underway, or have been completed, officials estimate. The construction agenda will require a hefty investment for a city the size of Kansas City, and the impact is already being felt. Culturally, the city's assets are increasing and becoming more visible within the community, say residents, who emphasize that citizens have given generously to aid in these endeavors. These investments are big business and already are helping to shape real estate investment, urban design, and planning decisions across the region. Among the arts and cultural expansions and redevelopments are:

- The Nelson-Atkins Museum of Art—with 28,000 works of art, one of the most distinguished art museums between the Great Lakes and the Pacific Ocean—has begun construction on a $133.5 million, 150,000-square-foot expansion. To be named the Henry W. and Marion H. Bloch Gallery of Art for museum trustee and well-known area philanthropist Bloch and his wife, the new building will occupy mostly underground space, topped by five luminous glass boxes that will dot the landscape and diffuse natural light into the art galleries below. Designed by internationally known architect Steven Holl, the structure is slated to open in late 2005. To date, the Nelson-Atkins Museum has raised more than $200 million for expansion, renovation, and program endowments, including increased educational outreach.

- Liberty Memorial, the only World War I memorial in the nation, will reopen in May following an extensive $100 million renovation. Dedicated in 1926 (President Calvin Coolidge attended the ceremony when the cornerstone was laid two years earlier), the Egyptian Revival–style edifice was closed to the public in 1994 because of structural damage.

- The Kansas City Public Library is renovating the old First National Bank Building at Tenth Street and Baltimore in a $46.7 million project that includes rehabilitation of 170,000 square feet of space and construction of a 450-vehicle parking garage west of the building. New libraries lure people into the downtown area, say developers, who applaud the adaptive use of a grand and historical building at the heart of the city.

- The Truman Presidential Museum & Library in nearby Independence has undergone a $22.5 million renovation that includes expanded educational programs and a new permanent exhibit on the Truman presidency featuring a highly interactive exhibit. Nearly $12.5 million of the funding came from private contributions, $8 million in federal funds through the National Archives and Records Administration (NARA), and $2 million from the state of Missouri.

- The Starlight Theater in Swope Park—one of Kansas City's favorite summertime spots—has completed a $10 million, 12,000-square-foot renovation that resulted in a new air-conditioned, ten-story covered stage. Careful planning by the architects ensured that the new construction blended in with the existing pair of brick towers that have become a symbol of the Starlight. The stage will be named the Jeannette and Jerome Cohen Community Stage after the

pair who donated more than $1 million for the project.

- Penn Valley Community College is building the $5 million Anna & Kemper Carter Center for Visual Arts and Imaging Technology, which will more than double the college's visual arts facilities. Slated for completion in spring 2003, the 25,000-square-foot structure will comprise a new ceramics lab, a gallery and exhibit area, and photography labs and other amenities. Says Jackie Snyder, president of the college: "This will be a signature piece for our campus architecturally. We have always had a great faculty and a wonderful art program, and now we will have the building to match our program. It will also be a tremendous addition to the art community in the midtown areas."

- The new Belger Art Center at the University of Missouri at Kansas City will, according to donor Dick Belger, house the Belger family collection of contemporary art in the former Midwest Motor Freight building on Volker Boulevard and Brookside Boulevard. The 39,000-square-foot space is expected to take several years to complete and will include studio, demonstration, and various gallery spaces to encourage the creative process.

- The city's once crumbling monument to the "good old days"—Union Station—has undergone a $250 million restoration, described as the largest historic building renovation in Kansas City. It now includes Science City, a youth-oriented technology center.

- The Folly Theater, known for its jazz series and its children's theater productions, completed a $2 million renovation last summer in time for its centennial season.

"It is an exciting time to be a resident of Kansas City and to be part of the arts community," says Albert Kerr, principal of Walter P. Moore's Kansas City office. "For many years to come, people will be enjoying the

craftsmanship and functionality of the buildings that are growing up around the metropolitan area. You don't have to be an art lover to appreciate the beauty of the facilities and the skill it takes to design them."

The Arts as Big Business

Arts and cultural activities in Kansas City are important not only to art aficionados but also to businesses and companies seeking to recruit a talented workforce to the area. The area's chances of attracting and retaining top businesses improve as quality-of-life issues become increasingly important in corporate decisions on where employees will live and work, officials say. Cultural and artistic attractions become significant when more highly educated employees are being recruited.

Designed by Steven Holl, the Nelson-Atkins addition will consist of underground space topped by five glass boxes that diffuse light to the galleries below.

Bob Marcusse, president and CEO of the Kansas City Area Development Council (KCADC), says that because Kansas City has a vibrant economy and low unemployment, the region has set a goal of attracting not just any jobs but the best possible jobs to the metropolitan area. "That means headquarters jobs, research and development jobs, and jobs in certain high-skilled technical fields," Marcusse continues. "All of those jobs are in demand everywhere. Consequently, companies now look beyond the job to the community where the job would be located." Clearly, this means the selected community must offer an excellent educational system, sports, recreational facilities, and increasingly, cultural arts.

A vibrant arts and cultural scene is essential if Kansas City is to attract the best and the brightest, Marcusse says. "That's one of the reasons this community is focusing on an already strong arts sector," he says. "You build on your strengths, and an appreciation of the arts is something that permeates the community. We have been blessed with philanthropists who selected the arts for their various forms of philanthropy."

And, being corporate chiefs, most philanthropists understand that the arts themselves could become big business—something that is especially true in Kansas City. The Kansas City metropolitan area offers a wide variety of arts and cultural amenities, including internationally renowned fine and modern art museums, historic performing arts theaters, scenic amphitheaters, fine and modern art programs at area universities, and more than 375 arts organizations.

> **The Kansas City metropolitan area offers a wide variety of arts and cultural amenities, including internationally renowned fine and modern art museums, historic performing arts theaters, scenic amphitheaters, fine and modern art programs at area universities, and more than 375 arts organizations.**

Accordingly, cultural organizations have become a powerful economic and social force within the greater Kansas City community. In addition to employing some 4,500 people—which, if taken in the aggregate, places the cultural arts industry among the metropolitan area's top ten employers—Kansas City's arts and culture industry helps increase regional employment, contributes significant tax dollars to the economy, strengthens the business climate, and enhances the overall quality of life.

Last year, an economic study by the Denver office of Deloitte & Touche painted a robust picture of the local arts scene, noting that Kansas City's top cultural organizations in 2001 attracted a bigger audience than did the Kansas City Chiefs football team and the Kansas City Royals baseball team, generated revenues equal to those of Vanguard Airlines, and employed as many people locally as did Southwestern Bell.

The $280 million in spending generated by the arts in Kansas City amounts to about $160 per resident more than spending generated by the arts in a number of cities of comparable size, including Atlanta, Denver, and Portland. Joan Israelite, president and CEO of the Arts Council of Metropolitan Kansas City, calls the study an eye opener: "There wasn't an understanding before that the arts are an important component of our economy."

The Arts as Good Business

One characteristic of a great city is that it contains a vibrant arts and cultural community, adds David Oliver, a partner in the Kansas City law firm of Berkowitz, Feldmiller, Stanton, Brandt, Williams & Shaw LLP, who is chairman of the Business Committee for the Arts. "It is good for business and good for the community," he asserts. "In recent years, our Civic Council and the Chamber of Commerce have recognized that the arts play an important role in economic development. I attribute much of this awareness to the efforts of leaders in the arts, who continually visit with business and civic leaders."

With the new construction and renovations, Oliver believes Kansas City is poised to make a quantum leap in the cultural arts. He notes that the Nelson-Atkins was built a generation ago, as were most of the area's performance halls. "We have been fairly successful at saving some old theaters, but we also lost a good number of them with the decline of our downtown," he observes. "There is a great deal of effort now being put into revitalizing our downtown. It is a huge project, but the area needs a hub, and arts and culture help create that hub."

Kansas Citians proudly point to the Metropolitan Kansas City Performing Arts Center, a world-class attraction. The 400,000-square-foot center will house a 1,800-seat concert hall and a 1,900-seat theater. It will be home to the Kansas City Ballet, the Kansas City Symphony, the Lyric Opera, and productions by other organizations, most likely including Broadway shows.

> **The Anna & Kemper Carter Center will more than double Penn Valley Community College's visual arts facilities.**

Officials note that the PAC and the Nelson-Atkins Museum of Art's expansion will be the foremost attractions in the city's cultural landscape. Adds Israelite: "They will be the catalysts for raising our region's cultural vitality to another level."

> **Kansas City's cultural landscape is expanding community assets and an appreciation for the arts.**

Plans to expand the Nelson-Atkins Museum of Art were in the works for nearly eight years, notes Marc F. Wilson, director/chief executive officer of the museum. "This new building is the embodiment of the will of the community. Our long planning effort was designed to achieve that will in quantifiable steps through a rigorous process that tested proposals against dreams." Kansas City residents point out that the arts have always played a big role in the city. ULI trustee Jeannette

Nichols notes that Kansas City historically has focused on cultural development. "We have been blessed with visionary leaders, who celebrate our city and want to share it with others. Throughout the years, they have helped support a strong arts community."

There are many reasons why investments in art and culture are good for real estate and other industries, notes Steve McDowell of the Kansas City office of BNIM Architects. Expansion in arts and cultural facilities almost always ensures that cultural assets and appreciation grow within the community, he says. Because children gain from exposure to and knowledge of music and art, it helps them develop intellectual and creative thinking abilities that better prepare them for life in many ways. "Investments in major institutions can make them magnets for other types of development," says McDowell, "helping to establish confidence in the real estate market, land use, valuation, tax base, and so forth. Investments like these are healthy for the community because they demonstrate confidence and commitment for the future."

For decades, many routes across the United States have led to Kansas City—the center of the country—giving the city a distinct advantage in commerce. Now, more than 200 years after explorers Meriwether Lewis and George Rogers Clark stood on a rocky bluff deep in the American wilderness and gazed down at what would eventually become Kansas City, arts and culture are becoming the city's gateway. And that, civic and cultural leaders in Kansas City will tell you, is simply good business.

MIKE SHERIDAN IS A HOUSTON-BASED FINANCIAL JOURNALIST.

midwestern *momentum*

Momentum for urban redevelopment
is building as cities across the Midwest
move forward with revitalization plans
already set in motion.

BETH MATTSON-TEIG

From Chicago to St. Louis, midwestern cities nowadays have one thing in common—an aggressive pursuit of urban redevelopment. Old warehouses are turning into trendy lofts, parking lots are giving way to office towers, and brownfields are becoming ballparks. "Revitalization opportunities exist in many of these midwestern cities," says Ron Flies, vice president of project management at the Detroit Economic Growth Corporation, the municipal redevelopment agency. Detroit is in the early stages of redeveloping a five-block area that is anticipated to generate more than $2 billion in new development.

The urban revival sweeping the midwest has been a long time coming. The 1970s and 1980s were marked by an exodus of residents and businesses that fled downtowns in exchange for homes in the suburbs. A rebounding economy in the mid-1990s, however, created both means and opportunities for cities to breathe new life into their floundering neighborhoods and business districts. Despite the recent economic downturn, momentum for urban redevelopment is building as cities move forward with revitalization plans already set in motion.

The primary objective of major midwestern cities is to create a 24-hour environment with a balance of commercial and entertainment components, as well as a strong residential base. "More and more downtowns are becoming entertainment areas and not just office areas," says Maureen Pero, president of the Downtown Dayton Partnership, the strategic planning and management organization for downtown Dayton, Ohio. The municipality has a three-pronged approach to revitalizing its downtown that encompasses the growth of job, housing, and entertainment opportunities, she says.

Recent Dayton success stories include the $23 million Fifth Third Field, a minor league baseball stadium, which opened in 2000 and is home to the Dayton Dragons. The first phase of the city's new $21.7 million riverfront park, RiverScape, opened in May 2001 and features an outdoor aviation museum walk that tells the story of Dayton's contribution to aviation innovation. Other major projects underway include a $130 million performing arts center that is scheduled to open in March 2003.

The first phase of the city's new $21.7 million riverfront park, RiverScape, opened in May 2001 and features an outdoor aviation museum walk that tells the story of Dayton's contribution to aviation innovation.

The return of businesses and residents to urban centers is the intended result of cities' economic development initiatives. "I think there is an interest in coming back downtown," says John McLinden, a partner at Chicago-based Centrum Properties Inc. As of late, the city of Chicago has experienced a surge in demand for downtown housing from an eclectic group of people ranging from empty nesters to recent college graduates, he notes. McLinden's firm and New York–based Angelo, Gordon & Company are in the midst of creating Kingsbury Park, a new residential redevelopment in Chicago's River North neighborhood.

The Clarian Metrorail project will connect three hospitals in Indianapolis.

Bringing complex urban revitalization projects to fruition, however, is no easy task. Downtown communities present challenges in areas such as transportation, safety, and land assembly. As a result, cities are taking note of the successes—and failures—of their midwestern neighbors. Each municipality has different cultural, economic, and political characteristics, notes Flies of Detroit Economic Growth Corporation. But cities can learn from each other and gain a better understanding of the revitalization process, he adds.

Exemplary Indianapolis

Cities across the country have looked to Indianapolis as a model of urban revitalization. In the 1990s alone, the city invested $3 billion of public and private funds in downtown projects. "We now are a very competitive entertainment destination and premier office center," says Tamara Zahn, president of Indianapolis Downtown Inc.

Major projects in recent years include the new $175 million Conseco Fieldhouse, which is home to the NBA's Indiana Pacers and the WNBA's Indiana Fever. The National Collegiate Athletic Association opened its $50 million headquarters and Hall of Champions in downtown's White River State Park in 1999. During the same year, Emmis Communications Corporation, a diversified media company, built its $32 million headquarters on the city's Monument Circle, while the Indiana Historical Society opened a new $35.7 million headquarters on the Downtown Canal.

Indianapolis's development momentum continues, with 66 projects totaling $1.4 billion that either are planned or are under construction. Major facilities include the Indiana State Museum, scheduled to open in May in White River State Park. Indianapolis also has experienced tremendous growth in life

sciences due to projects such as the expansion of Eli Lilly's headquarters, Clarian Hospital, and Indiana University School of Medicine.

"The goal that we currently are working on is creating new residential opportunities," Zahn says. Twenty of the 66 projects planned or underway are residential developments, which account for about $209 million in new investment. "The other opportunity that we are very excited about in downtown is the old Market Square Arena," she says. The arena was torn down after the new Conseco Fieldhouse opened in 1999. The four-acre parcel presents an ideal redevelopment opportunity in the heart of downtown. The site is expected to accommodate a mixed-use development with a strong residential component, and the city plans to put out requests for proposals late this year or in early 2003, Zahn notes.

Active in Omaha

Nebraska's largest city is experiencing a phenomenal level of redevelopment. "There is so much momentum that it is a terribly exciting time in downtown Omaha and along the riverfront," says Jay Noddle, chairman of Pacific Realty/Grubb & Ellis in that city. Omaha has established a 422-acre redevelopment site in and around the former Union Pacific rail yards. The most significant project underway is a new $291 million convention center and sports facility that is set to open in late 2003. In addition, the 33-block area surrounding the convention center has an estimated $1 billion in construction projects proposed over the next decade.

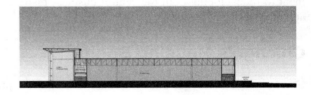

The most significant project underway in Omaha is a new $291 million convention center and sports facility that is set to open in late 2003.

One project that has helped to spark development activity is a 42-floor headquarters for First National Bank. Construction on the new office tower is scheduled for completion in the fourth quarter of 2002. Development activity has snowballed since the bank committed to remain downtown, Noddle says. Its chairman, recognizing the impact that NationsBank has had on Charlotte, North Carolina, realized that First National could have a similar impact on downtown Omaha, he adds.

Among the corporations to follow First National's lead is the New Jersey–based Gallup Organization, which is proceeding with plans for a 112-acre riverfront redevelopment project that includes its own operational headquarters on 65 acres. The first phase of the project is Gallup University, a 300,000-square-foot training facility slated for completion by October 2003. The site also will accommodate an 80,000-square-foot regional headquarters for the National Park Service that is expected to open by early 2004.

The Union Pacific Railroad Company has started site work for its 1.4 million-square-foot headquarters. In conjunction with that, the city is building a 1,400-space parking facility. Meanwhile, at least eight housing projects comprising 25 to 150 units each have commenced, Noddle says. Plans also are underway to build an elementary school that would serve the growing downtown residential base.

Two new hotels—a Hilton Garden and a Marriott Courtyard—have already opened, and the convention center is expected to attract additional hotel development. In addition, the Omaha Performing Arts Society recently formed with the objective of building a new $100 million performing arts center. The project currently is in the site selection phase.

Considering the city's relatively small population of 390,000, the amount of current activity is staggering. "One of the things that makes all this work in Omaha is that we have a very generous and extremely philanthropic business community," Noddle says. Local businesses, as well as individuals, contributed tens of millions of dollars in private money to get the projects started and to create true public/private partnerships, he says. The city administration also has a strong commitment to redeveloping both the central business district (CBD) and the riverfront, he adds.

Chicago's Housing Boom

Chicago has numerous successful redevelopment projects under its belt. A notable one currently underway is the 31-acre Kingsbury Park, which will undergo phased construction and is to be fully developed within the next five years. A group led by Centrum Properties and Angelo, Gordon & Company is transforming the former Montgomery Ward headquarters and catalog warehouse into a new residential neighborhood.

In Chicago, the development of Kingsbury Park involves the conversion of an old, vacant property into vibrant riverfront real estate.

The master plan calls for 2,000 to 2,500 residential units, a riverwalk, a marina, restaurants, bars, retail uses, and 1.5 million square feet of commercial office space. "Strategically, it is a significant development for the city simply because of its size," says Centrum's McLinden. The project investment will total approximately $1 billion when it is fully built out.

Kingsbury Park is located in the River North neighborhood, a vibrant area that is home to young professionals, as well as galleries, restaurants, and commercial space. The project is strategically located six blocks from Michigan Avenue and six blocks from the Loop. The master plan encompasses a variety of different housing types ranging in price from $170,000 to $3 million. Twelve subprojects feature residences such as lofts and single-family homes.

The development of Kingsbury Park involves the conversion of an old, vacant property into vibrant riverfront real estate. Restaurants and cafés will be developed along the half-mile stretch of the riverwalk. The project also will have a variety of boat slips at its marina, as well as space for kayaks and canoes.

Downtown Detroit

The multiphase Campus Martius development is expected to have a significant impact on Detroit's CBD. "It is envisioned as a rebirth or a rekindling of development at the commercial heart of the city, where the office area meets the retail spine of Woodward Avenue," says Flies.

The 2.5 million-square-foot, mixed-use development will house office and retail space, entertainment, and parking on five blocks—Crowley, Hudson, Kerns, Kennedy, and Monroe. The focal point of the $2 billion development will be the two-acre Campus Martius Park at the junction of Woodward, Michigan, and Monroe avenues.

The vision for creating a downtown hub dates back to the 1805 city plan adopted by the Michigan Territory. The city incorporated the same idea in its current Campus Martius master plan. Community, business, and civic leaders worked together in 1998 to develop a strategy for revitalizing the CBD. "The plan envisioned trying to develop an attraction at the heart of downtown that would lead people to redevelop office space," Flies says.

The two-acre Campus Martius Park will serve as the centerpiece of the redevelopment area, where the city has been slowly acquiring land since the 1960s. Compuware, a software and service firm, already has snapped up two blocks for its headquarters, which currently is under construction. The 1.1 million-square-foot first phase is expected to be completed by early 2003. The headquarters will feature a 2,200-stall parking garage, and there is room for a 320,000-square-foot second phase.

Detroit-based Kern Woodward Associates LLC has landed a deal with the city to develop the remaining three blocks—Hudson, Monroe, and Kennedy. The group is a partnership of local firms including Schostak Brothers & Company, Sterling Group, and Melvin Butch Hollowell. Under the city's agreement, the group has 24 months to put together the first package on any one of the three blocks, Flies notes.

Entertaining in Minneapolis

The Block E redevelopment, which is currently under construction and expected to open this fall in downtown Minneapolis, will fill a critical gap between the city's CBD and the neighboring entertainment district. "One of the city's objectives was to try to re-create a centerpiece for the entertainment district downtown," says Phil Handy, a senior project coordinator at the Minneapolis Community Development Agency.

Gameworks, Hard Rock Café, and Crown Theatres will anchor the 210,000-square-foot, mixed-use project. Borders Books and Music also has signed a lease for a 25,000-square-foot store. And a 250-room Marriott Renaissance Hotel is planned for the second phase.

The Block E redevelopment, which is currently under construction and expected to open this fall in downtown Minneapolis, will fill a critical gap between the city's CBD and the neighboring entertainment district.

The immediate benefit derived from Block E will be the tax revenue. Another benefit is that it fills a gap between the CBD and the neighboring entertainment district that has been there for 15 to 20 years, says Handy. The project also will provide skyway links from the downtown office core to the Target Center, a sports and entertainment venue, as well as several commuter parking ramps. In addition, the development will complement the neighboring theater district along Hennepin Avenue.

Block E has been in the works for more than a decade. "It is reflective of the situation that entertainment and retail uses alone have a difficult time putting together a financially feasible project in the center of a city," Handy says. Projects often require a use offering greater economic density, such as an office. "The problem always has been finding a two- to three-year time period in which the market and financing conditions were suitable for pulling together the entertainment components, and whatever economic engine was necessary to pull that train," he says.

In this case, the Marriott Hotel provided the necessary economic boost. The city also is subsidizing the $134 million project with about $38 million—provided largely through land acquisition costs and tax increment financing.

Historic Rehabilitation in St. Louis

The $35 million rehabilitation of the Old Post Office in downtown St. Louis is expected to be the catalyst in revitalizing the entire district in which it is located. "For some time, there has been a recognition that the district is in dire need of revitalization, and that the Old Post Office itself is the key to making it happen," says Gwen Knight, a vice president at DESCO Group, a local development firm.

DESCO and DFC Group Inc., also a St. Louis–based developer, have teamed up to convert the 240,000-square-foot Old Post Office building to a Class A office, retail, and education center. The 117-year-old structure is a historic landmark, and it ranks as the sixth most historic building in the General Services Administration's national inventory of structures. A $38.6 million parking garage is planned in conjunction with the Old Post Office renovation. Work on the project is expected to begin this fall.

Perhaps the biggest job facing the developer is convincing potential tenants that the Old Post Office renovation is only the first step in revitalizing the whole district. "In order for this building to be a success, tenants are going to want to see the other 1.8 million square feet leased up or at least see a plan to revitalize the area," Knight says.

Tenants never want to move into an area where they are surrounded by vacant, rundown buildings. So DESCO and DFC needed a plan that would spur additional redevelopment, and the creation of a parking structure was an integral part of that strategy, Knight notes. The proposed 1,050-stall facility is expected to satisfy the immediate parking need, and it also will house street-level retail and a bus transfer center serving two states.

The Old Post Office rehabilitation is expected to spark an estimated $213 million in additional office, retail, and residential development in surrounding historic structures. As with most major revitalization efforts, the post office's redevelopment is moving forward due to strong public support. "We have had tremendous cooperation and support from the different agencies involved in this, including federal, state, and city government, as well as corporate St. Louis," Knight says.

BETH MATTISON-TEIG is a freelance writer based in Minneapolis, Minnesota.

Saving Buffalo From Extinction

Refugees from war-torn countries could help revive a dying city—but first, they'll have to stop fleeing it.

By David Blake

Soe Soe and Hla Ohn met in a Thai refugee camp. Both belonged to separate rebel forces battling Burma's ruling military junta, which had killed or enslaved 30,000 people in the last 10 years. They spent seven years in the camp, where they fell in love, married and had their first child, Khin Hsint. In the spring of 2000, they moved into an apartment on 14th Street, in the West Side, one of the poorest neighborhoods in one of America's most woebegone cities: Buffalo, New York.

The West Side is known for transvestite prostitution and other trades of the underground economy, conducted mostly after dark. But during fine-weather days like this one, the street buzzes with playing children—there's a bottomless metal milk crate nailed to a telephone pole—and dueling stereos, an amalgam of Latino and African-American pop rhythms. The old houses here are well built: Soe Soe and Hla's apartment is spacious, with high ceilings, hardwood floors, nice woodwork and relatively large rooms.

The refugee resettlement agency that found them the apartment, the International Institute, also helped Soe and Hla apply for social services and find work. One of their neighbors, Thein Lwin, who goes by his pen name of Thara, was another Burmese refugee who had been in Buffalo for more than five years and had recently landed a job with Radio Free America there. A writer and an intellectual with over 60 books to his credit, all banned in his homeland, Thera is an unofficial godfather to Buffalo's small but expanding expatriate Burmese community. He speaks

English, a language neither Soe nor Hla know, and was able to help them with both translation and transition. Soe would get a job; the kids would go to school. Hla was pregnant again. "We were happy," says Soe, Thera translating. "We wanted to stay."

These are people who need a place, living in a place that needs people. At the turn of the 20th century, Buffalo was one of the largest cities in the world—a national icon of growth, prosperity and optimism. Buffalo's own heyday had everything to do with the arrival of outsiders, mainly German, Irish, Italian and Polish immigrants, as well as a few African-Americans—for escaped slaves, Buffalo was the last stop before Canada on the Underground Railroad.

Today, the symbols of the city's identity are snowstorms, chicken wings and an unrelenting economic deterioration. Buffalo entered a long, slow spiral of decline when traditional industries like steel and shipping began to erode. As its industrial base withered, the city's population began to slip away, declining to just over half its 1950 high of 580,132. The lost tax revenue sunk the city's economy even deeper into its already mortal regression. In 2000, the U.S. Census put Buffalo's population under 300,000 people—292,648, to be precise—for the first time since 1890. As it thus drops in rank from a second-tier to a third-tier city, Buffalo stands to lose $2.8 million in federal block grants, and possibly one or two congressional seats as well.

This past December, after being forced to lay off 433 public school teachers, the city's government began to consider a drastic solution it had always rejected before: letting Erie County swallow it whole and dissolving its own city government, effectively committing civic suicide.

Yet Buffalo has one remarkable advantage, one that defies its status as a national weather joke: This flat, swampy, snowy, isolated city has world-class geography.

The city's proximity to Canada—less than an hour away by car—along with that country's more tolerant citizenship laws, makes Buffalo a natural way station for refugees. Since 1984, thousands of asylum-seekers have filtered through Buffalo, seeking refugee status in Canada. The wandering populations come from wherever the world's latest atrocities crop up: Last October, four Afghans managed to find their way here, and in November, the number of Pakistanis spiked to 32. In the 1990s, the number crept up steadily; last year alone, at least five thousand exiles came to Buffalo to wait, making the city the crucial last stage of a journey that begins with escape from torture, starvation or death, and ends with a new life in a new country.

Roughly a thousand more refugees come to Buffalo each year to be integrated into American life by the city's four resettlement agencies. The ones who seek status in Canada could conceivably do the same: Though they're more likely to get refugee status in Canada than in the U.S., it's not unheard of for refugees to be rejected in Canada and later apply to and be accepted by the Immigration and Naturalization Service.

But in Buffalo, almost as a rule, they don't. Of the five thousand refugees who passed through Buffalo last year seeking Canadian citizenship, most are like Nasrat Mohamed: A Tanzanian who fled both political persecution and domestic abuse, she found Buffalo a desperate place. She felt sorry, she said, for people who must live there, expressing her pity to a local photographer for having grown up and lived in Buffalo all his life. She was on her way back to Canada; the idea of living in Buffalo horrified her. Of the refugees who pass through Buffalo, less than 1 percent of them try to stay.

So this class of temporary citizens continues to pass through, getting by on whatever public money they can, but never becoming a permanent part of the city or its economy. "It's kind of like they're on a train, and we're the final stop before they reach their destination," says Chris Owens, who runs Vive la Casa, the shelter where refugees wait to get their tickets into Canada. "And there's not much point in getting off here. But I wish they would."

He's not the only one. Owens and a few other local visionaries are suggesting an innovative solution to Buffalo's population problem: fill it up with refugees. "We need these people to move into our area, fill up some empty houses, fill up some jobs, bring some vitality," urges Greg Olma, a local politician.

"Historically, immigrants have been a great source of energy for New York [City], as well as other places, and that's a great thing to bring to upstate cities," agrees Robert B. Ward, director of research for the Public Policy Institute, a business-backed Albany think tank that studies New York State's economy. Last June, Ward wrote an op-ed in the *Buffalo News* suggesting the city replenish itself with refugees.

Urban growth and vitality in the U.S. has always depended on the resettlement of people from other places. The people who run cities know this, and in the past decade, those losing population have looked to refugees for salvation. Louisville, Kentucky, which created a new city office to coordinate translation and community support services, gained 20,000 immigrants and refugees in the 1990s. Boston created an Office of New Bostonians, and gained 32,000 Latino and Asian immigrants. Pittsburgh, as bereft an old steel town as Buffalo—like Buffalo, it lost about 10 percent of its population in the 1990s alone—is trying to attract refugees and other immigrants as well. Last April, a private foundation awarded four local nonprofits $800,000 to help lure immigrants with the promise of jobs. The hope is that they'll settle in, help fill up a depleted labor market—especially those ubiquitous low-wage, unskilled labor positions—buy homes and use their various talents to rebuild communities.

In Buffalo, where good jobs are scarce but low-wage jobs go begging, Ward thinks refugees could help keep local businesses in town. "We have traditionally looked at the fact that every community needs employers. If you don't have employers, people are certainly going to leave, and we certainly saw that all across western New York," he says. "But the other side of the coin is that if people move away, then employers can't make it either. You need to have workers."

Other upstate cities have done it: Ward cites Utica, an even smaller, struggling upstate city, which manages to successfully resettle over 700 refugees a year. A study conducted at Hamilton College in upstate's Mohawk Valley found that in the first years of resettlement, refugee households cost the local economy in resources—mainly education, public assistance and Medicaid. But once they stay a certain number of years—in the Mohawk Valley, it was 13—the net economic benefits to the workforce and to the tax base begin to accumulate, and add up for as long as they stay.

But in order for Buffalo to hit that point of increasing returns, it's going to have to convince refugees to remain. These days, even some of the refugees who come expressly to Buffalo to start new lives there leave. Thara, the venerated elder of the Burmese expats, is looking to move somewhere else; Texas, he's heard, is not bad.

Soe and Hla are also finding their lives in Buffalo supply more misery than other parts of America have to offer. Soe got a job working for a pallet company in Tonawanda, north of the city. But the job only pays minimum wage, and he has to leave daily at 11 for a two o'clock shift. Without a car, it's a trip that includes three changeovers and a three-mile walk from the last bus stop. When I ask Soe why he would take a job that pays so little and is so far away, Thara, interpreting, explains that when the agency finds you a job, you are obliged to take it, or else you're on your own.

What's more, he says, the weather is unbearably frigid, and the big apartment is expensive to heat in the winter. They received heating cost assistance last year, but by the time they figured out all the paperwork and got it processed, it was already March. "The weather here is too cold," says Thara, "even in the summer."

Mostly, though, Soe wants to make more money. Living in a larger Burmese community may take some of the edge off the family's loneliness as well. There's a Burmese refugee community in Fort Wayne, Indiana, he tells me, where a worker can get a better wage. Since neither Soe nor Thara can afford to move just yet, for now they're waiting it out. "They want to move someplace warmer, where they can make more money," Thara explains. "They can get welfare anywhere."

In the end, refugees flee this dying city for the same reasons natives do: poverty, hopelessness, poor housing, worse transportation. "Why are people leaving Buffalo like crazy?" asks one refugee from Vietnam who has stayed. "It's simple. Look at Buffalo."

Vive La Casa is located off a small side street on the East Side, in an abandoned Catholic school with bars on the windows, in a neighborhood visitors are usually warned to stay away from. The refugees who stay here are cautioned not to drift too far from the grounds, but there are always a few who get mugged.

Inside, long, poorly lit corridors lead to classrooms turned into dormitories, one for men and one for women and children. People here are dressed in the clothing of their cultures: bright colored shirts and skirts, shawls, turbans, loose-fitting and light colored for warm-weather climates—whatever they showed up here with. (One African man walked the miles from the downtown Greyhound station in a blizzard, wearing nothing but his best dinner jacket and an elegant Ascot.) Some never remove their winter hats. Others, awkwardly outfitted in old suits from charity donations, look like they could be auditioning as extras for *Casablanca*. They are all waiting, coming or going to and from nowhere in particular, playing pool, talking in clusters according to language. In the basement cafeteria someone's written *Russia Rules* in red marker on one of the walls. Underneath it, someone else wrote *Russia Sucks*.

Within the exile community, these are the lowest of the low. Even Soe and Hla's helpful neighbor Thara, the Burmese political exile and novelist who wrote about "the common man," refers to Vive's residents as "dirty illegals" and "liars," although he has never met one of them.

Five thousand people come through Vive every year, more than all the refugee resettlement agencies in Buffalo combined. All are searching for some place and possibility, but with the clerical distinction that they don't have the proper documentation and are therefore considered illegal aliens. If they were not at Vive, they would be in an INS detention facility or on the streets.

Nearly all are seeking asylum in Canada because chances of acceptance are greater there (48 percent) than they are in the U.S. (23 percent, and that was before September 11). Besides providing food and shelter, Vive helps them with their residency applications, and provides those who have been denied on their first try in Canada—and therefore must leave the land of the maple leaf for 90 days before they can reapply—a place to sit it out and hope for better luck next time.

Owens would like to encourage more of them to stay, and he has reached out to both local foundations, hoping they would sponsor a Pittsburgh-style population effort, as well as to the city's resettlement agencies. (He's also seeking international funding, since Vive functions as a de facto nongovernmental intermediary between countries.) But it's slow going: These are tough times for both Buffalo and refugees, and funding a grand international urban experiment is not high on anyone's list of priorities. Only two schools in Buffalo have resources to serve children who don't speak English, and they're both filled to capacity. Buffalo's budget crisis means there's little hope that things will get better.

Vive also has its own problems to attend to. Since late September, the agency has been filled to double capacity with refugees desperately seeking to get into Canada before this June, when strict new immigration laws prompted by 9/11 take effect there. (Among them, asylum-seekers will now have just a single opportunity to apply for Canadian citizenship before they must go back home or into the limbo of detention.) And in 1996, federal welfare reform removed New York State's obligation to fund certain services for legal immigrants. The result, for Vive, was a $400,000 budget cut. Vive would have gone out of business entirely had Erie County not decided to channel funds from other sources to the organization.

"Refugees are the largest and most silent homeless population in Buffalo," says Alex Priebe, Vive's former development officer. "When you apply for asylum in the United States, you cannot work, you cannot receive benefits. You are dependent on the kindness of anyone who will give it to you. Unless you come with money in your pocket—a lot of these people come with only the clothes on their backs—you are an orphan in a system not set up to be kind."

On a run-down section of Broadway Street, among liquor stores, bars, tattoo shops and abandoned houses, you'll find the low-slung office of the last politician who set out to make Buffalo a refugee haven. Until he lost at the polls this November, burly maverick Greg Olma was a Democratic county legislator.

The walls of Olma's office are bare, with two exceptions. On one there are the police mug shots of the actor Hugh Grant and Divine Brown, the prostitute he was picked up with a few years back. On the other is a life-size, smiling cardboard cutout of Buffalo's Common Council President, James Pitts, the powerful Democrat and political leader of Buffalo's black East Side. He's also a well-known Olma nemesis. Next to the cutout a carefully positioned cartoon balloon reads, in neat block letters: GREG OLMA IS A VERY SMART MAN!

Olma has a reputation for being outspoken and controversial, which, along with allegations of corruption (he denies them), probably contributed to his election defeat. Breaking from the fulsome provincialism and sophistry standard among the city's elected officials, he may be the only local politician who'll speak candidly about the city's pattern of spiraling decline and realistically about its prospects for revival. As county legislator, he was certainly the only one considering immigrant and refugee recruitment as part of any redevelopment plan.

"Buffalo's a sad case. It's not as bad as Youngstown, Ohio, or Gary, Indiana, or Newark, but it's pretty damn close to that," he said in an interview conducted before his defeat. "Our only hope would be to encourage immigration of people from countries that will work and maintain a partisan and ethnic enclave."

But Olma's attempt to revive the glory years of the urban immigrant political machine ran into some hitches. For one thing, Buffalo's refugee agencies are not well coordinated: They operate independently and

sometimes competitively, spending their limited resources on services—like English language classes and job placement programs—that often duplicate one another.

Olma's vision, for which he got some local support but ultimately too little funding, was to combine their efforts into one comprehensive community development initiative, making it easier for refugees to buy houses right away and begin building their new lives. "Essentially, what you got to have are people from poor countries without anything," says Olma. "There's a lot of those out there, and Buffalo's a good place to bring them, because they will help build us up again."

Olma's no stranger to the power of refugees in community revitalization. In the 1980s, the city built a low-rent housing project in the Broadway-Fillmore district, the Walentynowicz Apartments, designed for post-Solidarity refugees from Krakow. Noted for its strong ethnic ties, the district became a bustling Polish neighborhood, the symbol and center of which remains the Broadway Market—a large indoor bazaar with small kiosks selling everything from ethnic food to televisions. (Regularly mired in patronage scandals, Broadway Market also became a symbol of Buffalo's tradition of graft.)

But Broadway-Fillmore's comeback faded quickly when the immigrants headed for the suburbs. The way Olma sees it, that was because the refugees weren't poor enough or desperate enough. "What you have to have to build a community—to build an ethnic community in the inner city—you've got to have lower-income immigrants who come from a certain kind of poverty situation," he explains. "The problem with European immigrants, Eastern European, is that they watched Western TV. They think this country's like *Dynasty*. And so, you get good workers and stuff; it's good for the community; it's good for your restaurant selection—if you get enough immigrants you'll get some interesting food and things like that, parties to go to. But you don't get a real community from that kind of situation.

"A lot of it has got to do with education," he continues, oblivious that he's getting into sensitive territory. "A lot of these people from Poland had some college education, or they're more Westernized, so to speak."

There are, believe it or not, things Olma doesn't say. One of them is that one reason so many Polish residents were moving out was because African-Americans were moving in. At the same time, Broadway-Fillmore, like many other parts of the city, became run down with unemployment, declining property values and hard poverty. The tiny white enclave that remains is called the Iron Triangle, as much a reference to its siege mentality as its East European flavor. "I think that's the same thing that's going to happen with the Bosnians. There's some Bosnians moving in," says Olma. "But generally speaking, they're climbers and they're going to climb right out."

For Olma, a desire to settle, stay and build a life is what distinguishes the Vietnamese from some of the other immigrating populations. "Since the Polish dried up we've had a lot of Somalians, Bosnians, Vietnamese," he says. "And the Vietnamese," he declares, "were the ones that were the most durable."

It's this "Vietnamese-type of immigrant" that serves as the model for Olma's visions of refugee-fueled revival. He describes them as being "like the old immigrants," which is to say that they buy houses in his district and tend to bring over their extended families, which means more votes—preferably for him. "They're Catholics, most of them, which is good for the Catholic parishes," he points out. "They're savers, they're frugal, and they're not glory-seekers."

This is a point Olma stresses: that the earth's truly wretched will be grateful to live in Buffalo. "To me, the best thing for refugees is not doctors and lawyers," he says. "The best refugees are able-bodied workers who have some education but are not looking for the stylized American lifestyle. They just want to get ahead, you know... they don't pull themselves out and live in [suburban] Amherst, like the doctors and lawyers do. They're not that enculturated. I don't know if this sounds bad or not, but it makes perfect sense to me: Not every immigrant is as good as the other one."

Minh Tran is Olma's dream personified. He lives in a pleasant two-story house on the Lower West Side. On the corner directly opposite the house is his family's store, a tiny building so overcrowded with products and advertising that stepping inside is enough to trigger a swarming disorientation.

Minh's family arrived here in 1981 via South Vietnam, after a year in a Hong Kong refugee camp. Minh's father, a former officer in the South Vietnamese army, died in the camp, leaving Minh, his mother, two sisters and a baby brother to carry on without him. "My mother never took social services; she refused," says Minh, in a tone about as humble as a statement like that can be.

The family came over with some savings, but not enough to save Minh, who at 19 was the oldest son, from having to take a sewing job in Buffalo's old garment district to help support them all while his younger sisters and brother went off to school and, later, college. When he wasn't working, Minh was busy helping his mother run the store; to this day, he himself has never taken a college class. As a result his English, while not quite broken, is still thick with accent.

That kind of experience can cause bitterness, but there's no sense of that in Minh. Confident and charismatic, he's become a leader in Buffalo's close-knit, small, yet relatively powerful Vietnamese community. He is also a case manager at the International Institute, the agency that helped resettle his family. He gets calls at all hours from his clients, refugees new to the area who get lost, don't know how to call a taxi or need to find the nearest hospital.

Minh's *querencia*, his place of strength, comes from a mixture of individual will and genuine compassion. His success and kindness make him a local legend, but he deflects individual credit. "A lot of people help me out," he says, and specifically mentions Greg Olma.

More than once, Olma has driven across town to sit at Minh's table and talk to the local Vietnamese leaders, asking them what services they need and checking to see how many of them have registered to vote.

It was Olma who helped arrange a deal with the city so they could purchase space for a Buddhist cultural center. For those who are Catholic, it was Olma who helped them find a priest for their church.

"Greg, he welcomes people. He wants to build community," Minh says, struggling to fit a tile around a tricky corner. We are sitting on plywood that for the moment is passing as Minh's dining room floor, drinking cans of beer, while Minh is carefully measuring and laying new floor tiles. Not liking the fit, he peels it up, frowning, and tosses it over his shoulder. "There goes 99 cents," he says with a light laugh.

There are lots of pictures on the walls: family portraits, a painting of Jesus and other religious artifacts, including a large cross. I ask Minh if he's Catholic. "Yeah," he laughs, "but what is Catholic anyway, you know."

Minh thinks the whole Buffalo population crisis is way overblown. "The Census got it wrong," he insists. "Refugees weren't counted, for one; they don't know what those Census forms are or how to fill them out. And when the people come to the door to ask they come during business hours when the refugee is at work."

I ask Minh if he's concerned that Buffalo has trouble attracting immigrants and refugees who are willing to stay, and what that ultimately means for the community. "What problem?" he says. "In my mind, they all stay."

Once Minh leaves to go pick up his son from day care, though, his younger brother, Thom, says he can see why people are leaving Buffalo. "I'm not complaining; Buffalo treated me well," he adds quickly. Thom, which is not his real name but the only one he's willing to provide, went to SUNY-Buffalo and got a business degree. Now, he works at the Walentynowicz Apartments, a job Olma got him. For $7.50 an hour, he cleans apartments and collects rents from less fortunate, more recently arrived refugees. "I know it's hard for them. They only get the minimum wage jobs," he says. "But what am I supposed to do? I have to do my job."

Sitting on the porch, after a few beers, Thom begins talking about his life here, his childhood in Ho Chi Minh City, venal politicians. About trouble and the need, sometimes, for a new start. "I would like more, of course," he says, "but people have to accept reality."

David Blake is a writer who used to live in Buffalo. Brendan Bannon, who provided additional reporting for this story, has been photographing refugees in Buffalo for over two years.

From *City Limits*, February 2002, pp. 18-25. Copyright ©; 2002 by City Limits Community Information Service, Inc. www.citylimits.org Reprinted by permission.

Movers & Shakers

How immigrants are reviving neighborhoods given up for dead

By Joel Kotkin

For decades the industrial area just east of downtown Los Angeles was an economic wreck, a 15-square-block area inhabited largely by pre–World War II derelict buildings. Yet now the area comes to life every morning, full of talk of toys in various South China dialects, in Vietnamese, in Korean, in Farsi, in Spanish, and in the myriad other commercial languages of the central city.

The district now known as Toytown represents a remarkable turnaround of the kind of archaic industrial area that has fallen into disuse all across the country. A combination of largely immigrant entrepreneurship and the fostering of a specialized commercial district has created a bustling marketplace that employs over 4,000 people, boasts revenues estimated at roughly $500 million a year, and controls the distribution of roughly 60 percent of the $12 billion in toys sold to American retailers.

"In December we have about the worst traffic problem in downtown," proudly asserts Charlie Woo, a 47-year-old immigrant who arrived in 1968 from Hong Kong and is widely considered the district's founding father. During the holiday season, thousands of retail customers, mostly Latino, come down to the district seeking cut-rate toys, dolls, and action figures, including dubious knock-offs of better-known brands. For much of the rest of the year, the district sustains itself as a global wholesale center for customers from Latin America and Mexico, which represent nearly half the area's shipments, as well as buyers from throughout the United States.

Few in L.A.'s business world, City Hall, or the Community Redevelopment Agency paid much attention when Woo started his family's first toy wholesaling business in 1979. "When Toytown started, the CRA didn't even know about it," recalls Don Spivack, now the agency's deputy administrator. "It happened on its own. It was a dead warehouse district."

How dead? Dave Zoraster, an appraiser at CB Richard Ellis, estimates that in the mid-1970s land values in the area—then known only as Central City East—stood at $2.75 a square foot, a fraction of the over $100 a square foot the same property commands today. Vacancy rates, now in the single digits, then hovered at around 50 percent. For the most part, Spivack recalls, development officials saw the district as a convenient place to cluster the low-income, largely transient population a safe distance from the city's new sparkling high-rises nearby.

To Charlie Woo, then working on a Ph.D. in physics at UCLA, the low land costs in the area presented an enormous opportunity. Purchasing his first building for a mere $140,000, Woo saw the downtown location as a cheap central locale for wholesaling and distributing the billions of dollars in toys unpacked at the massive twin ports of Long Beach and Los Angeles, the nation's dominant hub for U.S.-Asia trade and the world's third-largest container port. Woo's *guanxi,* or connections, helped him establish close relationships with scores of toy manufacturers in Asia, where the vast majority of the nation's toys are produced. The large volume of toys he imported then allowed him to take a 20 percent margin, compared with the 40 to 50 percent margins sought by the traditional small toy wholesalers. Today Woo and his family own 10 buildings, with roughly 70 tenants, in the area; their distribution company, Megatoys, has annual sales in excess of $30 million.

"Immigrants are hungrier and more optimistic," says Harvard's William Apgar. "Their presence is the difference between New York and Detroit."

Toytown's success also has contributed to a broader growth in toy-related activity in Southern California. The region—home to Mattel, the world's largest toy maker—has spawned hundreds of smaller toy-making firms, design firms, and distribution firms, some originally located in Toytown but now residing in sleek modern industrial parks just outside the central core. Other spin-offs, including a new toy design department at the Otis College of Art and Design in West Los Angeles and the Toy Association of Southern California, have worked to secure the region's role as a major industry hub.

Woo envisions Toytown as a retail center. But whatever its future, the district's continuing success stands as testament to the ability of immigrant entrepreneurs and specialized industrial districts to turn even the most destitute urban neighborhoods around. Woo notes: "The future of Toytown will be as a gathering point for anyone interested in toys. Designers and buyers will come to see what's selling, what the customer wants. The industry will grow all over, but this place will remain ground zero."

For much of the 19th and early 20th centuries, immigrants filled and often dominated American cities. With the curtailment of immigration in the 1920s, this flow was dramatically reduced, and urban areas began to suffer demographic stagnation, and in some places rapid decline. Only after 1965, when immigration laws were reformed, did newcomers return in large numbers, once again transforming many of the nation's cities.

This was critical, because despite the movement of young professionals and others into the urban core, native-born Americans continued, on balance, to flee the cities in the 1990s. Only two of the nation's 10 largest metropolitan areas, Houston and Dallas, gained domestic migrants in the decade. As over 2.5 million native-born Americans fled the nation's densest cities, over 2.3 million immigrants came in.

The impacts were greatest in five major cities: New York, Los Angeles, San Francisco, Miami, and Chicago. These cities received more than half of the estimated 20 million legal and 3 million to 5 million illegal immigrants who arrived over the past quarter century. Without these immigrants, probably all these cities would have suffered the sort of serious depopulation that has afflicted such cities as St. Louis, Baltimore, and Detroit, which until recently have attracted relatively few foreigners.

In this two-way population flow, America's major cities and their close suburbs have become ever more demographically distinct from the rest of the country. In 1930, one out of four residents of the top four "gateway" cities came from abroad, twice the national average; by the 1990s, one in three was foreign-born, five times the norm. Fully half of all new Hispanic residents in the country between 1990 and 1996 resided in the 10 largest cities. Asians are even more concentrated, with roughly two in five residing in just three areas: Los Angeles, New York, and San Francisco.

In places such as Southern California, immigration has transformed the economic landscape. Between 1992 and 1999, the number of Latino businesses in Los Angeles County more than doubled. Some of these businesses have grown in areas that previously had been considered fallow, such as Compton and South-Central Los Angeles. In these long-established "ghettos," both incomes and population have been on the rise largely because of Latino immigration, after decades of decline.

A similar immigrant-driven phenomenon has sparked recoveries in some of the nation's most distressed neighborhoods, from Washington, D.C., to Houston. Along Pitkin Avenue in Brooklyn's Brownsville section, Caribbean and African immigrants, who have a rate of self-employment 20 to 50 percent higher than that of native-born blacks, have propelled a modest but sustained economic expansion.

The recovery of such once forlorn places stems largely from the culture of these new immigrants. Certainly Brooklyn's infrastructure and location remain the same as in its long decades of decline. Along with entrepreneurship, the newcomers from places such as the Caribbean have brought with them a strong family ethic, a system of mutual financial assistance called *susus*, and a more positive orientation to their new place. "Immigrants are hungrier and more optimistic," notes William Apgar of Harvard's Joint Center for Housing Studies. "Their upward mobility is a form of energy. Their presence is the difference between New York and Detroit."

It is possible that newcomers to America might even be able to revive those cities that have not yet fully felt the transformative power of immigration. A possible harbinger can be seen on the South Side of St. Louis, a city largely left out of the post-1970s immigrant wave. Once a thriving white working-class community, the area, like much of the rest of the city, had suffered massive depopulation and economic stagnation.

"Bosnians," says one immigrant, "don't care if they start by buying the smallest, ugliest house. At least they feel they have something."

This began to change, however, in the late 1990s, with the movement into the area of an estimated 10,000 Bosnian refugees, along with other newcomers, including Somalis, Vietnamese, and Mexicans. Southern Commercial Bank loan officer Steve Hrdlicka, himself a native of the district, recalls: "Eight years ago, when we opened this branch, we sat on our hands most of the time. We used to sleep quite a lot. Then this place became a rallying place for Bosnians. They would come in and ask for a loan for furniture. Then it was a car. Then it was a house, for themselves, their cousins."

In 1998, largely because of the Bosnians, Hrdlicka's branch, located in a South St. Louis neighborhood called Bevo, opened more new accounts than any of the 108-year-old Southern Commercial's other six branches. Over the last two years of the 1990s, the newcomers, who have developed a reputation for hard work and thrift, helped push the number of accounts at the branch up nearly 80 percent, while deposits have nearly doubled to $40 million.

A translator at the Bevo branch, 25-year-old Jasna Mruckovski, has even cashed in on the Bosnians' home-buying tendencies. Moonlighting as a real estate salesperson, she has helped sell 33 homes in the area over the past year, all but one to Bosnian buyers. In many cases, she notes, these homes were bought with wages pooled from several family members, including children. Mruckovski, a refugee from Banjo Luka who arrived in St. Louis in 1994, observes: "St. Louis is seen as a cheap place to live. People come from California, Chicago, and Florida, where it's more expensive. Bosnians don't care if they start by buying the smallest, ugliest house. At least they feel they have something. This feeling is what turns a place like this around."

Immigration also helps cities retain their preeminence in another traditional urban economic bastion: cross-cultural trade. Virtually all the great cities since antiquity derived much of their sustenance through the intense contact between differing peoples in various sorts of markets. As world economies have developed through the ages, exchanges between races and cultures have been critical to establishing the geographic importance of particular places. Historian Fernand Braudel suggests, "A world economy always has an urban center of gravity, a city, as the logistic heart of its activity. News, merchandise, capital, credit, people, instructions, correspondence all flow into and out of the city. Its powerful merchants lay down the law, sometimes becoming extraordinarily wealthy."

Repeatedly throughout history, it has been outsiders—immigrants—who have driven cross-cultural exchange. "Throughout the history of economics," observes social theorist Georg Simmel, "the stranger appears as the trader, or the trader as stranger." In ancient Greece, for example, it was *metics,* largely foreigners, who drove the marketplace economy disdained by most well-born Greeks. In Alexandria, Rome, Venice, and Amsterdam—as well as the Islamic Middle East—this pattern repeated itself, with "the stranger" serving the critical role as intermediary.

As in Renaissance Venice, the increasing ethnic diversity of America's cities plays a critical role in their domination of international trade.

As in Renaissance Venice and early modern Amsterdam or London, the increasing ethnic diversity of America's cities plays a critical role in their domination of international trade. Over the past 30 years, cities such as New York, Los Angeles, Houston, Chicago, and Miami have become ever more multiethnic, with many of the newcomers hailing from growing trade regions such as East Asia, the Caribbean, and Latin America. The large immigrant clusters in these cities help forge critical global economic ties, held together not only by commercial bonds but by the equally critical bonds of cultural exchange and kinship networks.

These newcomers have redefined some former backwaters into global trading centers. Miami's large Latino population—including 650,000 Cubans, 75,000 Nicaraguans, and 65,000 Colombians—has helped turn the one-time sun-and-fun capital into the dominant center for American trade and travel to South America and the Caribbean. Modesto Maidique, president of Florida International University, who is himself a Cuban émigré, observes: "If you take away international trade and cultural ties from Miami, we go back to being just a seasonal tourist destination. It's the imports, the exports, and the service trade that have catapulted us into the first rank of cities in the world."

Like the *souk* districts of the Middle East, diversified cities provide an ideal place for the creation of unique, globally oriented markets. These *souks,* which are fully operational to this day, are home mostly to small, specialized merchants. In most cases, the districts consisted of tiny unlighted shops raised two or three feet from street level. Stores are often grouped together by trade, allowing the consumer the widest selection and choice.

The emergence of the Western *souk* is perhaps most evident in Los Angeles, home to Toytown. Within a short distance of that bustling district are scores of other specialized districts—the downtown Fashion Mart, the Flower district, and the jewelry, food, and produce districts are crowded with shoppers, hustlers, and buyers of every possible description. These districts' vitality contrasts with the longstanding weakness of downtown L.A.'s office market, which has been losing companies and tenants to other parts of the city.

Similar trade-oriented districts have arisen in other cities, such as along Canal Street in New York, in the "Asia Trade District" along Dallas's Harry Hines Boulevard, and along the Harwin Corridor in the area outside the 610 Loop in Houston. Once a forlorn strip of office and warehouse buildings, the Harwin area has been transformed into a car-accessed *souk* for off-price goods for much of East Texas, featuring cut-rate furniture, novelties, luggage, car parts, and electronic goods.

These shops, owned largely by Chinese, Korean, and Indian merchants, have grown from roughly 40 a decade ago to more than 800, sparking a boom in a once-depressed real estate market. Over the decade, the value of commercial properties in the district has more than tripled, and vacancies have dropped from nearly 50 percent to single digits. "It's kind of an Asian frontier sprawl around here," comments David Wu, a prominent local store owner.

Indeed, few American cities have been more transformed by trade and immigration than Houston. With the collapse of energy prices in the early 1980s, the once booming Texas metropolis appeared to be on the road to economic oblivion. Yet the city has rebounded, in large part because of the very demographic and trade patterns seen in the other Sun Belt capitals. "The energy industry totally dominated Houston by the 1970s—after all, oil has been at the core of our economy since 1901," explains University of Houston economist Barton Smith. "Every boom leads people to forget other parts of the economy. After the bust, people saw the importance of the ports and trade."

Since 1986, tonnage through the 25-mile-long Port of Houston has grown by one-third, helping the city recover the jobs lost during the "oil bust" of the early 1980s. Today, Smith estimates, trade accounts for roughly 10 per-

cent of regional employment and has played a critical role in the region's 1990s recovery: By 1999 a city once renowned for its plethora of "see-through" buildings ranked second in the nation in total office space absorption and third in rent increases.

Immigrants were the critical factor in this turnaround. Between 1985 and 1990, Houston, a traditional magnet for domestic migrants, suffered a net loss of over 140,000 native-born residents. But the immigrants kept coming—nearly 200,000 over the past decade, putting the Texas town among America's seven most popular immigrant destinations.

Among those coming to Houston during the 1970s boom was a Taiwan-born engineer named Don Wang, who in 1987 founded his own immigrant-oriented financial institution, Metrobank. Amid the hard times and demographic shifts, Wang and his clients—largely Asian, Latin, and African immigrants—saw an enormous opportunity to pick up real estate, buy homes, and start businesses. Minority-owned enterprises now account for nearly 30 percent of Houston's business community.

Says Wang: "In the 1980s everyone was giving up on Houston. But we stayed. It was cheap to start a business here and easy to find good labor. We considered this the best place to do business in the country, even if no one on the outside knows it.… When the oil crisis came, everything dropped, but it actually was our chance to become a new city again."

Increasingly, the focus of immigrants—and their enterprise—extends beyond the traditional *souk* economy to a broader part of the metropolitan geography. Most dramatic has been the movement to the older rings of suburbs, which are rapidly replacing the inner city as the predominant melting pots of American society. This trend can be seen across the nation, from the Chinese- and Latino-dominated suburbs east of Los Angeles to the new immigrant communities emerging in southern metropolitan areas such as Houston, Dallas, and Atlanta. This move marks a sharp contrast to the immediate postwar era, when these suburbs, like their high-tech workforces, remained highly segregated.

The demographic shift in the near suburbs started in the 1970s, when African-Americans began moving to them in large numbers. In the ensuing two decades, middle-class minorities and upwardly mobile recent immigrants have shown a marked tendency to replace whites in the suburbs, particularly in the inner ring, increasing their numbers far more rapidly than their Anglo counterparts. Today nearly 51 percent of Asians, 43 percent of Latinos, and 32 percent of African Americans live in the suburbs.

This development is particularly notable in those regions where immigration has been heaviest. Among the most heavily Asian counties in the nation are such places as Queens County in New York, Santa Clara and San Mateo counties in Northern California, and Orange County, south of Los Angeles. Queens and Fort Bend County, in suburban Houston, rank among the 10 most ethnically diverse counties in the nation.

> **The melting pot has spilled into the suburbs. About 51 percent of Asians, 43 percent of Latinos, and 32 percent of African Americans live in the suburbs.**

Today these areas have become as ethnically distinctive as the traditional inner cities themselves, if not more so. Some, like Coral Gables, outside of Miami, have become both ethnic and global business centers. Coral Gables is home to the Latin American division headquarters of over 50 multinationals.

Other places, such as the San Gabriel Valley east of Los Angeles, have accommodated two distinct waves of ethnic settlement, Latino and Asian. Cities such as Monterey Park, Alhambra, and San Gabriel have become increasingly Asian in character; areas such as Whittier and La Puente have been transformed by Latino migration. Yet in both cases, the movement is predominantly by middle-class homeowners. "For us this isn't a dream, this is reality," notes Frank Corona, who moved to the area from East Los Angeles. "This is a quiet, nice, family-oriented community."

The reason the melting pot has spilled into the suburbs lies in the changing needs of immigrants. In contrast to the early 20th century, when proximity to inner-city services and infrastructure was critical, many of today's newcomers to a more dispersed, auto-oriented society find they need to stop only briefly, if at all, in the inner cities. Their immediate destination after arrival is as likely to be Fort Lee as Manhattan, the San Gabriel Valley as Chinatown or the East L.A. barrios. Notes Cal State Northridge demographer James Allen: "The immigrants often don't bother with the inner city anymore. Most Iranians don't ever go to the center city, and few Chinese ever touch Chinatown at all. Many of them want to get away from poor people as soon as possible."

As proof, Allen points to changes in his own community, the San Fernando Valley, which for a generation was seen as the epitome of the modern suburb. In the 1960s, the valley was roughly 90 percent white; three decades later it was already 44 percent minority, with Latinos representing nearly one-third the total population. By 1997,

according to county estimates, Latinos were roughly 41 percent of the valley population, while Asians were another 9 percent.

Similarly dramatic changes have taken place outside of California. Twenty years ago, Queens County was New York's largest middle-class and working-class white bastion, the fictional locale of the small homeowner Archie Bunker. Today it is not Manhattan, the legendary immigrant center, but Queens that is easily the most diverse borough in New York, with thriving Asian, Latino, and middle-class African-American neighborhoods. Over 40 percent of the borough's businesses are now minority-owned, almost twice as high as the percentage in Manhattan.

This alteration in the suburban fabric is particularly marked in the American South, which largely lacks the infrastructure of established ethnic inner-city districts. Regions such as Atlanta experienced some of the most rapid growth in immigration in the last two decades of the millennium; between 1970 and 1990, for example, Georgia's immigrant population grew by 525 percent. By 1996, over 11.5 million Asians lived in the South. Yet since most Southern cities lacked the preexisting structure of an ethnic Asian or Latino community to embrace the newcomers, most new immigrants chose to cluster not in the central city but in the near suburbs.

"Well, we still have one fried-chicken place left somewhere around here," jokes Houston architect Chao-Chiung Lee over dim sum in one of the city's heavily Asian suburbs. "It's a kind of the last outpost of the native culture lost amid the new Chinatown."

Yet if the successes of immigrants represent the success of the melting pot, the demographic shift also presents some potential challenges. In addition to a swelling number of entrepreneurs and scientists, there has been a rapid expansion of a less-educated population. For example, Latinos, the fastest-growing group in Silicon Valley, account for 23 percent of that region's population but barely 7 percent of its high-tech work force. Part of the problem lies with education: Only 56 percent of Latinos graduate from high school, and less than one in five takes the classes necessary to get into college.

Indeed, as the economy becomes increasingly information-based, there are growing concerns among industry and political leaders that many of the new immigrants and, more important, their children may be unprepared for the kind of jobs that are opening up in the future. Immigrants may be willing to serve as bed changers, gardeners, and service workers for the digital elites, but there remains a serious question as to whether their children will accept long-term employment in such generally low-paid and low-status niches.

George Borjas, a leading critic of U.S. immigration policy and professor of public policy at Harvard's John F. Kennedy School of Government, suggests that recent immigration laws have tilted the pool of newcomers away from skilled workers toward those less skilled, seriously depleting the quality of the labor pool and perhaps threatening the social stability of the immigration centers. "The national economy is demanding more skilled workers," Borjas says, "and I don't see how bringing more unskilled workers is consistent with this trend.... When you have a very large group of unskilled workers, and children of unskilled workers, you risk the danger of creating a social underclass in the next [21st] century."

> ## *No longer "lily white" enclaves, suburbs must draw their strength, as the great cities before them did, from their increasingly diverse populations.*

In the coming decades, this disconnect between the labor force and the economy in some areas could lead to an exodus of middle-class people and businesses to less troubled places, as happened previously in inner cities. Across the country, many aging suburbs, such as Upper Darby near Philadelphia and Harvey outside Chicago, are well on the way to becoming highly diverse suburban slums as businesses move farther out into the geographic periphery. Others—in regions including Boston, New Orleans, Cleveland, St. Louis, Dallas, and Indianapolis—now struggle to retain their attractiveness.

If unchecked, a broader ghettoization looms as a distinct possibility, particularly in some of the older areas filled with smaller houses and more mundane apartment buildings. These areas could become—as have some suburbs of Paris—dysfunctional, balkanized losers in the new digital geography. "It's a different place now. We can go either way," says Robert Scott, a former L.A. planning commissioner and leader of the San Fernando Valley's drive to secede from Los Angeles.

Scott grew up in the once all-white, now predominantly Latino community of Van Nuys. "The valley can become a storehouse of poverty and disenchantment," he says, "or it can become a series of neighborhoods with a sense of uniqueness and an investment in its future." As Scott suggests, for these new melting pots, the best course may be not so much to try clinging to their demographic past as to find a way to seize the advantages of their more diverse roles, both economically and demographically. No longer "lily white" enclaves, such communities increasingly must draw their strength, as the great cities before them did, from the energies, skills, and cultural offerings of their increasingly diverse populations.

Joel Kotkin (jkotkin@pacbell.net) is a senior fellow with the Pepperdine University Institute for Public Policy and a research fellow of the Reason Public Policy Institute. Excerpted from the book The New Geography: How the Digital Revolution Is Reshaping the American Landscape *by Joel Kotkin. Copyright © 2000 by Joel Kotkin. Reprinted by arrangement with Random House Trade Publishing, a division of Random House Inc.*

UNIT 5
Urban Politics and Policies

Unit Selections

Key Points to Consider

- Using John Lindsay and Richard Daley as examples, explain how differing mayoral attitudes on race can affect urban life.

- How has Michael Bloomberg defined his mayoralty? What issues seem most important to him?

- What makes a successful mayoralty? What makes a successful city?

 **Links: www.dushkin.com/online/**
These sites are annotated in the World Wide Web pages.

Munisource.org
http://www.munisource.org
U.S. Department of Housing and Urban Development
http://www.hud.gov
Virtual Seminar in Global Political Economy/Global Cities & Social Movements
http://csf.colorado.edu/gpe/gpe95b/resources.html

Liberal politics and policies helped spur the urban decline of the 1970s and 1980s. The first article, "Mayors and Mayorality: Daley and Lindsay Then and Now" provides a broad historical perspective that contrasts the different approaches and reputations of the past mayors of Chicago and New York. Their distinct approaches to race, public safety, quality of life, and neighborhoods help frame the urban experience in the second half of the twentieth century. "Beyond Safe and Clean" looks at how Business Improvement Districts have gone beyond their original mandate of safety, order, and cleanliness to work toward historical preservation and other goals that dovetail with the new urbanism. "Bloomberg So Far" looks at the first two years under Gotham's new mayor, and determines that while the city hasn't slid back to the morass of the pre-Giuliani days, nor is it making further progress.

Mayors and Morality: Daley and Lindsay Then and Now

FRED SIEGEL

Chicago's traditional tribalism looks remarkably similar to the modern multiculturalism of the Democratic Party.

—Paul McGrath, high-ranking advisor to former Chicago mayor Jane Byrne

HISTORY SEEMS TO HAVE come full circle for the Daleys of Chicago. In 1960 Mayor Richard J. Daley, who had been elected with black votes, temporarily made himself a hero to liberal Democrats when he played a key role in electing John Kennedy president. Forty years later his oldest son William Daley, working with Jesse Jackson, ran the campaign to put Al Gore into the White House. Over the past forty years of racial politics the Daleys have gone from darlings to demons and back again.

Political archetypes sometimes play tricks on us. Consider John Kennedy and Ronald Reagan. They were born just six years apart yet JFK is frozen in our memory as forever youthful, while few can imagine Reagan as anything but doddering. Mayors John Lindsay of New York and Richard J. Daley of Chicago are remembered as the antithetical embodiments of the 1960s urban crisis. Yet New York and Chicago are anything but typical. "New York," notes Saul Bellow, "is a European city though of no known nationality." While only a Bertolt Brecht could imagine that Chicago, a city of Slavs governed by Irishmen along the lines of European Christian Democracy, was typically American. Neither man's national reputation seemed to have survived the era's cauldron of racial politics. Both men reached their nadir in 1972: Lindsay in his brief but disastrous run for the presidency; Daley when his delegation was refused admittance to the Democratic convention only to be replaced by a group led by Jesse Jackson.

Nonetheless, the two mayors became ideograms frozen in the paratactic moments of urban rioting. The image of Lindsay that still endures is of a caring man walking the streets of Harlem, courageously keeping the city relatively calm as other cities went up in flames. The primary author of the Kerner Commission report on urban riots, Lindsay saw racism not only as a scourge but as virtually the sole explanation for African-American poverty. The jowly Daley by contrast was as rough-edged as Lindsay was smooth. His frustrated press secretary once blurted, "Print what he means not what he says." One of his most famous malapropisms was, "The policeman isn't there to create disorder; the policeman is there to preserve disorder." Daley's infamous "shoot to kill" arsonists order during the 1968 riots as well as the police riots that accompanied the Democratic Convention of that year are often the first things his name brings to mind.

Daley's and Lindsay's names were taken as the pole stars of city politics. Here's how *The Boston Globe* described the once-promising career of Mayor Kevin White when he left office: "Elected in 1967 as Boston's answer to John Lindsay, New York's young reform mayor, White left in 1984 as Boston's Richard Daley, the aging and resented Chicago machine boss." In the mid-1960s, Lindsay, his picture on the cover of all the newsweeklies, was seen as nothing less than the Second Coming of JFK. His youth, vigor, and moral commitment to racial equality gave him an extraordinary aura. There was even talk—talk that Lindsay encouraged—that he was likely to be president some day. But if Lindsay was once revered, this New York mayor who was supposed to represent the future of urban America has since been largely forgotten, while Daley, the man reviled as a dinosaur, is not only remembered but extolled as forerunner of today's successful new-wave mayors.

While Lindsay has been ranked as one of the worst big city mayors, the same poll of political scientists and historians selected Daley as the single best mayor of the late twentieth century and one of the ten best in American history. Today Daley's son, Richard M. Daley, reigns virtually unchallenged as his father's legatee. And at a time when mayors like to think of themselves as efficient managers rather than the social conscience of the country, the phrase "Boss Daley," popularized by Mike Royko, has, says Alan Ehrenhalt, "lost the evil connotation for most people that it seemed to have a quarter-century ago."

Why the reversal? In part, says political analyst Jim Chapin, it is a matter both of exoticism and of subtly shifting standards. In the sixties, jowly, aging, overweight machine politicians were old hat, a dime a dozen; the blow-dried dynamic Lindsay seemed different and promising. But today, in an era of smiling empty suits, Lindsay's style no longer looks promisingly authentic. Instead, a nostalgic haze glosses over the cigar chomping, backroom corruption, and police brutality of the Daley years. Today we can chuckle at the informal slogan of Fred Roti, a longtime First Ward alderman: "Vote for Fred Roti and no one gets hurt." The notorious mob-run First Ward also had Jackie "the Lackey" Cerone who, when described by the Associated Press as a "minor gangland figure," called to complain about the "minor."

At a time when liberals have largely given up on universalism, Daley's tribalism no longer seems so egregious. In retrospect, notes Paul McGrath, Daley was the least racist mayoral candidate of the 1950s and '60s in a city whose whites seethed with anti-black animus. Daley first won election in 1955 against the backdrop of a two-year-long, sometimes violent campaign by whites to keep blacks out of the far South Side of Chicago. The white incumbent Martin Kennelly openly courted backlash voters, while black voters backed Daley in order to bring down Kennelly. It was a measure of Daley's skill that he was endorsed by both *The Chicago Defender*, the city's leading black newspaper, and by white groups on the far South Side. Unable to adapt to the new climate of civil rights, Daley tried, with mixed success, to fit blacks into the machine politics mold. As he famously put it, "Why don't they act like the Poles, Jews, and the Irish?"

But if Daley was unable to see how the history of racism made the black condition distinctive, for Lindsay blacks were *sui generis*. Lindsay governed a liberal city that had already experienced something of a civil rights movement in the late 1940s and '50s. Yet by confronting the issue of race as simply a matter of white racism, Lindsay, the patrician paternalist, so empathized with black anger that he left his city far more polarized than he found it. While Daley couldn't see why the grandchildren of slaves and the children of semi-enslaved sharecroppers needed special help, Lindsay exempted African-Americans from any code of conduct. He explained away any and all behavior by those who claimed to speak for black anger.

Lindsay believed that government could save the cities and right innumerable wrongs. But three decades of HUD policy makes it hard to maintain that optimism. President Clinton's first HUD secretary, Henry Cisneros, testified to Congress in June 1993: "HUD has in many cases exacerbated the declining quality of life in Amer-

ica's cities." A dramatic case in point: the 1968 National Housing Act created the Section 235 program to provide subsidized loans to low-income families, with special assistance for welfare mothers, to buy houses. When the vast majority of the new owners defaulted on these loans there was widespread abandonment and devastation. Carl Levin, then Detroit City Council President, now a liberal Democratic senator, called the upshot "Hurricane HUD." *The Chicago Tribune* wrote that "no natural disaster on record has caused destruction on the scale of the government's housing programs...." For a Gotham analog we have only to look to East New York in the 1960s, where urban renewal and HUD policy produced massive foreclosures in private properties bought with federal aid. More recently a real estate revival in Harlem has been stalled by a new HUD scandal in which the Section 203(K) program created in 1978 to bring stability to low-income neighborhoods has been used, explains *The New York Times*, by "real estate speculators, mortgage lenders and nonprofit groups involved in a complex scheme in which they pocketed millions in rehabilitation money and profits from selling and reselling the buildings in quick succession."

As the passions of the sixties cooled and the costs of that era became apparent, Lindsay's moralism seems less alluring and his managerial failings seem more significant. New York's City Club (Lindsay himself was a member) complained that the mayoralty was "in the hands of people who know all about management—or its vocabulary—except how to get a job done." If Lindsay often viewed issues through a veil of abstraction aimed at impressing *The New York Times* editorial board, Daley emphasized the mundane housekeeping elements of the mayor's job which anticipated today's concern with quality of life issues. What Daley couldn't grasp was the liberal-moralist dimensions of racial politics. When Daley was confronted by Martin Luther King in 1968, he told the civil rights leader that "your goals are our goals" but offered very little in the way of either concrete changes or symbolic acknowledgment of white guilt. King was taken aback when Daley threw the ball back into his court, asking him, "What are your solutions, how do you eliminate slums and blight overnight?" When Jesse Jackson got his first audience with Daley, the mayor offered him a job as a toll-taker.

Daley had an immensely personal concern with the city, extending from everything: from individuals—it's said that he knew half of the city's forty thousand workers personally—to keeping the city clean and attractive. Today it is his son who has completed his vision of cleaning up the Chicago River for recreation.

Daley may have been dubbed a dinosaur in the 1960s, but Lindsay, the self-styled progressive, was on the wrong side of history when it came to the central issues of property and homeownership. While Daley was the champion of property-owning democracy, one of the few prominent Democrats in the sixties who empathized with the middle class, Lindsay was the product of New York political culture which mixed bohemianism, upper-class pretension, and leftist ideology into a coalition of contempt for the homeowning petty bourgeoisie. Lindsay had nothing but disdain for what his administration described, and I quote, as "the ticky-tacky" homes of Archie Bunker's Queens. The first-generation homeowners of the outer boroughs, fearful that their newly acquired middle class status might be stripped from them, returned the hostility. Lindsay seemed comfortable only with those too wealthy to need to work or those unable or unwilling to work. Daley, who had emerged from the ranks of the lower middle class, always understood the importance of homeownership for those newly arrived in positions of relative prosperity. He was the favorite of those white Chicagoans who owned modest homes in the "Bungalow Belt."

The hidden issue of homeownership produced an often unexamined clash between the two American ideals—the rights of private property and the right to equality of opportunity, both essential to the American creed. Lindsay honored the American ideal of equal opportunity by using city hiring to expand black employment opportunities. But his attempts to build housing for poor, racially oppressed black families with high rates of criminality in the midst of lower middle class white neighborhoods was a threat to American ideals of private property, particularly a home safe from government depredations. Lindsay was too arrogant, too sure that his was necessarily the path of righteousness, to be a hypocrite on these matters.

But Daley, like most effective politicians, was a practiced hypocrite. He protected the property rights of white homeowners at the cost of containing even black middle class families in the festering conditions of the inner city. Daley dragged his feet on expanding homeowning opportunities for African-Americans on political grounds. There was an intense and violent opposition when a black family moved into his own neighborhood of Bridgeport in 1955; the house was dismantled almost brick by brick. And the only time he was challenged politically came in 1963 from white critics who, shortly after the Robert Taylor homes had been constructed, said he had done too much for blacks. At the time, the Robert Taylor homes were seen as a big improvement, and they were built in black congressman William Dawson's district at his request and as his reward for service to the machine. Daley won re-election that year with overwhelming black support, while losing a majority of white voters.

A new book by photographer Wayne Miller chronicles the arrival of the people who moved into Robert Taylor. The modern viewer is struck by the still Southern character of the migrants as seen in photos of rabbits strung up across the sidewalk. Even more striking was the housing which looked like the rickety shacks that had been left behind in the Mississippi delta, except these were shacks piled up three and four stories high. These ramshackle homes were the site of innumerable fires, collapsed porches and buildings, garbage-strewn alleyways, rats rampant, an absence of indoor plumbing, disease.

Later, when they became vertical disasters, Daley's critics argued that he maliciously packed forty-thousand newly arrived African-Americans into the high-rise slum of the Robert Taylor homes. They note that "Robert Taylor construction was 'gold plated,' a gift to politically connected contractors. A licensed electrician belonging to a Daley-allied union had to be on site every time a refrigerator was plugged in." And federal money that might have gone into maintaining the vast complex was siphoned into the hands of Daley cronies who operated law firms and insurance companies. And if that wasn't bad enough, the Dan Ryan Expressway, like the Robert Taylor homes built with federal money "Daley was so good at getting," sealed the projects off from the rest of the city.

But Daley fought against high-rise buildings; "when I see my neighborhood I see all the neighborhoods of Chicago," he explained. In Washington he argued for walkups and row houses of the sort that other groups occupied as their first step on the housing ladder, but he was rebuffed by housing officials who insisted that only highrises could meet federal cost concerns. In other words, if we ask if the Taylor homes were a product of Daley's racism, the answer is both *yes* and *no*.

If liberals thought high-rises were reactionary in Chicago, they found them quite progressive when Lindsay proposed to build three twenty-four-story high-rise apartment buildings in the heart of a middle class Jewish neighborhood, Forest Hills, in Queens. Black and Italian middle class areas were vehemently opposed to the project, but Lindsay assumed the Jewish liberals who had voted for him in 1965 wouldn't object, and when they did he spoke of the project's "moral imperative" and denounced the opponents as "racists"—his favorite epithet. The residents of Forest Hills, it seems, were often people who had fled from Brownsville, Crown Heights, Hunts Point, and Far Rockaway into the safety of a pleasant neighborhood, and they didn't want to have to flee again.

Lindsay's narrow emphasis on race seems dated today. Consider the current controversy in Baltimore over an ACLU lawsuit designed to move welfare families into integrated working-to-middle-class neighborhoods in Northeast Baltimore with Section 8 vouchers. (Unsurprisingly, the ACLU lawyer who initiated the suit lives in a tony neighborhood entirely free of Section 8 tenants.)

City Council president Sheila Dixon and State Senator Joan Conway, both black representatives of Northeast Baltimore, are fighting the decision. Their city, they note, has a terrible track record in these matters. Keith Norris, a council member from the district who is also black, explains that he grew up in Park Heights and "witnessed firsthand its gradual decay…as a result of flawed public policy." He sees property ownership not only as an emblem of achievement but as a guarantee of social stability that is now threatened by government action.

"As a homeowner now," says Norris, "I don't want wilting property values to sap the spirit of residents…nor do I want to see the community used as a stage for a courtroom drama." If people are to be brought in "what must be different this time is the amount of support these families get…[such as] classes in home maintenance, landscaping, money management, and child care."

When I spoke to people in Northeast Baltimore, they snorted that "the government specializes in sending welfare populations into weak targets." "You won't see any welfare families sent to Roland Park," one black man snapped at me, referring to the Scarsdale-like neighborhood that resembles Rock Creek Park in the District of Columbia.

In other words, Daley's caution in these matters was more than a matter of racism, it was also—as a recent Chicago experiment with homeowners equity insurance suggests—a matter of helping lower middle class people protect their nest eggs. Derided as "black insurance" when the idea was proposed thirty years ago by the radical Saul Alinsky, homeowners equity insurance enables low-income homeowners to insure the current value of their property in order to prevent white flight. It was initially defeated by pressure from both real estate interests and black politicians, like Tim Evans, who were more concerned with maintaining black political majorities than better housing.

In the ten years since the program finally began under Daley Jr. in 1990, only ten homeowners on the Southwest Side have filed claims. Though the white population has shrunk to about 20 percent of the total (with the rest divided almost evenly between blacks and Hispanics), it is still far greater than in most surrounding areas. Perhaps most telling, property values have steadily climbed. The only catch is that participating residents are required to wait at least five years before a sale below the assessed value entitles them to file a claim. That catch has been crucial. Having committed to live with their new neighbors for at least a few years, many longtime white residents discovered that integration wasn't the horror they had expected.

Neighborhoods, notes *The Wall Street Journal's* Jonathan Eig, are class as well as race-sorting mechanisms:

> The home-equity program serves as a reminder that racial integration often is a matter of economic assimilation. Many of the black families that moved in a decade ago are now enrolling in the program because they fear that the new wave of Hispanic home buyers will damage property values, and Hispanic buyers are signing up because they're not so sure about the next generation of Hispanics.

Today the older Mayor Daley looks like a man ahead of his time on a variety of issues. He had doubts not only about high-rises but also about the social programs of the 1960s. He asked, "Is poor housing the cause of murder and arson?" Similarly, long before broken-windows policing became a great success, he understood that a city has to take care of the small things to maintain its quality of life.

The Lindsayites, however, seem stuck in the past. Recently I took part in a debate at the City University of New York Graduate Center on the question of whether John Lindsay was the worst New York mayor of the twentieth century. The event doubled as a Lindsay alumni reunion so the audience was packed with Lindsayites. And here I should note that the phrase "limousine liberal" is not merely a metaphor—after the debate, as I left the auditorium to go out onto Fifth Avenue, both sides of the street were lined with long black stretch limos.

During the course of the discussion the Lindsayites replied to every disaster, from the doubling of the welfare rolls in the midst of an economic boom to the bankruptcy Lindsay's policies visited on the city, with one of two responses. The first was that Lindsay was a "compassionate man": "Why, he even cried at the death of a black colleague's father." The other was to argue that no one who wasn't a part of the administration could understand or evaluate it. "You had to be there, you had to be inside the administration" to judge it, they insisted time and again. This argument, it so happens, was the favorite of the Lindsayites' archnemesis, Archie Bunker. When Bunker's son-in-law tried to explain to Archie why Vietnam was wrong, Archie replied that "Meathead" didn't know "nuttin'." If you wanted to judge a war, "you had to be there" just like Archie had been there in "the big one, World War II." The Lindsayites' sanctimony had not only effectively sealed them off from learning from their failures, it had reduced them to the caricature they had once mocked.

Still, in putting Lindsay in his proper place we ought not elevate Daley beyond his. The Chicago mayor faced an impossible situation inadequately. But he wasn't nearly as bad as the critics of his time suggested, nor was he as good as nostalgists suggest. We can judge Daley senior in part by what his son has done differently in a Chicago largely shorn of both machine politics and patronage. Once the tough among cities, in the words of Lincoln Steffens, Chicago has turned soft, so to speak. Symbolically, the son has left the family's ancestral home in working-class Bridgeport, which is now slowly gentrifying, for the more cosmopolitan climes of downtown. And while Chicago still suffers from police and government corruption, both Daleys paid inordinate attention to detail. Like his father, Richard M. Daley is planting trees at every opportunity. But the son runs a far more inclusive regime.

Richard M. Daley has done far more than his father to Lindsay-like bring African-Americans into government while improving the services offered to the rapidly growing number of black homeowning neighborhoods. In 1960s terms he has co-opted the black opposition more effectively than his father ever did. Both father and son courted black ministers but Richard M. has done far more to include blacks in city pork, as when he cut African-American politicians in on the lucrative food franchises at the city-owned O'Hare Airport. And black contractors were given a sizable chunk of the action when Daley built the new police headquarters in the historically African-American neighborhood of Bronzeville. Young Daley has supported affirmative action, criticized police brutality, and subsidized church loans for social service corporations. He is now in the process of tearing down the high-rise projects his father built and then generally neglected in favor of dispersing the welfare population into low-rise walk-ups. In three terms as mayor, Daley has gone from 3 percent of the black vote in 1989 to 45 percent last year when he defeated Congressman and former Black Panther Bobby Rush in a landslide even greater than those won by his father. In short, the Daleys have adjusted to a powerful African-American political presence, and most of the black leadership has adjusted to Chicago's one-party political culture.

The "Boss's" mantra of emphasizing "loyalty, hard work, and playing by the rules" was revived for Democrats by the centrist Democratic Leadership Council. The council's chair, Bill Clinton, picked up Daley's themes in his successful 1992 run for president. "Daleyism," referring to the father, was recently defined by John Judis writing in *The New Republic*, as a "cross-racial, working-class and lower middle class voting majority with the financial support of business—which is what every Democrat wants to bottle and imbibe these days." That is one reason why older brother Bill Daley ran Al Gore's campaign.

If there's merit to Richard J. Daley's revival, it's oddly enough because the elder Daley was a man behind the times. In the 1960s he was a fish out of water, a localist in an era that demanded a universalist racial ethic. But as cities have, for the most part, become more racially inclusive, they've generally been able to return to the time-honored approaches that have always worked. Daley's passion for both private homeownership and the details of city life point to the policies of today's most successful mayors. But it's only as race has receded as a defining issue that Daley's parochial perspective, which sees affirmative action as just another way of dividing the spoils, could once again define the Democrats. In Chicago, an inclusive tribalism looks remarkably similar to the multiculturalism of Jesse Jackson and the liberal wing of the Democratic Party.

Fred Siegel is the author of *The Future Once Happened Here* (1997).

From *Partisan Review*, Spring 2001, pp. 218-227. © 2001 by Fred Siegel. Reprinted with permission.

BEYOND
Safe and Clean
BIDs help create design guidelines for historic downtown Los Angeles.

BRIDGET MALEY, CATHLEEN MALMSTROM, AND KELLIE PHIPPS

In the revitalization efforts of numerous downtowns, authentic urban streetscapes are being rehabilitated using both public subsidies and private investment. Nearly always, historic building rehabilitation and reuse are at the core of these efforts. Each city has its own formula for balancing public and private involvement, mandatory and voluntary preservation practices, and local historic architectural traditions and newer cultural influences within the community. Design guidelines for historic commercial buildings that involve—or are sponsored by—local business organizations and that embrace local design traditions have a greater chance of being implemented, and thus are more likely to contribute to downtown revitalization.

There is no single formula for rehabilitating historic areas, but there are standards. The U. S. Secretary of the Interior's *Standards for Rehabilitation,* known as the Standards, are an important tool in creating a framework for preservation—an action often linked to valuable tax credits for private sector developers. However, the Standards do not address every relevant issue, as each rehabilitation project entails its own specific concerns. Applying the Standards while also employing important local cultural practices can serve to enhance a project in the long run; recent efforts to develop design guidelines for historic downtown Los Angeles offer a model.

For years, developers, architects, historians, and tourists alike have believed that Los Angeles has no urban center—no heart. Although downtown Los Angeles, once the city's entertainment, commerce, and retail hub, has undergone great change since the 1940s, many buildings of an earlier era remain. Greater Los Angeles's extensive suburban expansion, however, left the older, historic core behind—and almost forgotten.

In the latter half of the 20th century, a number or events contributed to the decline of Los Angeles's historic downtown. They include changing demographics, removal of trolley car lines, new access to the west side of downtown from the Harbor Freeway, razing of residential Bunker Hill and subsequent commercial redevelopment, changes in the entertainment industry and banking institutions, and abandonment of downtown for other areas with the Los Angeles basin. However, recent urban patterns, including congested freeways and the high cost of housing, as well as a broader appreciation of historic areas, have created a renewed interest in Los Angeles's historic center. (See "L.A. Pieces," page 50, February 1999, *Urban Land.*)

The drive to create design guidelines for historic buildings in Los Angeles's downtown core is the result of a collaborative effort by property owners, business improvement districts (BIDs), preservation advocates, and merchants. The goal is to develop standards flexible enough to embrace existing local cultural traditions, but firm enough to encourage rehabilitation, reuse, and revitalization to uncover the area's rich architectural legacy.

Throughout the country, BIDs have been established to help maintain and support urban revitalization. Although BIDs often focus on improved security and clean streets, several area BIDs in Los Angeles have moved beyond their "safe and clean" tasks to include preservation and design issues concerning their historic buildings and streetscapes. Working with the Los Angeles Conservancy (a local preservation advocacy organization established in 1978), the Historic Core, Downtown Center, and Fashion District BIDs developed a grant proposal for the Getty Grant Program's Preserve L. A. program. Upon receipt of the October 2000 grant, these three BIDs and the Los Angeles Conservancy embarked on a process to develop guidelines for historic building and storefront rehabilitation along Hill, Broadway, Spring, and Main streets, between Third and Ninth streets, in the center of the city.

During the late 1920s, the introduction of sound in movies resulted in a new wave of movie palaces along Broadway, and several major department stores also opened in the vicinity, further enlivening the streetscape.

Shown here are an example of the existing condition of representative storefronts (inset) and a sketch from the design guidelines for historic downtown Los Angeles, which include a requirement that signage not conceal historic features and materials.

Spring Street developed as Los Angeles's banking and financial center, and was often dubbed the "Wall Street of the West." Most of these commercial buildings, and Broadway's elaborate theaters, have richly decorated and, in some cases, colorful facades that are largely intact. While there is great interest in these architectural gems, there also are threats to this important group of early 20th-century structures. Existing design review policies address only those structures individually landmarked, not the overall urban fabric, leaving many historic resources unprotected—and at risk.

Today, Broadway Street is a lively and profitable shopping area, with first-floor retail uses catering to the Latino community; however, the upper floors of these buildings are partially or completely vacant. Like Broadway, many upper stories in structures along Spring, Main, and Hill streets also are underused. Since the time when businesses abandoned the older commercial center, the built environment of historic downtown has remained essentially the same with only a few buildings demolished or extensively altered. On dozens of blocks, the upper stories of buildings look generally as they did between 1920 and 1940. However, at the street or storefront level, significant change has occurred; in many cases, signage and displays of merchandise obscure the remaining historic fabric. In more extreme cases, storefronts have been completely removed.

Currently, downtown Los Angeles is catching up with its sprawling suburbs, as new commercial and residential projects such as the Spring Tower Artist Lofts and the Old Banking District Lofts unfold in the area. At the center of this revitalization is the Los Angeles Conservancy, which has been instrumental in preservation efforts across the Los Angeles basin. It has been particularly active in preserving Broadway's historic theaters and in promoting revitalization efforts in the historic downtown area. The

Conservancy's "Broadway Initiative" seeks to return Broadway to an entertainment district and to create a mixed-use, 24-hour live/work environment in the historic downtown. Working with area BIDs, local developers, and financial institutions, the Conservancy is attempting to draw new development to and encourage rehabilitation projects in the downtown area. Its action plan also calls for physical building and streetscape improvements, which will be aided by the new design guidelines.

"Downtown Los Angeles's greatest assets are its architecture and history. We want to promote them to attract economic investment," explains Amy Anderson, who leads the Broadway Initiative for the Conservancy. "It was important to work with the property owners to develop the design guidelines. Involving the BIDs in a collaborative process helps to accomplish that goal." Building owners frequently are skeptical of guidelines or regulations that limit their flexibility. However, in this case, through the BIDs, owners were asked to contribute extensively to develop the guidelines—not just to respond to legislation being imposed by a governmental agency. The Conservancy and the three BIDs see their role as an educational one, informing the property owners that a standard of quality design will help to improve their assets, protecting them against neglect and insensitive renovations, and generating additional investment in nearby properties. The educational orientation of the guidelines, coupled with the fact that they will be voluntary, has sparked widespread interest and participation from property owners.

After the Conservancy and the BIDs adopt the guidelines, the next step will be for these groups to assist property owners in implementing the recommendations. Various future incentives—including non-governmental design review, low-interest loans, and improvement

Restoring Tinsel to Tinseltown

Early this part November, the curtain rose on Hollywood with the fanfare and spectacle reminiscent of the area's past. The long-awaited debut of the $615 million Hollywood and Highland mixed-use development adjacent to the famed Grauman's Chinese Theatre has been touted as the cornerstone for Hollywood's renaissance. (See "Hollywood Face-Lift," page 50, February 2001 *Urban Land*.)

Yet, the rebirth of Hollywood is more than the retail entertainment complex at the corner of the famous intersection that shares its name. According to the Hollywood Chamber of Commerce, approximately $1.6 billion is being reinvested in the historic neighborhood. During the 1950s and 1960s, the neighborhood of Hollywood changed dramatically. The seeds of blight were being sewn when many Hollywood stars moved to Beverly Hills, taking with them elegant shops and restaurants. Soon thereafter, other businesses began departing to the rapidly developing Los Angeles suburbs.

Over the years, Hollywood succumbed to increased crime, graffiti, and high vacancy rates. As the area continued to experience depreciating property values and economic and social maladjustments, the city of Los Angeles, through its community redevelopment agency (CRA), adopted in May 1986 the Hollywood Redevelopment Plan, responsible for an area spanning more than 1,100 acres. The Hollywood project area, bound approximately by La Brea Avenue to the west, Santa Monica Boulevard to the south, Western Avenue to the east, and Franklin Avenue to the north, is one of the largest redevelopment project areas in Los Angeles.

A 79,000-square-foot office building in the Hollywood and Highland area of Los Angeles, 6565 Sunset Boulevard is undergoing a $3 million architectural and technological renovation.

"There has been much talk about the on-again, off-again renaissance in Hollywood, especially with the successful opening of Hollywood and Highland," says Donna DeBruhl-Hemer, the CRA's project manager for the Hollywood project. "In actuality, changes were beginning to take place more than a decade ago." According to DeBruhl-Hemer, the CRA has worked with both the public and private sectors for the past 15 years to address the problem of blight in Hollywood. As a result, it has championed more than 150 public, residential and service, and commercial and industrial development projects within the redevelopment area, among them the Hollywood and Highland project.

The impetus created by the CRA and projects like Hollywood and Highland, Cinerama Dome, and Sunset and Vine can be seen in improvements occurring at the grass-roots level. For example, construction is nearly complete on the $3 million architectural and technological renovation of 6565 Sunset Boulevard, a five-story, 79,000-square foot office building adjacent to the Hollywood Athletic Club. The building's original south-facing aluminum-and-glass facade has been replaced by a reflective glass curtain wall, and an elliptical-shaped lobby is being constructed entirely of frameless structural glass. Interior upgrades at nearby 6464 Sunset, a vintage 1970s 11-story office building, are nearly completed and plans already are underway to renovate the exterior.

The reinvestment in Hollywood by Paramount Contractors and Developers, owners of 6565 and 6464 Sunset and other local building owners, such as local developer Tom Gilmore, who is spending $6 million on the renovation of the historic Equitable Building on Hollywood Boulevard, has resulted in numerous entertainment companies returning to and/or expanding in Hollywood, one of the CRA's major goals. According to the *Hol-

lywood Economic Development Update 2001,* recently published by the Hollywood Chamber of Commerce Economic Development Committee, leases totaling approximately 250,000 square feet were signed by entertainment companies alone in 2001. Universal Television and Paramount Pictures (no relation to Paramount Contractors) recently signed lease expansions and renewals at 6565 Sunset Boulevard. Atom Films, TV Guide, Time Warner Entertainment, and USA Studios also have inked deals in Hollywood this past year.

To create an effective redevelopment plan for the area, the CRA and the Metropolitan Transit Authority in the mid-1980s conducted a study of potential development around what were then the three planned Hollywood Metrorail portal sites (all now in operation): Hollywood and Highland, Vine Street, and Western Avenue. The joint agency study provided clear direction for the CRA as it identified three distinct districts within the redevelopment area, each with its own specific needs: entertainment and retail space at Hollywood and Highland; theater and market-rate residential uses at Vine Street; and affordable housing and community-serving retail at Western and Santa Monica.

Sitting atop the Metrorail station at Hollywood and Highland is the new 1.2 million-square-foot Los Angeles-based TrizecHahn Development Corp. project, which includes 225,000 square feet of specialty retail, 100,000 square feet of restaurants and live venues, and the 3,500-seat Kodak Theatre—permanent home to the Academy Awards. The project is credited with attracting several new restaurants and clubs to the district, including the New York music club Knitting Factory and Mel's Drive-In, which was featured in the 1973 movie, *American Graffiti.* Down the street, the historic Pig 'n' Whistle restaurant, a 1920s landmark that had been closed for a number of years, reopened last March after a $1 million renovation.

To the east is the Vine Street Theater District, which, in sharp contrast to the Boulevard improvements to the west, is being planned in large part for use by corporate entities and local residents instead of tourists. The Metrorail portal at Hollywood and Vine is across the street from the Pantages Theater, which reopened in October 2000 after a $10 million facelift. It since has been home to Disney's stage production of *The Lion King.*

Less than a mile south near Sunset Boulevard are two major components of the redevelopment of Vine: Sunset and Vine and the Cinerama Dome Entertainment Center. Sunset and Vine is a mixed-use development located on the former site of the Merv Griffin TAV Celebrity Theater, build originally in 1937 as a broadcast studio for the American Broadcasting Company. The first major residential mixed-use project in Hollywood, Sunset and Vine features community-serving retail at street level, including Costs Plus and Borders Books stores, and provides the first new market-rate housing to be built during the current wave of Hollywood redevelopment. The residential component will feature 300 loft apartments ranging in size from 550 to 1,200 square feet.

The success of Sunset and Vine is viewed by some as the first step in the transformation of the immediate area into a 24-hour, pedestrian-oriented community, where residents can walk to work or shop. Adjacent to Sunset and Vine is the Doolittle/Ricardo Montalban Theater, built in 1926 with 1,142 seats. Purchased last year by Montalban's Nosotros Foundation, which is raising an additional $8 million for rehabilitation and operating endowment, the theater is expected to give Hispanic artists a high-profile venue for special performances.

Anchoring the Vine District is the Cinerama Dome Entertainment Center, a $90 million development that will surround the famous Cinerama Dome Theater with 34,000 square feet of stores and restaurants and a 50,000-square-foot health club. The center will be served by a much-needed public parking structure, financed entirely by the CRA, that can accommodate more than 1,700 automobiles.

(continued)

These two projects are credited with spawning activity around the Sunset and Vine hub. One block west on Sunset Boulevard, one of San Francisco's most popular music stores, Amoeba Music, opened its southern California flagship last summer in a new 45,000-square-foot building. Across the street at 6353 Sunset is the new headquarters of Klasky Csupo, best known as the creators of *The Rugrats.* Experiencing major growth, Klasky Csupo, which became the first non-Disney studio to break the $100 million domestic box-office mark with an animated feature film in March 1999, needed a facility to consolidate its operations. Also new to the area is Cooltoons, Klasky Csupo's street-level retail store featuring a collection of merchandise from the company's animated motion picture and television features.

At 6353 Sunset is the new headquarters of the film studio, Klasky Csupo, which includes a streeet-level retail store, Cooltoons.

On the easternmost border of the redevelopment area, near a Metrorail station at Western Avenue and Santa Monica Boulevard, was a third and totally different district, far from the glamour and glitter of Tinseltown, yet considered equally important to Hollywood's total redevelopment. The densely populated area is characterized by older retail uses and inadequate housing for what is largely a lower-income Hispanic and Asian population, many of whom work in and around Hollywood. There, more than 200 affordable housing units have been constructed near Western Avenue; among them, the 60-unit Western Carlton, located on the site of a former earthquake-damaged slum apartment building on the southwest corner of Hollywood and Western. Across the street, construction has started on Hollywest, a 115,000-square-foot, community-serving retail center anchored by a Ralph's Grocery market and a Ross Dress for Less. Due to open in December, Hollywest also will provide the community with 100 housing units for seniors.

While each of the three districts has its own unique needs, the interplay among the three is considered critical to Hollywood's renaissance. For example, not only will residents of the affordable housing units have the opportunity to benefit from new retail being developed within their neighborhood, but also projects like Hollywood and Highland, bound by "first-source hiring," offer employment opportunities. "Redevelopment is more than helping the business community," says CRA's DeBruhl-Hemer. "A great measure of our success is what's done to improve the social fabric of the community."

Among the businesses that have been drawn most recently to Hollywood's allure and, at the same time, most responsible for contributing to it are the area's new nightclubs and restaurants. One of the first to see Hollywood's promise was Michel Larry, owner of Le Deux Cafés, one of L. A.'s hottest restaurants. Others followed, including Deep, a restaurant/nightclub on Hollywood and Vine Street that was featured in the recent movie,

Ocean's 11. Across the street is the Hollywood and Vine Diner, which opened in January at a cost of $3.5 million. Located on the ground floor of the newly renovated Hollywood Equitable Building, originally built in 1929, the diner also includes the Ultra Lounge operated jointly by Capitol Records, which will feature some of its recording artists regularly at the nightspot. CineSpace, which bills itself as a unique supper club and digital cinema lounge, opened last January and is the first venue of its kind in southern California, allowing patrons to dine while viewing the latest in entertainment programming.

While the recent developments in the Hollywood and Highland area are viewed as a boon for the area, civic and business leaders are trying to ensure that Hollywood is not turned into a theme park. "We need an electric mix of retailers that will enhance the urban fabric," says the Hollywood chamber's Gubler. "We want and need the Gap, but there's also a place for the wig shops and tattoo parlors. We need to maintain the character that is Hollywood; that's part of its attraction."

A new 115,000-square-foot community retail center, Hollywest, is due to open in December.

The large development projects have inspired local business owners to create several business improvement districts (BIDs) in Hollywood. The first, the Hollywood Entertainment District, was formed in 1996 and spans an 18-block stretch of Hollywood Boulevard, from LaBrea on the west to Gower on the east and includes the Hollywood and Highland project. Today, this BID oversees a budget of $2.1 million—raised by assessing property owners within the district—to pay for private security patrols; maintenance of sidewalks and gutters; removal of trash and graffiti; marketing and promotion of the area; and administration.

The BIDs also serve as advocates for the property owners within their boundaries. "An important role is to bring the voices of our stakeholders to city hall and to improve the area," points out Mary Lou Dudas, executive director of the Hollywood Media District, a BID that encompasses the area south of Fountain Avenue between Highland and Vine. Last year, the Hollywood Media District raised $600,000 primarily for a clean-up program. However, with the assistance of local consulting firm Kyser Marston, the BID was able to generate $1.2 million in grant funding from the city for streetscape improvements.

As a result of the success of and support for the two existing BIDs, a third BID, the Central Hollywood Coalition, is now being formed with 35 of the 200 property owners in support of the 63-block BID area along Sunset Boulevard from Highland eastward to the Hollywood Freeway and along Vine Street from Selma Avenue to Melrose. Among its members are CBS Television, Amoeba Records, Pacific Theaters, Klasky Csupo, and the Post Group. The three BIDs cover roughly 40 percent of the CRA's Hollywood project area.—**Brian Folb,** a *principal of Paramount Contractors and Developers, a Hollywood, California-based commercial real estate firm*

grants—have been discussed. The recent investment and development activity in the downtown already has resulted in an appropriation of federal funds for revitalization of Broadway. The Conservancy will establish a forgivable loan program to financially support facade renovations that are consistent with the design guidelines. In addition, seven downtown Los Angeles BIDs and two other organizations currently are working together to develop wayfinding signage for vehicles and pedestrians for use throughout the downtown areas.

There are many who agree that bringing residential uses into older commercial centers is key to their renewal. This is

true in Los Angeles, where the city recently has instigated a powerful incentive in the form of the Adaptive Reuse Ordinance. This preservation tool promotes compatible uses of historic office buildings, such as residential use. This new incentive, in conjunction with use of California's historic building code, allows for alternative means to meet building safety requirements. As a result, a number of local developers and building owners have converted older office structures into residential lofts, which has helped to bring people back to downtown Los Angeles.

Both the Conservancy and the BIDs have stressed the need for the design guidelines to address the ethnic influences and evolving community traditions within the historic core, particularly the Latino *mercado* tradition that has developed in recent years along Broadway. As Los Angeles's Latino population has increased, markets catering to it and offering merchandise ranging from produce to blue jeans have economically sustained portions of downtown. Existing storefronts and large "swap meets" in some of the city's historic theaters provide substantial income for both merchants and their landlords. These relatively unplanned businesses are quite profitable because of the sheer number of sales generated within or just outside the building. Income from existing street-level retail establishments can be so high that building owners in downtown Los Angeles have felt no need and little incentive to invest in the substantial rehabilitation required to attract tenants to the upper floors. As a result, the lack of interest in the upper floors has led to deterioration of many building components.

> *Because the historic identity of a district can serve as a "brand," it is in the interest of BIDs to become advocates for preservation within their districts.*

The appropriation of sidewalks and building walls for displays of enormous quantities of goods, wares, and signage, including the exuberant use of color and graphics, can be considered both an asset and a detriment to downtown Los Angeles. As a positive element, these features provide a vibrant streetscape. However, the *mercado* tradition of merchandise display sometimes leads to the complete removal of historic storefronts to allow for retail expansion out onto the sidewalk. Without the storefront building elements, metal roll-down doors are required to secure the shops when they are closed. The combination of nighttime desolation, stark roll-down doors, limited storefront glazing, few additional uses and activities, and cultural unfamiliarity leads to a perception by some people that the area is unsafe. On Broadway in downtown Los Angeles, the streets are active from 9 to 5, after which time shops close, roll-down doors descend to the street, and the sidewalks are virtually abandoned.

An issue important to both the Conservancy and the BIDs while developing the historic downtown Los Angeles design guidelines was the need to support economic activity by juxtaposing historic resources with the ongoing life of the street. Design parameters can complement existing historic resources and maintain the ethnic diversity that gives the district its vitality. The concern about providing secure storefronts dovetails with the tradi-

tional "safe and clean" tasks initiated by the BIDs, yet there is agreement that the nighttime appearance of a seemingly continuous facade of metal roll-down doors is a detriment to the area.

Design guidelines for historic buildings can address ways to enhance both the actual security of an area and the appearance of security. For example, the solid metal pull-down panels can be replaced by a variety of open grilles, allowing merchandise to be protected and simultaneously creating a connection between pedestrians and interior storefronts.

"Broadway was once the city's entertainment and shopping corridor," says Kent Smith, executive director of the Fashion District BID. Today, it is a Latino-oriented shopping district. The signage guidelines promote the use of color and light, rather than size or quantity, as the primary means of sending a marketing message. It is hoped that this will help deter use of excess signage while retaining the vibrancy of the street. The Grand Central Market on Broadway, for example, has already achieved reasonable controls on signage and displays imposed by the landlord without diminishing the atmosphere of a vibrant market.

Design guidelines are only one element in a successful downtown revitalization strategy. Other components include an incentive package, educational programs, and design review processes. Design guidelines for historic buildings can help to build political will by engaging property owners and tenants, addressing their competing priorities, and helping them to find common ground and direction. Such guidelines can become a tool for educating stakeholders as diverse as those in downtown Los Angeles on the value of preservation and on the methods of signage and display that both serve their commercial needs *and* complement the historic character of the area.

Through their established outreach efforts, BIDs can effectively encourage revitalization. Because the historic identity of a district can serve as a "brand," it is in the interest of BIDs to become advocates for preservation within their districts. They can serve as partners in creating flexible design guidelines for historic buildings that can promote the unique character of commercial downtowns. Although the three Los Angeles BIDs still are involved in "safe and clean" activities, they have moved beyond their traditional role in revitalization, becoming agents of economic development and design enhancements within downtown Los Angeles.

BRIDGET MALEY, CATHLEEN MALMSTROM, AND KELLIE PHIPPS ARE ARCHITECTS AND HISTORIANS AT THE SAN FRANCISCO–BASED ARCHITECTURE FIRM ARCHITECTURAL RESOURCES GROUP, WHICH ASSISTED THE BIDS AND THE LOS ANGELES CONSERVANCY IN COMPLETING THE DESIGN GUIDELINES FOR HISTORIC DOWNTOWN.

Bloomberg So Far

Fred Siegel & Harry Siegel

WHEN MICHAEL BLOOMBERG was elected mayor in 2001, New Yorkers had little idea what to expect from him. A liberal Democrat by disposition turned Republican by opportunity, the billionaire media baron had no previous political experience. He had used his fortune to conduct a stealth campaign, bombarding the public with direct mailings and television advertising and making virtually no unscripted appearances. Wrapped only in the halo of outgoing mayor Rudolph Giuliani's belated endorsement, and widely expected to lose, the would-be mayor was barely questioned, let alone tested, before he took office.

In the immediate wake of 9/11, Bloomberg's conciliatory and willfully apolitical style turned out to be well suited to the city's sense of trauma. The political neophyte seemed to promise Giuliani-like results without the ex-prosecutor's abrasive, stentorian style. Now, halfway through his tenure and with talk of the next mayoral election already in the air, Bloomberg has a record and an established public personality. He is far more of a known quantity, even if much of what can now be said about him is neither especially flattering nor encouraging for the future of New York.

TO HIS credit, and despite his sometimes graceless efforts to escape his predecessor's shadow, Bloomberg has consolidated and even extended a number of Giuliani's most important achievements. Contrary to the expectations of many commentators, there has been no increase in crime in New York City, nor a renewed sense of urban dread and menace. In fact, since Bloomberg took office, the crime rate has dropped a further 10 percent, thanks in no small measure to the latitude that he has given to his police commissioner, Raymond Kelly. Moreover, as the mayor noted in his recent State of the City address, "We've done all this while protecting the nation's most important city against the constant threat of terror."

Bloomberg has also built upon the success of Compstat, the block-by-block breakdown of crime statistics that Giuliani instituted as a way to assign responsibility for public safety. Now the city has a similar system for quality-of-life problems, based on phoned-in complaints. By replicating the Compstat ethos of tracking data and quickly spotting undesirable trends, Bloomberg has made the city more responsive to the petty annoyances—potholes, noise violations, inadequate garbage pickups, cell-phone dead spots—that can make life in New York a daily trial.

Bloomberg's most significant accomplishment to date has been winning back mayoral control of the city's schools. For years, 110 Livingston Street, the Board of Education's downtown Brooklyn address had been shorthand for Byzantine bureaucracy and wanton waste. Giuliani had paved the way

for the takeover with his tough talk about the need to "blow up" the Board of Education; but the former mayor's enemies in Albany, where such decisions are made, refused to give him the victory. State lawmakers proved more receptive to Bloomberg's calm and conciliatory style.

From a purely administrative point of view, Bloomberg's reorganization of the schools has thus far been highly successful. Textbooks are delivered on time, and supplies are available. The powerful custodians' union, which has been ripping off the city for years, is being brought to heel through the partial privatization of janitorial services. More important, a mayor can no longer hide behind the Board when schools perform poorly while stepping forward to take credit for any and all signs of educational progress. Bloomberg has repeatedly said that if he fails to reform the education system, he should be voted out of office—a commendable pledge of accountability.

But there are other items than these on Bloomberg's ledger sheet, and too many of them fall decidedly into the debit column. Though there is no denying the importance of his having won mayoral control of the schools, his use of that control with respect to the curriculum has been irresponsible, even reckless. As a candidate, Bloomberg spoke of the need for a back-to-basics approach to education. But the instructional program imposed by the mayor and his schools chancellor, Joel Klein (formerly the Justice Department's lead counsel in the Microsoft case), is straight out of the left-wing fever swamps of Columbia Teachers College. Advised by Diana Lam, a well-known advocate of "progressive" education, Klein abandoned a variety of phonics programs that had shown some success in improving reading scores, replacing them with a one-size-fits-all "whole language" approach that has a long history of failure. Worse, the literacy effort has been micromanaged from Klein's office, which has told even experienced and successful teachers how to arrange every minute of their day and every inch of their classrooms. Blackboards, for example, are prohibited, as is arranging chairs in rows with the teacher in the front. (According to the slogan of progressive education, a teacher must act not as "a sage on the stage" but as a "guide on the side.") This attack on pedagogical authority has even extended to school discipline, emboldening unruly students and generating a surge in violence against teachers.

Education aside, Bloomberg has expended valuable political capital on various pet causes. The most notorious of these has been his anti-smoking campaign. He used much of the good will of his honeymoon in office to pass a draconian law that banned smoking in bars and other heretofore unregulated places and dramatically raised the cigarette tax—an issue he had not mentioned as a candidate. The predictable result has been a new and violent black market in out-of-state cigarettes and vastly increased noise levels outside bars, some of which have lost considerable business. Even voters sympathetic to his cause were offended when the mayor promoted it by warning the citizenry, with missionary zeal, that "more people [would] die from second-hand smoke than were killed in the World Trade Center."

A worthier effort, if one handled just as badly, was Bloomberg's campaign in 2003 to persuade voters to approve a ballot initiative establishing nonpartisan elections for mayor and City Council. The proposal was hardly revolutionary. Nonpartisan elections—already in place in eight of the country's ten largest cities—open up municipal government to a wider range of interests. In New York City, such a reform would help to break the powerful hold of the public-sector unions, whose highly organized members dominate the all important Democratic primary.

But it takes time to explain how nonpartisanship would make elections more competitive and politicians more accountable. Bloomberg insisted on rushing the matter, placing it on the ballot only a few months after it was officially proposed by a charter commission that he had appointed. Trying to replicate the stealth tactics that had helped him win the mayoralty, he blitzed voters with a last minute, $7.5-million direct-mail campaign. The results were predictable. Although nonpartisanship enjoyed a slight majority of support among the electorate as a whole, the 12 percent who bothered to vote in this off-year ballot—many of them drawn from the same pool of public-sector employees whose influence Bloomberg was trying to limit— defeated the proposal by a margin of more than 2 to 1. In what Dan Janison of *Newsday* called his "Evita moment," the mayor declared that what mattered was not the outcome but the effort: "I was a big winner yesterday."

EVEN A reform as intelligent as nonpartisan elections is no substitute for dealing more directly with the public-sector interests that have long been the fiscal albatross around New York City's neck. Like Giuliani before him, Bloomberg was given a poor economic hand. The city was in recession even before 9/11, and the new mayor was saddled with rising pension and Medicaid costs imposed during Giuliani's boom years. He arrived in office facing a budget deficit of $4 billion. But unlike Giuliani, Bloomberg played his poor hand poorly, especially in his dealings with his "friend," Governor George Pataki, on one side and with the public-sector unions on the other. In both cases his watchword was "partnership"—in contrast, presumably, with Giuliani's vaunted confrontationalism. Thus, lavishing praise on the Republican governor and donating $1 million of his personal money to the state GOP, Bloomberg went so far as to support an obviously unpopular fare hike imposed on the city's buses and subways by the Pataki-controlled transportation authority. What he got in exchange was worse than nothing. Pataki refused Bloomberg's reasonable request to help reinstate the city's small but symbolically important commuter tax, while permitting him to raise the city's sales and income taxes, already the highest in the region.

The story was similar with the public-sector unions. Perhaps the most dramatic incident occurred in December 2002, when Roger Toussaint, the radical president of the Transit Workers Union, threatened to strike rather than accept changes in work rules that would allow, among other things, subway cleaners to change light bulbs and do minor painting. Placed in a similar situation, Giuliani had made clear how much damage he could do to the union under the law; Bloomberg, instead, spoke plaintively of how much damage the union could do to the city. "A strike," he said, "would be more than inconvenient. It would endanger human life and devastate our economy." Toussaint largely got his way.

The pattern of behavior that Toussaint capitalized on had been set earlier. In what he declared to be a new "partnership" between the city and its public sector unions, Bloomberg had announced, before even sitting down to bargaining sessions, that he would do everything he could to avoid layoffs. Where Giuliani had restrained hiring through a vacancy-control board, Bloomberg quickly abolished the board. Where Giuliani had used the threat of privatization to win concessions from unions, Bloomberg promised to avoid such measures wherever possible. He also made no effort to renegotiate the unions' health, benefits, and pension plans, all of which are far more generous than similar plans in the private sector and in most other big cities.

In exchange for this new spirit of cooperation, Bloomberg expected good will from the other side. Naturally, it never materialized. But the mayor's naive expectation was costly, causing him to wait almost a year before imposing any kind of serious controls on hiring and spending. The results were devastating for the city's overall financial health. Where Giuliani reduced spending by 3 percent in his inaugural year, Bloomberg increased spending by almost as much—increments that amounted to much more than peanuts in New York City's massive budget. As the Manhattan Institute's E.J. McMahon has noted, if Bloomberg "had duplicated Rudy's spending restraint in his first two fiscal years, the city would now be spending about $2.5 billion less, and most of Bloomberg's tax and fee hikes wouldn't have been necessary.

"That Bloomberg has, in fact, closed the city's budget gap primarily through those "tax and hikes" has been especially galling to many who supported him. Bloomberg ran for office on a ringing pledge of no new taxes, confirming this in his first speech as mayor when he warned that higher taxes would only "drive people and business out of New York." But within a year, he had sharply raised cigarette, sales, and income taxes. Over the noisy protests of middle-class homeowners in every borough, he also pushed through a whopping 21-percent increase in the property tax. All of these hikes, insisted the mayor of a city that was already the most taxed in the nation, were unavoidable.

BY THE last quarter of 2003, Michael Bloomberg had achieved the unhappy distinction of possessing the lowest approval rating ever held by a modern mayor of New York. To explain his deep unpopularity, it is not enough, though, to catalogue his policy missteps. Bloomberg is disliked, even hated, not just because of what he has done but perhaps in equal measure because of how he has done it.

A self-made man who has accumulated a personal fortune of $4.5 billion, Bloomberg possesses an overweening self-confidence, acting at times as if it were demeaning to have to explain himself to others. Plainly, he is someone accustomed to having his word taken as law. But City Hall is a very different place from the boardroom, and rarely has a mayor shown himself, by temperament or forethought, to be less prepared to govern a major city.

Like Bloomberg, Giuliani had never held elected office prior to his victory in 1993. But Giuliani had spent years in the public sphere as a federal prosecutor. More important, he had already made one unsuccessful run for mayor, and after his defeat had gone to work studying every aspect of city policy. Once elected, Giuliani was single-minded in the performance of his job, immersing himself for eighteen hours a day in the details of government operations while at the same time keeping the big picture in sight.

What has stood out with Bloomberg, by contrast, is his aloofness, not just from the city (he often quietly escapes by private jet for weekends at his home in Bermuda) but from city government itself. Unlike his predecessor, he has neither taken a direct hand in running the city's maze of bureaucracies nor tried to give specific guidance to his appointees.

Moreover, for a hard-headed businessman who now presides over a budget larger than that of all but eight states, Bloomberg can seem appallingly naive. When he insisted (to guffaws) that "corruption, waste, and meaningless programs hardly exist in city government," he was declaring himself content with business as usual, and essentially denying that the city faced any sort of crisis.

For a great many New Yorkers whose wonted relationship to their mayor is visceral and intimate, this detachment has been too much to bear. Time and again, Bloomberg has proved that he simply does not understand average New Yorkers or empathize with their travails. As the possibility of a subway strike loomed, he dragged reporters along to watch him buy a $600 bicycle, and suggested that others should meet their transportation needs in the same way. At a time when middle-class New Yorkers were outraged by his tax hikes, he jauntily told an elite Manhattan business group that the city was "a high-end product, maybe even a luxury product." Further stoking the anger of his critics, he jibed that he, for one, was perfectly willing to pay higher taxes.

HAS BLOOMBERG learned anything from the rocky first years of his tenure? Perhaps. In his State of the City address this January, he seemed intent on relaunching his mayoralty with an appeal to New York's outer boroughs. The highlight of the speech was a proposal to issue a $400 rebate against the huge property-tax increase he had imposed. Striking, too, was the tone of the address, with its stress on crime control and the city's quality of life—clear echoes of Giuliani's priorities. For the first time, the mayor seemed to be talking to—instead of at—voters.

What remains unclear is whether Bloomberg now understands the deeper issue for New York: the enduring and now-desperate need to shrink and reform the city's bloated public sector. If nothing else, he has certainly placed himself on a collision course with the unions, virtually all of whose major contracts are up for renegotiation this year. Working to close an estimated $2-billion deficit—and, thanks to his proposed rebate, with less money at hand—he has stipulated that any salary increase will have to be paid for by improvements in productivity. Needless to say, this position is fiercely opposed by the unions.

The grim reality facing New Yorkers concerned about the future of the city is that the billionaire incumbent, an accidental mayor who seems to have run for office primarily to test himself with a new challenge, may be their best hope among the available alternatives. Since the defeat of the initiative for nonpartisan elections, Left-liberal rivals have been making ready their campaigns. They include Fernando (Freddy) Ferrer, an ally of Al Sharpton who almost won the Democratic mayoral nomination the last time around, and Gifford Miller, the speaker of the City Council and a young and willing accomplice of the city's spending interests. In short, Bloomberg could well be defeated in 2005 by a candidate backed by and ready to accommodate the same interests that are slowly strangling the city and driving away its middle class.

It is hard to exaggerate the danger of such a relapse. Bloomberg is fond of reassuring audiences that "smart people have to be here if they want to be successful." This, however, has become less true with each passing year, especially as New York's costs have risen in relation to those of its competitors. The last recession set a telling precedent. Usually the city and the region rise and fall together, but this time New Jersey and Connecticut, which have diversified their economies by attracting industries once based overwhelmingly in New York, recovered quickly—and left the city behind.

Behind the sparkle and dynamism of today's New York is the mundane fact that, with the exception of San Francisco, no other American city has lost residents at a higher rate over the past several years. Poor and ill-educated immigrants have continued to flow into the city, while highly skilled people with intellectual capital continue to decamp for places that offer them more and tax them less. For the city's Democratic politicians and the public employees they represent, this may be good news; the middle class has always been the chief political obstacle to their hold on power. For New York City as a whole—even for those precincts of it inhabited by the likes of Michael Bloomberg—such news is a portent of dark days ahead.

Fred Siegel is a professor at Cooper Union and was a member of the 2003 charter commission appointed by Mayor Bloomberg. Harry Siegel, the editor-in-chief of New Partisan, is writing a book on gentrification in New York.

Brain-Gain Cities Attract Educated Young

By Blaine Harden

SEATTLE

In a Darwinian fight for survival, American cities are scheming to steal each other's young. They want ambitious young people with graduate degrees in such fields as genome science, bio-informatics and entrepreneurial management.

Sam Long was easy pickings. He was born, reared and very well educated in Cleveland. With a focus on early stage venture capital, he earned his MBA at Case Western Reserve University. Venture capital is in Long's blood. His great-great-grandfather invested in Standard Oil of Ohio, the company that John D. Rockefeller built in Cleveland in the late 19th century.

In the early 21st century, Cleveland desperately needs entrepreneurs, but it never had a shot at keeping Long. He wanted to sail in Puget Sound, ski in the Cascades and swim in Seattle's deep pool of money, ideas and risk-taking young investors.

He now runs a small venture capital company. It sniffs out software ideas, many of them incubated in the computer science department at the University of Washington. "Birds of a feather, you know," said Long, who arrived here in 1992, when he was 28. "There are more people like me in Seattle."

Long is part of an elite intercity migration that is rapidly remaking the way American cities rise and fall. In the 2000 Census, demographers found what they describe as a new, brain-driven, winner-take-all pattern in urban growth. "A pack of cities is racing away from everybody else in terms of their ability to attract and retain an educated workforce," said Bruce Katz, director of the Center on Urban and Metropolitan Policy at the Brookings Institution. "It is a sobering trend for cities left behind."

"In our business, you have to cannibalize," said Ron Sims, the county executive of King County, which surrounds Seattle, and a Democratic candidate for governor of Washington state. "Many cities don't fight back very well." In addition to Seattle, the largest brain-gain cities include Austin, Atlanta, Boston, Denver, Minneapolis, San Diego, San Francisco, Washington, and Raleigh and Durham, N.C.

The rising tide of well-schooled talent has created a self-reinforcing cycle. Newcomers such as Sam Long have made a handful of cities richer, more densely populated and more capable of squeezing wealth out of the next big thing that a knowledge-based economy might serve up.

The Seattle area lost more than 60,000 jobs in the past four years, as average wages declined and population growth stagnated. But this city and those like it remain national leaders in the availability of venture capital, and demographers say they appear to have kept most of their educated young people, who hang on even without good jobs.

The winner-take-all pattern of the past decade differs substantially from the Rust Belt decline and Sun Belt growth of the 1970s and '80s. Then, manufacturing companies moved south in search of a low-wage, nonunion workforce. Now, talented individuals are voting with their feet to live in cities where the work is smart, the culture is cool and the environment is clean.

Migrants on the move to winner-take-all-cities are most accurately identified by education and ambition, rather than by skin color or country of birth. They are part of a striving class of young Americans for whom race, ethnicity and geographic origin tend to be less meaningful than professional achievement, business connections and income.

The Sun Belt is no sure winner in this migration. Such cities as Miami and El Paso are struggling to keep college graduates, who are flocking to such foul-weather havens as Minneapolis, Seattle and Ann Arbor, Mich.

Among the country's 100 largest metro areas, the 25 that entered the 1990s with the largest share of college graduates had, by the end of the decade, sponged up graduates at twice the rate of the other 75 cities, according to a Brookings analysis of the census.

These cities tend to have a high percentage of residents who are artists, writers and musicians, as well as large and visible gay communities. They often have pedestrian neighborhoods, with good food, live music and theater. The percentage of foreign-born residents is also high in these cities, reflecting a significant population of college-educated imports.

With the exception of Austin, none of the 10 fastest-growing U.S. cities of the 1990s ranked among the top 25 cities for increases in the percentage of residents with college degrees. The fastest-growing city, Las Vegas, leads the nation in attracting more high school dropouts than college graduates. "Really fast-growing places, like Las Vegas and Phoenix, have needs not associated with college education, like the construction industry and service workers for retirement communities," said William H. Frey, a demographer at the University of Michigan.

Another peculiarity of brain-gain cities is that they have a tendency to lose residents of lesser educational attainment, even as they vacuum up more college graduates.

New York, Chicago and Los Angeles are perennial magnets of high-end talent, but their size and the constant churning of their population make it difficult for demographers to discern the winner-take-all pattern identified in mid-size cities.

What is easy — and depressing — to see in brain-drain cities is the extraordinary cost of losing talent. The departure of people such as Sam Long from these cities has stalled growth, lowered per-capita income and prevented the formation of a critical mass of risk-takers who can create high-paying jobs. Besides Cleveland, these cities include Baltimore; Buffalo; Detroit; Hartford, Conn.; Milwaukee; Miami; Newark; Pittsburgh; St. Louis; and Stockton and Lodi, Calif.

The graduates most likely to leave the Cleveland area have degrees linked to innovation. A recent series in the Plain Dealer found that the higher their degree, the more likely young people were to move. The newspaper found that about two-thirds of doctoral graduates in engineering, the sciences and the creative arts cleared out of Ohio between 1991 and 2001. A recent Census Bureau report reinforced that finding of brain drain, saying the Cleveland region lost young, single college graduates to other parts of the country in the late 1990s. It was one of only three of the nation's 20 largest metropolitan areas to do so.

Cities such as Cleveland have become painfully aware of what they are losing, and their leaders have come to regard cities such as Seattle as mortal enemies. "Are they a threat to the survival of Cleveland? Absolutely," said Manuel Glynias, a Cleveland-born scientist and entrepreneur. "Are they a threat that we haven't figured out how to answer yet? Absolutely."

His own story is not encouraging — unless you live in a winner-take-all city. In 1996, he created a successful bio-informatics company called NetGenics, which employed 100 people in downtown Cleveland and won accolades in the local media as a harbinger of the city's high-tech future. His employees wrote software that allowed drug companies to make better use of vast amounts of research data.

But NetGenics did not grow as fast as its primary competitor, the German company Lion. Part of the problem, Glynias said, was that he could not find marketing people in Cleveland who understood high-tech. Lion bought NetGenics last year and has moved many of its jobs to San Diego, a major biotech center. The last jobs left Cleveland this summer.

"It was felt that there were better places to do business in a high-tech sort of way," Glynias said. "If Cleveland can't find a way to stop this, I will be visiting my children and grandchildren in San Diego or Austin or Seattle."

It might seem unfair to set up Cleveland as a foil for Seattle, like arranging a prizefight between a has-been and a cocky contender. But the comparison mirrors a national reality, as Austin, Minneapolis and Boston routinely poach talent — and steal the future — from cities such as San Antonio, St. Louis and Hartford.

"It is a totally unfair fight, and it is the way the market works now," said Michael Fogarty, director of the School of Urban Studies at Portland State University and former professor of economics at Case Western. Cleveland and Seattle are about the same size, with about a half-million residents inside the city limits and 2 million-plus in the metro region. Both cities have a history of big money. Each produced the richest men of its era (Rockefeller and Gates). In an explosion of capitalistic energy, they became world-famous centers for technical innovation, entrepreneurial creativity and a bullying business style that pushed — and sometimes broke — the limits of the law.

These bursts of prosperity, of course, were separated by nearly a century. Cleveland flowered in the second half of the 19th century and peaked by 1930, when productivity started to slide in steelmaking and metalworking. As with many cities in the Rust Belt, the population began to decline in the 1960s. Racial segregation played a chronically corrosive role, as poverty rose, public schools nose-dived and whites fled to the suburbs.

Sprawl was encouraged and hugely subsidized by Ohio's tax policy. It sucked gas taxes out of Cleveland and other cities, and the state spent the money on roads in rural areas that often blossomed into affluent suburbs. At the same time, Cleveland failed to become a "gateway city" for new immigrants. Large waves of Asian or Latin American immigrants did not pour into the city or its close-in suburbs (as occurred in Seattle and Washington) to replace those who had been vacuumed out by subsidized sprawl.

The success of U.S. cities, demographers agree, is not related to racial composition but rather to education levels. High levels of immigration by nonwhite college graduates in the 1990s to such cities as Seattle, Austin and San Francisco have been a major factor in their prosperity. At the same time, the relative dearth of college-educated immigrants of any race to cities such as Cleveland is viewed as a key reason for their decline.

Although Cleveland has sprawled without growth, Seattle has grown while winning a come-from-behind fight against sprawl. After losing population to the suburbs for 30 years, it turned a corner in the '90s, growing by 9 percent, with many newcomers moving to housing near the waterfront.

State law has forced more than 80 percent of new housing construction to occur inside designated urban zones in King County. Population growth continues in Seattle, although the recession slowed it to a crawl.

More than a half-million people moved to King County in the past two decades and about 10,000 millionaires were minted, mostly at Microsoft. Forty-seven percent of Seattleites have at least a bachelor's degree, about twice the national rate and four times higher than Cleveland's.

More households have access to the Internet (80.6 percent) than in any other U.S. city, and Seattle ranked second in the country (after Minneapolis) in a recent survey of literacy. The city also ranks among the top five high-tech cities in percentages of creative artists, foreign-born residents and gays. The emergence of winner-take-all cities is usually linked to the presence of a dominating research university. Seattle is no exception. The University of Washington, which is in the city, has doubled its research budget in the past decade and is the country's leading public university as measured by federal funding.

Among urban scholars, business leaders and big-city politicians, there is a chicken-and-egg debate over what exactly makes a high-tech city grow. Does technology come first and lure talent? Or does the mere presence of talent, through some creative alchemy, hatch technology that spawns high-paying jobs? A look at a recent software start-up in Seattle suggests the answer is both. The new company, called Performant Inc., emerged from an idea that Seattle investors quickly grasped and bathed in a nourishing pot of money. One of them was Sam Long, the venture capitalist who moved here from Cleveland. Three years ago, Long got a call from Ashutosh Tiwary, an Indian immigrant and doctoral student at the University of Washington's School of Computer Science and Engineering.

Tiwary had an idea that came to him while he was working part time at Boeing, where he was troubleshooting design software for new aircraft. He found a way to diagnose why computer systems at major companies often slow to a crawl. His software could speed them up. He took the idea back to the university, where a professor and a senior software researcher from Microsoft (an adjunct professor) saw its potential. They helped him refine, patent and market a product. They also hooked him up with a venture capital company run by wealthy Microsoft retirees. That company, in turn, gave him Long's phone number. Long quickly invested $750,000, part of the $10 million that Tiwary and his partners raised during the teeth of Seattle's recession. This spring, they sold the company, doubling their investors' money. Thirty jobs created by the company are staying in Seattle. Tiwary said he never would have come up with the idea — or made money from it so quickly — had he not been in Seattle. He moved there in the late 1990s, by way of India, Texas and California.

"There is a business ecosystem here that is both creative and technical," said Tiwary, now a vice president at Mercury Interactive Corp., the company that bought him out. "It starts with people who understand technology, have built successful things before and want to do it again. It is a little bit of an addiction." At the very top of the entrepreneurial food chain in Seattle, the addiction to risk-taking is being turned loose on biotech.

Scholars who study U.S. cities agree that Cleveland has probably tried harder — and achieved more — than any other major brain-drain city. It has substantially rebuilt its downtown, winning national attention as a "comeback city" with the Rock and Roll Hall of Fame, as well as new complexes for professional baseball, basketball and football. The percentage of residents with high school degrees has increased and concentrated poverty has been reduced.

The fastest-growing neighborhood in Cleveland is the downtown core. There, city government has worked with developers to turn warehouses and abandoned department stores into apartments that appeal to young professionals. Cleveland's leading university, Case Western, is urging students and faculty to live in the city. It is spending hundreds of millions of dollars for new housing and for a retail neighborhood near the university. "You must position yourself as the place people want to move to, rather than from," said the school's new president, Edward M. Hundert. He is demanding that the school's researchers work with, rather than compete against, other local research centers, such as the Cleveland Clinic and University Hospitals of Cleveland.

"This is a city that, against all odds, is getting its act together," said Katz, whose Urban Affairs Center at Brookings monitors most major U.S. cities. *"I believe that if Cleveland had not tried so hard, it would look like St. Louis or Detroit."* And yet, in Cleveland — as in many other brain-drain cities that are trying to fight back — the loss of talent continues. Throughout the '90s, even as Cleveland made its highly publicized comeback, it continued to lose college graduates and income. It lost about $35 billion because it could not keep the people and maintain the per-capita income it had in 1990, according to an analysis in the Plain Dealer.

A critical mass of money, ideas and risk-taking has not coalesced in Cleveland, said David Morgenthaler, one of the country's most eminent venture capitalists. He manages $2 billion and lives in Cleveland. Morgenthaler said he would love to invest more money in his home town. But he does not do so because the city "does not breed enough good horses to bet on."

His judgment is echoed in Cleveland's dismal ranking among the 50 largest cities as measured by venture capital as a percentage of the metro economy. Cleveland ranks 42nd, while Seattle ranks second, behind San Francisco. "Cleveland lives off the past, and the executives from these old industries are still the community leaders," Morgenthaler said. "The city has made progress, but it is not close to where it has to be." A decade after leaving Cleveland for Seattle, Sam Long wishes his hometown well, but says he cannot conceive of a reason he would live there. He just built a four-bedroom house near Lake Washington in one of Seattle's most expensive neighborhoods. At regular dinners with friends from the computer science department at the University of Washington, he schemes about turning ideas into money. "We talk of pie in the sky," he said. In Seattle, unlike his home town and many other cities that keep losing young talent, pie in the sky has a way of turning into high-paying jobs and companies that own the future.

UNIT 6

Regentrification and Urban Neighborhoods

Unit Selections

Key Points to Consider

- Describe the effects of racial and class segregation at the neighborhood level.

- What does gentrification mean to the existing residents of a neighborhood?

- Can a city prosper without gentrification? If so, how?

- Can a neighborhood attract an affluent or upwardly mobile population without pushing out poorer residents? Can a city do the same? If you said "yes" to either question, how?

 **Links: www.dushkin.com/online/**
These sites are annotated in the World Wide Web pages.

Center for Democracy and Citizenship
 http://www.publicwork.org
Civnet/CIVITAS
 http://www.civnet.org/index.htm
The Gallup Organization
 http://www.gallup.com

Even at the nadir of urban decline, city neighborhoods varied enormously, from wealthy enclaves rich in amenities to areas with high rates of poverty, joblessness, segregation, and abandoned buildings. Leading scholars continue to debate the persistence and meaning of racial (and, to some extent, social class) segregation at the neighborhood level, raising important substantive and methodological issues.

Neighborhoods, a relatively undeveloped unit of analysis in sociological theory, are the building blocks of cities. How and to what extent have cities rebuilt their most devastated neighborhoods, and what institutions and strategies have helped most (and least) in these efforts? The economic upturn of the 1990s and the serious reductions in crime in many cities brought widespread upscaling, and gentrification replaced abandonment in the urbanists' lexicon. The economic downturn of the early 2000s combined with the vogue for attracting members of the "creative class" have increasingly led to cities with rich and poor and a shrinking middle and working class separating the two extremes.

The case study about neighborhood revitalization "The Essence of Uptown," explore the causes and consequences of gentrification, the processes by which more affluent people move into an area; "The Gentry, Misjudged as Neighbors," reports surprising research findings about the effects this has on longer-term, poorer residents. The article "The Geography of Cool" offers a global perspective on the brew of mysterious qualities that allows a neighborhood to become hip. In San Francisco, a downturn following an economic boom has led to conflict between the city's entrepreneurial and bohemian classes, with the latter group gleefully retaking the spaces used by businessmen in better times, a battle detailed in "Amid Office Shuffle In San Francisco, Bohemian Rhapsody." "Windows Not Broken" looks at the uneasy and unequal relations between gentrifiers and longtime neighborhood residents in New York's Williamsburgh.

The comeback of the front porch, now competing with the backyard deck as a feature of choice among contemporary homebuyers, is reported in the article "Rocking-Chair Revival." As the author (like the new urbanists before him) points out, the front porch has significant social implications for neighborhood and street life.

The Gentry, Misjudged as Neighbors

By JOHN TIERNEY

WE all think we know how gentrification works. Developers and yuppies discover charm in an old neighborhood, and soon the very people who created the neighborhood can't afford it anymore. Janitors and artists are forced out of their homes to make room for lawyers and bankers.

This process has been routinely denounced in neighborhoods like Harlem and Park Slope in Brooklyn. But when researchers recently looked for evidence of such turnover, the results were surprising.

Gentrification does not cause an exodus of the poor and the working class, according to a study in New York and another in Boston. Just the opposite happens: people with relatively little income and education become more likely to stick around. The rate of turnover declines, apparently because people don't like to leave a neighborhood when it's improving.

You may have a hard time believing these results, but you can't dismiss them as propaganda from developers. The New York study was done by Lance Freeman, a professor of planning at Columbia University, and Frank Braconi, an economist and the executive director of the Citizens Housing and Planning Council, a well-respected nonprofit research organization with a centrist position in New York's housing wars.

There are always, of course, some people who move out of gentrifying neighborhoods. But then, some people would move out even if the neighborhood didn't change. To see how gentrification affects turnover, Dr. Freeman and Dr. Braconi analyzed the city's Housing and Vacancy Survey, which is gathered by revisiting the same 15,000 housing units every three years.

According to the survey, only 5 percent of the New Yorkers who moved during the late 1990's reported being forced to move by high rents. That percentage was a little lower than during the real estate doldrums of the early 1990's, when there was less gentrification going on.

For a more precise measure, Dr. Freeman and Dr. Braconi looked at the survey data in seven gentrifying neighborhoods: the Lower East Side, Chelsea, Harlem and Morningside Heights in Manhattan, and Williamsburg, Fort Greene and Park Slope in Brooklyn. In those neighborhoods, the poor and working-class tenants—those who had low incomes or who lacked a college degree—were about 20 percent less likely to move during the 1990's than were socioeconomically similar tenants in the rest of the city.

"You've got two competing forces in a gentrifying neighborhood," Dr. Braconi said. "The prices are going up, which gives low-income people an incentive to leave. But the neighborhood's getting nicer, so people have more incentive to stay. There's been an assumption by community activists that the incentive to leave is stronger, but that turns out to be wrong. You don't displace the poor. You actually slow down the process of people moving out of the neighborhood."

In the past, Dr. Braconi has argued that rent regulation can be useful in preventing displacement, and he said that was borne out by the research. The tenants in rent-regulated apartments were especially likely to remain in place. But even tenants in unregulated apartments were more likely to remain in gentrifying neighborhoods than elsewhere, he said.

THESE results jibe with those of a new study by Jacob L. Vigdor, an economist at Duke University, who tracked changes at 3,000 houses and apartments in Boston and its suburbs from 1985 to 1993. Fewer than 10 percent of the apartments were covered by rent control, but the trend was the same as in New York: low-income and less-educated residents of gentrifying neighborhood were more likely to remain in place than were similar residents in other neighborhoods.

How did the poor manage to stay? "I didn't find much evidence of more people crowding into the homes," Dr. Vigdor said. "For the most part, people simply paid more." About 3 percent of the people, typically elderly tenants on fixed incomes, complained that the higher rents weren't accompanied by improvement in living conditions, but most people said they were benefiting from improvements to their dwellings and their neighborhood as well as better public services. Most people's income rose at least as fast as the rents, in some cases presumably because of new jobs that came into the neighborhood.

When you add up all these advantages, it may seem hard to imagine how the opponents of gentrification could keep up the fight. If the neighborhood's improving and old-timers aren't being displaced, what's not to like? But let's see what new complaints they come up with.

The essence of Uptown

Can the latest hot neighborhood move up without leaving itself behind?

By A.T. Palmer, Special to the Tribune

When Eric Snyder moved to Chicago from Atlanta last spring and started scouting North Side neighborhoods for housing, he had absolutely no intention of buying in Uptown, he claims.

The 2.3-square-mile neighborhood, bounded by Lake Michigan, Irving Park Road, Clark Street and Montrose, Ravenswood and Foster Avenues, "looked like a dive," recalls the 34-year-old banker.

Yet, Snyder's purchase in August was a $214,000 two-bedroom, 1.5-bath condominium in southeast Uptown. And, it's already appreciated $56,000, the result of some bathroom and closet upgrades, he boasts.

Why Uptown?

"Where else in the city can I make a return of 20 percent? Plus have the lake, easy access to transportation and fewer crowds than Lincoln Park?" he says.

"There's a Starbucks, a gym, and hopefully a Fresh Fields [grocery] and Borders [bookstore] coming soon. This is becoming a middle-class neighborhood."

Latest figures from the Multiple Listing Service of Northern Illinois, which compiles a quarterly report of median sale prices of local housing listed with real estate agents, concurs. The median price of a home in Uptown rose to $215,000 in the third quarter from $192,000 in the year-earlier period. That exceeds median prices for such desirable suburbs as Palatine ($190,000) and Flossmoor ($195,000).

According to Mimi Slogar, Uptown Community Development Corp. chairman, Uptown is among the top five areas citywide in condo conversion volume—on a par with the West Loop.

"I couldn't even use the word 'Uptown' 6 to 12 months ago when I was marketing property there," says Scott Kruger, a Koenig & Strey GMAC broker, longtime Uptown resident and six-flat owner there.

"It had a connotation of poor housing stock and streets that weren't pretty," he says. "Now, people specifically ask to see Uptown properties. There's new construction and rehabbing attractively priced on almost every block. It's such a transformation."

This transformation isn't being greeted with the same enthusiasm by other long-time residents, such as State Rep. Larry McKeon (D-34th).

When he moved into his one-bedroom rental apartment at Ravenswood and Montrose Avenues 10 years ago, the monthly rent was $550. Now it's $1,000.

"As a renter, I'm being priced out of my own district," complains McKeon, looking for rental housing in areas to the north that were recently annexed to his district—North Andersonville (part of Edgewater) and Rogers Park.

"There's been little development in the mid-range for firefighters, social workers and government workers like me," he says. "There's been tremendous displacement of the most vulnerable people—seniors on fixed incomes and welfare-to-work people, who must live near work when they find jobs. I'm not against development and gentrification. But, balanced development must be protected."

Snyder and McKeon represent two sides of the multi-faceted debate over Uptown's dramatic changes.

Built as a luxury lakeside summer resort in the 1890s and which became one of the nation's feature film production headquarters after World War I, Uptown was hit hard by Great Depression economics. Many big homes were divided into rental apartments, priced cheaply.

Since then, Uptown has become Chicago's port of entry for newcomers—Southerners, immigrants from Vietnam, Cambodia, Ethiopia and Bosnia, plus deinstitutionalized patients from state psychiatric facilities, says Sarah Jane Knoy, executive director of Organization of the Northeast (ONE), a community action group.

State and not-for-profit social service agencies established offices in the neighborhood to serve this clientele. But, now Uptown's changing: 4,000 property parcels vacant in 1990 have dwindled to 1,000, according to latest census data.

One parcel, at 4848 N. Sheridan Rd., is the future home of The Alexa, a 70-unit condominium midrise. The one- to three-bedroom units, base-priced from $170,000, and up to $450,000 for the 1,700-square-foot penthouse, are more than 40 percent sold, reports Victor E. Cypher, president of Chicago-based ViCor Development Co.

"Eight years ago, $250,000 bought a lake view," says Chip Long, broker at Lakefront Group Realty Associates Inc. "Now two- and three-bedroom condos that sold for $150,000 are going for $200,000 to $350,000."

Commercially, this neighborhood of primarily small owner-operated shops and a vibrant Asian commercial strip on Argyle Street from Sheridan to Broadway is also changing.

Neighborhood residents have seen final plans to renovate the long-vacant Goldblatt's Department Store into a mixed retail/residential building with a 25,000-square-foot Border's Books & Music, other retailers, and 37 condominiums.

The historic Uptown Theatre received a recent $1 million grant from the Albert Goodman Foundation to help rehab the theater, one of the country's largest.

But, growth has an underside, community leaders warn. Uptown has lost about 2,000 to 3,000 families since 1990, says McKeon. The number of children under age 18 is down more than 20 percent.

New census data about Uptown's 63,551 residents show population is down marginally (0.45 percent). Anglo-Caucasians increased to 42 percent of the population from 38 percent, while the number of African-Americans dropped to 21 percent from 24 percent, Hispanics, to 20 percent from 23 percent, and Asians, to 13 percent from 14 percent.

Gentrification and its impact on Uptown's property values, affordable housing and racial and ethnic diversity elicit a range of reactions from long-time residents, newcomers, community activists, real estate brokers and urban experts.

There's some excitement by homeowners about rising property values, an increasing middle class and plans for brand-name retail stores; some dismay over the changing look of some residential streets and loss of some local citizenry; and worry because there's no comprehensive, long-range neighborhood plan.

"I'm happy that gentrification has finally come," says Bob Peterson, president of the Gunnison Block Club in northeast Uptown. Bought 15 years ago for $115,000, his duplex condo has more than doubled in value.

"Diversity should include middle-class families," he says. "That's the biggest change gentrification has brought to Uptown. We have a stronger group of middle-class families committed to staying and sending their children to school here. That will strengthen the neighborhood."

Rae Mindock, a chemical engineer and Beacon Neighbors Block Club member, shares Peterson's happiness. Her two-bedroom condo in southwest Uptown appreciated to more than $250,000 from $100,000 in 10 years. But, she's worried about other aspects of gentrification.

"There are lots of affluent individuals who've moved in," she says. "That's not bad. What's difficult is their inability to accept the neighborhood they've moved into 'as is'— with homeless and other residents.

"I'm also worried too many condos will destabilize our neighborhood," she adds.

Neighborhood destabilization also concerns Syd Mohn, president of Heartland Alliance, a not-for-profit social service association serving the poor. Since 1996, Heartland's Uptown client list of 8,000 has dropped 15 to 20 percent.

Rising apartment rents have prompted about half of Uptown's 8,000 Cambodian residents to relocate, says Kompha Seth, executive director of the Cambodian Association of Illinois. The association itself moved to Albany Park from Uptown earlier this year. "It was heartbreaking leaving Uptown," says Seth. "I feel very isolated now."

This trend is troublesome to newcomers attracted by Uptown's racial and ethnic diversity.

"I picked Uptown over Lincoln Park or Andersonville," says 24 year-old Jackie Aicher, a supermarket retailer who moved from Evanston into a rental in Uptown in September.

"Uptown's more individual, more local and not corporate," she says. "This area won't be special if Border's comes in. They're everywhere. I'm also afraid that gentrification will displace the African-Americans, Hispanics and Asians that I came here to live with."

"I'm African-American and wanted a neighborhood where I'd see a black, white and Hispanic when I walk down the street," adds Andrew Stroth, 34. The sports and entertainment attorney moved from Lake View ("all yuppies," he says) into a three-bedroom condo near Truman College in May. "This neighborhood is vibrant."

Uptown's community leaders are dealing with gentrification issues with innovative programs.

The neighborhood is one of the first citywide to implement Chicago's Purchase Price Assistance Program. Developers voluntarily set aside 10 percent of their building's units for sale to low- and middle-income individuals. The city subsidizes down payments. The Alexa and proposed Goldblatt's development are participants.

Community leaders helped 10 federally subsidized apartment buildings convert to ownership by tenants, not-for-profits or for-profit companies that pledge to maintain affordable housing, says Knoy, ONE's executive director.

"Loyola University Chicago is preparing the first comprehensive set of baseline data on real estate in a Chicago community—Uptown," says Rep. McKeon, the project's catalyst. "Available next spring, this data will include all federal, state, county and municipal housing information and will be available for all stakeholders," he says. "Sometimes, this data is not readily available. When it is, it's for purchase only.

"Because there's been a lack of viable and reliable data on housing, Uptown has been divided into 'those that have' and 'those that don't' in this debate," he claims. "We've ended up with two political extremes. This lack of information increases the intensity and acrimony of arguments."

"It's easy to get emotional about gentrification with a few inflammatory sentences," says Cindi Anderson, president of the Uptown Chicago Commission, another citizen group, who also complains about the dearth of information. "Conversations about the 'big picture' don't occur here."

Will these solutions be enough to retain Uptown's uniqueness amid gentrification? It's unclear, but residents, real estate professionals and community activists are determined.

"Uptown can be strong in growth and diversity," says the Heartland Alliance's Mohn. "This community needs to come together to decide what to preserve and what to become."

"Uptown must learn how to stay Uptown," adds Mindock, the Beacon Street resident. "People are learning to have conversations with people who are different from themselves. This is a start."

Windows Not Broken

by Harry Siegel

It's not that I take pleasure in seeing anyone get hurt, but I can't say I was upset when the natives violently crashed the pioneer party in Williamsburg. There were 25 or so hipsters, umbrellas, space pirates, or whatever you like to call them on the roof blazing copious quantities of high grade skunk, another six on the fire escape drinking loudly, and a brick holding the apartment's outside door open, Dr. Dre booming from a stereo system that well exceeded the monthly rent, plugged into a pricey new Apple loaded up with mp3s. I'd been there about an hour, with friends who had come to see friends of theirs, and still had no idea whose apartment I was in. It didn't seem to matter. Several people had apparently just ambled in, drawn by the noise, crowd, drugs, and women, uninvited and unchallenged.

Then come the Hispanics. Four, all men, one of them easily larger than anyone else at the party. Hip hop clothes, gold chains, one with a couple of knife scars on his cheek. Someone puts the music down and suddenly there's a lot more murmuring than yelling. As the noise goes does, the newcomers tense up. Quantum uncertainty in practice — the newcomers are trying discreetly to examine the party, the party is trying discreetly to examine them and everyone is stuck staring. One of the newcomers asks for a cigarette in a neutral voice — half the hipsters are smoking, no one offers a smoke. Within five minutes all the women in the room have retreated to the roof. Five minutes later, three fellows descend from it, trying to look serious and purposeful but coming off stoned and spooked. One of them steps up to the newcomers, and, to quote "Airplane," starts talking jive— "Yo fellas, I'm sayin, yo, no disrespect, knowh'Imean , but this is a private party, yo" — then puts his hand on the biggest guy's shoulder, as though to steer him to the door. Even after the young jive talker was smacked around, I still wasn't clear if he was the host of the party, but in any event no one stepped in to help him. The Hispanics left after that, unchallenged, and the party quickly petered out.

It's a testament to how much the city has changed since the Dinkins years that the hipsters at the party, many of them newcomers to the city, lacked the danger sense shared by most all New Yorkers. There is an almost unprecedented expectation of safety in Hipster Williamsburg (which shares little but a name with Hispanic Williamsburg and Hasidic Williamsburg), with its population of underemployed, oversexed recent college graduates and their ilk. There's a shared expectation that the L is a safe means of transportation at three in the morning, that there's nothing wrong with sitting in a park with a $2,000 laptop or leaving your apartment door open while throwing a party.

But this detachment is from the police as well as from hard men and low lives. The Giuliani revolution in controlling crime is barely noticed, taken as a given. Unlike those who live in poor or working class neighborhoods, the city's young hipsters feel neither compunction nor fear about smoking a joint while at home or at a party. While the poor and working class continue to face consequences for smoking pot, middle class pot use has been all but decriminalized — and this is, for the most part, a good thing.

Ask a hipster fresh off the boat or however it is they get here about juice bars, and odds are you'll hear about some spot on Houston Street that mixes a great blueberry smoothie. Ask about weed, and odds are you'll hear about a delivery service, some young entrepreneur from the neighborhood moving quarter-ounces.

But a decade ago, as the East Village, the Lower East Side, and Alphabet City were just beginning to gentrify, just about every juice bar in those areas — and there was a fair handful of them — sold nickel and dime bags. The quality was fairly low, ranging from dusted or otherwise laced up to pure schwag, but the quantities were generous. Most of the spots sold a particular brand of weed, or at least sold weed in little plastic bags branded with little logos, so that seeing the empty bags strewn on the sidewalk, anyone, smoker or otherwise, much plugged in knew where they came from — other than the police, evidently. The IRS could have conducted a half decent audit by collecting the bags in the neighborhood, which is where most all the weed was smoked — you left, went to a bodega for papers or a blunt, and then lit up outside.

The other classic setup was the bodega full of dusty cans and without any customers younger than 14 or older than 35. During the day, customers would buy a soda or a bag of plantain chips and the weed bag would be dropped in the paper bag. At night, all business was conducted from a bulletproof glass window facing the street. I've actually gone to such spots late night in search of household super basics, like garbage bags, only to be told, less politely, that "We don't do that now."

There were many variations. For a while there was an ice cream truck in on the action, taping bags to the bottom of ice cream cups — once or twice I saw parents buy their kids an ice cream while treating themselves.

Spots did get busted here and again, but new ones opened up, hydra-like. Those too impatient for word of mouth would drop in on a new deli that had that look, drop a ten spot, and see what ended up in their paper bag. If the ten was snickered at or disdainfully ignored, you knew you were in a coke or smack spot.

Nearly all these spots sold extremely low quantities that the police were evidently willing to overlook, or at least not go out of their way to find. But in consequence, most users were sparking up right after leaving the store, on the street. But of course these spots and street users added up to a classic broken windows scenario. Turning a blind eye to the spots (easily identified, among other ways, by the tremendously poor care they took of their stores and storefronts) told their customers it was alright to smoke in the streets, seeing people smoke in the streets gave the sign that it was alright to get rowdy, fight, and otherwise seriously disrupt the neighborhood's life, and so on. In short, the spots were central to a pervasive feeling of lawlessness and incivility.

Like many people about my age (25) who were born here, I have certain nostalgia for all that lawlessness and chaos and the weirdness and adventures that intermittently popped up around it.

But who in their right mind wants to live above a drug spot, with people getting high all around — yelling, fighting, pissing in the streets, and worse — or open a business adjacent to one? Some storeowners and neighborhood residents objected, but the response was most always some variation of "This is how it is" or "What do you expect living here?"

Rudy changed all that. Few people remember how controversial the whole idea of proactive, Broken Windows policing was in 1993. Today the idea that small crimes are signposts that larger crimes are acceptable, and that those who commit small crimes are likely to be involved in larger ones, seems conventional. But at the time, the idea of focusing on small crimes in a city overwhelmed by big ones was dismissed by Al Sharpton, the New York Times, and much of the city as absurd, if not outright villainous.

We now know that the idea was spot on. When Rudy's first police chief, Bill Bratton, started conducting massive arrest sweeps of turnstile jumpers, it turned out that one of every seven people arrested had an outstanding felony warrant. In little time, crime began to plummet, and as went the fare jumpers and squeegeemen, so went the drug fronts. By 1996, there was nary a spot left in Manhattan (Note to newcomers: Manhattan here is Bloomberg's luxury product, going only as far north as about 110th Street. Uptown is, of course, understood as a distinct sixth borough. I'm talking about the Manhattan you see on taxi maps.).

In their place came delivery services, stepping into the vacuum that the spots had left in Manhattan, Park Slope, Brooklyn Heights, Williamsburg, and the rest of the places the young, better off, and sometimes beautiful choose to live. Even low level delivery services tend to have a minimum sale of about an eighth of an ounce and to sell a higher grade of weed than did the five and dime spots.

The delivery quantities were too small, though, to be worth robbing, especially since most services had fairly small clienteles, gained through word of mouth and recommendations from trusted clients. This, combined with the price barrier to entry goes a fair ways toward filtering out the younger and wilder crowd. Often one or two man operations, with the delivery guy doubling as the CEO, they are for the most part discreet affairs that help to separate the drug economy from the criminal and quality of life concerns that accompany open air drug use and sales. Outside of their operations, these new dealers tend to be disconnected from the criminal economy, as do their clients, outside of their smoking. Neither tend to interact with any other sort of criminal element either during the sale or otherwise.

In short, all drug sales are not the same — spots have far more impact on the surrounding community than do delivery services. As George Kelling, co-author of the seminal 1982 Atlantic article "Broken Windows" that introduced the theory of the same name puts it, however distasteful it might be, "Suburban drug use…doesn't compare with the violence associated with the fight for drug markets that has literally wiped out neighborhoods. The drug trade threatens the stability of poor neighborhoods — very few middle class neighborhoods are threatened by drug dealing or drug use."

I sat down in the big playground at Washington Square Park with Nancy — names have been changed to protect the guilty — an attractive (but married) red haired, chain smoking Hispanic woman in her late 20s, while her six year old son played on the swings. A lifelong Brooklynite and waitress at a popular Village restaurant, devoted martial artist, and former casual heroin user, she's been selling weed from a friend's place in the Village for the last six months, pocketing an extra $1,200 or so a month on about six ounces. "I'm thinking of expanding to low poundage," she told me. "If I was contactable, I could easily expand, but I've got no beeper and only answer my house phone when I recognize the number. No one can find me except physically. It's very Victorian."

Nancy entered into the pot business almost by accident, when her personal source vanished "and my new guy only sold in larger quantities than I could smoke, so I moved some along down the food chain, thus the better to help friends, make money, and live a happy life." After unsuccessfully staring down an eavesdropping mother staring daggers at us, Nancy expressed concern that the other mother might call the city's child services bureau and we moved the conversation out of the park, leaving her son to play with Nancy's sister.

When I then asked what concerns, moral or otherwise, she had about the business, Nancy, who has never had an encounter with the police while selling, said, "I don't think it's a problem or a vice anymore than cigarettes or chocolate. I'm not into the legalization people. It's not a moral issue … I don't think I'd sell to high school kids — it feels like mixing the crimes. I am conscious of the risks just because of the college student clients, who think oh no, I got a bright future. It's this chick who's, you know, not in college.' The clients are not very paranoid about the police, and neither am I, but I'm sometimes paranoid about the clients."

To her, the job means always having a bit of her own weed to smoke and "the difference between working full time to pay the bills and having money to spend. It's putting my child through private elementary school."

When I asked Kelling about delivery services, he surprised me by arguing that limited police resources necessitate a degree of tolerance for discrete delivery services. "I have never been an advocate of legalization but at the same time the ideas that we are going to have a drug free society or stop all drug dealing is a joke. The top priority of the police has to be with drug markets that threaten the stability of cities, and to come down very hard on such groups. It seems to me that if one is able to make substantial gains the threshold might change. At one moment in time the pattern of a group or gang might be minimally appropriate but once you've changed the threshold, you demand even more discrete drug dealing."

Given police success, the hope is to eventually define deviancy back up, but in the short haul, so long as the sellers are policing themselves and staying off the streets, the cops have other priorities. At this moment in the cycle, at least, the practical result is the essential decriminalization of low level middle class drug use. Suddenly, the window is all but unbroken, the war on drugs distinct from the war on crime on the local level. It is the extension of the free and open use of coke in high end bars otherwise free of disruptive or criminal dealings, and that handle what trouble does emerge in house. This is a whole new spin on the old adage, often invoked when the cops or other sorts of trouble approach, to "master your high." In short, to the extent that drug use in a neighborhood is distinct from other criminal or publicly disruptive activities, it becomes less and less of a police and prosecutorial priority.

Daniel is another example of a dealer below the present threshold. A non descript white guy in his mid-20s, Brooklyn born and raised, he has been selling for half a decade, first at college and then in Park Slope, and has yet to encounter the police. He nets about $2,500 a month, labeling it "a decent bartender's salary, and I prefer my line of work."

He got his customers through socializing, a free mix of business and pleasure— "I have a pretty small client base of about 15 people … I'm a local to my neighborhood. You know people — I play softball with some people, I play poker with other people, friends refer friends. Almost all my people are in the Slope and Prospect Heights."

Like Nancy, he has no moral qualms, and little fear of the police. "I don't really get worried when I carry. Maybe in the beginning, but at this stage in the game I'm pretty comfortable with everything. I don't meet people in the street — either in their homes or in a car. I don't have that guilty conscience. I really don't believe I'm doing anything wrong or that anyone has reason to think I am."

Julia Vitullo-Martin, the crime columnist for GothamGazette.com, makes a distinction similar to those of both Kelling and Daniel. "It comes back to the federal drug war and our motives for doing this. Do we have this war against drugs because like turn-of-the-century Protestants we think drugs, like alcohol, nicotine, gambling, and coffee are immoral? Is that what's driving this or is it because we object to drugs because with drugs come crime and it's really crime we don't want. I really don't care what anyone does at home if that person is not robbing, raping, or murdering. The war on drugs is premised on the idea that the addiction itself is what we should go after… I hesitate because I don't want to see anybody selling drugs on my street. I don't object to any low level dealer selling in his apartment but any selling on the street I object to because I think it always triggers bad stuff. I'd like to see the NYPD turn a blind eye to this low level stuff whenever it becomes private but as soon as it becomes public I object." The difficulty is in codifying common sense, and applying limited resources in a way that is both reasonable and fair, which are two very different, and sometimes contrary goals.

The upshot is that those with their own place, a fair amount of discretionary cash, and minimal prudence, most all of whom live within delivery zones such as Hipster Williamsburg, slide while nickel and dime bag buyers, like those in Hispanic Williamsburg, get no such free ride. I asked Vitullo-Martin, is this an unfair use of policing and prosecutorial discretion or an intelligent application of limited law enforcement resources?

Referring back to the crack epidemic of the 1980s, she replied that, "In cycles of public policy there is such a thing as shock treatment in which you're on some kind of downward spiral and you're just going to keep going down unless something shocking and practically brutal happens. Then the question becomes, how do you get out of that shock treatment, which is where we are right now. The shock treatment did work, but now what? … Some kind of basic equity requires that if you're going to bust the crack user with a small amount you've also got to slam the privileged kid drug user."

Daniel doesn't want to hear this. Now that he no longer sells to high school students — "These kids looks so suspicious, its ridiculous, and they have no sense of how things are supposed to flow" — he's had not even close shaves with cops or hardcore crooks. "I haven't been involved in any real shady shit. My partner who does his thing in the city had a gun put to his head and had 10 Gs taken in any attempted transaction. I only go out of my network if I get a referral. I carry no weapon. I'm not dealing with those kinds of clients and those kind of areas. I'm in a family biz and a family neighborhood."

On the subject of families, Nancy's husband "knows, but doesn't want to. As far as he's concerned, it's no moral issue, but breaking the law is liable to get you into trouble, and we have enough trouble anyway. It seems kind of sleazy. I think that's the main issue — it seems kind of low brow."

Or, as Vitullo-Martin has it, however much safer the city is these days, "this is not Greenwich, Connecticut."

Amid Office Shuffle In San Francisco, Bohemian Rhapsody

Artists and Activists Invade The Buildings Once Held By the Bygone Dot-Coms

By NICK WINGFIELD,
The Wall Street Journal

SAN FRANCISCO — In the South of Market district here, the two-story building at 690 Fifth St. is packed with quirky fixtures of the old dot-com workplace. A fountain trickles in the lofty atrium. Hip-hop music pulses from glass-walled offices as people peck at computers. Rice-paper screens obscure an elegant conference room.

These were once the offices of Netcentives Inc., an Internet flop that marketed worker-incentive and loyalty programs. But look who's here now: a Tibetan rug maker, an Irish arts foundation and an Asian-American theater company. There are also filmmakers, a record label, fiction writers and a couple of dozen nonprofits and artistic groups.

"This will be the beginning of the biggest renaissance in creativity in San Francisco history," says David Latimer, who manages the building. He's encouraged because these are the very folks the dot-coms began squeezing out of the prime real estate just a few years ago. Their displacement sparked street protests, anti-growth measures and fears about the loss of this liberal city's cultural life and its historical soul.

But they're back, the artists and the activists, reclaiming the neighborhood that once was the epicenter of the thriving Internet scene. The city rode the dot-com boom as startups piled into town, bringing with them lavish launch parties, jobs and prosperity. Now, amid the bust, the rental market has cooled, allowing the dislocated to reclaim turf they were priced out of just a few years ago.

Here in San Francisco, one of the cradles of bohemian culture, artists and gold-diggers have alternately reshaped neighborhoods like no other city in the country. In the 19th century, poets and writers were drawn by the natural beauty, raucous saloons and free-wheeling culture. The Beat movement attracted artists of all stripes to the coffee houses and jazz clubs in the 1950s. In the 1960s, the Haight-Ashbury neighborhood was the prime urban stomping ground for the nation's counterculture movement. And the city has long had a thriving gay community contributing to the cultural milieu.

"People come here looking to find themselves," says Larry Harvey, the founder of Burning Man, a San Francisco organization that holds a popular arts festival in the Nevada desert. "If they're sincere in that pursuit they tend to stay."

But the city has also been a center of manic capitalism. The gold rush of 1849 established San Francisco as a hub of finance. By the end of that century, the city's bohemian community had settled into cheap studios in the Montgomery Block building — also known as Monkey Block — downtown. It was one of the city's first major office buildings, abandoned when San Francisco's mining and banking interests moved to other parts of the city. Almost a century later, the pyramid-shaped Transamerica building was erected on the site, a distinctive icon on the San Francisco skyline.

In recent decades, nearby Silicon Valley brought an influx of technology, banking and other businesses, but San Francisco retained its reputation as a bulwark of liberal politics. And a unique mix of businesses and bohemians crammed into a city less than a sixth the size of New York City.

That precarious balance between the two groups, for a time, seemed threatened as never before by the Internet frenzy. And South of Market, or Soma, as locals affectionately call it, is something of an archaeological record of that boom and bust. Long home to light manufacturing, Soma was also a favorite of dance clubs, museums and artists. The roomy lofts and warehouses appealed to the irreverent sensibilities of Internet companies more than the pricier offices of the nearby financial district. In the late 1990s, Soma came to be known as Multimedia Gulch.

Much of that bustle is gone now. San Francisco and two nearby counties, Marin and San Mateo, have lost more than 73,000 jobs since late 2000. While less than 1 percent of offices South of Market were vacant three years ago, almost half sit empty now, by far the highest vacancy rate downtown. "It's as if a neutron bomb went off — the people are gone but everything else is here," says Daniel Ben-Horin, executive director of CompuMentor, a nonprofit that supplies technology products and services to other nonprofits.

While Soma's economic frenzy may be gone, in its place are survivors such as the businessman on nearby Bluxome Street who calls himself Tardon Feathered. Sitting in a 7,200-square-foot loft cluttered with microphones, drum kits and speakers, Mr. Feathered (the name he has gone by for decades) considers the change in fortunes of his business, Mr. Toad's, a recording and video-production studio.

During the boom, many of his aspiring-musician clients disappeared, nabbing steady paychecks instead from Internet companies. Adding to Mr. Feathered's strain two years ago: a threatened tripling in his rent. After the real-estate bust, that never materialized. In Soma, in fact, average annual rents for a common class of offices South of Market run only $17.08 a square foot, roughly a quarter the price several years ago, according to real-estate-brokerage firm Grubb & Ellis Co.

Mr. Feathered's business has since picked up. Artists and musicians are "society's economic equivalent of cockroaches," he says, able to survive during meltdowns.

The bust "has lit a fire under people to be expressive," adds Austin Lewis, a former tech worker, now a clown with Xeno, a circus group in San Francisco.

In many cases, nonprofits are capitalizing on the amenities Internet companies left behind. After cramming its 70 employees into converted apartments in two buildings, CompuMentor now occupies a spacious, 21,000-square-foot place that started out as a Soma warehouse. Later it housed Pets.com Inc. and, when that Internet retailer folded, Netcentives. The previous tenants left behind row after row of expensive cubicles and fancy office chairs. "They're better than what our butts are accustomed to," says Mr. Ben-Horin, CompuMentor's executive director.

At 690 Fifth St., Netcentives left loads of gear at its former building, including cubicles, office chairs and $100,000 of computer servers, estimates Mr. Latimer, the building manager. He stores beer for office parties in a server room where a thermostat keeps the brew, and the computers, cool. "You still need five levels of security to get to your beer," he jokes, fumbling with an access card at the door of the server room.

For Mr. Latimer, finding an eclectic set of tenants has become a mission. He has run an assortment of magazines, including one about psychedelic drugs called "High Frontiers." A longtime San Francisco resident, Mr. Latimer, 48, moved to New York during the Internet boom, after selling "Res," a film festival and publication, to an Internet venture there.

By the time he returned to San Francisco last summer, many of his friends had left. "I said, 'What is gone from the city? All the cool people who had to leave because they couldn't afford it anymore,'" Mr. Latimer says. So he set out to change that. He persuaded real-estate developer Merritt Sher, an investor in one of Mr. Latimer's magazines, to put him in charge of renting Mr. Sher's empty Netcentives offices. Mr. Latimer charges about $250 a month for a large cubicle, Internet access and shared use of the building's conference room.

Tenants here say they like the communal atmosphere of the place, which Mr. Latimer calls Space 690. Before moving in, Nicole Avril, regional director of GenArt, a nonprofit arts group, says she couldn't find an affordable office with open, airy spaces, perks she had grown accustomed to at a dot-com called I-Drive. She left there early last year to return to nonprofit arts administration. That's the field she was headed to, she says, before getting "sucked into the dot-com thing."

Rocking-chair
revival

Nostalgic front porch makes a comeback in a new century

By Leslie Mann

Special to the Tribune

It was gone, but not forgotten, and now is back—in force.

The American front porch nearly disappeared during the second half of the 20th Century, except for a blip on the screen during the '70s and '80s when some builders attached pretend porches to the facades of faux-Victorians.

They looked good on paper, but, in real life, you couldn't cram a rocking chair into them with a crowbar.

Now, front porches seem to be enjoying a retro revival, along with comfort foods and Radio Flyer wagons.

Not just ornamental, pretend porches, but deep, roomy porches that invite passers-by to come on up, put their feet up and have a glass of lemonade.

Front porches and their backyard cousins are nothing new, of course. The word "porch" derives from the Latin word "porticus." Early American homes, including George Washington's Mount Vernon and Thomas Jefferson's Monticello, had porches.

From the start, they were decorative (dressing up Plain-Jane homes or embellishing the already ornate) and/or functional (adding square footage and offering free air conditioning).

"The late 1800s to WWI were the heydays of the front porch and the front stoop," says Emily Talen, professor of urban and regional planning at the University of Illinois. "Then our culture became a car culture and the garage went up front."

Builders trace the current front-porch craze back to the mid-1990s, when Walt Disney Co. built the much-publicized Celebration community outside Orlando. It was billed as the flagship for the neo-traditional housing trend, which pushed garages to the backs of lots, resurrected alleys and clustered homes closer together.

As backyards shrunk, front porches became the new gathering spots. According to the National Association of Home Builders (NAHB), the number of porches (front and back) on new homes grew from 42 percent in 1992 (the first year it tallied them) to 50 percent in 2000.

'The neighbors walk by and say hi. The porches give the neighborhood a Mayberry, small-town kind of feeling.'

Homeowner Stacy Connor

"Whether you use the front porch or not, it makes for a better streetscape," says Talen. "The garage doors out front say, 'Cars live here.' Front porches say, 'People live here.'"

Builders say the front-porch passion crosses demographic lines.

"Front porches are appealing to all kinds of buyers—young families and older couples," reports Naperville-based builder John Schillerstrom, who has built dozens of custom and semi-custom homes with front porches in the last few years. "The common thread—they like to socialize with their neighbors."

"The front porch was pleasant, not exciting," recalls William Geist in his book, "Towards a Safe & Sane Halloween & Other Tales of Suburbia" (Random House).

"It was a place to sit. To sit and talk—something called visiting—about anything that came up.

"Sometimes nothing was said for several minutes, just sharing the silence, the sound of the crickets, the lawn sprinkler, or whatever. It was okay to be silent then, not a failure to communicate that you had to seek professional help for."

Then came TV, says Geist in his 1985 book. Then, the central air.

By the 1950s, recalls Geist sarcastically, "A body'd have to be a fool to sit out on the front porch talking with his next-door neighbor when he could be in his air-conditioned 'TV room' being talked at by

Photo for the Tribune by Steve Lasker

Antique furniture and planters, as well as benches, rocking chairs and swings, are common fare on porches at HomeTown Aurora.

the big stars from Hollywood and New York."

The trend started before 9-11, but now people are staying home even more. The front porch is a place they can relax.

Front porches are selling at all price points, too, from modest, subdivision homes to the over-$350,000 homes Schillerstrom builds.

Prices in a wide range

Like the houses they adorn, their prices run the gamut, he says, "from a $3,500, simple one with a concrete floor to a $10,000 to $15,000 one with a beadboard ceiling and canned lights. The sky's the limit."

Municipal land planners like front porches "because they help create safe, feel-good neighborhoods," says Mark Elliott, president of the Elliott Group in Morton Grove, which builds custom and semi-custom homes in the $500,000-and-up market.

"But it's not just the curb appeal they add," reports Elliott. "People are really us-

ing them." "We're out there spring, summer and fall, and eat out there in the summer," says Stacey Connor, of the porch that wraps around her two-story, four-bedroom home in HomeTown Aurora, built by Palatine-based Bigelow Homes.

"We [Connor and her husband, Keith] sit there and watch the kids play in the tot lot next door. The neighbors walk by and say hi. The porches give the neighborhood a Mayberry, small-town kind of feeling."

Furniture is abundant

Surrounded by wooden railings, the Connors' porch is deep enough to accommodate plenty of patio furniture, she says.

"When the kids get older, I'll put a porch swing out there, too," she says.

Research showed that people "yearned for more connected, social neighborhoods, and front porches are part of this," says Bigelow's vice president of sales and marketing, Jamie Bigelow.

"They no longer want to be prisoners of their backyards like they were in the '70s, '80s and '90s."

Bigelow says about 70 percent of the buyers in his neo-traditional HomeTown communities in Aurora, Oswego and Romeoville choose the front-porch upgrade.

Bigelow offers several versions—wrap-around, two-thirds, full-front and double-decker (plantation-style).

The average cost of $7,000 includes cement floors, wooden columns and railings. The homes range in base prices from $121,900 to $180,000.

"Buyers are willing to forgo interior upgrades such as wooden floors, ceramic tile or oak [stairway] railings for front porches," says Bigelow.

Roger Mankedick, executive vice president of Concord Homes in Palatine, agrees.

"Buyers give up other amenities or just pay more for porches, which they say remind them of their grandmothers and of simpler times," he says.

Front porches are hot tickets at Concord's neo-traditional communities—Montgomery Crossing in Montgomery and Madrona Village in Round Lake, where base prices range from $177,990 to $245,990.

Although front porches seem especially popular in the new, neo-traditional neighborhoods, they are sprouting in new subdivisions with more traditional layouts, too.

Rolling Meadows-based Kimball Hill, for example, features two-story front porches at its Fisher Farms development in west suburban Geneva, where homes go for $235,900 to $430,000.

Distinctive Homes of Orland Park builds wrap-arounds on its Prairie Trail homes in Plainfield, priced from $159,000 to $225,000.

A notch up the price ladder, Joe Keim Builders of Geneva has full front porches on its Majestic Oaks homes in St. Charles, where pricetags range from $500,000 to more than $1 million.

Front porches help soften the look of new homes on teardown properties, says Schillerstrom. While neighbors and village boards don't always take kindly to garage-nosed monstrosities replacing teardowns in older neighborhoods, "houses with front porches are good fits," he says.

As the front porch trend saturates the single-family market, it is spilling into the multi-family market, too. A local case in point is the townhouse line-up at Sho-Deen Inc.'s Mill Creek in Geneva.

"Now we're even seeing them in public housing," reports Talen.

At least one family, Carla and Michael Perry of Palatine, are repeat buyers of front porches. Their last home, a townhouse, had one. So a front porch topped their list of amenities when they bought a single-family home recently in Concord's new Concord Estates.

"We even changed lots to make sure we had the right elevation for the porch," says Carla Perry.

This summer, she says, they plan to spend evenings on their new front porch, getting to know their new neighbors.

"We have two rocking chairs on order," she says. "I can't wait."

From *Chicago Tribune*, June 8, 2002, pp. 1, 4. © 2002 by the Chicago Tribune. Reprinted by permission.

THE GEOGRAPHY OF COOL

What defines cool in a city, and why does the temperature change? We look at seasonal shifts in London, New York, Berlin, Paris and Tokyo

LONDON never set out to be cool. Indeed, London never set out to be anything, which may be the secret of its success. The British capital is essentially a conservative city: communes belong in Paris, springs in Prague and revolutions in St Petersburg. London has never used its built environment to proclaim a sense of change. Even today, of the billions of pounds of lottery money being spent in the capital, most is going on fixing up existing structures, such as the Royal Opera House and the new Tate Bankside gallery. London will never get a pyramid in the forecourt of Buckingham Palace.

Then again London has never had a politician to carry out such a plan. Even the new mayor won't have the power of his counterparts in Paris, Barcelona or New York to push through grandiose schemes. Officially sanctioned modernising projects usually fall flat in London. And Londoners are often the first to deride projects like the hapless Millennium Dome. The Pompidou Centre (co-designed by a Briton) was built in Paris, not London.

No. Cool in London is a village affair. Uniquely, London is a haphazard conglomeration of villages. And the villages were shaped into a city more by the accidents of history than by the imperatives of town-planning. Sometimes a village manages to capture the spirit of the age, to reflect a wider social and cultural phenomenon. Chelsea did so in the "swinging sixties". In the mid-1990s, "Cool Britannia" was supposed to be spilling out on to the streets of Camden and Islington.

Thus creating "cool" in London is a uniquely organic and authentic process. It is this very authenticity which makes the city such a magnet for the youth of Europe. So how does a London village become trendy in the first place? Here is a step-by-step guide:

- To begin with the area has to be relatively seedy and poor, with a plentiful supply of cheap, but solid, housing. Fortunately, London's villages are well provided with an abundant stock of large Victorian and Georgian accommodation.
- This means that young, trend-setting bohemians—active agents from London's enormous number of art schools—can afford to move into the area when they are at their penniless but creative best. Since the 1960s, artists have been joined by rock musicians, fashion designers and the like.

- For real bohemia you also need immigrants. These are essential to create cultural diversity and to challenge the complacent mono-culture of the resident English. Two of the trendiest parts of London in recent years, affluent Notting Hill and upcoming Brixton, were both hosts to large numbers of West Indian immigrants in the 1950s, because they could afford the cheap rents in the areas.
- The ethnic mix of the areas have contributed to the sense of edginess and roughness that first attracted the trendsetters to the area. Since the late 1950s Brixton and Notting Hill have both seen violent riots.
- This sense of danger is a strong draw for the more adventurous members of the middle and upper classes, as long as the violence can be viewed from a safe distance. They bring money into the area, and institutionalise bohemia into shops and cafés. Most of the trendy areas have been spillovers from the smarter parts of town. Thus Notting Hill from Kensington, Islington from the City and Chelsea from Belgravia.
- All this has to be fuelled by a plentiful supply of drugs. Drugs were

as essential to the 1960s as they were to creating the clubbing and dance scene of the 1990s. Though Britain has some of the harshest drug laws in Europe, its capital has one of the most flourishing drug economies.

Put these ingredients together, and a village will reach critical mass—but only for a while. Thus Chelsea was the trendiest part of town in the Victorian era, boasting painters such as James Whistler and writers such as Oscar Wilde amongst its residents. The Chelsea Arts Club survives to this day as a reminder of this vanished era.

Notting Hill started to take off in the late 1960s, when artists and designers like David Hockney and Ossie Clark moved in. Jimi Hendrix died there in

1970, and "The Clash" made it into a centre of punk rock in 1976. Islington began to move in the late 1970s, and the upwardly mobile middle classes (such as Tony Blair) arrived en masse in the late 1980s.

To be "cool", all these villages had to strike a delicate balance between holding on to enough of the danger, the seediness and the ethnic and cultural mix that made them chic in the first place, while surrendering enough of it to make it safe for incomers to enjoy. The moment it becomes too comfortable, trendification leads inexorably to gentrification, accompanied by rapid house-price inflation. At which point the party moves on.

By the time the film "Notting Hill" internationalised the appeal of that particular village, the game was up. Notting Hill's estate agents now trade on an er-

satz trendiness. A two-bedroom maisonette in the All Saints Road, once London's dingiest drugs den, now sells for half a million. But then it is in the middle of a "very trendy" area.

So where is cool now? Hoxton, just east of the City of London, has been the centre of the "Britart" movement during the 1990s. White Cube, an offshoot of London's smartest art gallery, opens there this week. It looks set to start a stampede as the more avant-garde galleries migrate across town from Mayfair and St James's. But the arrival of so many dealers, let alone the imminent opening of the Prince of Wales's school of architecture, spells the end of the Hoxton scene. And for the future? Watch out for Brixton, which still has some way to go, and Hackney Downs.

The best of mates

According to the young Americans described by Ethan Watters
in Urban Tribes, we don't need our families any longer.
Andy Beckett looks at the new grouping

Andy Beckett

On weekday afternoons in San Francisco, the sunlit, airy cafés that seem to stand on every street corner are always puzzlingly full. Not with pensioners or parents with babies, but with single people in their 20s and 30s in well-cut casual clothes. Most Americans of that age and apparent level of wealth are stuck in offices, but in San Francisco and other liberal American cities a different form of young middle-class life seems to flourish.

Ethan Watters calls them "urban tribes", and describes them as "the fastest-growing demographic group in America". They have been to university, they have confidence and money, but they are uninterested in what comes next in the conventional middle-class life: a structured career, marriage, children. Instead, Watters's subjects form groups with like-minded peers, and spend the decades between early adulthood and middle age going out together, bonding and gossiping with their new extended family, earning money by freelance means, and drinking a great number of leisurely coffees.

A few of the many tribe members Watters interviews live in Britain and other nations besides the United States. The phenomenon he has identified, he implies, is becoming apparent in all wealthy countries. But essentially this is a book about America. Foreign readers are expected to understand its references to "Seinfeldian" situations and "Costco-sized" supermarket products and—as with all the other trendspotting American popular sociology books that have crossed the Atlantic in recent years, such as The Tipping Point by Malcolm Gladwell and John Seabrook's Nobrow—to consider the insights here about American society as relevant to non-American lives.

Watters, a freelance writer in his 30s, lives in San Francisco. Until recently, he was a member of exactly the kind of peer group he writes about here, and he cites his and his friends' experiences at length. But the whiff of narcissism about this book feels entirely appropriate. The world Watters describes is inward-looking, self-sufficient, cut off from the rest of society. "In certain hipster areas," he writes, "you could literally go days without seeing a child." Working and playing in their small peninsular city at the very edge of America, he and his fellow bohemians can ignore the traditional family values of the Bush era: "I lived in a social microculture to such an extent that the national zeitgeist was felt only as a small shifting of the breeze."

Watters writes vividly about his tribe's existence: a perpetual present of parties, noisy dinners and group excursions, whole years passing in a pleasant blur in the seasonless San Francisco weather. The group share houses, collaborate on freelance writing and art projects. They drive to a festival in the desert to build a sculpture. For them, and their counterparts in Seattle and New York and elsewhere, money is not much of a worry. They have saleable skills and contacts—a hippyish-sounding artist mentioned here turns out to be making a chandelier for the architect Frank Gehry. They do each other favours—the writer Po Bronson, another member of Watters's group, provides a favourable cover quote for this book. And they know their actual families, with whom they remain in sporadic contact, may one day hand them substantial inheritances. The property and savings acquired by more conventional generations usefully underwrites the urban tribes' years of fun and experiments: as Watters says with commendable but slightly shocking directness, "Why worry about saving for retirement when your parents have done it for you?"

He is sufficiently self-aware to see that the lives he depicts can seem "comically selfish and self-absorbed". But he argues, quite convincingly, that urban tribes cannot simply be dismissed in those terms. The spirit of cooperation and mutual reliance also present in these gangs of friends is presented here as a throwback to the collective American traditions that existed before modern working patterns and consumer capitalism created a nation of office addicts and lonely shoppers.

All this material is presented in a conversational, informally researched way. At one point, he mentions "searching the web with words like 'friendship', 'loyalty', 'meaning of'". There is little of the erudition and sharp-elbowed argument that animates the older, non-American tradition of writing about city subcultures, exemplified by Peter York and Dick Hebdige in the 70s and 80s. They defined urban tribes in a more political and class-connected way—as skinheads, punks, Sloane Rangers—that fitted a more overtly political era; Watters's soft-edged portrait of a generation fits its time and its subject matter, but at times feels a bit unfocused and shallow by comparison.

There is not much here about ageing, or the biological difficulties of having children late. There is a long section speculating about why the author and his peers have delayed getting married that could be a vaguely argued women's magazine article. But the book regains its momentum in the final chapter, as Watters's train of thought heads off in an unexpected direction.

He has hinted already that being in a tight gang of friends well into your 30s might have a time-filling aspect. The relentless, heavily ritualised activities of the groups he describes—weekly group dinners, group parties held at the slightest excuse—do suggest a fear of being alone and thinking about the trajectory of your life. In the long term, he says, this has a cost: "[You] dam up certain desires, hopes, and plans. With each passing year, the pressure builds a little."

Yet close groups do not always let their members leave easily. Watters is good on the ways groups have of discouraging relationships with outsiders: the murmurs against "unsuitable" partners, the maintenance of an "ambient sexual charge" within the group itself, through "long-standing flirtations, unexpressed crushes, and glimmers of mutual attraction".

By the end of the book, Watters's urban tribes feel less free and appealing. Abruptly, he reveals he has left his and got married. Perhaps a conventional career awaits him after all, as a repenting bohemian in the Daily Mail. But he'll have to harden up his prose style.

UNIT 7

Urban Problems: Crime, Education, and Poverty

Unit Selections

Key Points to Consider

• How has the application of the "broken windows" theory—the concept of order maintenance in crime prevention—led to New York's dramatic decline in crime? What other examples of a change in thinking about crime can you describe, and what effect would these changes have on crime rates?

• What makes a successful public housing project? How can subsidized housing be constructed to create such results?

• What is the difference between bilingual education and English as a Second Language (ESL)? Which of the two approaches, in your opinion, helps urban schools better educate its children? How does the problem of segregation in the school system enter into your thinking?

• Can different classes, especially the rich and the poor, prosper at the same time in a city, or is success a zero sum game?

 **Links: www.dushkin.com/online/**
These sites are annotated in the World Wide Web pages.

The Center for Innovation in Education, Inc.
http://www.center.edu
Justice Information Center
http://www.ncjrs.org
National Institute on the Education of At-Risk Students
http://www.ed.gov/offices/OERI/At-Risk/
The Urban Institute
http://www.urban.org

Educational reform has been called the civil rights battleground for the twenty-first century, the institutional arena where equal opportunity will be expanded or curtailed. Urban schools have in general either stagnated or declined academically over the past quarter century, driving out middle class students, leaving behind the poor trapped in a system with no exit. Students in these schools suffer from slack standards and social promotion even when they do manage to graduate. A number of reform efforts have sprouted over the years to challenge or provide alternatives to large urban school systems. Currently, the most important ideas, from charter schools to vouchers, all provide low-income parents with a greater degree of school choice, something that middle class and more affluent parents take for granted.

School choice question also entered the debate over the recent referendum in California that limited the number of years students can spend in bilingual classes. Parents of Spanish-surnamed children complained about having their kids forced into dead-end, bilingual programs that were largely monolingual in Spanish. School choice won a momentous legal victory in June 2002 when the Supreme Court upheld Cleveland's publicly funded voucher program.

The fact that cities have begun to solve some of their most egregious problems should not blind us to those that remain. Crime, in fact, falls into both categories. Steep declines have occurred in some cities, but others like Washington, D.C., have yet to see any improvement. New York has had steep declines both in crime and in police violence against civilians.

Any discussion of crime in contemporary American cities can profitably begin with James Q. Wilson and George Kelling's very influential essay "Broken Windows." Wilson's 2002 update, "How an Idea Drew People Back to Urban Life," connects the history of the broken windows idea to actual changes in policing that drove down the crime rate in various cities. William Bratton, who as Giuliani's first police commissioner, applied Broken Windows policing to New York is now trying to repeat his famous success in Los Angeles, as Heather Mac Donald reports. "Crossing the Line" examines the police strategies in one of Brooklyn's high-crime neighborhoods, examining the impact on public housing residents (including parolees and probationers), as well as gentrifiers and local businesses. As crime continues to drop, neighborhood activists are increasingly embracing these strategies and trying to improve police-community relationships, as Bob Roberts details in "Police Line-Do Cross."

But while crime rates are down, the economic downturn of the past few years has again brought poverty to the forefront, In "In New York City, Fewer Find they Can Make It," Michael Powell reports that while New York is prospering, it is at the same time hollowing out, as fewer middle and working class citizens can afford to stay, leaving the poor and wealthy to share their connected cities. Aaron Bernstein sees things differently in "An Inner-City Renaissance," arguing that the poor prospered during the boom of the 1990s, as crime went down, and employment and incomes in the inner city neighborhoods shot up.

The police and neighborhood safety

BROKEN WINDOWS

BY JAMES Q. WILSON AND GEORGE L. KELLING

IN THE MID-1970S, THE STATE OF NEW JERSEY ANNOUNCED A "Safe and Clean Neighborhoods Program," designed to improve the quality of community life in twenty-eight cities. As part of that program, the state provided money to help cities take police officers out of their patrol cars and assign them to walking beats. The governor and other state officials were enthusiastic about using foot patrol as a way of cutting crime, but many police chiefs were skeptical. Foot patrol, in their eyes, had been pretty much discredited. It reduced the mobility of the police, who thus had difficulty responding to citizen calls for service, and it weakened headquarters control over patrol officers.

Many police officers also disliked foot patrol, but for different reasons: it was hard work, it kept them outside on cold, rainy nights, and it reduced their chances for making a "good pinch." In some departments, assigning officers to foot patrol had been used as a form of punishment. And academic experts on policing doubted that foot patrol would have any impact on crime rates; it was, in the opinion of most, little more than a sop to public opinion. But since the state was paying for it, the local authorities were willing to go along.

Five years after the program started, the Police Foundation, in Washington, D.C., published an evaluation of the foot-patrol project. Based on its analysis of a carefully controlled experiment carried out chiefly in Newark, the foundation concluded, to the surprise of hardly anyone, that foot patrol had not reduced crime rates. But residents of the foot-patrolled neighborhoods seemed to feel more secure than persons in other areas, tended to believe that crime had been reduced, and seemed to take fewer steps to protect themselves from crime (staying at home with the doors locked, for example). Moreover, citizens in the foot-patrol areas had a more favorable opinion of the police than did those living elsewhere. And officers walking beats had higher morale, greater job satisfaction, and a more favorable attitude toward citizens in their neighborhoods than did officers assigned to patrol cars.

These findings may be taken as evidence that the skeptics were right—foot patrol has no effect on crime; it merely fools

the citizens into thinking that they are safer. But in our view, and in the view of the authors of the Police Foundation study (of whom Kelling was one), the citizens of Newark were not fooled at all. They knew what the foot-patrol officers were doing, they knew it was different from what motorized officers do, and they knew that having officers walk beats did in fact make their neighborhoods safer.

But how can a neighborhood be "safer" when the crime rate has not gone down—in fact, may have gone up? Finding the answer requires first that we understand what most often frightens people in public places. Many citizens, of course, are primarily frightened by crime, especially crime involving a sudden, violent attack by a stranger. This risk is very real, in Newark as in many large cities. But we tend to overlook or forget another source of fear—the fear of being bothered by disorderly people. Not violent people, nor, necessarily, criminals, but disreputable or obstreperous or unpredictable people: panhandlers, drunks, addicts, rowdy teenagers, prostitutes, loiterers, the mentally disturbed.

What foot-patrol officers did was to elevate, to the extent they could, the level of public order in these neighborhoods. Though the neighborhoods were predominantly black and the foot patrolmen were mostly white, this "order-maintenance" function of the police was performed to the general satisfaction of both parties.

One of us (Kelling) spent many hours walking with Newark foot-patrol officers to see how they defined "order" and what they did to maintain it. One beat was typical: a busy but dilapidated area in the heart of Newark, with many abandoned buildings, marginal shops (several of which prominently displayed knives and straight-edged razors in their windows), one large department store, and, most important, a train station and several major bus stops. Though the area was run-down, its streets were filled with people, because it was a major transportation center. The good order of this area was important not only to those who lived and worked there but also to many others, who had to move through it on their way home, to supermarkets, or to factories.

The people on the street were primarily black; the officer who walked the street was white. The people were made up of "regulars" and "strangers." Regulars included both "decent folk" and some drunks and derelicts who were always there but who "knew their place." Strangers were, well, strangers, and viewed suspiciously, sometimes apprehensively. The officer—call him Kelly—knew who the regulars were, and they knew him. As he saw his job, he was to keep an eye on strangers, and make certain that the disreputable regulars observed some informal but widely understood rules. Drunks and addicts could sit on the stoops, but could not lie down. People could drink on side streets, but not at the main intersection. Bottles had to be in paper bags. Talking to, bothering, or begging from people waiting at the bus stop was strictly forbidden. If a dispute erupted between a businessman and a customer, the businessman was assumed to be right, especially if the customer was a stranger. If a stranger loitered, Kelly would ask him if he had any means of support and what his business was; if he gave unsatisfactory answers, he was sent on his way. Persons who broke the informal rules, especially those who bothered people waiting at bus stops, were arrested for vagrancy. Noisy teenagers were told to keep quiet.

These rules were defined and enforced in collaboration with the "regulars" on the street. Another neighborhood might have different rules, but these, everybody understood, were the rules for *this* neighborhood. If someone violated them, the regulars not only turned to Kelly for help but also ridiculed the violator. Sometimes what Kelly did could be described as "enforcing the law," but just as often it involved taking informal or extralegal steps to help protect what the neighborhood had decided was the appropriate level of public order. Some of the things he did probably would not withstand a legal challenge.

A determined skeptic might acknowledge that a skilled foot-patrol officer can maintain order but still insist that this sort of "order" has little to do with the real sources of community fear—that is, with violent crime. To a degree, that is true. But two things must be borne in mind. First, outside observers should not assume that they know how much of the anxiety now endemic in many big-city neighborhoods stems from a fear of "real" crime and how much from a sense that the street is disorderly, a source of distasteful, worrisome encounters. The people of Newark, to judge from their behavior and their remarks to interviewers, apparently assign a high value to public order, and feel relieved and reassured when the police help them maintain that order.

Second, at the community level, disorder and crime are usually inextricably linked, in a kind of developmental sequence. Social psychologists and police officers tend to agree that if a window in a building is broken *and is left unrepaired*, all the rest of the windows will soon be broken. This is as true in nice neighborhoods as in run-down ones. Window-breaking does not necessarily occur on a large scale because some areas are inhabited by determined window-breakers whereas others are populated by window-lovers; rather, one unrepaired broken window is a signal that no one cares, and so breaking more windows costs nothing. (It has always been fun.)

Philip Zimbardo, a Stanford psychologist, reported in 1969 on some experiments testing the broken-window theory. He arranged to have an automobile without license plates parked with its hood up on a street in the Bronx and a comparable automobile on a street in Palo Alto, California. The car in the Bronx was attacked by "vandals" within ten minutes of its "abandonment." The first to arrive were a family—father, mother, and young son—who removed the radiator and battery. Within twenty-four hours, virtually everything of value had been removed. Then random destruction began—windows were smashed, parts torn off, upholstery ripped. Children began to use the car as a playground. Most of the adult "vandals" were well-dressed, apparently clean-cut whites. The car in Palo Alto sat untouched for more than a week. Then Zimbardo smashed part of it with a sledgehammer. Soon, passersby were joining in. Within a few hours, the car had been turned upside down and utterly destroyed. Again, the "vandals" appeared to be primarily respectable whites.

Untended property becomes fair game for people out for fun or plunder, and even for people who ordinarily would not dream of doing such things and who probably consider themselves law-abiding. Because of the nature of community life in the Bronx—its anonymity, the frequency with which cars are abandoned and things are stolen or broken, the past experience of "no one caring"—vandalism begins much more quickly than it does in staid Palo Alto, where people have come to believe that private possessions are cared for, and that mischievous behavior is costly. But vandalism can occur anywhere once communal barriers—the sense of mutual regard and the obligations of civility—are lowered by actions that seem to signal that "no one cares."

We suggest that "untended" behavior also leads to the breakdown of community controls. A stable neighborhood of families who care for their homes, mind each other's children, and confidently frown on unwanted intruders can change, in a few years or even a few months, to an inhospitable and frightening jungle. A piece of property is abandoned, weeds grow up, a window is smashed. Adults stop scolding rowdy children; the children, emboldened, become more rowdy. Families move out, unattached adults move in. Teenagers gather in front of the corner store. The merchant asks them to move; they refuse. Fights occur. Litter accumulates. People start drinking in front of the grocery; in time, an inebriate slumps to the sidewalk and is allowed to sleep it off. Pedestrians are approached by panhandlers.

At this point it is not inevitable that serious crime will flourish or violent attacks on strangers will occur. But many residents will think that crime, especially violent crime, is on the rise, and they will modify their behavior accordingly. They will use the streets less often, and when on the streets will stay apart from their fellows, moving with averted eyes, silent lips, and hurried steps. "Don't get involved." For some residents, this growing atomization will matter little, because the neighborhood is not their "home" but "the place where they live." Their interests are elsewhere; they are cosmopolitans. But it will matter greatly to other people, whose lives derive meaning and satisfaction from local attachments rather than worldly involvement; for them, the neighborhood will cease to exist except for a few reliable friends whom they arrange to meet.

Such an area is vulnerable to criminal invasion. Though it is not inevitable, it is more likely that here, rather than in places where people are confident they can regulate public behavior by informal controls, drugs will change hands, prostitutes will solicit, and cars will be stripped. That the drunks will be robbed by boys who do it as a lark, and the prostitutes' customers will be robbed by men who do it purposefully and perhaps violently. That muggings will occur.

Among those who often find it difficult to move away from this are the elderly. Surveys of citizens suggest that the elderly are much less likely to be the victims of crime than younger persons, and some have inferred from this that the well-known fear of crime voiced by the elderly is an exaggeration: perhaps we ought not to design special programs to protect older persons; perhaps we should even try to talk them out of their mistaken fears. This argument misses the point. The prospect of a confrontation with an obstreperous teenager or a drunken panhandler can be as fear-inducing for defenseless persons as the prospect of meeting an actual robber; indeed, to a defenseless person, the two kinds of confrontation are often indistinguishable. Moreover, the lower rate at which the elderly are victimized is a measure of the steps they have already taken—chiefly, staying behind locked doors—to minimize the risks they face. Young men are more frequently attacked than older women, not because they are easier or more lucrative targets but because they are on the streets more.

Nor is the connection between disorderliness and fear made only by the elderly. Susan Estrich, of the Harvard Law School, has recently gathered together a number of surveys on the sources of public fear. One, done in Portland, Oregon, indicated that three fourths of the adults interviewed cross to the other side of a street when they see a gang of teenagers; another survey, in Baltimore, discovered that nearly half would cross the street to avoid even a single strange youth. When an interviewer asked people in a housing project where the most dangerous spot was, they mentioned a place where young persons gathered to drink and play music, despite the fact that not a single crime had occurred there. In Boston public housing projects, the greatest fear was expressed by persons living in the buildings where disorderliness and incivility, not crime, were the greatest. Knowing this helps one understand the significance of such otherwise harmless displays as subway graffiti. As Nathan Glazer has written, the proliferation of graffiti, even when not obscene, confronts the subway rider with the "inescapable knowledge that the environment he must endure for an hour or more a day is uncontrolled and uncontrollable, and that anyone can invade it to do whatever damage and mischief the mind suggests."

In response to fear, people avoid one another, weakening controls. Sometimes they call the police. Patrol cars arrive, an occasional arrest occurs, but crime continues and disorder is not abated. Citizens complain to the police chief, but he explains that his department is low on personnel and that the courts do not punish petty or first-time offenders. To the residents, the police who arrive in squad cars are either ineffective or uncaring; to the police, the residents are animals who deserve each other. The citizens may soon stop calling the police, because "they can't do anything."

The process we call urban decay has occurred for centuries in every city. But what is happening today is different in at least two important respects. First, in the period before, say World War II, city dwellers—because of money costs, transportation difficulties, familial and church connections—could rarely move away from neighborhood problems. When movement did occur, it tended to be along public-transit routes. Now mobility has become exceptionally easy for all but the poorest or those who are blocked by racial prejudice. Earlier crime waves had a kind of built-in self-correcting mechanism: the determination of a neighborhood or community to reassert control over its turf. Areas in Chicago, New York, and Boston would experience crime and gang wars, and then normalcy would return, as the families for whom no alternative residences were possible reclaimed their authority over the streets.

Second, the police in this earlier period assisted in that reassertion of authority by acting, sometimes violently, on behalf of the community. Young toughs were roughed up, people were arrested "on suspicion" or for vagrancy, and prostitutes and petty thieves were routed. "Rights" were something enjoyed by decent folk, and perhaps also by the serious professional criminal, who avoided violence and could afford a lawyer.

This pattern of policing was not an aberration or the result of occasional excess. From the earliest days of the nation, the police function was seen primarily as that of a night watchman: to maintain order against the chief threats to order—fire, wild animals, and disreputable behavior. Solving crimes was viewed not as a police responsibility but as a private one. In the March, 1969, *Atlantic*, one of us (Wilson) wrote a brief account of how the police role had slowly changed from maintaining order to fighting crimes. The change began with the creation of private detectives (often ex-criminals), who worked on a contingency-fee basis for individuals who had suffered losses. In time, the detectives were absorbed into municipal police agencies and paid a regular salary; simultaneously, the responsibility for prosecuting thieves was shifted from the aggrieved private citizen to the professional prosecutor. This process was not complete in most places until the twentieth century.

In the 1960s, when urban riots were a major problem, social scientists began to explore carefully the order-maintenance function of the police, and to suggest ways of improving it—not to make streets safer (its original function) but to reduce the incidence of mass violence. Order-maintenance became, to a degree, coterminous with "community relations." But, as the crime wave that began in the early 1960s continued without abatement throughout the decade and into the 1970s, attention shifted to the role of the police as crime-fighters. Studies of police behavior ceased, by and large, to be accounts of the order-maintenance function and became, instead, efforts to propose and test ways whereby the police could solve more crimes, make more arrests, and gather better evidence. If these things could be done, social scientists assumed, citizens would be less fearful.

A GREAT DEAL WAS ACCOMPLISHED DURING THIS TRANSITION, as both police chiefs and outside experts emphasized the crime-fighting function in their plans, in the allocation of resources, and in deployment of personnel. The police may well have become better crime-fighters as a result. And doubtless they remained aware of their responsibility for order. But the link between order-maintenance and crime-prevention, so obvious to earlier generations, was forgotten.

That link is similar to the process whereby one broken window becomes many. The citizen who fears the ill-smelling drunk, the rowdy teenager, or the importuning beggar is not merely expressing his distaste for unseemly behavior; he is also giving voice to a bit of folk wisdom that happens to be a correct generalization—namely, that serious street crime flourishes in areas in which disorderly behavior goes unchecked. The unchecked panhandler is, in effect, the first broken window. Muggers and robbers, whether opportunistic or professional, believe they reduce their chances of being caught or even identified if they operate on streets where potential victims are already intimated by prevailing conditions. If the neighborhood cannot keep a bothersome panhandler from annoying passersby, the thief may reason, it is even less likely to call the police to identify a potential mugger or to interfere if the mugging actually takes place.

Some police administrators concede that this process occurs, but argue that motorized-patrol officers can deal with it as effectively as foot-patrol officers. We are not so sure. In theory, an officer in a squad car can observe as much as an officer on foot; in theory, the former can talk to as many people as the latter. But the reality of police–citizen encounters is powerfully altered by the automobile. An officer on foot cannot separate himself from the street people; if he is approached, only his uniform and his personality can help him manage whatever is about to happen. And he can never be certain what that will be—a request for directions, a plea for help, an angry denunciation, a teasing remark, a confused babble, a threatening gesture.

In a car, an officer is more likely to deal with street people by rolling down the window and looking at them. The door and the window exclude the approaching citizen; they are a barrier. Some officers take advantage of this barrier, perhaps unconsciously, by acting differently if in the car than they would on foot. We have seen this countless times. The police car pulls up to a corner where teenagers are gathered. The window is rolled down. The officer stares at the youths. They stare back. The officer says to one, "C'mere." He saunters over, conveying to his friends by his elaborately casual style the idea that he is not intimidated by authority. "What's your name?" Chuck." "Chuck who?" "Chuck Jones." "What you doing, Chuck?" "Nothin'." "Got a P.O. [parole officer]?" "Nah." "Sure?" "Yeah." "Stay out of trouble, Chuckie." Meanwhile, the other boys laugh and exchange comments among themselves, probably at the officer's expense. The officer stares harder. He cannot be certain what is being said, nor can he join in and, by displaying his own skill at street banter, prove that he cannot be "put down." In the

process, the officer has learned almost nothing, and the boys have decided the officer is an alien force who can safely be disregarded, even mocked.

Our experience is that most citizens like to talk to a police officer. Such exchanges give them a sense of importance, provide them with the basis for gossip, and allow them to explain to the authorities what is worrying them (whereby they gain a modest but significant sense of having "done something" about the problem). You approach a person on foot more easily, and talk to him more readily, than you do a person in a car. Moreover, you can more easily retain some anonymity if you draw an officer aside for a private chat. Suppose you want to pass on a tip about who is stealing handbags, or who offered to sell you a stolen TV. In the inner city, the culprit, in all likelihood, lives nearby. To walk up to a marked patrol car and lean in-the window is to convey a visible signal that you are a "fink."

The essence of the police role in maintaining order is to reinforce the informal control mechanisms of the community itself. The police cannot, without committing extraordinary resources, provide a substitute for that informal control, on the other hand, to reinforce those natural forces the police must accommodate them. And therein lies the problem.

SHOULD POLICE ACTIVITY ON THE STREET BE SHAPED, IN important ways, by the standards of the neighborhood rather than by the rules of the state? Over the past two decades, the shift of police from order-maintenance to law-enforcement has brought them increasingly under the influence of legal restrictions, provoked by media complaints and enforced by court decisions and departmental orders. As a consequence, the order-maintenance functions of the police are now governed by rules developed to control police relations with suspected criminals. This is, we think, an entirely new development. For centuries, the role of the police as watchmen was judged primarily not in terms of its compliance with appropriate procedures but rather in terms of its attaining a desired objective. The objective was order, an inherently ambiguous term but a condition that people in a given community recognized when they saw it. The means were the same as those the community itself would employ, if its members were sufficiently determined, courageous, and authoritative. Detecting and apprehending criminals, by contrast, was a means to an end, not an end in itself; a judicial determination of guilt or innocence was the hoped-for result of the law-enforcement mode. From the first, the police were expected to follow rules defining that process, though states differed in how stringent the rules should be. The criminal-apprehension process was always understood to involve individual rights, the violation of which was unacceptable because it meant that the violating officer would be acting as a judge and jury—and that was not his job. Guilt or innocence was to be determined by universal standards under special procedures.

Ordinarily, no judge or jury ever sees the persons caught up in a dispute over the appropriate level of neighborhood order. That is true not only because most cases are handled informally on the street but also because no universal standards are available to settle arguments over disorder, and thus a judge may not be any wiser or more effective than a police officer. Until quite recently in many states, and even today in some places, the police make arrests on such charges as "suspicious person" or "vagrancy" or "public drunkenness"—charges with scarcely any legal meaning. These charges exist not because society wants judges to punish vagrants or drunks but because it wants an officer to have the legal tools to remove undesirable persons from a neighborhood when informal efforts to preserve order in the streets have failed.

Once we begin to think of all aspects of police work as involving the application of universal rules under special procedures, we inevitably ask what constitutes an "undesirable person" and why we should "criminalize" vagrancy or drunkenness. A strong and commendable desire to see that people are treated fairly makes us worry about allowing the police to rout persons who are undesirable by some vague or parochial standard. A growing and not-so-commendable utilitarianism leads us to doubt that any behavior that does not "hurt" another person should be made illegal. And thus many of us who watch over the police are reluctant to allow them to perform, in the only way they can, a function that every neighborhood desperately wants them to perform.

This wish to "decriminalize" disreputable behavior that "harms no one"—and thus remove the ultimate sanction the police can employ to maintain neighborhood order—is, we think, a mistake. Arresting a single drunk or a single vagrant who has harmed no identifiable person seems unjust, and in a sense it is. But failing to do anything about a score of drunks or a hundred vagrants may destroy an entire community. A particular rule that seems to make sense in the individual case makes no sense when it is made a universal rule and applied to all cases. It makes no sense because it fails to take into account the connection between one broken window left untended and a thousand broken windows. Of course, agencies other than the police could attend to the problems posed by drunks or the mentally ill, but in most communities—especially where the "deinstitutionalization" movement has been strong—they do not.

The concern about equity is more serious. We might agree that certain behavior makes one person more undesirable than another, but how do we ensure that age or skin color or national origin or harmless mannerisms will not also become the basis for distinguishing the undesirable from the desirable? How do we ensure, in short, that the police do not become the agents of neighborhood bigotry?

We can offer no wholly satisfactory answer to this important question. We are not confident that there *is* a satisfactory answer, except to hope that by their selection, training, and supervision, the police will be inculcated with a clear sense of the outer limit of their discretionary authority. That limit, roughly, is this—the police exist to help regular behavior, not to maintain the racial or ethnic purity of a neighborhood.

Consider the case of the Robert Taylor Homes in Chicago, one of the largest public-housing projects in the country. It is home for nearly 20,000 people, all black, and extends over ninety-two acres along South State Street. It was named after a distinguished black who had been, during the 1940s, chairman of the Chicago Housing Authority. Not long after it opened, in

1962, relations between project residents and the police deteriorated badly. The citizens felt that the police were insensitive or brutal; the police, in turn, complained of unprovoked attacks on them. Some Chicago officers tell of times when they were afraid to enter the Homes. Crime rates soared.

Today, the atmosphere has changed. Police–citizen relations have improved—apparently, both sides learned something from the earlier experience. Recently, a boy stole a purse and ran off. Several young persons who saw the theft voluntarily passed along to the police information on the identity and residence of the thief, and they did this publicly, with friends and neighbors looking on. But problems persist, chief among them the presence of youth gangs that terrorize residents and recruit members in the project. The people expect the police to "do something" about this, and the police are determined to do just that.

But do what? Though the police can obviously make arrests whenever a gang member breaks the law, a gang can form, recruit, and congregate without breaking the law. And only a tiny fraction of gang-related crimes can be solved by an arrest; thus, if an arrest is the only recourse for the police, the residents' fears will go unassuaged. The police will soon feel helpless, and the residents will again believe that the police "do nothing." What the police in fact do is to chase known gang members out of the project. In the words of one officer, "We kick ass." Project residents both know and approve of this. The tacit police–citizen alliance in the project is reinforced by the police view that the cops and the gangs are the two rival sources of power in the area, and that the gangs are not going to win.

None of this is easily reconciled with any conception of due process or fair treatment. Since both residents and gang members are black, race is not a factor. But it could be. Suppose a white project confronted a black gang, or vice versa. We would be apprehensive about the police taking sides. But the substantive problem remains the same: how can the police strengthen the informal social-control mechanisms of natural communities in order to minimize fear in public places? Law enforcement, per se, is no answer. A gang can weaken or destroy a community by standing about in a menacing fashion and speaking rudely to passersby without the law.

W E HAVE DIFFICULTY THINKING SUCH MATTERS, NOT SIMPLY because the ethical and legal issues are so complex but because we have become accustomed to thinking of the law in essentially individualistic terms. The law defines *my* rights, punishes *his* behavior, and is applied by *that* officer because of *this* harm. We assume, in thinking this way, that what is good for the individual will be good for the community, and what doesn't matter when it happens to one person won't matter if it happens to many. Ordinarily, those are plausible assumptions. But in cases where behavior that is tolerable to one person is intolerable to many others, the reactions of the others—fear, withdrawal, flight—may ultimately make matters worse for everyone, including the individual who first professed his indifference.

It may be their greater sensitivity to communal as opposed to individual needs that helps explain why the residents of small communities are more satisfied with their police than are the residents of similar neighborhoods in big cities. Elinor Ostrom and her co-workers at Indiana University compared the perception of police services in two poor, all-black Illinois towns—Phoenix and East Chicago Heights—with those of three comparable all-black neighborhoods in Chicago. The level of criminal victimization and the quality of police–community relations appeared to be about the same in the towns and the Chicago neighborhoods. But the citizens living in their own villages were much more likely than those living in the Chicago neighborhoods to say that they do not stay at home for fear of crime, to agree that the local police have "the right to take an action necessary" to deal with problems, and to agree that the police "look out for the needs of the average citizen." It is possible that the residents and the police of the small towns saw themselves as engaged in a collaborative effort to maintain a certain standard of communal life, whereas those of the big city felt themselves to be simply requesting and supplying particular services on an individual basis.

If this is true, how should a wise police chief deploy his meager forces? The first answer is that nobody knows for certain, and the most prudent course of action would be to try further variations on the Newark experiment, to see more precisely what works in what kinds of neighborhoods. The second answer is also a hedge—many aspects of order-maintenance in neighborhoods can probably best be handled in ways that involve the police minimally, if at all. A busy, bustling shopping center and a quiet, well-tended suburb may need almost no visible police presence. In both cases, the ratio of respectable to disreputable people is ordinarily so high as to make informal social control effective.

Even in areas that are in jeopardy from disorderly elements, citizen action without substantial police involvement may be sufficient. Meetings between teenagers who like to hang out on a particular corner and adults who want to use that corner might well lead to an amicable agreement on a set of rules about how many people can be allowed to congregate, where, and when.

Where no understanding is possible—or if possible, not observed—citizen patrols may be a sufficient response. There are two traditions of communal involvement in maintaining order. One, that of the "community watchmen," is as old as the first settlement of the New World. Until well into the nineteenth century, volunteer watchmen, not policemen, patrolled their communities to keep order. They did so, by and large, without taking the law into their own hands—without, that is, punishing persons or using force. Their presence deterred disorder or alerted the community to disorder that could not be deterred. There are hundreds of such efforts today in communities all across the nation. Perhaps the best known is that of the Guardian Angels, a group of unarmed young persons in distinctive berets and T-shirts, who first came to public attention when they began patrolling the New York City subways but who claim now to have chapters in more than thirty American cities. Unfortunately, we have little information about the effect of these groups on crime. It is possible, however, that whatever their effect on crime, citizens find their presence reassuring, and that they thus contribute to maintaining a sense of order and civility.

The second tradition is that of the "vigilante." Rarely a feature of the settled communities of the East, it was primarily to be found in those frontier towns that grew up in advance of the reach of government. More than 350 vigilante groups are known to have existed; their distinctive feature was that their members did take the law into their own hands, by acting as judge, jury, and often executioner as well as policeman. Today, the vigilante movement is conspicuous by its rarity, despite the great fear expressed by citizens that the older cities are becoming "urban frontiers." But some community-watchmen groups have skirted the line, and others may cross it in the future. An ambiguous case, reported in *the Wall Street Journal*, involved a citizens' patrol in the Silver Lake area of Belleville, New Jersey. A leader told the reporter, "We look for outsiders." If a few teenagers from outside the neighborhood enter it, "we ask them their business," he said. "If they say they're going down the street to see Mrs. Jones, fine, we let them pass. But then we follow them down the block to make sure they're really going to see Mrs. Jones."

Though citizens can do a great deal, the police are plainly the key to order-maintenance. For one thing, many communities, such as the Robert Taylor Homes, cannot do the job by themselves. For another, no citizen in a neighborhood, even an organized one, is likely to feel the sense of responsibility that wearing a badge confers. Psychologists have done many studies on why people fail to go to the aid of persons being attacked or seeking help, and they have learned that the cause is not "apathy" or "selfishness" but the absence of some plausible grounds for feeling that one must personally accept responsibility. Ironically, avoiding responsibility is easier when a lot of people are standing about. On streets and in public places, where order is so important, many people are likely to be "around," a fact that reduces the chance of any one person acting as the agent of the community. The police officer's uniform singles him out as a person who must accept responsibility if asked. In addition, officers, more easily than their fellow citizens, can be expected to distinguish between what is necessary to protect the safety of the street and what merely protects its ethnic purity.

But the police forces of America are losing, not gaining, members. Some cities have suffered substantial cuts in the number of officers available for duty. These cuts are not likely to be reversed in the near future. Therefore, each department must assign its existing officers with great care. Some neighborhoods are so demoralized and crime-ridden as to make foot patrol useless; the best the police can do with limited resources is respond to the enormous number of calls for service. Other neighborhoods are so stable and serene as to make foot patrol unnecessary. The key is to identify neighborhoods at the tipping point—where the public order is deteriorating but not unreclaimable, where the streets are used frequently but by apprehensive people, where a window is likely to be broken at any time, and must quickly be fixed if all are not to be shattered.

Most police departments do not have ways of systematically identifying such areas and assigning officers to them. Officers are assigned on the basis of crime rates (meaning that marginally threatened areas are often stripped so that police can investigate crimes in areas where the situation is hopeless) or on the basis of calls for service (despite the fact that most citizens do not call the police when they are merely frightened or annoyed). To allocate patrol wisely, the department must look at the neighborhoods and decide, from first-hand evidence, where an additional officer will make the greatest difference in promoting a sense of safety.

One way to stretch limited police resources is being tried in some public-housing projects. Tenant organizations hire off-duty police officers for patrol work in their buildings. The costs are not high (at least not per resident), the officer likes the additional income, and the residents feel safer. Such arrangements are probably more successful than hiring private watchmen, and the Newark experiment helps us understand why. A private security guard may deter crime or misconduct by his presence, and he may go to the aid of persons needing help, but he may well not intervene—that is, control or drive away—someone challenging community standards. Being a sworn officer—a "real cop"—seems to give one the confidence, the sense of duty, and the aura of authority necessary to perform this difficult task.

Patrol officers might be encouraged to go to and from duty stations on public transportation and, while on the bus or subway car, enforce rules about smoking, drinking, disorderly conduct, and the like. The enforcement need involve nothing more than ejecting the offender (the offense, after all, is not one with which a booking officer or a judge wishes to be bothered). Perhaps the random but relentless maintenance of standards on buses would lead to conditions on buses that approximate the level of civility we now take for granted on airplanes.

But the most important requirement is to think that to maintain order in precarious situations is a vital job. The police know this is one of their functions, and they also believe, correctly, that it cannot be done to the exclusion of criminal investigation and responding to calls. We may have encouraged them to suppose, however, on the basis of our oft-repeated concerns about serious, violent crime, that they will be judged exclusively on their capacity as crime-fighters. To the extent that this is the case, police administrators will continue to concentrate police personnel in the highest-crime areas (though not necessarily in the areas most vulnerable to criminal invasion), emphasize their training in the law and criminal apprehension (and not their training in managing street life), and join too quickly in campaigns to decriminalize "harmless" behavior (though public drunkenness, street prostitution, and pornographic displays can destroy a community more quickly than any team of professional burglars).

Above all, we must return to our long-abandoned view that the police ought to protect communities as well as individuals. Our crime statistics and victimization surveys measure individual losses, but they do not measure communal losses. Just as physicians now recognize the importance of fostering health rather than simply treating illness, so the police—and the rest of us—ought to recognize the importance of maintaining, intact, communities without broken windows.

James Q. Wilson is Shattuck Professor of Government at Harvard and author of Thinking About Crime. *George L. Kelling, formerly director of the evaluation field staff of the Police Foundation, is currently a research fellow at the John F. Kennedy School of Government at Harvard.*

From *The Atlantic Monthly*, March 1982, pp. 29-36, 38. © 1982 by James Q. Wilson and George L. Kelling. Reprinted by permission.

How an Idea Drew People Back to Urban Life

Twenty Years After 'Broken Windows,' **James Q. Wilson** Assesses the Theory

Two decades ago, George Kelling and I published an article in the Atlantic Monthly entitled "Broken Windows: The Police and Neighborhood Safety." Maybe it was the catchy title, maybe it was the argument, but for some reason the phrase and maybe the idea spread throughout American policing, and now is being taken up by the police in many other countries. Today, I sometimes hear a police official explain to me that they have adopted the "broken windows" strategy as if I had never heard of it.

The idea was simple. Citizens want public order as much as they want crime reduced, and so the police ought to worry about public disorder as much as they worry about catching crooks. Disorder arises from minor offenses such as aggressive panhandling, graffiti sprayed on the outside of buildings, alcoholics wandering the streets, and hostile teenagers hanging around bus stops and delicatessens.

Even though chasing away or arresting people who did these things may not do much to reduce crime immediately and in any event would constitute at best a minor pinch that police officers rarely took seriously and that courts were likely to ignore, recreating public order would do two things: Convince decent citizens that they and not some hostile force were entitled to use the streets and (perhaps) reduce crime over time by inducing good people and discouraging bad ones from using the streets.

The idea arose from Mr. Kelling's study of the effects of foot patrol on crime and public attitudes in New Jersey. He worked for the Police Foundation as it carried out a rigorous evaluation of foot patrol in Newark when Hubert Williams was the police chief. The neighborhoods where the experiment took place were largely inhabited by blacks and the officers who did the patrolling were largely white. The theory was that foot patrol would make the streets safer.

By and large, police chiefs did not believe this; after all, an officer on foot could not do much to chase a burglar in a car, and besides thieves could easily avoid the streets where foot patrol officers were walking. Police officers did not much care for foot patrol either. Standing outside on a cold or rainy night in Newark was a lot less pleasant than sitting in a warm patrol car, and the arrests you were likely to make while on foot would probably be of small-time offenders that would not do much to advance your police career.

The research showed that the police chiefs were right: Foot patrol did not cut crime. But it showed something else as well: The citizens loved it.

Explaining this puzzle is why we wrote the article. Were the citizens just fooling themselves by liking foot patrol? Did the whole project mean that the cops got better public relations just by conning the voters? Or maybe the citizens were right. Maybe they valued public order as much as they valued less crime. Perhaps public order would later on reduce the chances of crime rates rising if enough good folk used the streets and fewer roughnecks did.

We think the citizens were right. Getting rid of graffiti, aggressive panhandling, and wandering drunks made the citizens happier and increased their support for the police. Moreover, the cops on foot actually liked the work because they got to meet a lot of decent people and learn how they thought instead of just getting out of a patrol car to arrest a crook. We went on to offer the speculation—and at the time it was only a guess—that more orderly neighborhoods would, over the long haul, become less dangerous ones.

Our idea survived the predictable onslaught. Many civil rights organizations began to protest against efforts to control panhandling. Such efforts, they argued, were directed at the poor, blacks and the homeless. The ACLU filed suits in some cities against aspects of broken-windows policing. They must have forgotten, or perhaps they never knew, that broken-windows policing was first tested in poor black neighborhoods that enthusiastically endorsed it.

Civil libertarians also complained that stopping begging in the New York subways denied people free speech, and even got a federal judge to agree with them. But the appeals court threw out the argument because begging was not speech designed to convey a message, it was simply solicitation for money.

Slowly our idea grew until now it is hard to find a police department that does not claim to practice community-oriented policing and follow a broken-windows strategy. Just what the police chief means by these terms is not always very clear; to some extent, these words have become buzz phrases, backed up by a federal government policy of giving money to cities if they practice community policing, somehow defined.

In 1996, Mr. Kelling and his wife, Catherine Coles, published a book, "Fixing Broken Windows," that reviewed what has been done by Robert Kiley, David Gunn, and William Bratton to restore decency and safety to the New York subways and Bratton's later efforts to cut crime citywide after he became commissioner of the New York Police Department. Similar efforts took place in Baltimore, San Francisco, and Seattle.

The New York Transit Authority experience was especially telling. Long before he became the NYPD commissioner, Mr. Bratton, working with Messrs. Kiley and Gunn, had cut crime dramatically in the city's subways by holding his subordinates accountable for reducing offenses and getting rid of the graffiti. The people and the editorial writers cheered and in time the number of cops on duty underground could be safely cut.

Everyone in New York will recall the key steps whereby the subway success became the whole city's achievement. Rudolph Giuliani got elected mayor after a tough anti-crime campaign. One of the first things the NYPD did after he took office was to emphasize a policy begun by former police commissioner Raymond Kelly (who is now commissioner

again) to get tough on "squeegee-men," males who extort money from motorists by pretending to wash (and sometimes spitting on) their car windows. Traditionally, officers would at best give only tickets to squeegeers, who would usually ignore the tickets or at worst pay a small fine. But then the NYPD began issuing warrants for the arrest of squeegee-men who ignored their tickets. Getting the warrant for non-appearance meant jail time for the recipient, and suddenly squeegee harassment stopped.

It may have been a little thing, but every New York motorist noticed it. Almost overnight, the city seemed safer. No one can say it was safer from serious crime, but it appeared safer and the people loved it.

After Mr. Giuliani took office, the crime rate plummeted. Lots of criminologists think that this happened automatically or as a result of some demographic change. No doubt serious crime fell in a lot of cities, but it fell faster and more in New York than almost anywhere else.

I do not assume that broken-windows policing explains this greater drop. Indeed, my instinct is to think that Mr. Bratton's management style, and especially his effort to hold precinct commanders accountable by frequently reviewing their performance in rigorous CompStat hearings, was the chief factor.

But Mr. Kelling has gathered a lot of evidence that a broken-windows strategy also made a difference. He measured that strategy by counting the number of misdemeanor arrests in New York precincts and showing that an increase in such arrests was accompanied by a decrease in serious crime, even in areas where unemployment rates rose, drug use was common, and the number of young men in their crime-prone years had increased.

So maybe a broken-windows strategy really does cut crime. But we know that it draws people back into urban life. And that is no trivial gain.

Mr. Wilson is an emeritus professor at UCLA and a lecturer at Pepperdine University.

MURDER MYSTERY

In the 1990s, New York and Boston achieved dramatic decreases in homicide.
One of them is still improving. The other is getting worse again. Why?

BY JOHN BUNTIN

TWO DOZEN YOUNG AFRICAN-AMERICAN MEN, wearing orange, blue and tan jumpsuits, are sitting in a semi-circle in a room at the Suffolk County House of Corrections in Boston. They are there because they are about to be released from prison, and because they are former gang members at high risk of returning to crime.

Sitting across from them is a whole battery of ministers, social workers, police and local and federal prosecutors. Each of them has something to offer the inmates. The ministers tell them about a mentoring program. The social workers say they can help arrange child support payments, get them IDs or driver's licenses, and find transitional living arrangements.

Then the prosecutors take over. Theirs is a different message: We're watching you, and if you return to your former lifestyle, we'll be there to make sure you regret it. "There are two messages," says Kurt Francois, who works for a program called the Safe Neighborhood Reentry Initiative: "It's time to change, and if you don't, you will bear the consequences."

There, in a nutshell, is Boston-style policing. It is based on an unusual collaboration between law enforcement agencies, social service organizations and local churches. It has given the city one of the nation's most admired police departments. Lately, however, local residents have been asking a blunt question: Does it really work?

Five years ago, the question would have seemed absurd. Between 1990 and 1999, as the Boston approach took hold, the city's homicide rate fell by 80 percent. Of course, other cities experienced big crime drops too, including some cities that did little in the way of innovative policing. But only two—Boston and New York—saw murder rates fall by double-digit figures year after year.

Both Boston and New York attributed the decline to new—and very different—approaches to policing. In New York, the police emphasized "quality of life" law enforcement, focusing on minor property and nuisance offenses as a key to serious crimes, and developed a high-tech mapping and accountability system to track police performance. Boston did some of that, but its emphasis was elsewhere: on the partnerships between police and parole officers, community leaders, "streetworkers," academics and ministers.

Because both systems produced impressive numbers, both departments became models for reform-minded policing across the country. But in the eyes of many, Boston had a clear edge: Whereas New York's reduced crime rate came at the cost of growing tension between police and minority activists, Boston accomplished the same result while police relations with the African-American community actually improved. U.S. Attorney General Janet Reno called it "the Boston Miracle."

Former New York chief William Bratton: Stopping crime is up to the police, not citizens.

It was almost too good to be true. And then the numbers started changing. Boston's homicide rate began creeping up again. It took a while for most of the country to notice, but New York noticed very quickly. Last December, in his nationally televised farewell address, Mayor Rudolph Giuliani made a pointed comparison. "In the last statistics put out by the FBI," the mayor said, "there has been a 67 percent increase in murder in Boston. During that same period of time, there was a 12 percent decrease in the city of New York. I don't know, which policing theory would you want to follow?" And then Giuliani answered his own question: "The reality is that the model that was adopted for dealing with crime in New York City is the very, very best way to assure that you can keep a city safe."

Officials in Boston wrote these remarks off as personal pettiness. "A shallow boast," sniffed the *Boston Globe* editorial board. "I can't tell you why he did it," said Boston Mayor Thomas Menino. "Maybe it was frustration because he wishes he could continue the job."

Whatever the motive, Giuliani's figures were accurate. In the past two years, Boston's homicide rate has increased by more than 100 percent. At the same time, the rate in New York City has continued to fall. Clearly, something must be going on. The question is what.

Does Boston's rising homicide rate reflect problems with the Boston model itself, as Giuliani charges, or is Boston suffering from new demographic trends that other cities can soon expect to see? It's a question whose answer has major implications for police departments around the nation. Looking at Boston and New York's divergent police styles isn't a bad way to begin studying this question.

Boston and New York began with a common problem. In the late 1980s and early '90s, both experienced a frightening epidemic of murder. In 1990, New York's homicide total hit the staggering number of 2,245— quadruple the figure in the 1960s. That same year, homicides in Boston reached 152—a number that sounds modest at first but in fact was almost identical to New York's on a per capita basis.

And the problem seemed certain only to get worse. "If there are two thousand murders this year," warned New York newspaper columnist Pete Hamill, "get ready for four thousand." A *Time* magazine survey found that 59 percent of New Yorkers would move out of town if they could. To many, it seemed the police had simply relinquished control of the streets to criminals.

The New York strategy was born in the waning days of Mayor David Dinkins' administration, when Commissioner Raymond Kelly publicly embraced the "broken windows" philosophy of policing, which held that "disorder and crime are usually inextricably linked." Kelly began with an aggressive crackdown on the notorious "squeegee men" who harassed the city's commuters.

Commissioner Paul Evans attributes the 'Boston Miracle' to a web of partnerships between police and the community.

The new approach wasn't enough to save Dinkins; he was unseated by Giuliani in November 1993. But Giuliani embraced "broken windows" and steadily built upon it. He replaced Kelly with William Bratton, the former Boston police commissioner, and Bratton added the critical innovation called Compstat.

The brainchild of Bratton's chief crime strategist, the late Jack Maple, Compstat married the idea of crime mapping with a new focus on precinct commander performance. Every week, precinct commanders from one of New York's eight patrol boroughs would come before the department's top brass to discuss the crime trends in their precincts. Commanders who failed to show sufficient familiarity with those trends, or who failed to come up with strategies for solving the problems, were quickly reassigned or demoted—two-thirds of the city's precinct commanders in all. The crime rate plummeted.

Criminologists continued to debate the effect of "broken windows" policing and Compstat, but the homicide rate continued to go down. It was 1,177 in 1995, 770 in 1997, 664 in 1999. Compstat quickly became one of the most admired innovations in American policing in decades.

But in the midst of the good news, some New Yorkers began to see a dark side to the aggressive style of policing that the New York system encouraged. Former Mayor Dinkins complained to the press that Bratton and Giuliani "seem more interested in 'kicking ass' than increasing peace." In 1999, when members of the elite Street Crimes Unit opened fire on Amadou Diallo, an unarmed African immigrant, much of New York's African-American leadership came out to protest against the NYPD.

Boston wasn't having those sorts of problems. And its murder rate was falling just as dramatically, from 152 in 1990 to 31 in 1999. Police officials there were quick to assert that the reason was their law enforcement philosophy, based on social service and neighborhood relations, not on the cold statistics and hard-nosed street tactics of the cops in New York. "It wasn't just tough enforcement," says Commissioner Paul Evans. "It was going out to the community, trying to prevent crime, trying to identify alternatives for young people, after-school programs, jobs." In short, he argues, it was the result of an extraordinary web of partnerships between local, state and federal law enforcement agencies, nonprofit organizations and social service agencies, and the city's African-American clergy.

The Boston strategy emerged, unlike New York's, not so much from numbers but from one horrifying event. In May 1992, a group of youths burst in on a funeral being held for a slain gang member at Morning Star Baptist Church in Mattapan. In the presence of 300 panicked witnesses, the youths repeatedly stabbed one of the mourners, whose presence they viewed as an insult to the deceased.

Boston responded to the Morning Star attack (and a string of youth homicides that followed) with a flurry of programs and partnerships, such as the 10 Point Coalition, a group of African-American ministers who decided to reach out to kids on the street and put aside their distrust of the police. The homicide rate started going down, but rather slowly. Between 1992 and late 1996, it declined to 70 deaths per year—a big improvement from 1990, but more than twice as many as the city's historical average.

Then in mid-1996, Boston's police added something new to its network of partnerships—the idea of "focused deterrence." It was the inspiration of an unlikely coalition: front-line police officers from the Youth Violence Strike Force; a neighborhood probation office; the Department of Youth Services; the Streetworkers, a youth outreach program; the FBI and Drug Enforcement Administration; the U.S. Attorney and county D.A.; and researchers from Harvard University's Kennedy School of Government. "Focused deterrence" began not with social work but with the recognition that a relatively small number of hard-core gang members were responsible for most of the carnage in Boston.

At first, this was a discouraging finding: These hard-core offenders scarcely seemed the type who would walk away from drug-dealing and gun-running for a temporary summer job. But officers in Boston decided to turn these kids' very criminality against them. Because these kids were so criminally active, they could potentially be deterred or punished in a number of ways. As the officers put it, there were "a lot of levers to pull." Kids who were on probation could be supervised more closely; kids who had been referred to the Department of Youth Services could be taken into protective custody and even transferred to rural western Massachusetts; kids who were repeat offenders could be subjected to federal prosecution and sent out of state.

The Youth Violence Strike Force had achieved good results using a limited trial of focused deterrence on a gun-happy Cape Verdean gang on Boston's crime-plagued Wendover Street: not only had there been an immediate drop in gun-related incidents, but many kids gave up their weapons voluntarily. Now the same approach was employed citywide, with police, probation officers and prosecutors all warning gang members that gun violence would bring down on them the full attention not only of local authorities but of the U.S. Attorney's Office, the DEA and the ATF.

This marked a major change from the way Boston police had dealt with homicide "hot spots" in the past. "Years ago," said Commissioner Evans, "we'd have shootings in neighborhoods and we'd do saturation patrols and warrant sweeps and we were going after anybody and everybody. Now… we know what's going on; we know who's involved in the shooting; we call them all in; they're all on probation; we use the levers. We tell them, 'Fellows, the violence stops…. We're not going to let you kill each other.'"

In August 1996, Boston police and federal agents arrested 21 members of the Intervale Posse, one of Boston's most notorious gangs. Then, in a series of forums with other gangs in the city, the Ceasefire group quickly got the word out: If the shooting doesn't stop, this will happen to you, too. One notorious gangster found with a single bullet in his possession was sent to federal prison for 10 years. Soon the city's homicide rate was in a gratifying freefall.

Boston isn't the only city where this sort of intervention worked. Minneapolis, a city not normally associated with violent crime, experienced an explosion of gang-related violence in the mid-1990s. In 1997, it responded with a Ceasefire program. The same thing happened as in Boston—homicides fell dramatically. The city ended the year with 58 murders, down from 86 the previous year. In Stockton, California, gang-related killings fell from 20 to four with Boston-style tactics. Indianapolis and the city of Winston-Salem, North Carolina, reported similar results.

New York, meanwhile, was finding equal success with its different emphasis. Maple, the NYPD's chief strategist, stressed four guiding principles: "accurate and timely intelligence," "rapid deployment," "effective tactics and strategies" and "relentless follow-up and assessment." Partnerships and reeducation meetings were not at the top of his list of effective methods.

Nearly all the media coverage of New York's declining crime rate stressed Compstat and the constant use of computer data. But within the department, many believed that the key element in keeping crime down was the fourth one on Maple's list: follow-up.

"We're great at initiatives, but it's the follow-up that's crucial," notes Elizabeth Glazer, chief of staff of the New York City Department of Investigation. "What Compstat does is ensure that there's always follow-up."

And that may offer a partial clue to the puzzling discrepancy between Boston and New York crime rates in the past couple of years. Researchers who have studied Ceasefire-style interventions say they are weak when it comes to follow-up. They tend to produce dramatic initial results—and then fall apart. "They're hard to sustain," admits Harvard criminologist David Kennedy. "They take an awful lot of assembly. They're basically simple, but it takes a lot of moving parts to put it together. Some are so dramatically effective that there comes a time when there's really not much work to do. People gather around a table and ask each other, 'Has there been any violence?' People say, 'No,' and if that goes on long enough, the partnership weakens. Violence picks up and people move on, and the script has been forgotten."

As Boston's homicide rate was plunging in the late '90s, the Ceasefire group met less frequently. Key players were promoted or moved on to other tasks. The grant that had supported work on the program at the Kennedy School was phased out. While the Youth Violence Strike Force continued to hold an occasional Ceasefire forum, the gang members no longer received the sustained "focused deterrence" they once did. They didn't seem to need it.

In retrospect, it seems they may have needed it after all. By the spring of 2000, Boston's violent crime remission was over. After years of decreases, the number of gun incidents in the gang strongholds of Roxbury and Dorchester started to creep up again. The increased gunplay soon translated into a rising homicide rate. In 2000, Boston had 40 homicides. In 2001, the number jumped to 66.

There are plenty of explanations for that change that avoid the issue of police tactics altogether, and stress demographics. Many believe, for example, that the return of homicide is connected to convicts completing their prison terms and returning to their old neighborhood, settling old feuds and trying to regain control of the drug trade.

"You want my quick and dirty analysis for the jump in the numbers?" probation officer Billy Stewart told the *Boston Herald*. "Simple: They're b-a-a-ck!… and they're back smarter. They're back embittered. And that seasoned bitterness makes them extremely dangerous."

Some statistics do buttress this argument. A decade ago, the average age of the city's homicide perpetrators was between 20 and 25. Last year, the department says, it was 31. The average age of inmates released from the Suffolk County House of Correction in January 2001 was 32—considerably older than the prison population a decade ago. "When you look at the Boston Miracle or the Boston model," says Commissioner Evans, "it was really geared toward youth violence. Now what we've seen in the last year is a much older individual."

On the other hand, the release of prisoners back into the community is hardly a new phenomenon. The prisoner population at the Suffolk County House of Corrections peaked in 1999, when approximately 3,700 offenders were released. It's possible that these ex-cons are behind Boston's recent murder increase, but commanders in the field discount the notion. "I can look at some neighborhoods—Bowdoin, Geneva—a couple of guys got out of jail, and we saw things happen," says Captain Robert Dunford, "but in terms of citywide, no."

In contrast to the "ex-con" theory, some analysts say the explanation for increased homicide is exactly the opposite: a tough new batch of young kids. Back in the mid-1990s, criminologists such as James Alan Fox and John DiIulio were warning of a whole generation of "super predators"—teenage criminals more ruthless and more dangerous than any cohort that preceded them. "Although we would never use the term 'super predator,'" says the Reverend Eugene Rivers, co-chair of the National 10 Point Leadership Foundation, "this kid that we [have seen] emerging fits that description of that uncertain term.... A younger cohort of more violent young people [have been] surfacing."

Body Count

Number of homicides

	BOSTON	N.Y.
1985	87	1,384
1986	105	1,582
1987	76	1,672
1988	93	1,896
1989	99	1,905
1990	143	2,245
1991	113	2,154
1992	73	1,995
1993	98	1,946
1994	85	1,561
1995	96	1,177
1996	59	983
1997	43	770
1998	34	633
1999	31	664
2000	40	671
2001	66	642

Note: Data up through 1999 are from BJS, 2000-2001 are from PDs.

Source: Bureau of Justice Statistics, Boston Police Department, New York Police Department

There are problems with this explanation as well. Boston's youth population was growing steadily throughout the '90s, even as crime began to fall. In 1991, the percentage of homicide victims aged 24 and under (victim numbers generally track perpetrator numbers pretty well) was 48 percent. Last year, it was 41 percent. The story is much the same nationwide. According to a March report by the Urban Institute, a nonpartisan think tank in Washington, D.C., the youth population increased by 13 percent between 1990 and 2000. During that same period, the juvenile crime rate fell by a third, to its lowest level in two decades.

Given the inconsistencies in both of the demographic theories, it begins to seem more plausible to return to the issue of police strategy. And this is just what Boston is doing. However, rather than reinvigorating its efforts at "focused deterrence," the Boston police department seems to be redoubling its efforts at building partnerships, expanding social services and involving the community in the fight against crime.

This past January, the Boston police department laid out what it calls "Boston Strategy Part 2." It calls for redoubling the department's emphasis on "prevention, enforcement and intervention," for pushing more authority to the district commander level, and for creating a new law enforcement community coordinating group to direct the department's actions. "You can see with all of our strategies, we're not moving away from partnerships," says Superintendent Paul Joyce. "You can't put the responsibility of dealing with crime issues on the police or on the probation officer; it's really too much."

That's the kind of sentiment that Giuliani and his police commissioners scoffed at. "I'm from the school of thought that the average citizen doesn't want to be engaged in patrolling their own neighborhood," says Bratton, the police commissioner who first introduced community policing to Boston in the early '90s, before becoming Giuliani's first commissioner in 1993. "When I come home at night, I don't want to be looking over my shoulder or coming upstairs to get my flashlight, my armband, and go out and patrol the neighborhood. That's what the police are for." Indeed, the idea that the police couldn't reduce crime on their own was one of the ideas that Giuliani and Bratton set out to demolish. When Bratton was appointed police commissioner, he promised Giuliani that under his watch the NYPD would reduce crime by 30 percent in three years—and it did.

The NYPD doesn't exactly repudiate the partnership idea. "It's critical," says Deputy Commissioner Michael Farrell, "that there be productive relationships with communities, particularly with cities that have as much diversity in their makeup as we do." On the other hand, Farrell acknowledges, the department's emphasis continues to be placed on those strategies it believes are working: Compstat and quality of life.

Boston police are hopeful that their new efforts will work, too. They say they're encouraged by early indications that the homicide increases are leveling off in 2002. They're optimistic that initiatives such as the prisoner reentry program and the ongoing efforts to provide more resources to district commanders will further depress crime rates.

Still, Superintendent Joyce doubts that Boston will soon return to the homicide levels of a couple of years ago. "Most likely, we've seen our best days," he admits. "Crime will move up. It's how you monitor that and how you deal with that as crime trends start to move up again."

Meanwhile, in the first quarter of 2002, the homicide rate in New York City was down another 29 percent.

CROSSING THE LINE

Police do everything it takes to protect booming brownstone
Fort Greene—from the projects on the other side of "Murder Avenue."
Is neighborhood profiling here to stay?

BY SASHA ABRAMSKY

"We used to be able to just chill in front of our door," says Jermaine, 22, who lives in Fort Greene's Ingersoll Houses. He can't anymore. The neighborhood's too safe. "I had a cop come up," recalls Jermaine. "He told me I cannot sit in front of my building. He said if I'm there when he comes back in five minutes he's gonna arrest me."

Jermaine spent his teenage years in and out of juvenile institutions and jail for robbery and assault before moving back in with his mother four years ago. In the years since, Jermaine, tall with a scraggly beard, a blue headband and a silver earring in his left ear, has been given tickets for spitting on the sidewalk. He has received more tickets—most of which he says courts subsequently dismissed—for owning dogs without a license. He has also been picked up by the police and held for questioning about his friends' involvement in crimes.

As far as the cops are concerned, Jermaine deserves the extra attention. Last year, he was arrested for petty larceny—he says, vaguely, that he was running a small internet scan—and put on three years' probation. Since then, he says the police have arrested him four times, all on charges relating to his dogs.

In recent years, Fort Greene has become known for its swift gentrification—for increasingly pricey historic brownstones and a blossoming of new cafes and bars. Close to half of all small residential buildings have changed owners in the past six years. None of those are rent-regulated; the newcomers are paying market rents and mortgages. All of that was made possible by a tremendous drop in crime—over 60 percent since the early 1990s.

"The cops, they harass you," says one local 21-year-old African American man, who asked not to be named, working as a counselor at a

summer jobs program near the projects. His hip-hop image—gold chains and rings, gold teeth-coverings, long hair and bandanna—puts him firmly into the police profile of a likely criminal. "You can't even walk outside peacefully without having to pull your I.D. out. I look like an average boy in the hood."

Although he claims he's never been convicted of any crime, is on his way to college and has never gotten into real trouble, he says that he has been arrested 14 times in the past three years. "They run up on you. Frisk you for no reason," he says angrily, as coworkers nod in agreement. "I ain't got no record. Fourteen times for bullshit. Dismissed. Dismissed. Dismissed. Wasting taxpayers' dollars putting us through the system. You want to run, just to avoid the contact."

It's not just the police. At the instigation of the NYPD, parole officers have become sometimes-reluctant players in aggressive crime prevention efforts in the Fort Greene projects—part of a push to target people on parole. "Maybe half my friends are on parole or probation," says Jermaine. "One of my friends got violated. He had two years of probation left. He got locked up for riding a bike on the sidewalk. He had no I.D. on him." Police have found other friends of his in violation of their parole "for trespassing. Being caught in a sweep. Being somewhere you're not supposed to be. A lot get locked up for weed, for drinking outside."

Inevitably, people here in the projects blame it on the newcomers on the other side of Myrtle Avenue, who have met extensively with the police to demand a safe neighborhood. Both the public housing and the brownstones are part of the 88th Precinct. Darnel Canada, 42, a one-time prisoner who served seven years for assault, now heads the Fort Greene Empowerment Organization, a group that seeks employment for residents in the projects. "Ten years ago," says Canada, "you'd hear shots for a while and no police. Now, anything you call the police for now, there's an over-response. Since property values went up there's a difference. The police response is, 'You're messing up our block and we're not having it.' A lot of people in the development feel it's a property issue. Now the police run in here like crazy."

The September 11 attack dramatically altered police priorities. For a while, it also muted what had been a torrent of criticism of NYPD practices. The attack and its aftermath highlighted just how vital the police are to the city's survival, and how brave officers can be in times of danger.

The NYPD did not return numerous phone calls and interview requests related to this article. But clearly, policing a tract of public housing is a task as complex as any the police take on. "Many residents have social issues that need to be addressed—employment, poor health care, poor diet, domestic violence, teenage pregnancy, lack of maintenance to buildings they live in," notes Eric Adams, a lieutenant at Fort Green's 88th Precinct and co-founder of the group One Hundred Blacks In Law Enforcement, a long-time critic of Giuliani administration police leadership. He believes that many residents "look at police officials as representatives of the authority figure preventing some of these other issues being addressed."

Police are supposed to monitor local activities, such as the actions of convicted larcenist Jermaine, but also convince neighborhood residents that the cops are there for their protection. They must balance legitimate crime prevention strategies with equally valid local concerns about excessive, and selective, police interventions.

As a new mayor and an old police chief take office, basic concerns over police unfairly targeting different groups and neighborhoods have hardly gone away. During his campaign, Mayor Michael Bloomberg claimed that racial profiling didn't even exist. Not surprisingly, his recently stated commitment to end such practices hasn't convinced reformers that he's serious. "Problems like racial profiling do not disappear just because a great tragedy has hit the city," says Adams. "The officer who profiles pre-9/11 didn't suddenly turn over a new leaf."

The police once had every reason to identify Fort Greene as an area where crime demanded an overwhelming response. During the Reagan years, the city's infrastructure came apart at the seams: The crack wars started, and the tree-lined streets, whose historic brownstones had already started to attract gentrifiers, became some of the most violent in the city. In 1987, the 88th Precinct saw 26 murders, 49 rapes, over 1,500 robberies, nearly 650 felonious assaults, 1,350 burglaries, close to a thousand auto thefts or break-ins, and a multitude of other crimes. That year, 5,583 felonies were reported within the neighborhood. Locals started calling Myrtle Avenue, the dividing line between the projects and the brownstones, "Murder Avenue."

"Drugs started flowing heavy in this community in 1987," remembers Darnel Canada. "Real deep. The next thing you knew the crime statistics flew crazy high. The 16, 17 year-olds grab a gun and they develop a feeling of invincibility. And then you have a whole bunch of bystanders being shot." By the end of the 1980s, 88th Precinct and Housing Authority police were making over 1,700 felony arrests a year.

The brownstone-dwellers were hardly immune from violent crime. "My husband was mugged in the park once," recalls one longtime homeowner. "A bunch of kids jumped us. We were jogging on a Sunday afternoon. His front teeth were knocked out with brass knuckles."

Though it existed barely a decade ago, that crime-ridden neighborhood would be almost unrecognizable to people moving to Fort Greene today. Through mid-October 2001, COMPSTAT figures indicate only seven murders in the 88th Precinct, 15 rapes, 359 robberies, 177 felonious assaults and 192 burglaries, with a total of 399 arrests in the seven major felony categories. Similarly, in 2000 the precinct experienced nine murders, 19 rapes, 422 robberies, 198 felonious assaults, 267 burglaries and 358 car thefts or break-ins. Murders, robberies, felonious assaults and burglaries have all fallen by between 58 and 75 percent over the past seven years.

Crime has declined by a similar amount throughout the city—by 62.7% percent citywide in the last eight years, according to police department figures. But because Fort Greene started this period with a particularly high crime rate, the fall to more manageable levels has had a significant effect on the psychology of the neighborhood. And increasingly, what crime does remain in Fort Greene is contained within the sprawling public housing in its northern section.

Newly arrived Fort Greene residents are aware that their now-thriving streets haven't been safe for very long, and they've gone out of their way to make sure that those streets stay safe. Even as crime has fallen, new residents and business groups continue to insist that the police do even more. "More demands are put on the police already and even more are going to be put on the police in the future," says one local homeowner who has been involved in meetings between residents and police. At some of these invitation-only meetings, homeowners have asked neighbors, police lieutenants, detectives and local political figures to sit down in their living rooms and discuss how best to lower crime on their streets. "You have people moving into the neighborhood who expect better levels of service than in the past. It's an economic issue," says the homeowner.

POLICE AND PAROLE OFFICERS MAKE MIDDLE-OF-THE-NIGHT SURPRISE VISITS. PAROLE OFFICERS DON'T LIKE THE CRACKDOWN. THEY WORRY THAT PUBLIC HOUSING RESIDENTS NOW VIEW THEM AS INFORMANTS ENSNARING MORE PEOPLE IN THE CRIMINAL JUSTICE SYSTEM.

With his partner, Richard M. bought a house in the late 1980s for $400,000. He could now sell it for more than double that. The 48-year-old chef and caterer won't give his last name for fear of reprisals. He's well aware that crime could be much worse than it is: Mugged at knife- and gun-point six times in his life, including once in the Fort Greene area, he has not been victimized in the past five years. But he remains adamant that the police must protect his property and his quality of life. "I [have been] asking them to make

more arrests. Drug arrests mainly. Now they're making quality-of-life arrests, which is great," says Richard. Graffiti and drug dealing are two of his chief complaints. "From a police point of view there has to be more vigilance," he says.

In the spring of 2000, in the wake of a drug-related shooting on his street, Richard organized a large meeting in his house. Over 40 neighbors attended, as well as representatives from the police precinct and the local congressional and state assembly offices. The locals' demands appeared reasonable: They didn't want stray bullets whizzing past them when they stepped outside their doors, and they wanted the police to do whatever was necessary to make the area safe. "We asked them to be more responsive to what was going on in the neighborhood," Richard remembers.

In the months since then, while Richard still isn't entirely happy, he thinks the police are now responding more to homeowners' concerns. "Just getting people from standing on the corner. Drinking. Loitering. Things [the police] feel lead to bigger crimes. They've told us they stop card games because that leads to bigger things. Marijuana. Minimal things. There's much more of a major presence of the police in the area now."

Could crime return? "I don't think so," says Loretta Brown, owner of the Clinton Hill Simply Art gallery and chair of the Myrtle Avenue Merchants' Association. "I don't think the merchants or the community would tolerate it. But I don't know. The *elements* are here," she says, talking of local hoodlums. "You have an interesting mix of people."

Pressures from property and business owners do matter. Jeremy Travis, co-author of the Urban Institute report "From Prison to Home," notes that in transforming neighborhoods such as Fort Greene "the issue becomes more acute, because the [gentrification] change creates more demands upon the police." Caught between the urgings of newly arrived property owners and the

grievances of poorer residents, the police face a dilemma, says Travis. "Who do you listen to? Who is the community voice that helps you decide your priorities? Just the fact of urban renewal in a community policing environment causes problems that are not new but are accentuated."

In Fort Greene, says Bob Evans, chair of Community Board 2, the voice often comes from people who weren't there for the bad times. "You have people who are new to the neighborhood. They perceive the police as benign. Many ask for quality of life pressures—getting people off the street, not letting them sit on the stoop. It's been driven by economics—as much the call for middle-income minorities as for whites."

Fort Greene, of course, isn't the only place in the city where aggressive misdemeanor arrests have been a leading tool of law enforcement. After all, it was the centerpiece of former Mayor Rudolph Giuliani's zero-tolerance strategy, aggressive "broken windows" policing that cracks down on even the mildest manifestations of social disorder.

Citywide, as the high crime rates of the 1980s leveled out and then plummeted, misdemeanor arrests—for marijuana possession, public urination, the consumption of alcohol in parks and the like—increased. They went up by about 66 percent between 1987 and 1999, from 150,000 arrests to just over 250,000.

In Fort Greene, the statistics are even starker. In 1987, the local police arrested 1,104 people on misdemeanor charges. Three years later that number had declined to 846—less than one arrest for every four misdemeanor complaints received by the precinct. Then the numbers began to increase. By 1998, despite the dramatic falls in crime, the 88th Precinct received 4,001 misdemeanor reports and made 1,926 misdemeanor arrests—an increase of nearly 75 percent from a decade earlier. In the first half of 1999, that number ratcheted up still further, to 1,014 arrests in a six-month period, carried out by 88th Precinct police patrols, police assigned to the public housing, transit cops and traffic police.

For public housing residents, such policing has become a brutal fact of daily life. "They run up on our kids, slam 'em against a wall and search 'em," says tenant Edna Grant. According to Wallace Scott, who has been running tenant patrols against local drug dealers for the past few years, the problem runs even deeper: he contends that police don't conduct foot patrols of the projects to the extent they do on the middle-class streets, thus failing to establish the sort of peaceable community police presence credited with reducing crime in so many parts of the country. When police enter the public housing, they do with overwhelming force. "We have too many different officers coming into the area who are not familiar with the area or with our kids," Scott states. "And when they do come in, they come in swinging."

Misdemeanor arrests have soared during a period in which crime reports have declined 60 percent. This extremely proactive policing can be interpreted as a kind of success: Arresting more people for ever-more-trivial infringements of the law suppresses more serious criminal activity. That's the heart of broken windows policing.

But critics argue that these numbers also reflect a police culture that promotes a continued, often unnecessary, emphasis on high arrest rates at a time when serious crime has fallen to its lowest level in decades. "They're so driven by numbers now," ex-Police Commissioner William Bratton was quoted as saying in 1998, "that as they have less and less crime to work on, they start going after things that are really far-fetched."

Says Mike Jacobson, onetime city commissioner of parole and now a professor of criminal justice at New York City's John Jay College, "The cops now make far more misde-

meanor arrests than they ever used to make. It clearly comes with huge social and political costs."

The revolving door of the city's jail and court system, argue Jacobson and other experts, is leading to people losing wages and losing jobs, breaking down parent-children relationships, making people more vulnerable to homelessness and, in the long-term, undermining the stability of communities.

DARNEL CANADA USED TO BE IN PRISON. NOW HE HELPS EX-CONS FIND JOBS—AND KEEPS AN EYE ON THE COPS WHO WATCH THEM.

Jeremy Travis says that New York has much to learn from Boston's experience sustaining lower crime rates. There, beginning in the mid-1990s, the police department, in conjunction with the grassroots-based Ten Point Coalition, scholars such as Harvard's David Kennedy, and a variety of community groups, worked with local teenagers, gangs, and others deemed to be at particular risk of inflicting harm or getting hurt, in an effort to eradicate crime. "It was a very targeted deterrence model," notes Travis, "involving meetings with police, gangs, churches." At its peak, Boston saw no teen murders for two years. Its model of interventionist policing is now being taken up by forces in Indianapolis, Minneapolis, Portland and other cities. "The lessons in Boston are powerful," Travis says. Unlike the NYPD's recent policy of massive sweeps against misdemeanor offenders, Boston's goal is "not arrest for arrest's sake. It's to change behavior."

A misdemeanor arrest is a burden for anyone. But for people who are on probation or parole, it can easily mean the end of their freedom. In Fort Greene, the number of people being released from jail continues to outpace the number of those going in. In 1993, 4,497 Brooklyn residents

were sentenced to prison, or a full 18 percent of all prison terms issued statewide. In 2000, at the end of a decade in which New York City's unemployment numbers fell steadily, the city's economic base expanded, and the crack epidemic subsided, only 1,895 Brooklyn residents were sent to prison, representing barely 10 percent of total commitments statewide.

In 2000, the 88th Precinct registered 262 parolees within its borders; another hundred-plus lived in the nearby Farragut public housing units just outside the precinct borders. Not far to the east, in Bedford-Stuyvesant the 75th Precinct had close to 800 parolees; in Crown Heights, the 77th Precinct included well over 500. Hundreds more, who have either served out their parole, or who were released from prison unsupervised after "maxing out" their sentence or because of good-time credits from the prison system, also live within the area, as do hundreds of others who have spent time in local jails.

Citywide, while fewer than 10 percent of parolees end up back behind bars within the first year of their parole, 40 percent return to prison within three years.

Since 1997, police (whose traditional responsibility has been to enforce the law) and parole (whose job is to monitor and also help ex-prisoners during their years of conditional release) in Brooklyn North and elsewhere have cooperated closely to monitor ex-offenders and find them in violation of parole for any infractions.

In Fort Greene, for example, police, parole and probation officers are going to great lengths to implement law enforcement programs such as Operation JAWS (Joint Absconder Warrant Squad), begun in 1999 to track down parole violators; Operation Gunslinger, which targets parolees for questioning about local drug activities; the Targeted Offenders Program to monitor parolees deemed to be a particular risk to the community; and Operation Night-watch, a particularly controversial program, started in 1997, that in addition to searches and drug tests involves middle-of-the-night surprise visits to parolees by teams made up of both parole and police officers. All of these are designed to ensure crime statistics stay low. Politically, they also serve to boost the NYPD's arrest numbers.

Says Willis Toms, council leader for Parole Division 236 of the Public Employees Federation, if a parolee is arrested on marijuana charges, "he is going to be violated. He'll probably serve another year." "One of our concerns," says Milton Stroud, a parole bureau chief working in downtown Brooklyn, "is the number of people being returned to state facilities as a result of drug arrests." He's speaking of men like 22-year-old Sace, who served three years in prison for a drug conviction, then had to do another year after a urine test indicated he had been smoking weed.

NEWLY ARRIVED RESIDENTS ARE TRANSFORMING FORT GREENE—AND DEMANDING UNPRECEDENTED POLICE PROTECTION.

When the results came in, recalls Sace, "my parole officer asked me to work for them and tell on people on the streets. I'd have to watch them and report on them. I wasn't willing to do that. I went on the run. I got caught and had to serve the year. It was a terrible experience: In order to stay out of jail, I'd have to put other people in jail."

The parole officers' union doesn't like the crackdown either; they say the NYPD is encroaching on their turf. Members also worry that heavy-handed tactics are undermining community trust in the Division of Parole, with public housing residents increasingly viewing parole officers as informants looking to en-

snare more people in the criminal justice system, rather than as allies helping released prisoners stay out of trouble. But with orders from on high, officers have to cooperate. "You drop in on these people, take them to the precinct and make them urinate," explains one high-ranking parole officer. "Taking them to the precinct allows the cops to question them about their knowledge of criminal activities."

The police are likewise exploiting parole officers' legal access to private homes. When a parole officer pays a visit to a parolee, he can search only the ex-offender's bedroom. However, when the police accompany a parole officer—thus bypassing the need to get a search warrant—the cops can search the entire apartment, and even arrest a parolee's relatives or roommates on gun or narcotics charges. "There was a few incidents like that in Ingersoll," says Canada. "Where they came in and as a result the family got evicted from city housing. Because there are drugs in the house and he [the parolee] doesn't admit they're his, everybody in the house gets arrested. As far as I know it's a new thing, because they used to come in with a warrant looking for a specific person."

Ｎew York is not alone in targeting people on parole for crackdowns. Nationwide, in 1980, 18 percent of those admitted to state prisons were put away for violations of parole. By 2000 that percentage had doubled, to 36 percent; almost half were busted for minor drug infractions. According to Travis' Urban Institute report, seven out of 10 parolees completed their parole terms in 1984, but by 1998 only 45 percent did so. Fully 42 percent of parolees were being returned to prison, the majority of them for technical parole violations. In California, 65 percent of prison admissions in 1998 were for parole violations.

As law enforcement clamps down on increasingly minor crimes and parole violations, parolees are caught in a cycle of incarceration, release, and reincarceration. "The problem is you have parole agencies with no resources," says Jacobson. "So once [paroles] start to violate, parole officers are in this bind—because they have nothing else, no intermediate steps they can take, they either have to ignore the violation or take the most expensive, punitive step and send someone back to prison. In an irrational environment, it's a rational decision."

It is a trend exacerbated by the hard economic truths faced by most ex-cons. According to Mindy Tarlow of the Center for Economic Opportunities, a Lower East Side organization that works with close to 2,000 citywide parolees each year, only about 65 percent of the group's clients find jobs; of those, fewer than half remain employed six months later. For the vast number of returning prisoners who receive no job placement assistance, the employment statistics are even grimmer. Not surprisingly, many resort to crime. "Eighty-three percent of people who violate probation or parole are unemployed. That's a staggering number," says Tarlow, citing state Department of Labor statistics.

Tarlow's organization sends out about 200 people each day to work as janitors at CUNY campuses and cleaners at city piers, among other jobs. The crews work four-day weeks and are paid from a pool of money allotted by New York State. "It essentially builds a little résumé for them," says Jacobson. "It's incredibly successful. In public safety and criminal justice terms these types of public works programs, and education programs, are the things that keep people from going back to crime."

On the fifth day, the ex-cons meet with an employment counselor, to prepare for finding work on their own. "If more people were employed," Tarlow argues, "you could break the cycle of incarceration." She believes public agencies and non-profits should coordinate to provide services, from job-finding to drug treatment, in neighborhoods with large numbers coming out of jail and prison. "It's about having a real service delivery system," Tarlow says.

Jacobson believes that, paradoxically, the recession could help ex-offenders—with money tighter than ever, the state might be persuaded to expand public works programs for the thousands of parolees returning to communities. The potential savings in diverting nonviolent parole offenders away from prison and into jobs, guesses Jacobson, could be up to $100 million a year.

Darnel Canada agrees that the price of doing nothing is high. "I'm seeing old faces," says Canada. "And they're coming out [of prison] looking for employment. I know without employment it isn't going to be too long before the situation arises that got them into prison in the first

place. Once I can take care of my three basic needs—food, shelter and clothing—then I can think about basic principles of morality. But until I can, I go into survival mode."

In a brutal economy, Fort Greene faces renewed challenges. It will somehow have to preserve lower crime levels and higher property values, without an ever-more-coercive police presence in poorer parts of the area. Police have to maintain public order without sweeping young men and women into jail on two-bit charges. Ex-cons need new job opportunities at a time when everyone's feeling the economic crunch, while drug users need something other than the criminal justice system as a front-line social service intervention. Above all, though, the challenge comes down to priorities: how to fairly provide police services to all residents.

In the summer of 1999, the residences of several Pratt Institute stu-

dents were burglarized. Police patrols were on practically every street looking for the culprit. Eventually, they caught him and charged him with possession of crack. When a parole violator ran onto the Pratt Institute's campus a few months later, police from the 88th Precinct surrounded, and cordoned off, the entire institute.

"People don't pay attention to crime in the projects," says one local parole officer. "But when someone walks into Clinton Hill and commits a crime, it's more serious. People take note. What's happening on the other side of the park, in the projects, people don't care about. And that's always been the attitude of Fort Greene."

Sasha Abramsky is a Brooklyn-based freelance writer. This article was supported by a grant from the Center on Crime, Communities and Culture of the Open Society Institute

Segregation in New York Under a Different Name

J. P. Avlon *Exposes the Separate and Unequal Status of Bilingual Education*

Segregation exists in New York City public schools under the name of bilingual education. What began as a well-intentioned program to aid non-English speaking newcomers has become an entitlement program that promotes separate classrooms and unequal results along ethnic lines. Having gained control over the school system, Mayor Bloomberg is suddenly in a position to mend—and possibly end—bilingual education as we know it.

Last February the Board of Education unanimously passed the first and only fundamental reform of bilingual education in the program's 26-year history. Among other things, the plan sought to give parents a new high-speed English immersion alternative to traditional bilingual education programs and began aiming in earnest to have students transition out of bilingual education within three years. This hard-won reform was trumpeted as one of the key victories of Harold Levy's tenure as Chancellor. He had succeeded where virtually every leader of the Board of Education had failed since the early 1980s. But after the fanfare died down, bilingual education reform died the lonely death of most reforms entrusted to the Board of Education—it was never implemented due to a fight over funding.

The losers were the roughly 160,000 "English Language Learners" in the public schools, who speak more than 145 different languages and dialects.

These students are split between traditional bilingual education classes, which are taught primarily in the student's native language, and English as a Second Language classes, which are taught primarily in English. In bilingual classes, 90% of the students are Spanish speaking. ESL courses tend to be offered to a linguistically and ethnically diverse array of students.

The stated purpose of bilingual education is to make students fluent in their native language before teaching them English—a process that bilingual advocates say can take between five and seven years. Bilingual education is also not limited to immigrant students—increasingly, native-born Americans who speak Spanish at home are placed in these programs. Many bilingual education teachers are not bilingual—they can't speak English themselves, and 27% are not certified.

Of the students who entered bilingual programs in the first grade, 22% were still enrolled in the program nine years later. 54% of students who began bilingual programs in the sixth grade in 1991 had not transitioned into a mainstream classroom by 1999; and 85% of the students who entered bilingual programs in ninth grade in 1991 did not transition out within four years—the traditional end of high school.

Bilingual education programs also have a negative effect on school scores. In 1999 only 6.9% of the middle school English Language Learner population who took the Citywide Reading Test could read at grade level. In the Citywide Math Test, which is givin in the student's native language, only 15% of middle school English Language Learners scored at or above grade level, and more than 55% of them fell below the 25th percentile.

And despite the fact that bilingual education classes were created in part to address high drop out rates, students who stay in bilingual programs beyond six years are nearly 50% more likely to drop out than students in the general population.

At every level, students in ESL classes performed better on tests and transferred into mainstream English-speaking classes more rapidly than their counterparts in bilingual. The 18-month study conducted by Mayor Giuliani's Bilingual Education Reform Task Force (on which I served as a staff member) confirmed the findings of the 1994 report commissioned by Chancellor Raymond Cortines, which stated that "Students in ESL-only programs consistently tested out of entitlement faster than students served in bilingual programs, even when baseline differences in English were taken into effect."

Mr. Bloomberg seems to understand the limitations of bilingual education, and the need for such programs to rededicate themselves to English acquisition. Beginning with next year's sophomore high school class, all students will be required to pass five Regents examinations, including English, in order to receive a diploma at the end of high school. Effective reforms must be enacted to avoid a debacle in 2005, which is incidentally an election year here in New York City.

California has successfully taken the bold step of ending bilingual education entitlement programs, replacing them with intensive English immersion programs. Critics and activists claimed that this an abandonment of non-English speaking students and predicted a steep decline in test scores. In fact, the opposite has happened—in the four years since the elimination of California's bilingual programs, test scores have gone up consistently in every category. California's success has spurred other states, including Arizona and Colorado, to dump bilingual education. Will New York be next?

Mr. Bloomberg could presumably implement the Board of Education's already approved reforms single-handedly now that he has control of the school system. But if he wants to end bilingual education in New York, he'll have to take his fight to court.

The Mayor will find that his ability to institute bilingual education reforms is severely restricted by the Aspira Consent Decree, which began bilingual programs for Spanish-speaking students here in the city of New York in 1974. The decree was originally intended to allow Spanish speaking students "full and equal educational opportunity" in the learning process while ensuring that students "avoid isolation and segregation from their peers."

But Aspira now undermines its original purpose. A 1975 Board of Education pamphlet defining Board policy at the outset of bilingual education stated that parents "are to be notified of their child's entitlement and of the nature of the program to be provided. Every effort is to be made to inform parents of the educational value of the [bilingual] program and no attempt is to be made to invite parents to withdraw from the program." This institutional bias in favor of bilingual education has had disastrous effects for several generations. It has created segregated educational programs rather than ending them. The results are separate and unequal.

The sad fact is that bilingual education has become an entitlement program. It is defended by those with an interest the status quo, despite the fact that the system is clearly broken beyond repair. Professional bilingual advocates are strikingly out of touch with the constituents they claim to represent. A Zogby poll measured support for "all public school instruction to be conducted in English, and for students not fluent in English to be placed in an intensive one-year English immersion program." Seventy-nine percent of all New York voters surveyed supported this proposal—72% of Democrats, 87% of Republicans, and 62% of Latino voters. This is consistent with a poll conducted by the non-partisan, non-profit group Public Agenda which showed that two out of three immigrant parents believe that "it is more important for public schools to teach English as quickly as possible, even if they fall behind in other subjects."

In 1644, a Jesuit missionary named Father Isaac Jogues visited our city and counted 18 different languages being spoken. Our city has always been a melting pot, and immigration has always been the secret to our success. For the most diverse city in the history of the world to thrive, it must have a common currency of communication. We have an important opportunity to emphasize in theory as well as practice that bilingual education exists to help the children of all immigrants as quickly as possible so that they might participate fully in the pursuit of the American dream.

Mr. Avlon's column appears weekly. His e-mail address is jpavlon@nysun.com.

In New York City, Fewer Find They Can Make It

By **Michael Powell**
Washington Post Staff Writer

NEW YORK — Michael Bloomberg, this city's billionaire mayor, looks at Manhattan's glittering economy and all but chortles. "Jobs are coming back to the Big Apple," he said recently. "Our future has never looked brighter."

The Wall Street bull is snorting. Investment bankers arm-wrestle for a $18 million Park Avenue apartment. Slots at prestigious private kindergartens retail for $26,000. Lines trail out of the latest, hot restaurants, and black limos play bumper car in Tribeca.

"New York," a recent newspaper article proclaims, "it's HOT."

Except that a closer look at this largest of U.S. cities reveals much that's not so hot. New York's unemployment rate jumped in January from 8.0 to 8.4 percent, the worst performance among the nation's top 20 cities. It has lost 230,000 jobs in the past three years. Demand for emergency food has risen 46 percent over the past three years, and 900,000 New Yorkers receive food stamps. Inflation, foreclosures, evictions and personal bankruptcies are rising sharply. Fifty percent of the city's black males no longer are employed.

President Bush will journey here this August for the Republican convention, and he is expected to celebrate the revival of the nation's financial capital since the Sept. 11,

2001, terrorist attacks. But at this point, that recovery is characterized more by its weakness — and by the stark disparities between rich and poor.

In the third quarter of 2003, the nation's gross domestic product grew at a rate of 8.4 percent; the comparable rate in New York grew by 0.3 percent.

"Our economy is polarized; our population is polarized," said Kathryn S. Wylde, president of the Partnership for New York City, which represents the city's 200 top private-sector chief executives. "The bonuses of a relative handful of very wealthy people are driving our economy."

The Invisible Poor

Around the corner from City Hall in downtown Manhattan, Arthur Harvey considers his economic prospects, which happen to stink. He is one of a record number of 40,000 homeless New Yorkers.

"My landlord raised my rent from $125 a week to $200, so I began to sleep in my mom's back yard in Queens," said Harvey, 40, with a goatee and hollowed-out eyes. "I used to work as a messenger, but the company's gone out of business.

"I'm in trouble, y'know what I mean?"

Seen from the perspective of Manhattan and the ever-more-swank streets of brownstone Brooklyn, these are curiously invisible hard times. Home prices spiral upward 10 percent or more each year, midtown is crowded and retail sales are strong, and the Wall Street bonus is back, $10 billion worth this year. A half-dozen new restaurants open each week, and a survey found that New Yorkers plan to eat out more than they did last year.

Nor is the current downturn as deep as recessions past. In the early 1990s, New York lost 360,000 jobs and the three horsemen of urban decline — AIDS, crack and crime — left its streets mean and forbidding. The plagues have stabilized, and the crime rate has plummeted. Bloomberg preserved many city services during the recession by raising property taxes.

"I live in Greenwich Village, and if you walked around the past few years, you'd never guess that 300,000 New Yorkers don't have a job," said Patrick Markee, a senior policy analyst with Coalition for the Homeless. "But if you venture out of the 'hot' neighborhoods, you find a lot of people doing phenomenally badly."

That *other* New York can be found in Chinatown and in Upper Manhattan, and across the East and Harlem Rivers in the Bronx and Brooklyn, where the unemployment rates stand at 10.3 and 8.5 percent, respectively. Queens is a proudly middle-class borough with thriving immigrant communities. But last year, 210 homeowners defaulted on their mortgages each month. Forty-five percent of those homes were auctioned off, twice the national foreclosure rate, according to Foreclosures.com, which analyzes national trends.

There are more harbingers of hard times. There has been a 20 percent rise over the past three years in the number of tenants being sued for nonpayment of rent. About 300,000 New Yorkers — 10 percent of the city's workforce — labor for less than $7 an hour.

"A lot of businesses have folded out here," said Al Titone, director of the Small Business Development Center at York College, which sits at the end of the E-subway line in lower middle-class Jamaica, Queens. "A lot of folks are in scary shape."

At the Yorkville Common Pantry, on the southern edge of East Harlem, director Jeffrey Ambers recently converted his food program for the poor into a 24-hour-a-day operation — and began serving 12,000 more meals. "We are serving more people, and some days we run out," Ambers said. "We're not seeing signs here of an improving economy."

New York's labor participation rate — the percentage of employed adults relative to population — fell from 65.6 percent in July 2002 to 57 percent now. The city comptroller's office recently framed that drop this way: "If the labor force participation rate had remained at the level of July 2002, the NYC unemployment rate [now] would … rise to 19.9 percent."

Harvey Robins served as a senior official in two mayoral administrations, and has analyzed the city economy for 20 years. "We talk on and on about the price of real estate, but the other city is ignored," Robins said. "The elites focus on the difficulty of getting a restaurant reservation but never hear about the restaurant worker who spends 50 percent of his salary on rent."

Worrisome Job Market

Juan Batista has arrived at his 62nd year without a job or health insurance. For decades, the East Harlem man threaded fabric through textile machines — until he was laid off in 2002. Now he leafs through the classified ads each morning and walks the streets. He sees rug stores but no longer the factories that make them.

His wife's salary is his sole support. "I don't want to retire, but I don't have the possibilities of youth," Batista said last week. "I'm worried. What can I do but wait for death?"

The talk of late on Wall Street is resurgent profits and young analysts hungry for their first Jaguar. But a survey of the job market finds worry in many corners. Manufacturing still employs 126,000 New Yorkers, but it has bled jobs for decades and lost another 1,100 jobs in January.

The private sector gained 20,600 jobs. But the Fiscal Policy Institute found that the sectors gaining jobs paid $34,000 less, on average, than the sectors that lost jobs. Health and education are the fast-growing sectors in Manhattan; the average salary for both is $42,000. But the cost of the average Manhattan co-op apartment is $983,000.

"It takes two of the jobs we've gained to make up for one that we've lost," said James Parrott, chief economist for the labor-funded Fiscal Policy Institute. "That does not bode well for the future."

Economic calamity has fallen with particular force on the shoulders of black males. The Community Service Society, a liberal social policy organization, discovered a sharp three-year decline in employment that has left 51.8 percent of black males holding jobs.

The city's core economic sector — securities trading and financial services — displays more strength. The Wall Street spigots are again running and profit margins are staggering. Securities firms recorded profits of $15 billion last year. This has fed a re-

vival in advertising, legal work, catering, and restaurants and hotels.

Still, Wall Street remains a slender version of its Gilded Age self. Many firms retain corporate suites in New York but have placed back offices in Long Island and Jersey City, or farther afield. Last year, the nation gained 120,000 finance jobs; the city lost 1,500.

"We lag behind the rest of the nation in job creation in our key sectors," said Jonathan Bowles of the Center for an Urban Future, a think tank that examines the city economy. "The national economy is outperforming New York."

Hiding Behind Sept. 11

It is a matter of secular faith among many local politicians that New York owes the severity of its hard times not to structural economic problems but to the devastating effects of the 2001 terrorist attacks.

Several influential economists, however, offer a dissent. They note that the city pitched into recession in January 2001 and job losses were mounting rapidly before the attacks. They say the popping of the stock bubble and the city's economic dependence on Wall Street accounted, chiefly, for the severity of the downturn.

"The terror attack created sizeable job and income losses, but the city's current downturn appears to stem largely from the national economy and the financial markets," Jason Bram, an economist with the Federal Reserve Bank of New York, wrote last year.

The hangover from those attacks has stifled frank discussion. Analysts of various ideological stripes say the city needs to retool its taxes and fees — which are among the nation's highest — restructure labor contracts, raise the minimum wage and address its extreme reliance on Wall Street. But that conversation is rarely heard.

"September 11th came along, and there was all this talk of how it pulled us closer together," said Richard Murphy of the Community Food Resource Center. "But, economically, we are further apart than ever, and no one talks about it."

Partnership for New York City president Wylde added that nothing about the city's economic dominance can be taken for granted. "We had done a good job of restoring the middle class, but it's very transient, very fragile," she said. "We have an economy where a lot of job growth is epitomized by restaurant jobs and nannies."

As if to underline this point, Bloomberg News Service reported that there are 15 applications for every $26,000 seat at the most prestigious private kindergartens. And last month, the Time Warner twin towers opened at Columbus Circle, occasioning fleets of Lincoln Town Cars and apple martinis and gymnastics by Cirque du Soleil. Undercover cops came in tuxes, as did reporters.

"It's like a mecca for everything," wrote one local newspaper scribe.

That same evening, three miles to the north, Clinton Campbell, 47, walked into a Community Food Resource Center in Harlem to have his tax forms prepared for free. An African American and New York native, he managed a McDonald's until he was laid off a year ago. Now he collects unemployment more often than he works.

Afterward, he walked down Eighth Avenue to a food pantry for dinner.

"I worked at a grocery store last month, but I was too old to lug boxes upstairs," Campbell said as he stood in line with a tray. "They say if you make it here, you can make it anywhere. But I'm hurting real bad."

With that he excused himself, said a prayer, and lifted his knife and fork.

Chief Bratton Takes on L.A.

Can he repeat his NYPD sucess with America's most battered police force?

Heather Mac Donald

The Los Angeles Police Department desperately wants to reclaim its sullied reputation; its new chief, former New York Police Commissioner William Bratton, would like to clinch his shining one. Their union could be historic. If Bratton can repeat his crime-busting success in this radically different city, he will destroy the criminologists' destructive myth that policing can't cut crime. In addition, he will show how to overcome the corrosive, racially charged anti-cop politics that dominated policing nationwide for the last decade and that brought the once-proud LAPD so low that it forgot its very reason for being.

Today, a dozen years after the 1991 Rodney King beating that—wrongly—made the department a byword for violent, racist policing, the LAPD operates under federal control, subject to rigid management constraints that check a strong chief like Bratton at every turn. Given these restrictions and the department's deep demoralization, no one should underestimate the magnitude of the new chief's task. He himself certainly doesn't. After a particularly murder-soaked week early in his tenure, he asked himself, "'What am I doing here? What the hell is going on here?' The department was messed up, worse than I thought."

Ironically, the LAPD was expressly crafted to prevent its getting messed up in just this way. In the 1950s, when corruption in big-city forces was still the norm, legendary chief William Parker labored to mold a department that the politicians couldn't touch. The result was a corps that for decades commanded respect as the pinnacle of efficient, incorruptible policing. And so it viewed itself. Recalls gang detective Jack Cota: "Our department was based on, 'We're the best; we have integrity.'"

The core challenge of L.A. policing has not changed since Parker's reforms: to cover a huge area with a woefully small force. Angelenos have always balked at funding a police department big enough for its responsibilities, perhaps because most of the tax revenue comes from neighborhoods with little crime: gangbangers don't do drive-by shootings in Bel Air. Today, 9,000 Los Angeles cops police 467 square miles, which works out to 19 cops per square mile. New York's 37,000 officers, by contrast, oversee 321 square miles—115 cops per square mile. So while New York's commanders, with one officer for every 216 residents, can throw manpower at problems, their Los Angeles counterparts, with only one officer for every 417 residents, must engage in constant triage.

Chief Parker's no-nonsense solution was to insist that officer quality would trump quantity. He gave cops up-to-the-minute technology and rewarded rapid response time to radio calls. Once on the scene, L.A. officers took control, got the information they needed, and returned to the road as fast as possible, wasting no time schmoozing with the citizenry. The attitude, recalls Hollywood officer Mike Shea, was: "I'm the police; I'll tell you what needs to be done to stop crime in your area; we're the experts; now shut up."

In an era when police authority was far less contested than today, Parker's cops asserted their power more aggressively than most. James Ellroy, author of the novel *L.A. Confidential*, remembers the LAPD of his youth as "buffed and turned out. If you ran, they would beat you up. If you mouthed off, you would get beat up." Even into the eighties, officers would "hijack" murder witnesses and take them to the station house to ensure their testimony, says a longtime LAPD vet.

This command-and-control manner alienated many black residents. And the LAPD, a creature of its time, was no model of racial sensitivity. George Beck, a retired deputy chief who wrote the nation's first police manual for Los Angeles, worked in Watts during the fifties and sixties. "Some cops were really racial," he says; "a lot were not, and some were in the middle." The LAPD was one of the first departments to try to stop crime before it happened by intervening in suspicious behavior; in practice, this meant that "in certain neighborhoods, if you were a black man with another black man, you would automatically be pulled over," recalls Ed Turley, a gang-intervention worker. And cops' behavior during a stop could be egregious: James Ellroy saw two white officers give a black driver a sobriety test in 1971 by making him scratch himself like an ape.

Even so, for years the LAPD rode high in national opinion, promoted tirelessly by its chief as the big blue machine, steely and untouchable. But Parker's public-relations success came back to haunt his beloved agency. A growing army of anti-cop advocates converted his carefully crafted image of the department into an insult, and used it to bludgeon the LAPD into submission, long after the department had ceased in any way to resemble the Parker corps.

Beginning in the late 1970s, cop-hostile politics began to reshape the LAPD. Typically, a politics-induced change would produce unintended negative consequences, which led to an even greater anti-LAPD backlash, in an ever-downward spiral. For instance, in 1981, in response to the emerging politics of "diversity," the department settled a lawsuit by agreeing to hiring quotas for women, blacks, and Hispanics. The result: lower standards of competence, character, and physique—even though the less physical strength an officer has, the more he (or she) will have to rely on weapons to subdue resisting suspects, provoking more excessive-force complaints.

In the same spirit, politics determined tactics. An outcry over civilian deaths from the improper application of the choke-hold, used to incapacitate violent offenders, understandably forced its ban. But without the choke-hold (which police professionals endorse, when used properly), officers had little alternative to the baton when suspects resisted. And use of the baton would provoke an even greater crisis in the Rodney King affair.

Politics shaped the LAPD budget, too. Mayor Tom Bradley loathed Chief Daryl Gates and expressed it by slashing police funding—just as violence between black and Hispanic gangs was exploding in East and South Central L.A. With the crime rate soaring 26 percent from 1984 to 1989, law-abiding citizens demanded a decisive police response.

The logic behind Chief Gates's answer was unimpeachable, though the result was not. Operation Hammer, launched in 1988, would compensate for the chronic manpower shortage by temporarily flooding high-crime areas with officers, and would use all available laws, including quality-of-life statutes, to get gangsters off the streets—much like 1990s New York policing. But inadequate supervision resulted in hundreds of indiscriminate stops of young black males, generating ill will that cop-haters nourish to this day.

For sheer devastating destruction of reputation and morale, however, nothing had ever approached the video of

three L.A. cops beating the struggling Rodney King in March 1991. Officers speak of the pre-King and post-King eras. After King, a "culture of cowardice," as one sergeant puts it, descended on the top brass, and criminals showed open contempt for a psychologically defeated force.

The common understanding of the King beating as racially driven brutality is wholly wrong, as Lou Cannon has demonstrated in his magisterial LAPD history, *Official Negligence*. When officers finally stopped the drug-addled King after a 115-mile-an-hour car chase, they tried to take him into custody without hurting him, using commands, a gang-tackle and handcuffs, and a Taser. Only after the powerfully built King charged at them did they resort to their batons. That charge was edited out of the videotape that was shown worldwide for months afterward, leaving 68 seconds of seemingly unprovoked baton blows. Officer Laurence Powell's frenzied counterattack did not grow out of a culture of official racism or violence in the LAPD, but out of his terror, his weakness compared with King (the result of lowered hiring standards), and his ineffectiveness with the baton. Had it been a white driver behaving similarly, his fate would have been the same.

But international public opinion instantaneously deemed the episode pure racial animus. And the influential commission charged with investigating both the event and the LAPD, headed by L.A. establishment lawyer and future U.S. secretary of state Warren Christopher, did little to dispel the widespread public misconception. The commission seized on a handful of radio messages to condemn the department for tolerating bigotry, even though many of those messages had nothing to do with race. The solution to this alleged bias problem, according to the commission: more racial and gender quotas. The commission also charged the department with tolerating excessive force and impeding civilian complaints about police conduct.

A year later, it became stunningly clear how thoroughly the anti-cop publicity machine had emasculated the LAPD, when the department failed completely to quell the riots that raged after the acquittal of the Rodney King officers. As the jury debated the assault charges, signs that violence was in the wings abounded, but, because of fears that riot preparation would provoke the "community," as Mayor Tom Bradley put it, the department did nothing. Once the violence started after the acquittals, management remained paralyzed, and, as rioters pulled drivers from their cars and beat them mercilessly, officers stood by passively. Unwilling to use the necessary force, the commander of the 77th Division, ground zero of the increasingly savage violence, ordered his officers to retreat, knowing full well that unsuspecting white, Asian, and Hispanic motorists, arriving at the intersection of Florence and Normandie, faced certain brutal attack. Trucker Reginald Denny, whose skull Damian Williams gleefully crushed with a brick, was a casualty of this shameful retreat. Even as the death toll mounted, police brass at the ill-equipped riot-command post, fearful of another brutality accusation, told officers not to engage or arrest the rioters.

"The common understanding of the King beating as racially driven brutality is wholly wrong."

With the violence spiraling out of control, Chief Daryl Gates went AWOL, attending a tony political fundraiser miles from the mayhem. When he returned, he still issued no orders. Other commanders, dutifully obeying the political mandate for outreach, went to a unity rally at the First African-American Methodist Episcopal Church, as if nothing were happening. The final toll: 54 lost lives, 2,328 hospitalizations, and nearly $1 billion in property damage.

Nothing—not even the King media circus—so destroyed rank-and-file morale as the department's abdication during the riots. Having to stand by as public order crumbled represented a galling betrayal of officers' oath to protect and serve. The message cops took from the episode was that, for their bosses, fear of criticism trumped public safety.

After the smoke cleared and Mayor Bradley forced Chief Gates out of office, the troops yearned for strong leadership to give them their pride back. They didn't get it. The key political consideration in selecting a new chief was that he be black, and Willie Williams, the corpulent and unkempt chief of the lackluster Philadelphia police, got the job. Added to his endemic inability to pass the mandatory police qualifying exam, the revelation that he had accepted gifts from Las Vegas casinos sealed his doom as a one-term chief.

Alas, his successor, LAPD insider Bernard Parks, was worse still. A tall, dashing African American with a square jaw and arrow glance, his tenure is a textbook example of the power of leadership to make or break an organization. Parks took office in 1997 surrounded by high hopes, since he had worked his way up the command ladder and knew virtually everything about the department. But, says Mike Downing, commander of the Hollywood division, he lacked "wisdom"—wisdom to delegate, to learn from subordinates, to change course.

Though Parks's initial moves were promising—above all, he implemented a version of Compstat, the NYPD's computer-assisted crime-analysis program that had driven New York's unparalleled crime drop in the 1990s—he also disastrously implemented the Christopher Commission's demand that the department thoroughly investigate every civilian complaint it received. Hitherto, field supervisors could dispose of patently unfounded complaints after pre-

liminary investigation. Now, a charge that a cop had stolen the *Apollo* lunar lander from the moon would have to be investigated all the way up to the top of the department, with reports from supervisors and commanders at every step. Within a year, complaints processed jumped 400 percent. Every station house had to dedicate three or four supervisors to complaint duty, leaving far fewer to oversee officers. Sergeants were crisscrossing southern California, tracking down witnesses to interview for clearly bogus complaints.

Officers shut down in fury. The no-discretion complaint system penalized good police work, since criminals routinely file complaints as payback for an arrest. Gang detective Jack Cota says: "Gangs knew that the easiest way to keep officers off the streets was to complain." The result: officers avoided law-enforcement actions with a high likelihood of retaliatory complaints.

Perhaps Parks, despite his martinet inclinations, would have made the complaint process more rational over time, but once the Rampart scandal broke, any chance that supervisors would be given more leeway evaporated. The Rampart area, a 7.4-square-mile district of small, closely clustered bungalows and bodegas just west of downtown skyscrapers, is mecca for about 30 Central American gangs, with some 8,000 members. Frequent contact with the gangs' violent indifference to human life develops in officers a politically incorrect loathing of gang culture, which most cops learn to live with, however uneasily. But a very few start fudging the law to ensure punishment for such depravity. The Rampart scandal grew in part out of this vigilante impulse, but the participants' own evil soon overwhelmed any pretensions they may have had as defenders of the good.

Ringleader Rafael Perez and his cronies in the Rampart division of CRASH—the LAPD's undercover gang unit—planted evidence on gangbangers to get them off the streets. They beat them up to get them to talk or to keep them from filing complaints. They also sold stolen drugs and shot people, usually gangsters.

The crimes of Perez and his colleagues would never have gone so far without a total breakdown in oversight. "Once an officer puts on dirt-bag clothes, you need good supervisors," says retired commander George Beck, and supervision is precisely what Rampart CRASH lacked. The division's two feuding top commanders were not talking to each other. At all hours, Perez and his partners had unmonitored access to their remote office, where they could beat up gangsters and uncooperative witnesses. They became a rogue gang within the LAPD.

Rampart CRASH's corruption didn't make the whole LAPD corrupt, but the media storm after the scandal broke in 1998 took just that line—one more body blow to the rank and file. "We felt helpless; we wanted to tear that guy's face apart," remembers Robert Duke, a downtown officer. "Being called a dirty cop—and you put up with *so much* on this job! Everyone had their secret desire to leave."

"'Being called a dirty cop—and you put up with *so much* on this job! Everyone had their secret desire to leave.'"

True to form, the LAPD just rolled over and played dead. It disbanded CRASH citywide, leaving no gang cops on the street. Chief Bratton marvels at this overreaction. "When we had the Dirty 30 in New York," he says, "we didn't dismantle all 75 precincts." When the department reconstituted an anti-gang detail, it made sure it was neutered, according to Bratton: "No plainclothes, no unmarked cars, no informants, no narcotics enforcement—it's like asking a carpenter to build a house without nails or a hammer." Cops across L.A. got the message: We don't trust you.

And now the LAPD's troubles really began. The U.S. Justice Department moved to put the department under federal control, invoking an ill-conceived 1994 law allowing Justice to sue local police forces for engaging in a "pattern or practice" of denying individuals their constitutional rights. The threat of terrifyingly costly federal litigation almost always leads local governments to give up local control and accept a federally appointed police monitor without a fight.

The Rampart scandal, however egregious, had revealed no pattern or practice in the LAPD of encouraging or tolerating such behavior—especially not after all the post-Rodney King discipline, diversity, and community-outreach measures. But the Clinton Justice Department's campaign against the LAPD was all about power, not reform—as witness DOJ's non-negotiable insistence that the department begin racial data collection to show if cops were "racially profiling," a Clinton Justice buzzword. The Rampart scandal, however, had nothing to do with alleged racial profiling, and Rodney King, even if the episode were a relevant marker of LAPD practices seven years and two chiefs afterward, was stopped for his speeding, not his race.

Chief Bernard Parks's greatest moment was fighting the Justice Department, something no other top cop has done as publicly. The LAPD, he said, was correcting the Rampart scandal. A consent decree's busywork would only drain resources away from his effort to tighten management controls. What do federal civil rights lawyers know about running a police department, anyway? he asked. They couldn't even keep track of ten boxes of sensitive records they had demanded from the LAPD—and

lost. Moreover, not only did his cops base their enforcement actions on suspicious behavior, not race, he said, but DOJ had no valid methodology for analyzing the racial data it wanted him to collect.

The chief's resistance earned him the contempt of the *Los Angeles Times* and the city's political elites. City attorney James Hahn—now the mayor—the City Council, and the Police Commission finally forced Parks to accept a five-year consent decree in 2000—without ever making Justice defend its baseless charge of a "pattern or practice" of civil rights violations at the LAPD.

Since the settlement, it gets clearer day by day how right Parks was. After eight years of decline, possibly due to changes in the city's demography, serious felonies rose for the first time in 2000, by 6.7 percent, and they went up alarmingly for the next two years. But the decree has hamstrung the department's ability to respond, by draining money and manpower away from crime busting— some $40 million the first year, and upward of $50 million every year thereafter, according to city estimates, in addition to 350 officers pulled from crime fighting to decree-tending so far. Meanwhile, current chief Bratton has been vainly begging the City Council for 320 new officers.

Justice attorneys, the consent decree makes clear, view policing not primarily as crime fighting but as report writing, with reports written upon reports upon reports. Some of those reports, such as audits of the accuracy of arrest data, represent good management practices. But the decree unwisely locks the department into a draconian and wholly inflexible schedule for completing them. Failure to reach full compliance with all 190 provisions by 2004 means that the decree can continue indefinitely beyond its scheduled expiration in 2006.

Full compliance may well be impossible, judging from the August report of the federal monitor, Michael Cherkasky, who heads the Kroll Associates security firm. A control freak with the most unforgiving interpretation of deadlines, Cherkasky seems unaware that the department sometimes has to tear itself away from report-generation to fight crime. For example, though captains managed to complete required reports on instances of non-deadly force, such as twisting someone's arm to cuff him, within the mandated 14 days 94.3 percent of the time, Cherkasky judged the department out of compliance—a remorseless standard of bureaucratic fidelity that few modern organizations could meet.

More troublingly, the consent decree rests on a highly dubious managerial philosophy. It presumes that brutality and racism are so ingrained that only oversight systems with zero managerial discretion can stem constant civil rights abuses.

Its rules for investigating deadly force, for instance, presume collusion in lawlessness right up the chain of command. This July, three cops happened to witness a gang shooting in a supermarket parking lot. They jumped out of their car, drew their weapons, and shouted, "Drop your guns." One gangster wheeled and shot; two cops shot back. Everybody missed.

For the rest of the night, each officer was guarded in a separate area of the parking lot, so the three couldn't talk to one another, while investigators canvassed the scene. Three sergeants taken off patrol duty for the rest of the night accompanied their every bathroom visit. At dawn, a separate car transported each officer to the station house. Deputy Chief Earl Paysinger, a rising departmental star, judges: "If you can't trust an unbiased supervisor to put two cops in his car and tell them not to talk to each other, we need to find other supervisors." Such obsessional regulation, he says, "compromises the fabric of that very elusive thing we call trust."

The department's mandated investigations of officer-involved shootings also suggest a perverse set of priorities. That night, twice as many detectives investigated the officers' self-defense shootings for possible civil rights or criminal violations as investigated the gangsters' attempted murder of the officers.

Reports will cascade forth, as is *de rigueur*. Say a cop struggles with a robbery suspect while arresting him, for instance. Even if the suspect admits he wasn't injured, the officer's sergeant still has to write a use-of-force report, interviewing the officer, the suspect, and all potential witnesses, and taking photos. "A two-page arrest report generates a 20-page use-of-force report," a frustrated sergeant grouses. "It may take you four to five hours to document. Then you get an investigation supervisor to study your report; it takes him four hours. Someone else reviews it. By the time everyone's finished, that's a $2,000 report." The racial data-report mandate has a similar effect. "You wouldn't believe what it does to slow my progress down," says a downtown officer, working on a tall stack of them after a night patrolling Skid Row.

By the time Bratton arrived on the job last November, the LAPD was a shadow of its former self. "We were going through the motions, as if running in mud," says Deputy Chief Paysinger. "We weren't doing police work," sums up a downtown cop.

What's more, the ugly battle to oust Chief Parks in 2002 had left a bitter racial aftertaste. While the city's left wing, including new mayor James Hahn, criticized the chief for not making enough progress on the consent decree and on "racial profiling," the black establishment stoutly defended him, showing that race politics is even stronger than anti-police and even anti-racial profiling politics. After his ouster, Parks promptly got elected to the council from a black district, where he lies in wait to ambush either the new police chief or mayor. Bratton understands the tension. As he told a group of community representatives in June: "Believe me, I had concerns

as a white coming in after two black chiefs, and after the controversy of the last removal."

But in choosing Bratton, the Police Commission showed how desperately the city wants to reclaim policing from race politics. The commission—and the mayor—wanted someone who would put modern management techniques into the relentless service of cutting crime. Bratton had jumpstarted New York's historic crime drop—bringing homicides down 44 percent and serious crime down 25 percent in 27 months—by holding managers accountable for measurable results: fewer shootings, homicides, and armed robberies, better quality of life across all neighborhoods.

Bratton is fashioning a powerful blueprint for repeating that success, and from the very start he set out to build support for his vision of policing. "In the first few days I don't think he slept at all," recalls police union president Bob Baker. "He was at every community meeting in the city." His message: the LAPD is getting back into the crime-fighting business, and it's going to win. "For the past five years, this department has been on the bench; it hasn't even been on the field," he tells audiences.

He has broken some prevailing taboos to speak the truth. At one community meeting, when activists started complaining about the big, bad LAPD and demanding that Bratton control his cops, Bratton shot back: "Control your kids!" He has stressed that crime-ridden communities cannot expect the police to solve all their problems—that parents and neighbors must take responsibility for stopping gang violence, too. At other events, he called criminals "mental nitwits" and gangs "domestic terrorists." He suggested that an appropriate response to a suspect who had fled from the police would be to "hang 'em high."

Such rhetoric was a shot of adrenaline to patrol officers, but the black elite, still nursing its wounds from the Parks ouster, blew up. Its members declared themselves deeply troubled by Bratton's language, and the entire left-wing commentariat piled on. Journalist Mike Davis, the Marxist fabulist of L.A. history, complained about Bratton's plans to attack graffiti, and anti-cop attorney Connie Rice penned an uproarious *Los Angeles Times* op-ed that reverentially quoted a member of the murderous Grape Street Crip gang who argued that—in essence-fighting graffiti was no different from drive-by shootings: "How they 'spect us to respect them when they act like us?" whined this sensitive Crip.

But then something remarkable happened. In a scathing editorial, the ultimate arbiter of fashionable opinion—the *Los Angeles Times*—broke ranks, mocking the black establishment's "selective war on words." It pointed out that Bratton's critics had failed miserably to quell street violence, and it said Bratton was right to call that violence domestic terrorism. In a hopeful augury for the future, the new chief's lock on the pinnacle of elite opinion has held firm. Not only has the *Times's* editorial page consistently backed his calls for more cops to fight crime, but Hollywood moguls Steven Spielberg and David Geffen have donated cash to help update the department's technology.

Following his New York playbook, Bratton searched for the talent among the command staff. His promotions of Jim McDonnell and Mike Hillman to assistant and deputy chief thrilled the rank and file, for they are tough crime-fighters whom the Parks regime had shunned—both marks of honor in the eyes of the street cop. Such personnel choices have convinced officers that their new chief will back them up for smart, assertive policing. Equally crucial to restoring morale has been Bratton's decision to return reasonable discretion to the complaint process. "Bratton is tough on discipline," union chief Baker observes. "But the only thing cops want to know is: 'Does he care?'"

Next, Bratton set priorities, with quelling gang violence at the top of the list. To do that, he put drug and gang enforcement under one command, since gangs dominate the L.A. drug trade. Gang czar Hillman has re-energized the gang units and ordered them to respond aggressively to shootings. "Do it right, do it legally, but don't wait three days for approval before acting," he tells them. Once-moribund multi-agency task forces—drawn from, for example, the city attorney, probation officers, and the LAPD—are finally cooperating effectively.

But these policy changes cannot be fully effective unless the beaten-down detective corps recovers its zeal and its mandate for crime-fighting. "In the old days," says LAPD chronicler James Ellroy, "when you had a murder, the detectives would roll on it till they dropped. They'd work through the night." Today, thanks to bureaucratic constraints, detectives spend most of their days filing reports on arrests that patrol officers have already made, not on solving crimes. And thanks to the politics of gender, they spend too much of their remaining time on domestic-violence cases, to meet politically correct state mandates.

Bratton's inner circle is trying to turn them back into detectives. The morning after a prostitute had been killed this August, Deputy Chief Paysinger asked the detective on the case what the vice officers had said about her. The vice officers don't get in until 2 PM, the detective replied, so he hadn't spoken to them yet. "They have phones, don't they?" Paysinger responded caustically. "For Christ's sake, someone's dead." The department is also requiring detectives to go to every shooting, even if no one was killed, instead of showing up only at homicides or near-homicides, as before. As Paysinger explains, "If we don't have a greater awareness of the most violent of crimes, as purveyors of the peace we're done."

The LAPD reengineers are hammering home to detectives how valuable search warrants are as a tool for preventing crime before it happens. "Even if you find nothing, as you search, you may see a parolee at large, or someone who wants to be a witness, or other weapons in plain sight," says Paysinger. "You're telling the crook: 'I will always be there watching.'" But until recently, few detectives even remembered how to write a search-warrant request to a judge.

Bratton is using Compstat, the crime analysis and command accountability sessions he pioneered in New York, to reinforce these lessons in proactive policing. A sign in the large Compstat room reads: WHO ARE THEY? WHERE ARE THEY? HAVE THEY BEEN ARRESTED?—the conceptual framework for the weekly Compstat meetings. During those meetings, top brass grill area commanders on their knowledge of crime patterns in their jurisdictions and their plans for solving them. Jim McDonnell, who heads the sessions, reminds commanders about some basic crime-fighting tools imported from New York, such as questioning all suspects about other unsolved crimes. After a gang shooting, he tells them, don't let your officers mill around guarding the perimeter of the scene; get them quickly into the shooter's home turf, in anticipation of a retaliatory drive-by.

Besides Compstat, Bratton's biggest New York policing innovation was to demonstrate the power of order-maintenance enforcement. When he headed the New York Transit Police, his troops began arresting turnstile jumpers and subway panhandlers—until then, viewed as harmless victims of poverty—and caught serious criminals. As NYPD commissioner, he cracked down on public drinkers and graffiti vandals, and by so doing moved once chaotic neighborhoods toward greater civility and safety.

Bratton is showcasing order-maintenance (or "broken-windows") policing in three Los Angeles neighborhoods—downtown's Skid Row, the sadly deteriorated Macarthur Park in Rampart, and Hollywood, with its hookers and hustlers. Skid Row (also known as the "Nickel" for the cheap flophouses that vagrants once used) is the greatest challenge.

The most amazing discovery a first-time visitor to the Nickel will make is that its few legitimate residents think it looks *good*—compared with before Bratton arrived. Until you've stood on Fifth and Wall, you haven't really seen a vagrancy problem. Nothing in New York's most chaotic days in the 1980s comes close to the squalor and madness that have taken over block upon block of the warehouse district. Addicted men and women fill entire streetscapes, some sitting in lawn chairs outside their tents, others sprawled out facedown on the sidewalk. Pushers peddle drugs hidden inside cigarette boxes spread out on the sidewalk. Outside the women's missions, teenagers strut threateningly, while their newest illegitimate siblings are parked in baby carriages on the sidewalk. Transvestites in bikinis gesture defiantly at the occasional passing squad car.

A few hardy toy and fish wholesalers remain. Holly Sea Food has sold fish downtown since 1923, but over the last few years, one-third of its neighbors have left. "You can't sell your business or hire help," laments owner Rick Merry, in his air-conditioned wood-laminate office. "We've had an ad in the *Times* for a bookkeeper. Candidates will just drive by without stopping. They later call: 'I'm sorry, but I won't work there.' The female postman put in for a transfer. Ladies were leaning up against her truck, defecating. The bad part is: my wife works here. Guys will walk right up to the gutter and whip it out, and there she is, staring at someone's privates."

Four months ago, a vagrant's tent across the street from Holly's warehouse exploded in flames as the occupant slept inside, payback for a bad drug deal. The target would have died had the surrounding bums not pulled him from his tent.

Downtown L.A.'s "homeless" problem may be unparalleled in scale and concentration, but its causes are the same as everywhere else: politics and misguided "compassion." The lawless bum life-style depends on the subsidy of self-proclaimed do-gooders, who provide everything legal that a street person could desire. At 6 AM one day this summer, a tangle of garments and half-eaten plates of food, which volunteers had doled out the night before, strewed an entire sidewalk block. The "homeless" left the city's sanitation service to clean up what they didn't want.

The brightly colored tents that fill the sidewalks were another gift of the homeless advocates—a gift intended to foil law enforcement, on the theory that, if the vagrants could claim ownership of their street domicile, rather than scrounging it from dumpsters every night, the police would not be able to remove encampments from the streets. The success of this strategy waxes and wanes with the politics of the moment.

Even before Bratton arrived, the former commander of downtown's Central Division, Charles Beck, had tried to stem the anarchy. "I was abhorred by it," he says. "It drove me nuts. My dream was to clean up downtown L.A. You need the collective will to say that this conduct is not allowed any longer."

But Beck made little progress: advocates had the City Council under their thumb. The shrillest activist, Alice Callahan, could call the council and say: "Do you know that an officer just told a homeless person to wake up?" and the police would get an incensed phone call in ten minutes, recalls officer Daniel Gomez. Business owners, by contrast, could tell the council: "We have a serious problem," and the response would be, "Yeah, *whatever*."

Now, though, some newly elected council members recognize the truth: conditions on the Nickel are unacceptable in a civilized society. Their election to the council could not be more timely. Chief Bratton needs all the political backing he can get to battle the advocates.

Every Bratton initiative to civilize Skid Row has sparked a lawsuit. The radical National Lawyers Guild sued to prevent arrests of parole and probation violators, while the ACLU asserts that enforcing a law against blocking sidewalks constitutes "cruel and unusual punishment." Undeterred, the LAPD continues to target drug dealing, violence, and other illegal behavior, without exempting people who choose to live on the streets. A team of officers patrols Skid Row every morning, referring people to housing and services, yes—but also making arrests for lawless conduct.

Bratton's attack on street disorder has dramatically improved public space downtown, according to local businesses. "Eight months ago, there were 50 tents across the street," says fish merchant Rick Merry. "You couldn't walk on the sidewalk." To a newcomer, the sidewalks still look perilous, but the regulars see tremendous progress. Patrol cops agree. "These guys [the homeless task force] have done an incredible job," says officer Robert Duke. "If they stopped for two days, it would be out of control; patrol can't handle it."

Developers are taking note as well. They are converting abandoned Beaux Arts office buildings and factories into hotly sought-after lofts, moving ever closer to the heart of the Nickel. If Bratton can continue to fend off the advocates and their judicial handmaidens, L.A.'s architecturally rich downtown may eventually throb with round-the-clock living for the law-abiding.

What Bratton needs most for all these initiatives to succeed is more manpower. In New York, as he and his deputies rolled out one new strategy after another, the department had ample staffing to implement them, and crime plunged immediately—16 percent after six weeks. In Los Angeles, by contrast, Bratton has had to backtrack. He had to dismantle an anti-graffiti squad, because he needed more patrol officers. He has scaled back his crime-reduction schedule from an originally promised 10 percent reduction in crime and a 25 percent cut in homicides in 2003 to a 5 percent drop in crime and a 20 percent cut in homicides. These goals are still exceedingly impressive, and he is already close to meeting them. As of September 13, homicides were down 23 percent compared with the year before, and all felonies were down 3.9 percent. But in his first year in New York, felonies dropped 12 percent.

When the City Council refused Bratton's plea for 320 new officers this spring, the chief lashed out, citing the urgency of fighting gangs and defending against terrorism. Putting police hiring on hold, he said, is like "placing a telephone call to Osama and saying, 'Osama, hold off for nine months till we get our act together here.' " The Council declared itself shocked by his tone. The *Los Angeles Times* told the legislators to get over it. When Bratton tried to free up existing cops by allowing them to ignore residential burglar alarms unless verified by the owner or alarm company, since over 90 percent of alarm calls are false, the council balked again, and the compromise that the mayor engineered—allowing homeowners two false alarms—will just engender more paperwork without unburdening patrol.

"Bratton's attack on street disorder has dramatically improved public space downtown, say local businesses."

It is critical to L.A.'s future that Bratton succeed. Effective policing is our most powerful urban reclamation tool: when cops make inner cities safe, commerce and homeownership revive, as happened in Central Harlem following its 80 percent drop in homicides and burglaries in the 1990s. Crime reduction also improves race relations. Bratton himself argued to a community meeting this June that as long as the black and Hispanic crime rate remains so high, whites and Asians—as well as some police officers—will continue to fear suspicious-looking blacks and Hispanics.

To get at least some of the manpower he needs, Bratton has a source at his fingertips: the 300-plus officers engaged full time in consent-decree duty. In addition, he could profitably redirect the thousands of hours that all other officers and commanders spend on consent-decree mandates, which undoubtedly add up to hundreds of full-time positions.

One of the best urban-policy moves that the Bush administration could make, since energetic policing is not a local issue but a national one, would be to free the LAPD from the consent decree. By doing so, the administration would also be boosting homeland security: alert cops are the country's second most important defense against another terror attack, after robust intelligence. That defense is useless, however, without enough cops to go around.

The consent decree is based on outdated stereotypes about the LAPD. If Attorney General John Ashcroft thinks that, without federal control, the LAPD would abuse people's rights, he should send his Justice Department lawyers to talk to people like the Reverend Leonard Jackson of the First African-American Methodist Episcopal Church. Asked if the police treat innocent black men abusively, Jackson responds emphatically: "No, no, no. They don't still work like that. It's been drummed into the heads of officers that everybody has rights."

Urban policing could be raised to a new height of professionalism by taking the shackles off the LAPD and letting Bratton turn the department into a national model of twenty-first-century policing, as it once was for the twentieth century.

POLICE LINE—DO CROSS

Crack's not back—but the drug trade has resurged
in the Bronx. To rein it in this time around, the NYPD and
the community must learn to work as partners.

By Bob Roberts

Standing in the half-light from the altar candle, Josefina Edwards, wearing a trim cloth coat, talks about her neighborhood while the members of her Charismatic prayer group file into their empty church. This Friday, as they have for the last five years, she and around a hundred of her fellow Our Lady of Refuge parishioners will make a procession around the church, at 196th Street and Briggs Avenue. At each street corner they will pause to sing hymns and offer a public witness to Jesus Christ over a hand-held loudspeaker. It's a social occasion as well as an act of worship—or was until recently. "Now we go right home," says Edwards. "There are so many people on the street you can't even walk down the sidewalk."

In the last two years the streets of the northwest Bronx neighborhood of Fordham Bedford have grown increasingly chaotic. At night, knots of drunken young men, many in their teens, lean against SUVs, stereos blaring at indescribable volume. Empty beer bottles explode against the sidewalk, and angry voices echo off brick walls, making sleep impossible.

During the day, junkies crowd the porch of a tumble-down house on Decatur Avenue, prepping their arms, while at a nearby Police Ath-

letic League "play street" at P.S. 54, run by Fordham Bedford Children Services, kids and staff are bombarded by eggs, batteries and ice cubes hurled by mocking rooftop gangs. According to residents, dealers and their crews are creating what John Garcia, director of Fordham Bedford Children's Services, calls "an atmosphere of lawlessness." Citizens haven't seen such blatant trafficking since the bad old days of the 1980s. Elsewhere on Decatur, surly teenage crews camp out on doorsteps, glaring at passersby. Over on Creston, a beauty parlor is raided for chairs so dealers can conduct street-level business in style. "We made it through the crack epidemic okay," says Garcia, who grew up on the street where Edwards lives. "But now it's starting to look bad again."

The police from the 52nd Precinct are trying to maintain order. The latest citywide anticrime initiative, called Operation Impact, has flooded high-crime spots with cops and made foot patrols a visible presence on the street. Still, there's a perception among neighborhood residents that the police aren't taking action. "I see cops on the corner writing out tickets for seatbelt violations while there's dealing across the street!" scoffs Ed-

wards' son Remy, who runs Fordham Bedford's Heiskell Learning Center.

The truth is that these days, it's getting harder for police to handle the drug problem—to make arrests and put dealers out of business. The 52nd Precinct, covering Fordham Bedford, Bedford Park, Norwood and University Heights, has always been known as a "busy" area for the police, particularly notorious for burglary and armed robbery. In some respects, things have gotten better. Consistent with a decline in reported incidents throughout New York City and the nation, for the last 10 years crime in the 52nd Precinct is down—at least according to Compstat, the data-tracking system the NYPD uses to identify trouble spots.

Since its inception under the Giuliani administration, Compstat has provided a statistical profile of crime in New York City. But it measures some crimes and not others. Burglaries, robberies, assaults, rapes and, of course, murders are counted. The spectrum of offenses related to the drug trade—possession, sale, loitering and so on—is not. Since the department uses Compstat to determine where to assign its personnel, this has a direct effect on how police do their jobs on the street.

These decisions are now more important than ever. The NYPD has been losing cops at a steady rate since the end of the Giuliani administration, down to 37,000 from a high of 40,000. The 52nd Precinct itself is at a 10-year low. At the same time, Operation Atlas, New York City's anti-terror effort, is putting new demands on the department's manpower. Not only are thousands of uniformed police from precincts like the 52nd subject to immediate deployment during an alert—such as the May 22 bomb scare on the Brooklyn Bridge—but more than a thousand detectives have been shifted away from the Organized Crime Control Bureau (which oversees the citywide Narcotics Division) and ordinary precinct assignments to the NYPD's intelligence activities.

As the police shift their manpower to high-profile terror targets, neighborhoods like Fordham Bedford are losing many of the men and women who have kept the drug business at bay. "It's creeping back," admits Community Affairs Officer Mark Morisi, a 12-year veteran of the 52nd Precinct. "We're doing more with less. People don't want to believe it, but it's true."

Running roughly from 183rd to 198th Streets, from Fordham University to Jerome Avenue, the neighborhood of Fordham Bedford represents about one-fifth of the total area of the sprawling 52nd Precinct—and more than 40 percent of its crime.

There's been no shortage of recent efforts to try to turn that around. In 1999, the NYPD's Central Bronx Initiative flooded the 52 and two adjoining precincts with special anti-narcotics teams. That same year, on the crooked two-block-long stretch of Valentine Avenue from Kingsbridge Road to 196th Street, the NYPD set up road blocks and floodlights as part of its Model Block Initiative, which sought to purge dealers from the area, and organize residents to keep them out.

Both efforts yielded mixed results. Despite a temporary respite for residents, dealers simply moved off the block for awhile, then moved back. Community organizing under police auspices collapsed beneath constant intimidation from drug crews.

A sense of mistrust between the police and community residents, not uncommon in high-crime neighborhoods, complicates police efforts. "Cops here don't know where they are!" complained Garcia at a September Neighborhood Security meeting, which until recently has been held the first Tuesday of each month in the auditorium of Our Lady of Refuge Church. Residents are torn between a desire for a strong and accessible police presence and the predictable apprehension bred by 20 years of roadblocks, "stop-and-frisk" and no-knock warrants.

What they want is a cop they know and who knows them. "Beat cops would be ideal," agrees Officer Morisi, "They know the good guys on the block from the bad guys." But community policing died with the Dinkins administration.

If the neighborhood has a public face when it comes to its relations with the NYPD, it's that of Monsignor John Jenik, pastor of Our Lady of Refuge. Jenik has always been defiant of the drug business—and has often taken his parish into the streets in an effort to put public pressure on the police department, which he sees as indifferent to the neighborhood's concerns. In the 1980s, he held vigils and even said mass at drug-dealing hot spots. CNN broadcast one (and all the tires of its news truck got slashed). On another occasion, Jenik brought Cardinal O'Connor on a tour of the neighborhood, forcing panicked cops to line every rooftop. Through actions like these, Jenik got the city and the police department's attention during the critical years of the crack epidemic.

He's also the chair of the board of Fordham Bedford Housing Corporation (FBHC), the parent organization of John Garcia's group. More than

two decades after a small group of activists started rehabbing a handful of abandoned buildings scattered throughout the neighborhood, the corporation has emerged as one of the city's more successful community development nonprofits. It has fixed more than 70 buildings, started a loan fund for neighborhood residents and built a nursing home from scratch. When it opened a shelter for women and children in 1983, it was Jenik who secured funding from the Diocese to keep it afloat.

Jenik is caustic, often withering, in his assessment of police efforts in his neighborhood, and he rarely misses an opportunity to point out what he sees as the NYPD's shortcomings. Contemptuous of efforts like the Model Block, he calls police brass who tout complex solutions "modern-day Gnostics" who believe themselves possessed of arcane knowledge inaccessible to ordinary citizens. When he hears talk of making "big busts" to flush drugs from the neighborhood he replies sharply, "I've been hearing that since [former Police Commissioner] Ben Ward!"

Jenik cites the case of Wilson Ramos as a particularly egregious example of police incompetence. In May 2000, Ramos was standing on Briggs Avenue drinking a soda when he was struck in the head by a stray bullet during a shootout between officers and a man who had robbed a pot dealer's house, then hijacked a bus. "We had been vigiling in front of that house for months and it came up at every one of our monthly meetings!" insists Jenik. The shooting remains a black eye for cops and a sore point in the community. The priest has battled with three of the last four commanders of the 52, and he doesn't give a fig how the cops view him: "I've never been liked at the precinct and I don't care."

Despite this, Jenik and Fordham Bedford Housing Corporation have forced the police to listen to him anyway. For the last nine years, the precinct leadership has been coming to monthly Neighborhood Security meetings in the auditorium of Our Lady of Refuge to hear community concerns and figure out ways to respond. Within the NYPD, it's extraordinary for top precinct officials to meet regularly with an independent community group. It's all the more remarkable because when they show up to Our Lady of Refuge, the cops often get no mercy from their hosts, particularly Jenik, and spend the nights sitting under fluorescent lights listening to a litany of their sins.

Last September, when the 52's new precinct commander, Joseph Hoch, attended his first—and last—Neighborhood Security Meeting, harassment charges dominated the evening. As he attempted to deliver a set speech about his philosophy of policing, Hoch was quickly interrupted by angry citizens. Remy Edwards, visibly shaking with rage, described how a simple traffic violation turned into a confrontation as six officers, hands resting lightly on their holsters, surrounded him on the sidewalk. Jenik related how a volunteer at the church's thrift shop was stopped while walking with her child, called a crackhead, and made to uncuff her jeans by two uniformed officers. (As with many accounts of police malfeasance from Jenik, this one turned out to be exaggerated: The woman in question, Bernice Gonzalez, says she was not with her child when she was stopped on 198th Street and actually was accused of purchasing marijuana from a local dealer.)

Jenik then proceeded to make one of his key points: Cops listen to confidential informants but not to residents. Though the inspector had just taken command, the four-year-old Ramos case was brought up. As Hoch became visibly angry, the auditorium buzzed with tension. At one point an oldtimer in the front row questioned Hoch's "Bronxhood." (He was born here.)

But by the end of the night, the dynamic in the room was very different. Far from haranguing the precinct brass, residents were clustering around Hoch to talk with their new

precinct commander about problems on their blocks.

It's this kind of communication between police and the community that Garcia, soft-spoken and diplomatic, has sought to cultivate in his year and a half of chairing Neighborhood Security Meetings. Since Fordham Bedford Children Services works with kids from three public schools, as well as Our Lady of Refuge's own parochial school, Garcia has a natural interest in seeing that schoolyards, playgrounds and student assembly areas are protected. While he shares many of Jenik's criticisms, he's still managed to maintain a close day-to-day working relationship, serving almost as a community liaison with the precinct. He makes a point of saying, "I always find the police helpful and professional when I talk to them." Officer Morisi has known Garcia for eight years and considers him "honest but fair."

Garcia knows that police harassment happens. He's experienced it himself. "The only time you deal with a police officer here is in a negative situation," observes Garcia. "Either you're getting stopped for a traffic violation or because you fit the identity of someone they're looking for." Three years ago, in an eerie echo of Diallo, he was stopped by officers with guns drawn as he was reaching under his shirt for his cell phone. "I took it in stride and said to myself, 'Man, that's the neighborhood.'"

The Our Lady of Refuge Neighborhood Security Meetings are currently in abeyance. Though Father Jenik doesn't want the issue to be "Jenik versus the precinct," there's little doubt that his antipathy toward the 52 is one of the main reasons that Inspector Hoch canceled regular police participation in the meetings. Says Hoch, "I never understood why one group gets a meeting all to themselves."

"**M**istrust of the police is ingrained in the culture of the

neighborhood," Remy Edwards maintains. But the police also sense that people in the community don't have cops' backs. On December 1, during the filming of a video for rap star Noriega on Decatur Avenue, a suspect who had been picked up on a possession warrant broke away from police. As they chased him down the block, cops were pelted with garbage from neighboring rooftops while the crowd cheered. Five shots were fired (no one was hurt, and the shooter was arrested the next day). When it comes to drugs, few residents are willing to come forward with the concrete details needed to make an arrest.

For people who live here, there's a sense of impotence. Most know who is selling what on which corner, and relations can become almost casual. "Every morning I see the local heroin dealer," relates Wanda Solomon, who lives on Valentine Avenue. "I say 'Hi' and 'Bye'—what else am I supposed to do? Once I saw him sweeping the sidewalk."

If you can look out your window on a Sunday morning and watch dealers in action, it's hard to figure out why the police aren't doing anything. Deputy Inspector Hoch, who took over the 52 last August after a stint leading the nearby 48th Precinct, hears complaints along those lines all the time. He says they are misguided. "I understand peoples' frustrations, but if you just call up and tell me that drugs are being sold on the corner, what can I do?" he asks. "My officers can't just walk up to [suspected dealers] and search them. Then they're breaking the law. At most, they can ask them to move on if they're somewhere they're not supposed to be. So the average person says, 'The cops did nothing.'"

What Deputy Inspector Hoch can do, if his precinct receives enough complaints, is deploy a Street Narcotics Enforcement Unit, or SNEU—a team of six officers and a sergeant—and begin the painstaking task of gathering enough information to make a legitimate arrest, using rooftop observation posts and criminal informants. Says Hoch, "It takes a little longer but it leads to better results."

Hoch happens to be an expert in this arena. Forty years old and rising rapidly through the ranks of the department, he served in the Bronx Narcotics Bureau before becoming a precinct commander. (He is also one of just a handful of orthodox Jews to hold high command in the NYPD.) The 52, in Hoch's estimation, merits two SNEU units. But since the precinct has lost close to a hundred officers in the last 10 years, he can only field one.

And that's not even the most critical shortfall Hoch is dealing with. Detectives from the Bronx Command of the NYPD's Narcotics Division provide critical support to precinct anti-drug efforts. Officers at the 52 won't talk about numbers, but David Palladino, vice-president of the Detective Endowment Association—who incidentally grew up in Fordham Bedford, attended Our Lady of Refuge's parochial school, and served in the 52 as a uniformed officer and a detective before retiring in 1991—explains the extent of the damage. According to his sources, more than 20 percent of Bronx Narcotics Division personnel have been shifted to counterterrorism work. Narcotics detectives confirm that the 52 has had its support teams cut from eight to three.

A shortage of undercover officers is also making a fundamental difference in how the precinct attacks drug trafficking, Palladino claims. Each undercover "module" consists of six officers, a sergeant, and two undercover cops. According to Palladino, there are now only two covering the entire 52 and the adjoining 47th Precinct. "The Bureau is starving for undercover cops," says Palladino, who maintains that even in the best of times it's tough to find volunteers for such a dangerous assignment. "They're the backbone of narcotics enforcement. Without them, cops have to rely on observation, and the dealers do surveillance too so they get 'made'"—recog-

nized and promoted in the business. "The whole process becomes hit-and-miss."

What Hoch does have at his disposal are 50 rookie cops, compliments of Operation Impact, the program cited by Mayor Bloomberg and Commissioner Kelly as instrumental in making New York City "the safest big city in America." In the 52nd Precinct last year, all of those officers were concentrated within two "impact sectors" (there are currently 22 across the city)—one in the perennial neighborhood hot spot on Decatur Avenue between 193rd and 198th streets, the other covering the area just to the north of that, including the streets around Our Lady of Refuge. Hoch can claim that Fordham Bedford now boasts the largest concentration of foot patrols in its history.

T he 52nd Precinct has reported a double-digit drop in Compstat crime in areas where the Operation Impact police officers have been deployed, and they're a welcome presence to residents. But they are not deterring "workers": professional drug dealers, masters of sleight of hand, who manipulate tiny glassine envelopes while surreptitiously pocketing cash.

The Impact cops, after all, are rookies, only months removed from a college classroom. They're naturally experiencing culture shock, in a multiethnic neighborhood with little to unite it socially or geographically. Nigerians work in the Arab chicken shop next door to the Mexican *carnecería*. The Cambodian grocery store does steady business. Men in dark suits stand in a long line outside an Albanian restaurant on a Friday night. And at its base, Fordham Bedford is still multiethnic Hispanic: Dominican, Puerto Rican, Mexican and Central American. It's overcrowded—doubling and tripling up among the increasing number of immigrants is common—and demographically it's one of the youngest neighborhoods in the Bronx. Despite

Fordham Bedford Housing Corporation's remarkable expansion, the neighborhood simply lacks much organized community presence—a tenant group, a block association—that makes itself felt at street level.

As much as possible, Hoch is trying to keep the Impact cops on the same blocks so they can learn the social terrain. But the final say on their deployment is had downtown. At the beginning of each year, assignments are made according to the current Compstat figures. Confident at the beginning of his tour that he would retain his allotment of 50 cops, Hoch now has to cope with a cut to 30, and they will be moved across the Concourse to patrol St. James Park, deserting Decatur Avenue and the heart of the Fordham Bedford drug trade. The best Hoch can do now is deploy an eight-man "post-impact team" to pick up the slack.

Jenik and Garcia maintain that it's the threat of violence that inhibits community organizing against crime. Cops acknowledge that the concern is legitimate, but Inspector Raymond Rooney, who commanded the 52nd Precinct for three years before leaving to become head of the Operations for the Bronx Detective Bureau, also offers a critique of FBHC's institutional culture: "Fordham Bedford, the only thing missing is getting their hands dirty."

Unlike his predecessors and Inspector Hoch, Rooney enjoys a warm personal relationship with Jenik, whom he calls a "catalyst for the neighborhood," and he credits FBHC and "Chairman Monsignor" as the prime reason that the Fordham Bedford neighborhood has survived relatively intact. But, he asks, "When was the last time the good people in the neighborhood said, 'Let's have a block party, let's clean up this vacant lot...outside of a Fordham Bedford function, something that they just got a grant to do?'"

It's unlikely that the NYPD will have the resources anytime soon to stage another intensive anti-drug effort like the Valentine Avenue

Model Block. Operation Impact may be an imaginative use of the department's limited resources, but—and both the cops and Father Jenik believe this—it's certainly no substitute for an adequately funded Narcotics Division.

Fordham Bedford can't do all the work the NYPD needs to help keep the community organized for order and safety, and the police still have a long way to go to connect with grass-roots organizations that could also get involved. Mention of police strategies, Operation Impact, or the new commander draws blank looks at the Decatur Avenue offices of Part of the Solution (P.O.T.S.), a community service group founded in the early 1980s. P.O.T.S. enjoys a good reputation with its neighbors thanks to its legal clinic, run by the Urban Justice Center, and its soup kitchen on Webster Avenue, which feeds as many as 450 people a day. The group works with residents on Decatur Avenue below 198th Street—the heart of the area's drug zone. But even though police regularly visit the soup kitchen looking for open warrants, the organization reports no formal contact with the precinct. John Hoffman, project coordinator of P.O.T.S, has noticed, and welcomes, the increased presence of young officers on patrol in his neighborhood. He's also grateful for the free turkeys cops drop off around the holidays.

But Hoffman gets more excited about the prospects for street-level organizing. When asked about the possibility of starting a block association, his eyes light up: "Wow, that's a really interesting idea!" He's not talking about citizen patrols armed with walkie-talkies. P.O.T.S. founder Ned Kelly is thinking about getting his neighbors together to pick up dog shit.

Our Lady of Refuge and Fordham Bedford Housing Corporation have gotten the NYPD's attention, and their efforts have resulted in Fordham Bedford receiving as much attention from the precinct as it does. But they've also monopolized the dialogue. There's little chance, after years of conflict, that anything cops do now will satisfy Jenik. If there is a possibility for real cooperation between the precinct and citizens, it will probably consist of a handful of neighbors wearing plastic gloves collecting trash while a cop quietly stands on the corner, rather than the latest "cutting-edge" anti-drug initiative or "new model" of community organizing.

Few expect miracles. It's more than likely that 10 years from now, heroin will still be for sale on Decatur Avenue. But the police have no choice but to look on the bright side. "Ten years ago people were worried about getting killed," notes Morisi. "So there's been progress." •

Bob Roberts is a Bronx-based freelance writer.

An Inner-City Renaissance

The nation's ghettos are making surprising strides. Will the gains last?

Take a stroll around Harlem these days, and you'll find plenty of the broken windows and rundown buildings that typify America's ghettos. But you'll also see a neighborhood blooming with signs of economic vitality. New restaurants have opened on the main drag, 125th Street, not far from a huge Pathmark supermarket, one of the first chains to offer an alternative to overpriced bodegas when it moved in four years ago. There's a Starbucks—and nearby, Harlem U.S.A., a swank complex that opened in 2001 with a nine-screen Magic Johnson Theatres, plus Disney and Old Navy stores and other retail outlets. Despite the aftermath of September 11 and a sluggish economy, condos are still going up and brownstones are being renovated as the middle classes—mostly minorities but also whites—snap up houses that are cheap by Manhattan standards.

It's not just Harlem, either. Across the U.S., an astonishing economic trend got under way in the 1990s. After half a century of relentless decline, many of America's blighted inner cities have begun to improve. On a wide range of economic measures, ghettos and their surrounding neighborhoods actually outpaced the U.S. as a whole, according to a new study of the 100 largest inner cities by Boston's Initiative for a Competitive Inner City, a group founded in 1994 by Harvard University management professor Michael E. Porter.

Consider this: Median inner-city household incomes grew by 20% between 1990 and 2000, to a surprising $35,000 a year, the ICIC found, while the national median gained only 14%, to about $57,000. Inner-city poverty fell faster than poverty did in the U.S. as a whole, housing units and homeownership grew more quickly, and even the share of the

population with high school degrees increased more. Employment growth didn't outdo the national average, with jobs climbing 1% a year between 1995 and 2001, vs. 2% nationally. Still, the fact that inner cities, which are 82% minority, created any jobs at all after decades of steady shrinkage is something of a miracle.

SCENT OF OPPORTUNITY

NOR ARE THE GAINS just the byproduct of the superheated economy of the late 1990s. Rather, they represent a fundamental shift in the economics of the inner city as falling crime rates and crowded suburbs lure the middle-class back to America's downtowns. After decades of flight out of inner cities, companies as diverse as Bank of America, Merrill Lynch, and Home Depot have begun to see them as juicy investment opportunities. National chains are opening stores, auto dealerships, and banks to tap into the unfulfilled demand of inner cities.

Wall Street, too, is jumping in, making loans and putting up equity for local entrepreneurs. "Smart businesspeople gravitate toward good opportunities, and it has become clear that inner cities are just that," says David W. Tralka, chairman of Merrill Lynch & Co.'s Business Financial Services group. In 2002, his group, which caters to small business, began formally targeting inner cities. It now offers financing and commercial mortgages for hundreds of inner-city entrepreneurs around the country.

Is it possible that America at last has started to solve one of its most intractable social ills? True, the progress so far is minuscule compared with the problems created by decades of capital flight, abysmal schools, and drug abuse. And some inner cities, like Detroit's, have made little sus-

tained progress. Ghettos also have been hit by the joblessness of this latest recovery. The national poverty rate has jumped by nearly a percentage point since 2000, to 12.1% last year, so it almost certainly did likewise in inner cities, which the ICIC defined as census tracts with poverty rates of 20% or more.

But as the economy recovers, a confluence of long-term trends is likely to continue to lift inner cities for years. The falling crime rate across the country has been a key factor, easing fears that you take your life in your hands by setting foot in an inner city. At the same time, larger demographic shifts—aging boomers turned empty nesters, more gays and nontraditional households without children, homeowners fed up with long commutes—have propelled Americans back into cities. When they arrive, slums suddenly look like choice real estate at bargain prices.

BEYOND PHILANTHROPY

POLITICAL AND CIVIC LEADERS helped lay the groundwork, too. After floundering for decades following the exodus of factories to the suburbs in the 1950s, many cities finally found new economic missions in the 1990s, such as tourism, entertainment, finance, and services. This has helped boost the geographic desirability of inner-city areas. New state and federal policies brought private capital back, too, by putting teeth into anti-redlining laws and by switching housing subsidies from public projects to tax breaks for builders. As a result, neighborhoods like the predominantly African-American Leimert Park in South Central Los Angeles are becoming thriving enclaves.

The outcome has been a burst of corporate and entrepreneurial activity that already has done more to transform inner

Inner Cities and Their Residents ...

The Boston-based Initiative for a Competitive Inner City has completed the first-ever analysis of the 100-largest inner cities in the U.S. and finds the once-dismal picture brightening

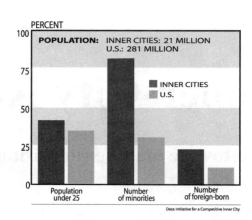

PERCENT

POPULATION: INNER CITIES: 21 MILLION
U.S.: 281 MILLION

■ INNER CITIES
▨ U.S.

Population under 25 / Number of minorities / Number of foreign-born

Data: Initiative for a Competitive Inner City

...Did Better than the Nation As a Whole in the 90s...

Change between 1990 and 2000 Census data

	INNER CITIES	U.S.
Population	24%	13%
Household income	20%	14%
Housing unit growth	20%	13%
High school graduates*	55 to 61%	75 to 80%
College graduates*	10 to 13%	20 to 24%
Home ownership	29 to 32%	64 to 66%
Poverty rate	34 to 30%	13 to 12%

*Of those 25 and over

...Although There's Still A Long Way to Go

2000 Census data

	INNER CITIES	U.S.
High school graduates*	61%	80%
College graduates*	13%	24%
Poverty rate	31%	11.3%
Unemployment rate	12.8%	5.8%
Home ownership rate	32%	66%
Average household income	$34,755	$56,600
Aggregate household income	$250 billion	$6 trillion

Data: Initiative for a Competitive Inner City

cities than have decades of philanthropy and government programs. "What we couldn't get people to do on a social basis they're willing to do on an economic basis," says Albert B. Ratner, co-chairman of Forest City Enterprises Inc., a $5 billion real estate investment company that has invested in dozens of inner-city projects across the country.

EMERGING MARKETS

THE NEW VIEW OF GHETTOS began to take hold in the mid-1990s, when people such as Bill Clinton and Jesse Jackson started likening them to emerging markets overseas. Porter set up the ICIC in 1994 as an advocacy group to promote inner cities as overlooked investment opportunities. Since then, it has worked with a range of companies, including BofA, Merrill Lynch, Boston Consulting Group, and PricewaterhouseCoopers to analyze just how much spending power exists in inner cities.

The new study, due to be released on Oct. 16, uses detailed census tract data to paint the first comprehensive economic and demographic portrait of the 21 million people who live in the 100 largest inner cities. The goal, says Porter, "is to get market forces to bring inner cities up to surrounding levels."

Taken together, the data show an extraordinary renaissance under way in places long ago written off as lost causes. America's ghettos first began to form early in the last century, as blacks left Southern farms for factory jobs in Northern cities. By World War II, most major cities had areas that were up to 80% black, according to the 1993 book *American Apartheid*, co-authored by University of Pennsylvania sociology professor Douglas S. Massey and Nancy A. Denton, a sociology professor at the State University of New York at Albany. Ghettos grew faster after World War II as most blacks and Hispanics who could follow manufacturing jobs to the suburbs did so, leaving behind the poorest and most

un-employable. Immigrants poured in, too, although most tended to leave as they assimilated.

In this context, the solid gains the ICIC found in the 1990s represent an extraordinary shift in fortunes. One of the biggest changes has come in housing. As cities have become desirable places to live again, the number of inner-city housing units jumped by 20% in the 1990s, vs. 13% average for the U.S. as a whole.

A number of companies were quick to see the change. BofA, for example, has developed a thriving inner-city business since it first began to see ghettos as a growth market six years ago. In 1999 it pulled together a new unit called Community Development Banking, which focuses primarily on affordable housing for urban, mostly inner-city, markets, says CDB President Douglas B. Woodruff. His group's 300 associates are on track this year to make $1.5 billion in housing loans in 38 cities, from Baltimore to St. Louis.

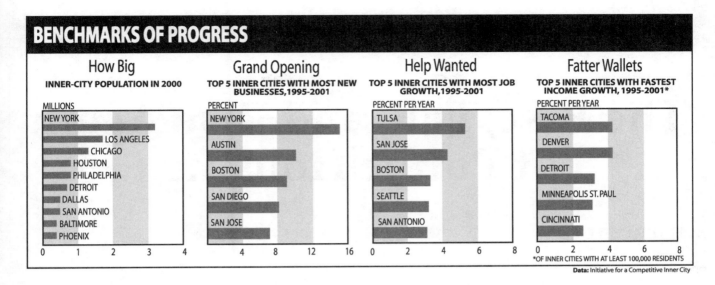

BENCHMARKS OF PROGRESS

How Big — INNER-CITY POPULATION IN 2000 (MILLIONS): NEW YORK, LOS ANGELES, CHICAGO, HOUSTON, PHILADELPHIA, DETROIT, DALLAS, SAN ANTONIO, BALTIMORE, PHOENIX

Grand Opening — TOP 5 INNER CITIES WITH MOST NEW BUSINESSES, 1995-2001 (PERCENT): NEW YORK, AUSTIN, BOSTON, SAN DIEGO, SAN JOSE

Help Wanted — TOP 5 INNER CITIES WITH MOST JOB GROWTH, 1995-2001 (PERCENT PER YEAR): TULSA, SAN JOSE, BOSTON, SEATTLE, SAN ANTONIO

Fatter Wallets — TOP 5 INNER CITIES WITH FASTEST INCOME GROWTH, 1995-2001* (PERCENT PER YEAR): TACOMA, DENVER, DETROIT, MINNEAPOLIS ST. PAUL, CINCINNATI

*OF INNER CITIES WITH AT LEAST 100,000 RESIDENTS

Data: Initiative for a Competitive Inner City

They will do an additional $550 million in equity investments, mostly real estate.

SHELLED OUT

PENSION FUNDS AND other large investors are putting in cash, too. The Los Angeles County Employee Retirement Assn. has sunk $210 million into urban real estate since 2000, including $87 million in August for a bankrupt, 2,496-room apartment complex in Brooklyn, N.Y. The plan is to do things like fix the broken elevators, hire security guards, and kick out nonpaying tenants. "We believe there are opportunities that weren't there before or that we weren't aware of," says board member Bruce Perelman.

One question is whether the ICIC's findings represent not so much progress by the poor as their displacement by middle-class newcomers. In other words, inner-city incomes could be rising simply because affluent new home buyers jack up the average. But experts think gentrification explains only a small part of what's going on. "It's certainly a local phenomenon, but if you aggregate 100 inner cities, gentrification is a small trend," says ICIC research director Alvaro Lima, who spearheaded the study.

In Chicago, for instance, a $65 million redevelopment of the notorious Cabrini-Green housing project has replaced three slummy high-rises with mixed-income units. The area has a new library, new schools, and a new retail center featuring a major grocery store, Starbucks, and Blockbuster (BBI)—all staffed by scores of local residents. "The goal is not gentrification, it's to integrate the classes," says Phyllis L. Martin, the head of a local committee that's trying to lure more than $50 million in private capital to help the city replace 3,245 public housing units in another blighted area, Bronzeville.

"We're just beginning to undo all the damage"

Despite the brightening picture, the decay of most inner cities is so advanced that half a dozen years of progress makes only a dent. The degree of poverty—a measure of how many poor people there are in a census tract—fell 11% in 60 large cities in the 1990s, according to an analysis by U Penn's Massey that parallels ICIC's approach. While that's a significant decline, it only begins to offset the doubling of poverty concentrations in prior decades, he found. "The gains are the first positive news since at least the 1950s, but we're just beginning to undo all the damage," says Massey.

BADGE OF SHAME

WHAT'S MORE, too many inner cities remain untouched. More than a third of the ICIC's 100 cities lost jobs between 1995 and 2001. Detroit's ghetto has seen little new development and shed one-fifth of its jobs over this period. Residents did gain from the booming auto industry, which hired many locals and pushed up their median incomes at a 3.2% annual pace in the 1990s—the third highest increase of the ICIC 100. But with auto makers now shedding jobs again, those gains are likely to be short-lived. More broadly, improving inner cities won't come close to wiping out poverty in the U.S. While the inner-city poverty rate of 31% is nearly three times the national average, the 6.5 million poor people who live there represent less than a fifth of the country's 34.6 million poor.

Still, America's ghettos have been a national badge of shame for so long that any real gain is news. The change in perspective also seems to be an enduring one, not just a 1990s blip. For evidence, consider Potamkin Auto Group, which owns 70 dealerships around the country and will break ground in Harlem in late October on a $50 million development that will include Cadillac, Chevrolet, Hummer, and Saturn dealers. Potamkin also has a project in another inner city and is mulling a national expansion. "We see opportunities there," says Robert Potamkin, president of the family-owned company. This view, that inner cities can be a good place to do business, may be the most hopeful news about the country's urban blight in decades.

—*By Aaron Bernstein in Washington, with Christopher Palmeri in Los Angeles and Roger O. Crockett in Chicago*

The Rise, Fall, and Rise Again of Public Housing

By HARRY SIEGEL

They tend to be isolated outposts: segregated from surrounding neighborhoods, folded in upon themselves, cut off from the street grid, avoided by outsiders other than troublemakers. More than their utilitarian ugliness, it is the red brick that gives them away, and how they huddle in masses so that each removes any doubt as to its neighbor's identity. Though of the city, public housing and its residents are too often set apart from its sprawling, mixed-use life.

Urban public housing came into vogue in the 1930s, when cities began to move beyond ward politics, and planners and politicians attempted to conceive of the city as a single unit or system, and to plan (and zone) housing accordingly. Modern in its ideas, architectural and otherwise, it was envisioned as a superior way of housing the poor replacing the run-down tenements. It continued in the years during and following World War II as a way to compensate for the sudden cessation in housing growth as resources were diverted into the war effort, and to prepare for the surge in population as veterans returned home and began having families.

The projects were also initially a source of valuable political capital, both in spreading construction monies and in housing the connected. Today they come to attention only during social or fiscal crises. And yet the great urban conflicts of the past half century—group versus individual rights, big government versus limited government, and of course race—have often been fought in these laboratories of social policy.

Professor Lawrence J. Vale, the head of MIT's department of urban studies and planning, has taken on the question of what makes a successful project in his new book. He focuses his attention on three Boston housing projects—Franklin Field, Commonwealth, and West Broadway—to see why the first is now considered a failure, the second a success, and the third a bit of each. What emerges is a picture of what successful public housing might look like, and the obstacles to creating such a system.

Public housing, Mr. Vale shows, is racked by competing interests. Should it strive to maintain a stable core of residents with a sense of ownership or to move residents up and on as quickly as possible? Should it be aimed at the poorest, who are often the most troubled, or at those with less need but more responsibility? Should residents of a neighborhood have priority for public housing? Mr. Vale uses the three projects to demonstrate the consequences of the varying implementation of public housing.

The three Boston projects he takes on are in different neighborhoods and serve very different tenant-constituents. All three opened in the decade following World War II and were intended primarily for white veterans and their families. In the time-honored manner of city politics, local and city leaders used the projects to spread wealth during construction and then to reward the politically loyal and connected with subsidized housing—evidenced by the large number of chauffeurs in residence.

Most of the city's projects originally excluded blacks through income and family structure criteria. This was brought to a halt by court orders in the 1960s, but because "standards" had served as a way to Jim Crow blacks, standards were done away with almost entirely. The Boston Housing Authority (BHA) began actively catering to the poorest and least capable applicants, including the mentally ill. This had deleterious effects on the quality of life of working-class residents, a situation exacerbated by the collapse of the BHA, which went into receivership in 1975, and the consequent erosion of the housing stock. Revitalization attempts began in the 1980s and have met with mixed success.

Though overwhelmingly white, West Broadway was always disliked in its predominantly Irish Lower End neighborhood. Initially more prosperous than the neighboring blocks, the project declined when the original residents took advantage of the low mortgage rates and loan opportunities of the postwar era, and left the neighborhood. Their replacements were poorer, and the project began a long downward spiral. (This pattern was typical of all the city's projects.) The few minority residents who dared to move in were met with pervasive hostility and violence that the police and the BHA for the most part ignored.

By contrast, Franklin Field—originally intended for Jewish war veterans and their families—was built in a Jewish neighborhood that was rapidly becoming black. As the Jewish residents migrated to the suburbs, a disastrous program encouraged black home ownership by providing mortgages for housing-in-disrepair with minimal down payments.

This was a con game dressed as social policy; more than 70% of these mortgages failed, and the neighborhood fell into severe disrepair.

The project and the neighborhood became a destination of last resort—a poorly maintained, crime-ridden slum with no shopping or bus service, adjacent to a dangerous and unkept park. The situation was compounded by the 1980s crack explosion. Residents felt completely powerless to get standard maintenance done, let alone effect change, and they lacked any political voice.

In the 1980s, the BHA set out to revive both projects. The money that went into West Broadway brought a renewed interest in its integration, although the violent hostility of neighborhood whites continued to be such that few minorities wanted to live there. A more radical renovation in the 1990s was largely successful in creating a greater sense of ownership on the part of the tenants, who except for a committed few had previously seen themselves as wards of the BHA. This improved the perceived quality of life, but has yet to translate into actual upward mobility.

Franklin Field has not fared nearly as well. An attempted renovation of the project in the late 1980s indulged in as much graft and shoddy workmanship as possible before declaring bankruptcy. It actually worsened conditions in the eyes of most residents.

The BHA had determined that Franklin Field was one of the places where a renovation was the least likely to succeed, and it received funding only as a black beard to allow predominantly white West Broadway to be renovated. Once the money was allocated, no one in power seemed to care how it was spent, and residents who felt powerless over their lives and environments to begin with felt even further removed from self-sufficiency and responsibility.

Commonwealth is the success story of the three, and the reasons why are obvious. It was set on prime property in an affluent neighborhood, and its neighbors invested in its success. Though the property rapidly deteriorated from 1975-80, tenants remained well-organized and active. The BHA allowed them to sign a deal with a private management company, which has worked exceedingly well.

But the success of Commonwealth has been more about improving the residents' frame of mind and quality of life than in creating or even encouraging an upwardly mobile lower class. The illegitimacy rate in the Boston housing projects is well over 50%, and employment is under 25%. The question is what should be done with the projects, particularly those deemed by reasonable factors to be beyond repair.

For this reason and others, public housing remains a difficult problem. Part of the answer lies in involvement by the residents themselves. The people who live in public housing must be held to a standard of conduct and be able to demand a standard of service.

If citizens and housing authorities are willing to do this, it may not be too late to return to the original vision of a lower class on the rise.

Mr. Siegel is a writer living in New York City.

UNIT 8

Urban Futures: Cities After September 11, 2001

Unit Selections

Key Points to Consider

- How did the events of September 11, 2001, affect the way Southerners see New York?

- How will 21st Century cities resemble 20th Century cities? How will they be different?

- How has economic restructuring produced different kinds of cities? What are some of these new cities like? Which one would you like to live in? Describe your own ideal city.

 **Links: www.dushkin.com/online/**
These sites are annotated in the World Wide Web pages.

Department of State International Information Programs
  http://usinfo.state.gov
Metropolis Archives: Sustainability
  http://www.metropolismag.com/html/content_1001/sup/index_b.html
SocioSite: University of Amsterdam
  http://www.pscw.uva.nl/sociosite/TOPICS/
United Nations
  http://www.unsystem.org
Urban Education Web
  http://iume.tc.columbia.edu

American cities face new challenges in 2004, even as they continue to build on major reforms introduced by a wave of innovative new mayors in the 1990s. The terrorist attack on September 11, 2001, exposed the vulnerabilities of cities, those dense concentrations of diverse people and modern sensibilities that create targets for massive destruction as well as markets and cultural centers.

Tough, brave, working class New York cops and firemen stand tall amidst the rubble and massive destruction that the terrorists inflicted, overshadowing and displacing, at least temporarily, those difficult New Yorkers whom the rest of the country loves to hate, in John Shelton Reed's "A View From the South." The internal contradictions within New York, America's most urban city, stood out during the heroic responses to September 11.

Yet there is still room, even after September 11 and the economic downturn that the attacks exacerbated, for cautious optimism: the revitalizing effects of some of the new immigrants, the growing awareness of economic opportunities in our cities, the successes of new wave mayors who've stopped looking to the federal government for their salvation, the surprising economic vitality of sophisticated new businesses, and the remarkable drops in crime and welfare in some of our most hard-hit, industrial cities.

City downtowns can offer the liveliness and energy lacking in even the most grandiose of suburban malls. A variety of older cities from Kansas City and Chicago to Cincinnati and Philadelphia are bringing people back into the downtown after working hours. Their aim is to make their downtowns into residential and recreational areas that attract a 24-hour population.

In "Model Cities" Joel Kotkin shows how Houston and Los Angeles have managed to again attract small businesses and businessmen. He proposes that New York, by again making its policies attractive to such entrepreneurs, can ensure it too has an economic future that includes a middle and working class.

Time to Think Small?

To remain a business capital, New York City needs more humility

By Joel Kotkin

John Shaw sits in the very midst of the beating heart of New York City, on the busy trading floor of a midtown financial firm. President of Jefferies and Company, a Wall Street trading business, he's a prototypical New Yorker—fast-talking, smart, quick on his feet, and, for now, worried about his city's future.

Like many, if not most, top executives in New York, Shaw lives elsewhere, in his case tony Westport, Connecticut. Now he notices that many of his top-drawer colleagues are giving up their second residences in Manhattan in favor of the suburbs, and that even some of his younger traders are pressing him—often at their wives' insistence—to work in offices elsewhere in the region. Thirty-five people from his Manhattan office are already getting transfers to the company's Stamford, Connecticut facility.

Some of this, he notes, is residue from September 11. "It tipped many people over the fence toward moving to the suburbs," Shaw maintains. "Now people are thinking about living a different way of life."

But other longer-term factors are also having an influence. Shaw notes that with new telecom technology a firm like Jefferies (with 538 employees in the New York City area, but only a third of them in Manhattan) no longer has a classic hub and spoke hierarchy. "None of our offices is a branch," he explains. "Each is interactive and equal within the firm." Instead of all heavy hitters concentrated in New York, the company's talent is scattered. The chief strategist resides in Boston. The chairman lives in Los Angeles. The CEO is in Stamford.

This is not merely an effect of the Twin Towers attack. It reflects lifestyle choices of people to live elsewhere, including far from New York City. Jefferies has long had a policy of allowing most of its top executives to work outside the confines of Manhattan, and the firm maintains large offices in places ranging from Short Hills, New Jer-

sey to Nashville, Los Angeles, Richmond, San Francisco, and Dallas.

"There are a lot of people who love this business but want to be elsewhere," Shaw says. "They don't want to schlep to New York City. We get people to work for us who we couldn't get otherwise by giving them other living options."

For many Americans, particularly the young, single, and culturally active, New York City remains an entrancing locale. Because of this magnetic effect, Manhattan boasts one of the nation's most educated populations (a sharp contrast to the demographics of the surrounding boroughs). These infusions of outside talent remain an essential economic asset of the city.

But while intelligence still gathers in New York, moving to Mecca is no longer necessary for the majority of America's most talented people. Back in mid-century, a trader at a firm like Jefferies, or anyone with ambitions in advertising, communications, fashion, publishing, or a host of other professions, had no choice but to live in New York. That is no longer the case. Levels of education in many regions—from northern Virginia to Boulder, Colorado—now exceed those in Manhattan.

The same is true for companies. Many which historically gravitated to Wall Street and midtown Manhattan now can operate just as well from elsewhere. Some urban theorists, such as Susan Fainstein and Saskia Sassen, maintain that "global cities" like New York may be able to resist this scattering trend. They argue that the rising importance of transnational information of various sorts, such as legal, accounting, and management services, increases the need for "centralized command and control," from a geographic epicenter.

Recent experience and today's technological revolution, however, make such assumptions somewhat dubious.

Throughout the 1990s, high-end services, particularly finance, have continued to see employment shifts toward the periphery. Even New York City's expensive decision to spend an estimated $900 million on a new stock trading complex won't guarantee Gotham's long-term domination of the financial service industry.

And financial services is one area where New York is *best* equipped to stay competitive. In many other economic undertakings the case is closed on New York's advantages. The nation's largest corporation, Wal-Mart, operates flawlessly out of Bentonville, Arkansas. Virtually all dominant American high-tech companies—Microsoft, Apple, Dell, Cisco, Hewlett-Packard, Intel—are based on the West Coast or in Texas. The nation's largest port is now Los Angeles, which is also home to the nation's biggest garment industry. And the creative focus of entertainment worldwide lies in the Big Orange, not the Big Apple.

New York should forget about being the "capital of the world," with the arrogance and massive white elephant projects that go along with that.

Increasingly, for more and more industries, it can no longer be assumed that the key players will locate in New York. Instead of migrating to critical physical institutions like exchanges, the prime economic imperative of many companies will be to find individual employees with the necessary knowledge and work habits, regardless of their location. In our post-industrial era, skilled jobs across a wide range of creative fields are essentially becoming artisan work, which can, and will, often be done from remote locales.

Post-9/11 security concerns, soaring insurance premiums for high-rise buildings, and a growing reluctance of workers with families to locate in downtown districts are accelerating the trend. Finally, there are the longstanding discouragements of heavy taxes, inflexible regulation, and age-old urban social problems. The cumulative result can be seen in the recent moves of several major investment banks like Goldman Sachs, Marsh & McLennan, and Morgan Stanley to settings outside New York City.

Jonathan Bowles, research director at the Manhattan-based Center for an Urban Future, suggests that all of this will require a new, more humble mindset on the part of New York City's leaders. In particular, the city needs a greater focus on the fundamental issues that attract or repel people and companies. He suggests that the vainglorious fixation of many New Yorkers on their city's position as "capital of the world" should be one of the first things to go. "The arrogance has to change," Bowles

believes. "For a long time we assumed that every major financial company needed to be in New York. Now that's not true. New York cannot afford to lay back."

New York City's hubris grows out of its past greatness and the remarkable ability of the city to maintain much of its status even in the face of the dispersing trends that dominated the last 50 years of American life. The heart of the city's greatness is that it has always been, first and foremost, a capitalist city. From its origins, New York has been a supremely commercial city (much like its original namesake, Amsterdam). New York was described by one observer in the early eighteenth century as "infatuated with trade." In contrast to Puritan Boston and Quaker Philadelphia, New York's social system was dominated early on by a high-spending pleasure-minded acquisitive class devoted to material accumulation.

New York's other great endowment was its magnificent harbor location and connection to the Hudson River, which after the opening of the Erie Canal in 1825 provided easy access to the great American hinterland to the west and north. No other eastern city save Baltimore had anything remotely as ideal for commerce. The port of New York became the nation's busiest in 1800, and by 1860 accounted for two-thirds of all imports to America.

This trade quickly transformed New York into the nation's commercial capital, and, by 1803, its most populated city. The city's merchant class congregated close to the wharves, and in the nearby area around Wall Street there grew "a veritable congregation of businessmen"— traders, financiers, insurers—clustered together in packed streets where they could arbitrage not only goods but also critical information. This provided the seedbed for the city's development into the nation's commercial front door.

These predominantly commercial—as opposed to industrial—origins helped New York adapt more successfully to post-industrial realities than other American cities. Although it also developed a powerful manufacturing economy, which once employed millions, the economic soul of the metropolis remained concentrated in the transactional and informational aspects of the economy. As a result, as the new millennium opened, New York still dominated many key sectors like financial services, law, advertising, and media.

Today, four of the top six accounting firms, six of the ten biggest consulting companies, five of the largest insurance companies, and all ten top securities firms are still headquartered in Manhattan. New York remains home base for two of the three largest television networks and the biggest media company (AOL-Time Warner), as well as the news operations of most of the others. These clusters of high-end services—as well as tourism, which has grown into a massive industry—have helped the city find a new role. That was badly needed in the face of a mass exodus of other large corporations from New York over the past three decades. In 1970, New York accounted for 131 of the Fortune 500; in the twenty-first century, the city claims little more than a quarter of the firms it had 32 years ago.

But this economic evolution has not come without a price. New York City's growing dependence on a handful of service industries has created an unusually bifurcated economy that offers great riches in some areas yet relatively little opportunity for vast portions of the city's population. The outer boroughs, once bastions of the white middle and working classes, have retained a preponderance of poor families. In Brooklyn and The Bronx, notes economist Robert Fitch, per capita family income is currently closer to the levels seen in inner Detroit than to the levels in Manhattan. As high as Manhattan stands in national income and education rankings, The Bronx sits close to the bottom.

New York's 1990s boom ameliorated some aspects of this "tale of two cities," while worsening others. The Wall Street bull market and the wild expansion of Internet firms created so much disposable wealth and drove housing prices so high that some neighborhoods in the outer boroughs—Williamsburg, Long Island City, Astoria—had tremendous increases in property values, and more new commercial development than had been seen in generations. Although New York's loud and dominant liberal intelligensia liked to portray Giuliani-era prosperity as "class warfare," the reality is that most poor and minority residents benefited from the growth. In neighborhoods such as heavily black Fort Green near the notorious Bedford-Stuyvesant slums, homeowners reaped huge benefits in higher real estate values. And driven both by new immigrants and aspiring young transplants, New York's total population soared by almost 700,000—the first big increase after decades of stagnation and decline.

Up until the 1950s and '60s, lower Manhattan boasted one of the nation's most vibrant collections of small industrial firms. These diverse enterprises, many of them employing 30 people or less, were involved in servicing local markets or processing imports and exports. The city's major industry, textiles and garments, was especially dominated by smaller firms. (Apparel manufacturing was never characterized by the kind of giantism associated with industries like steel or automobiles.) Collectively, these small firms kept New York City alive as a manufacturing metropolis, even as centers of mass assembly such as Detroit fell into decline, and they were a key employer of non-college-educated workers and recently arrived immigrants.

But by the 1970s there were clear signs of stress. Rising taxes, unfriendly regulation, declining public services, crime, and a general indifference to small businesses in New York were slowly undermining these firms. As recently as 1960, New York City's manufacturing industries employed over 900,000 workers. By 1974 that number had dropped to 610,000. Two decades later it was down to around 280,000. The manufacturing losses were most profound in the outlying boroughs—The Bronx, Brooklyn, and Queens—but large swaths of lower Manhattan were also affected.

For landlords in certain locations who were stuck with these dying industries as tenants, the broad urban recovery of the 1990s was like manna from heaven. With rents rising in elite business districts such as Wall Street and midtown, new employers and would-be residents sought out (initially low-cost) space carved from former industrial zones. (The barriers to fresh building are so massive in New York that most real estate expansion comes from adaptive re-use of existing structures.) And so the former workshops of blue-collar New Yorkers were converted into commercial offices and expensive residences.

As many New Economy companies chose locations in old industrial areas rather than traditional locations, the supply could not keep up with the demand, and prices rose precipitously—from as low as $8 per square foot to as much as $50. Even the legendary garment district has been transformed—and hit by soaring rents. Just since 1993, the proportion of Manhattan's private workforce employed in garment-making dropped by roughly a quarter.

New York needs to become more decentralized. Thriving districts that have their own culture and workforces must be encouraged in the outer boroughs.

For garment-makers, printers, and some other industrial users, the newfound passion for these older buildings has been less a blessing than a scourge. "We've been hit with rent inflation that is driving industries like printing out of town," laments Vicky Kennan, vice president of public affairs for the 600-member Association of Graphic Communications. Many of the Internet-related companies that drove the demand for new space have now crashed and disappeared. (Whereas Internet firms accounted for a full quarter of all new leases executed in Manhattan in early 2000, today they are the largest source of fresh vacancies.) Nonetheless, the real estate conversion process seems to have proceeded too far to be reversed.

Even amidst today's glut of vacated space available for re-lease, there will be no return of industrial tenants in most places. Landlords now used to getting $35 per square foot will never accept the $8 to $15 rents most industrial users can afford, believes Jim Stein, a leading commercial broker at Cushman and Wakefield's New

York offices. The Manhattan industrial buildings now deserted by the dot-coms have been so heavily upgraded there will be "no going back" to industrial uses, he predicts.

Ironically, there remain vast tracts of abandoned industrial buildings throughout New York, particularly along the waterfront. Many of these cry out for adaptive re-use, and getting them back into productivity—whether as residences, offices, or workshops—would be highly desirable. Unfortunately, New York's fractious neighborhood politics and gridlocked regulatory process have repeatedly blocked many proposed adaptations. And so the Brooklyn shoreline molders, while over in New Jersey construction cranes define the sky.

The budding struggle over redevelopment of the World Trade Center site encapsulates many of the issues discussed above. Ground Zero provides a rare opportunity to reinvent lower Manhattan, and parts of the broader city itself. Unfortunately, much of the initial focus has been on recreating the earlier paradigm of high-rise office buildings occupied primarily by large corporations. Large-scale incentives, financed by federal aid, are being offered to financial giants in order to keep the towers filled. "They are not talking about small businesses," complains Bowles of the Center for an Urban Future. "No one is talking about making the city, or lower Manhattan, a place that's good for growth companies."

This needs to change, and quickly. Ultimately, the "next" New York has to become a bit more like the rest of the country. In New York's archrival, Los Angeles, business activity is dispersing from a centralized downtown to numerous smaller, decentralized sub-locales (many of them self-governing as independent towns within the larger city) such as Pasadena, Glendale, Beverly Hills, West Los Angeles, Santa Monica, and Burbank. New York needs to become more multi-polar by encouraging thriving districts—including many in the outer boroughs—that have their own geographic centers, their own history and culture, their own workforces. These smaller localized centers will naturally enjoy a wider range of rent levels and local service options than are found in the official commercial districts in lower Manhattan and midtown.

"We need to look more at accommodating a small firm with 110 employees, rather than expecting large employers who are going to buy huge amounts of space," urges John Gilbert of Rudin Management, a leading Manhattan landlord controlling some 2 million square feet of space. This means a strong focus on maintaining basic city services, and on efficient regulation so start-ups and small companies aren't priced out of New York. Clean and safe cityscapes are important, as are good restaurants, shops, and festivals which make people want to live and work in the area. "You have to, first and foremost, make lower Manhattan livable," Gilbert says.

This will require a change in the city's consciousness, says Allison O'Rourke, president of the New York New Media Association. "There has to be an appreciation of the importance of entrepreneurial infrastructure," she urges. "The city has become so super-sized and dominated by a handful of giant corporations." The often-ignored reality is that New York's economy depends heavily on what happens to its smaller firms. Today, 89 percent of New York City companies have less than 20 employees, and in recent years small firms have created four to five times as many new jobs as big firms. City administrators must present a friendlier face to these small companies, and allow a more grassroots-based economy to grow.

In order to thrive in the future, New York City must find a way to blend its intrinsic strengths with a new sense of reality. It should forget about being the "capital of world," with the arrogance and massive white elephant projects (like the Twin Towers) that go along with that. Instead, Gotham needs to return to an earlier, more life-size version of itself, not only in lower Manhattan but throughout the city. Like any place in the digital age, New York can have a great future only if enough ambitious and talented people choose to be there instead of somewhere else. New York will remain great only if it continues to reinvent itself as a good place to live, and to work.

TAE *contributing writer Joel Kotkin is author of* The New Geography: How the Digital Revolution is Reshaping the American Landscape.

$\mathscr{A}$ View From the South

How New York City looks from way, way outside Manhattan

By John Shelton Reed

In the days after September 11, when Americans were watching a lot of television, many of us heard a Texas man-in-the-street tell a network interviewer something like, "Being a Texan or New Yorker just isn't very important right now. We're all Americans." Soon after that, we heard about some South Carolina middle-school students who raised the money to buy a truck for some Brooklyn firefighters who lost theirs (along with seven comrades) at the World Trade Center.

What's going on here? Texans and South Carolinians playing kissy-face with *New York City?* Isn't New York the heart of Yankeedom? Isn't it the city Southerners love to *hate?*

Well, like other Americans in that great red Republican interior on the 2000 Presidential election map, many Southerners do think at least occasionally of New York City as the Great Wen, the cesspool of iniquity, home of everything alien and vile. It has been suggested, not entirely in jest, that the city's evolution vindicates the Confederacy. The bill of particulars has several components.

First of all, there's a lot for *everybody* to dislike about New York: the welfare culture, deranged street people, dysfunctional public schools, periodic brushes with bankruptcy, wack-job politicians—even many New Yorkers complain about this stuff (often while taking a perverse sort of pride in being able to cope with it).

But Southerners have had some special reasons to dislike New York, starting with the fact that it is simply the most *urban* corner of America. A good many Southerners have seen city life as bad for both morals and manners. When Thomas Jefferson celebrated individual ownership of land and the farming life as the only sound bases for culture and society, he was writing in what was already an old Souther tradition. The most eloquent statement of the Southern case against big cities probably came in 1930, with a manifesto by twelve Southern men of letters called *I'll Take My Stand: The South and the Agrarian Tradition.* More recently, Hank Williams Jr. has often put the sentiment to music: In "Dixie on My Mind," for example, he complains, "These people never smile or say a word/ They're all too busy trying to make an extra dime."

In addition, although this may be changing, many Southerners have also taken a dim view of New York for serving as the great reception center and repository for foreign immigration. Our Chambers of Commerce, after all, used to brag about our "native-born" labor force, and Atlanta Brave John Rocker of Macon, Georgia is not the only Southern boy who thinks Americans ought to speak English.

The attacks have highlighted a different, less obnoxious kind of New Yorker, one many Southerners and other Americans find more sympathetic.

In general, ever since New York displaced Boston as the home of the ultra-Yankee, Southerners have tended to see whatever we dislike about Northerners as concentrated there. When we describe ourselves to pollsters as friendly, polite, hospitable, leisurely, traditional, conservative—well, it goes without saying who is *not* that way.

And what many of us *really* dislike about Northerners, and thus loathe in spades about New Yorkers, is their view of Southerners as yokels—if not as *Deliverance*-style Neanderthals. Wherever Northerners got their ideas of the South (and of course a Southerner wrote *Deliverance*), some of them have indeed been inclined to view us as a lesser breed. Consider Kirkpatrick Sale's scare-mongering 1975 book, *Power Shift: The Rise of the Southern Rim and Its Challenge to the Eastern Establishment*, which extrapolated from economic and demographic trends to project the sort of nightmare future in which Sales' Northeastern readers would have to choose between, say, a governor of Texas and a former senator from Tennessee for President. (One of the few pleasures of the 1992 Democratic convention for this Southerner was watching the expression on Mario Cuomo's face every time he said the word "Arkansas.")

I could go on, but the point is that there has been no love lost, in either direction, between New York City and the South. And in this, the South has merely been a 100-proof stand-in for places like Omaha, Idaho, Ohio, and many other parts of what some New Yorkers call "flyover country." We all know this, don't we?

But, of course, it hasn't been quite that simple. Southerners, like other American heartlanders, have always been of two minds about the city. Some have looked on New York and New Yorkers with admiration, occasionally envy. Most of us can find at least something to admire about the place and its people.

For decades, of course, New York looked pretty good to *black* Southerners. In the first half of the twentieth century, hundreds of thousands, especially from Georgia and the Carolinas, packed their worldly goods and box lunches and rode the Chickenbone Special out of the Jim Crow South, following the drinking gourd to seek a better life in Harlem and Bedford Stuyvesant.

Many whites joined this exodus, especially a certain type of young Southern intellectual for whom The City has always been where it's happening (whatever "it" may be). North Carolina's Thomas Wolfe set the pattern in the 1920s, and 40 years later Mississippi's Willie Mor-

ris epitomized it. Morris's wince-making memoir *New York Days* is awash in isn't-it-wonderful-that-I'm-a-part-of-you-New-York-New-York gush. Even as confident and self-aware an expat as Tom Wolfe the younger (the Virginian who pretty well peeled, cored, and sliced the Big Apple in *Bonfire of the Vanities*) once confessed, "I still find New York exciting, to tell the truth. It's not the easiest way to live in the world, but I still get a terrific kick out of riding down Park Avenue in a cab at 2:30 in the morning and seeing the glass buildings all around. I have a real cornball attitude towards it, I suppose, which I think only somebody born far away from there would still have."

Southern writers and artists have historically *had* to look north to New York, because that's pretty much where the literacy and artistic action was. Yet arty folk aren't the only ones who have feared, deep down, that nothing signifies unless it is noticed on that thin sliver of asphalt stretching between the Hudson and the East River; plenty of hardheaded businesspeople feel the same. Atlanta, in particular, is full of the kind of strivers Tom Wolfe nailed in *A Man in Full*, for whom "the one thing they can't stand is the idea that somebody in New York might be calling them Southern hicks." (Houstonians, for some reason, don't have as bad a case of what the Australians call "cultural cringe": On the rare occasions when they think of New Yorkers at all, they're likely to feel sorry for them because they're not Texans.)

No matter where we grew up, few of us have entirely escaped the romance of The City. We know about the mean streets, sure, but we can't shake the image of Gene Kelly dancing in them.

One might have thought that the South's astonishing economic development, the rise of Southern cities, and the end of *de jure* segregation—all of which have made the South more like New York—would make New York City less alluring to some, and less repugnant to others. Increasingly, Southerners don't have to leave home to find urban, cosmopolitan, polyglot settings. Now that we have our own street crime, pollution, and traffic problems, there should be less reason to feel superior. Now that we have our own operas and publishing houses and big-league sports, there would seem less reason to feel inferior. But we still think of New York as different, and, in some ways, special.

No matter where we grew up, few of us have entirely escaped the romance of The City. We know about the mean streets, sure, but we can't shake the image of Gene Kelly dancing in them. Thanks to *Mad* magazine and the

New Yorker, to Irving Berlin and Hollywood, I knew about Wall Street and Madison Avenue and Broadway and Coney Island and Harlem long before I ever set foot in New York. I recognized that socialites lived on Park Avenue, bums in the Bowery, bohemians in Greenwich Village. I understood who worked on Wall Street, and Madison Avenue, and Broadway, and Tin Pan Alley.

New York City is part of the mental furniture of all Americans, and—this is important—many of us think of the good things about New York as in some sense *ours.* We have proprietary feelings about the Metropolitan Opera, the Rockettes, the Statue of Liberty, and, yes, the World Trade Center. We feel attached to them whether we've seen them or not (and we may actually be more likely than the natives to have visited them). To say that those who destroyed the Twin Towers attacked New York City is like calling an assault on Mount Rushmore an attack on South Dakota.

But Iemínded us that the New Yorkers we most often hear from are not the only people who live there. When Southerners and other outsiders dislike (or fawn on) "New Yorkers," the people they usually have in mind are the media and show business figures, politicians, business titans, and intellectuals we encounter on television—in short, "the people who run things": sophisticated, worldly, cosmopolitan (if you admire them); supercilious, smug, arrogant (if you don't).

These people are still there, of course, and they sure can grate. Shortly after September 11, I heard Fran Leibowitz making snide comments on NPR about President Bush's reference to the "folks" responsible for the attacks. She apparently had that word associated with hayrides. But many of these obnoxious figures have been uncharacteristically subdued since last fall, and the attacks have highlighted a different kind of New Yorker, one many Southerners and other Americans find more sympathetic.

There has always been more to New York City than the "people who run things." Ever since the heyday of Jacksonian Democracy, an on-again off-again alliance has existed between ordinary Southerners (that is, most of us) and New York's working people. After the Civil War and Reconstruction, this coalition was famously described as one of "rum, Romanism, and rebellion." Later, it elected Franklin Roosevelt to four terms. Later still, it reassembled to elect Richard Nixon and Ronald Reagan.

Most Southerners who know New York (I lived there for five years) know that there's a kind of outer borough New York guy (it's almost always a guy) we get along with just fine. He is working-class and usually Irish, Jewish, or Italian, but these days sometimes black or Latino. He is what historian Paul Fussell called a "high prole," largely defined by his skills and "pride and a conviction

of independence." When Fussell identifies disdain for social climbing, fondness for hunting and gambling and sports, and unromantic attitudes toward women as his other traits, Southerners should recognize the Northern variety of what we used to call a "good old boy" (before the label escaped captivity and lost all precision). "A solid, reliable, unpretentious, stand-up, companionable, appropriately loose, joke-sharing feller," in the description of Roy Blount Jr.

> ## To say that those who destroyed the Twin Towers attacked New York City is like calling an assault on Mount Rushmore an attack against South Dakota.

The bond between Southerners and this kind of Northerner often does have to do with sports. Recall that "Broadway Joe" Namath of the New York Jets, the Pennsylvanian who became an archetypal New Yorker, launched his public persona as "Joe Willie" Namath of the Alabama Crimson Tide. (Namath even played a Confederate soldier in a seriously bad movie called *The Last Rebel*.)

Or consider Coach Frank McGuire, from St. Xavier High School and St. John's University in Queens, who steered the North Carolina Tar Heels to an undefeated season and a national championship, and later coached at South Carolina. The New York players McGuire recruited used to bemuse the locals with their habit of crossing themselves before foul shots. And then there's Coach Jimmy Valvano of North Carolina State University, another New Yorker who led a Southern team to a national championship and endeared himself even to fans of rival teams with his good-old-boy humor. (After his team blew a lead to lose to the arch-rival Tar Heels, Valvano claimed a fan wrote him "If you ever do that again, I'll come over and shoot your dog." Valvano said he wrote back saying he didn't have a dog and the man replied: "I'm sending you a dog. But don't get too attached to him.")

These are the kinds of New Yorkers we saw on television after September 11: policemen, firemen, rescue workers—ordinary folks. Their accents may have sounded funny to Southern ears, but they're our kind of Yankee: unpretentious, hard working when they have to be, offhandedly courageous. Mayor Giuliani may or may not be one of them by nature, but in that context he sure looked it, and most of us found him wholly admirable.

The post-9/11 fortitude and determination of New York's plain folk has led many of us to conclude that Tom Wolfe was wrong when, in one of his most famous essays, he described the stockcar racer Junior Johnson, from Ingle Hollow, Wilkes County, North Carolina, as "the last

American hero." We have learned that there are some guys from places like Red Hook, Brooklyn, New York, who qualify as well.

John Shelton Reed, a professor at the University of North Carolina, is author of Whistling Dixie *and other books on the South.*

Model Cities

What New York can learn from the economic recoveries in Houston and L.A.

By Joel Kotkin

NEW YORK'S ECONOMIC policy-makers probably don't spend a lot of time sitting around lamenting, "Why can't we be more like Houston?"

But maybe they should.

New Yorkers are not known for their willingness to look outside the City Limits for edification, but sometimes the experiences of other cities have important lessons for us.

Like New York today, Houston in the late 1980s and Los Angeles in the early 1990s were suffering from massive corporate downsizing and a devastating loss of civic direction. Yet under the leadership of strong, business-oriented mayors—Bob Lanier in Houston and Richard Riordan in L.A.—these two cities were able to stave off collapse by drastically remaking their economies. Today, even amid a stubborn national recession, both cities have been able to use their now highly diversified, small-business-oriented economies to stay on an even keel.

Some might thumb their noses at such comparisons. New Yorkers may prefer to look at other global cities, such as London or Paris, as models. Yet in reality New York is more like Los Angeles and Houston than it may want to believe: All three are highly immigrant-dominated magnets for young people with ideas.

At the moment, however, Houston and L.A. are doing much more to lever-age those assets into entrepreneurial strength. In several key indicators—including minority-business growth and expansion; the Inc. 500, *Inc.* magazine's annual ranking of the fastest-growing private companies in the United States; and the National Commission on Entrepreneurship's Growth Company Index—Houston and Los Angeles far outpace New York. New York would be better off seeking ways to boost its standing in these areas than worrying about the relative prestige of museums and restaurants in Paris, or the number of celebrity sightings in London.

Houston may be the strongest case. Back in the 1980s, the city went through a near-total economic meltdown; between 1982 and 1987, the area lost one out of every eight jobs. Dependent even more upon energy than New York is upon Wall Street, Houston's economy disintegrated when energy prices plummeted. "See-through" office towers—buildings with entirely vacant floors—replaced construction cranes as the metaphor for the city, which lost more than 200,000 jobs during this period.

Yet over the next decade, Houston reinvented itself and vastly diversified its economy. By the mid-1990s, the city had one of the highest rates of new-business formation in the nation. It had the third highest Growth Company Index—a measure of high employment growth—in the 1990s, according to the National Commission on Entrepreneurship's study of the 13 largest metro areas.

Houston's method for achieving this turnaround was a radical one: Unlike New York, which sees high real-estate prices as a *summum bonum* of economic development, Houston allowed "creative destruction" to take full force. Sagging real-estate prices helped draw a swarm of new entrepreneurs into the city.

Andrew Segal headed out to Texas to make his fortune after graduating from New York University Law School in 1994. Young, aggressive and full of entrepreneurial energy, Segal decided to stake his nest egg on properties in both Dallas and Houston—cities not fashionable at the time among the real-estate "experts" who saw Texas' oversupply of vacant office space as a disaster for investors.

But to Segal and others like him, Houston's predicament represented an enormous opportunity. "The whole real-estate infrastructure here was dead," Segal recalls. "These buildings had lost 90 percent of their value overnight in the oil bust. It was a totally open field."

Since then, Segal has accumulated some four million square feet of space in Houston. Segal says most of the demand for space has come not from oil companies or other traditional bulwarks of Houston's economy, but from a new generation of small firms covering everything from food processing to specialty chemicals. "There's the beginnings of explosive growth here, but very few people have focused on it," he says. "People still look for oil companies that can buy up big blocks of space. What I did is turn my focus on smaller companies and startups, because that's where the growth is."

Segal and other observers credit three factors for Houston's recovery: the city's entrepreneurial culture, immigrants and the six-year tenure of Mayor Lanier.

Immigrants and minorities, who now compose roughly two-thirds of Houston's population, have built some strong economic institutions there—something they have not achieved in New York. Perhaps the most important of these is Metrobank—founded by local entrepreneur Don Wang—which now has over $840 million in assets and stands as Houston's fourth-largest bank.

"In the 1980s, everyone was giving up on Houston, but we stayed," Wang observes in his brightly painted office in the city's second Chinatown, a few miles from the swank Galleria area. "It was cheap to start a business here and easy to find good labor. We consider this the best place to do business in the country—even if no one on the outside knows it."

Finally, government played an important role here. In 1992, Lanier, a former developer, became mayor. Like Mayor Rudolph Giuliani in New York, he concentrated on reducing crime—but he also made bringing services to the city's varied neighborhoods a priority. Lanier focused mainly on infrastructure—roads, sewers, street cleaning and other essential services—and gave no overwhelming preference to any part of the city. Not only did downtown recover, but many of the city's other neighborhoods came back as well.

Lanier took a similar approach to supporting business. His administration focused largely on making it easy for companies to start up—with a minimum of interference from City Hall. His goal was to diversify Houston's economy and create wealth across a broad spectrum of communities. Lanier said his primary goal was to improve the neighborhoods: "First you bring back the residents, and then the commercial flows, and then the jobs come back."

To a remarkable extent, he turned out to be correct. During the 1990s, Houston enjoyed one of the most buoyant economic expansions of any major American city, recovering all the jobs lost in the 1980s and then some. Even after the collapse of Enron, the city's economy has done somewhat better than the national average, outperforming those of most large metro areas and faring far better than New York's. Although some areas, particularly downtown, have seen an increase in vacancies as a result of the company's implosion, most other parts of the city have continued to do well, as smaller firms and the burgeoning medical sector have taken up the slack.

Los Angeles, by all accounts, did not recover as well, nor has it withstood the current recession nearly as comfortably as Houston. Yet the city, which shares liberal politics and high costs with New York, did stage a remarkable comeback from what might be considered an even deeper crisis. The first blow was structural: a meltdown of the once-dominant aerospace industry in the aftermath of the Cold War. The second was a massive escalation of costs for businesses, mostly imposed by state government in Sacramento. The third came from a sweeping withdrawal of Japanese capital following the onset of that nation's long recession.

Adding to these problems, Los Angeles suffered the worst riots in modern American history in May 1992. Fires, a major earthquake and floods all added to the devastation. By 1993, Los Angeles had lost 400,000 jobs, its unemployment rate was close to 10 percent and a great number of large, established companies—such as defense-industry giant Lockheed—were deserting the city.

Yet despite these problems, Los Angeles was able to turn itself around. As in Houston, one key to its success turned out to be the economic decline itself: When older firms moved out of the city, new ones, particularly those run by immigrants, stepped in. The vast upsurge of new businesses came in a host of fields, including mainstays such as entertainment, but also new ones such as digital media. Most notably, there was actually a surge of blue-collar job creation, particularly in the garment, textile, food processing and warehousing sectors. Unemployment dropped dramatically.

As in Houston, one critical factor in the recovery was the presence of large, minority-owned banks. By 2001, four of L.A.'s six largest financial institutions were run by minorities and immigrants. These and a host of much smaller community banks—most run by first-generation Asian immigrants—financed much of the growth that took place in the mid-1990s, when most national and mainstream banks were busily writing off Los Angeles as a hopeless dystopia.

> **By 2001, four of L.A.'s six largest financial institutions were run by minorities and immigrants.**

But government policy also made a difference. In sharp contrast to the actions of New York's leaders during the same period, L.A.'s Riordan, elected mayor in 1993, believed it to be the job of the city government to help all businesses, large and small, high-tech and low. Organizing what became known as "mayor's business teams," Riordan dispatched scores of his most trusted people to help firms leap regulatory hurdles. Some of these businesses were located around the downtown core, but many were in outlying sections such as the San Fernando Valley, the Eastside and even hard-hit south Los Angeles.

"What the business teams did is make firms feel welcome in L.A. and expedite things," explains Riordan, a retired venture capitalist and native of Flushing, Queens. "It didn't matter to us whether they were large or small, and we actually went after manufacturing firms because they created the jobs we needed."

Over the course of Riordan's eight years, the teams helped more than 3,000 businesses in an array of fields ranging from new media to food processing. This hard work has helped Los Angeles maintain a far more diverse economy than did many areas that depended on the stock market boom of the 1990s, such as San Francisco, Seattle and, of course, New York. As a result, the city has lost far fewer jobs—even in a bad economy and despite an unprecedented state budget crisis.

Houston and Los Angeles offer both specific and general lessons for New York. Using city resources to help a broad range of industries and neighborhoods is a notion that New York leaders have rejected for far too long. And focusing as Houston and L.A. did on such specifics as improving basic infrastructure and assisting small businesses could restore New York's long-lost status as an entrepreneurial hotbed.

Joel Kotkin is a Senior Fellow at the Davenport Institute for Public Policy at Pepperdine University and at the Center for an Urban Future. This column is adapted from "Engine Failure," a Center for an Urban Future report authored by Kotkin and the center's research director, Jonathan Bowles.

Index

Index

Test Your Knowledge Form

We encourage you to photocopy and use this page as a tool to assess how the articles in *Annual Editions* expand on the information in your textbook. By reflecting on the articles you will gain enhanced text information. You can also access this useful form on a product's book support Web site at *http://www.dushkin.com/online/*.

NAME: DATE:

_____

TITLE AND NUMBER OF ARTICLE:

_____

BRIEFLY STATE THE MAIN IDEA OF THIS ARTICLE:

_____

LIST THREE IMPORTANT FACTS THAT THE AUTHOR USES TO SUPPORT THE MAIN IDEA:

_____

WHAT INFORMATION OR IDEAS DISCUSSED IN THIS ARTICLE ARE ALSO DISCUSSED IN YOUR TEXTBOOK OR OTHER READINGS THAT YOU HAVE DONE? LIST THE TEXTBOOK CHAPTERS AND PAGE NUMBERS:

_____

LIST ANY EXAMPLES OF BIAS OR FAULTY REASONING THAT YOU FOUND IN THE ARTICLE:

_____

LIST ANY NEW TERMS/CONCEPTS THAT WERE DISCUSSED IN THE ARTICLE, AND WRITE A SHORT DEFINITION:

We Want Your Advice

ANNUAL EDITIONS revisions depend on two major opinion sources: one is our Advisory Board, listed in the front of this volume, which works with us in scanning the thousands of articles published in the public press each year; the other is you—the person actually using the book. Please help us and the users of the next edition by completing the prepaid article rating form on this page and returning it to us. Thank you for your help!

ANNUAL EDITIONS: Urban Society 05/06

ARTICLE RATING FORM

Here is an opportunity for you to have direct input into the next revision of this volume.
We would like you to rate each of the articles listed below, using the following scale:

1. **Excellent: should definitely be retained**
2. **Above average: should probably be retained**
3. **Below average: should probably be deleted**
4. **Poor: should definitely be deleted**

Your ratings will play a vital part in the next revision.
Please mail this prepaid form to us as soon as possible.
Thanks for your help!

RATING	ARTICLE
	1. Fear of the City, 1783 to 1983
	2. The Man Who Loved Cities
	3. The Death and Life of America's Cities
	4. Patio Man and the Sprawl People
	5. Is Regional Government the Answer?
	6. Downtown Struggles While Neighbor Thrives
	7. Unscrambling the City
	8. Are Europe's Cities Better?
	9. The Rise of the Creative Class
	10. Too Much Froth
	11. As Cities Move to Privatize Water, Atlanta Steps Back
	12. Packaging Cities
	13. Urban Warfare: American Cities Compete for Talent, and the Winners Take All
	14. Financing Urban Revitalization
	15. Ground Zero in Urban Decline
	16. Return to Center
	17. New Village on Campus
	18. The Fall and Rise of Bryant Park
	19. Culture Club
	20. Midwestern Momentum
	21. Saving Buffalo From Extinction
	22. Movers & Shakers
	23. Mayors and Morality: Daley and Lindsay Then and Now
	24. Beyond Safe and Clean
	25. Bloomberg So Far
	26. Brain-Gain Cities Attract Educated Young
	27. The Gentry, Misjudged as Neighbors
	28. The Essence of Uptown
	29. Windows Not Broken
	30. Amid Office Shuffle in San Francisco, Bohemian Rhapsody
	31. Rocking-Chair Revival
	32. The Geography of Cool
	33. The Best of Mates
	34. Broken Windows
	35. How an Idea Drew People Back to Urban Life

RATING	ARTICLE
	36. Murder Mystery
	37. Crossing the Line
	38. Segregation in New York Under a Different Name
	39. In New York City, Fewer Find They Can Make It
	40. Chief Bratton Takes on L.A.
	41. Police Line—Do Cross
	42. An Inner-City Renaissance
	43. The Rise, Fall, and Rise Again of Public Housing
	44. Time to Think Small?
	45. A View From the South
	46. Model Cities; What New York Can Learn from the Economic Recoveries in Houston and L.A.

(Continued on next page)

BUSINESS REPLY MAIL
FIRST CLASS MAIL PERMIT NO. 551 DUBUQUE IA

POSTAGE WILL BE PAID BY ADDRESEE

McGraw-Hill/Dushkin
2460 KERPER BLVD
DUBUQUE, IA 52001-9902

ABOUT YOU

Name   Date

_____

Are you a teacher? ☐   A student? ☐
Your school's name

_____

Department

_____

Address   City   State   Zip

_____

School telephone #

_____

YOUR COMMENTS ARE IMPORTANT TO US!

Please fill in the following information:
For which course did you use this book?

_____

Did you use a text with this ANNUAL EDITION? ☐ yes ☐ no
What was the title of the text?

_____

What are your general reactions to the *Annual Editions* concept?

_____

Have you read any pertinent articles recently that you think should be included in the next edition? Explain.

_____

Are there any articles that you feel should be replaced in the next edition? Why?

_____

Are there any World Wide Web sites that you feel should be included in the next edition? Please annotate.

_____

May we contact you for editorial input? ☐ yes ☐ no
May we quote your comments? ☐ yes ☐ no